HERMÈS
PHILOSOPHY

The author and editor would like to thank: Agostino Guerra, Rachel Koffsky and Talisa Mohammed of Christie's and Morgane Halimi, Alba Jang and Fei Yip of Sotheby's for their essential cooperation; and professors Jan Schoormans, Peter van der Bel and Beppe Vicenti for their contribution. A special thank you to Vittoria Bianchi, CEO of Faraone Casa d'Aste, for her invaluable input. The publisher would also like to thank Franco Jacassi of Vintage Delirium in Milan.

Unofficial and unauthorised

ISBN: 978-1-78884-335-5

First published in Italian under the title *Hermès Philosophy*
in 2025 by White Star s.r.l
WS whitestar® is a registered trademark property of White Star s.r.l.
This translation published by ACC Art Books in 2025
by agreement with White Star s.r.l.
© 2025 ACC Art Books Ltd

Italian Edition:
Project Editor: Valeria Manferto/Consulting D&D
Editorial Assistant: Giorgio Ferrero
Graphic Design: Paola Piacco

English Edition:
Translator: Katherine Kirby
Editors: Caroline Curtis, White Star; Sue Bennett, ACC Art Books
Typesetter/Technician: Steve Farrow, ACC Art Books

EU GPSR Authorised Representative:
Easy Access System Europe Oü, 16879218
Address: Mustamäe tee 50, 10621 Tallinn, Estonia
Email: gpsr@easproject.com Tel: +358 40 500 3575

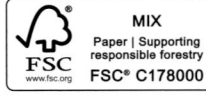

Printed in China by Beijing Allied Fortune Printing Ltd
for ACC Art Books Ltd, Woodbridge, Suffolk, UK
www.accartbooks.com

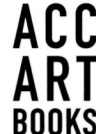

MARA CAPPELLETTI

HERMÈS
PHILOSOPHY

ACC ART BOOKS

CONTENTS

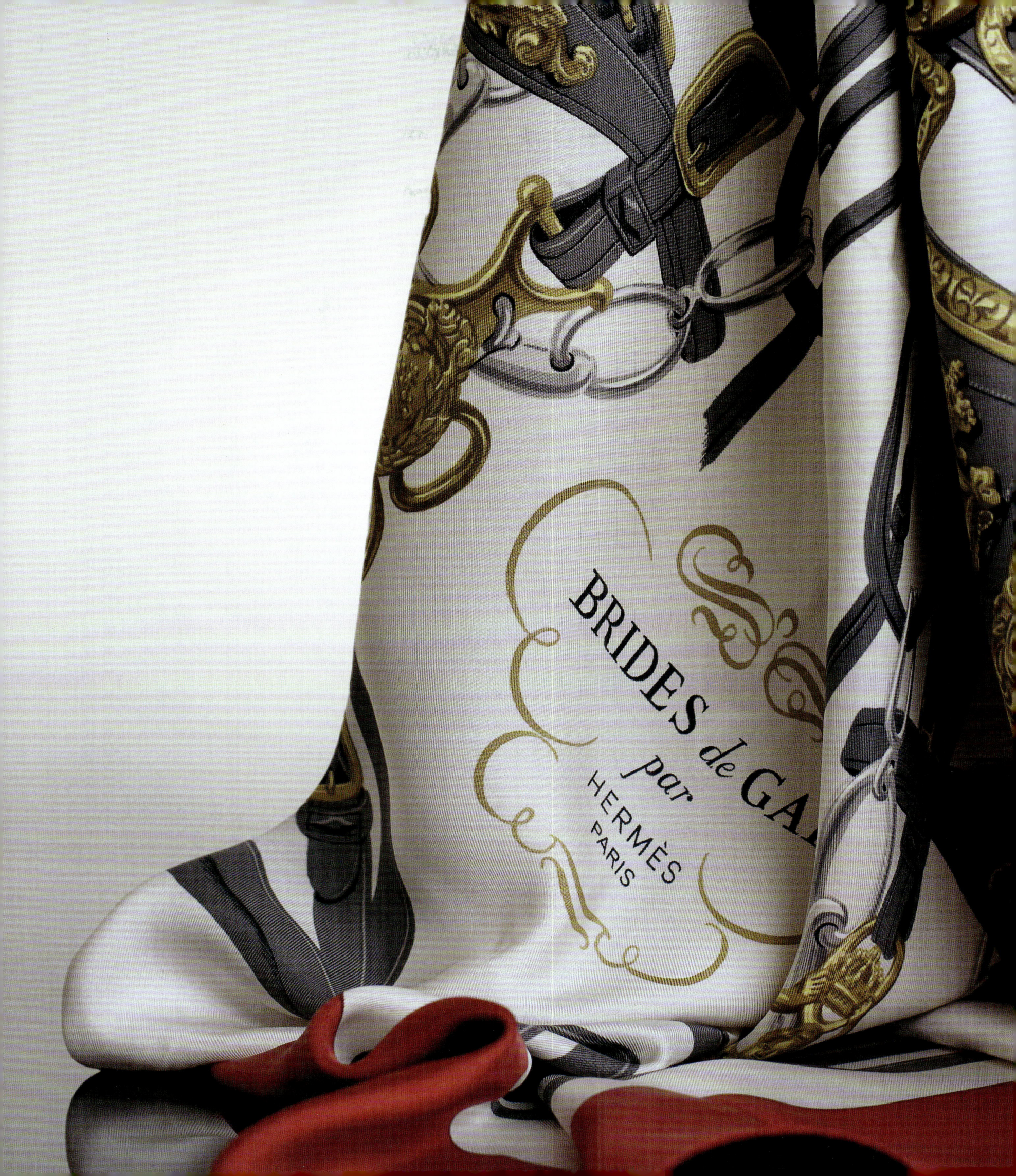

HERMÈS. NEVER TRENDY, ALWAYS IN FASHION

....

'Some brands, people just buy. Others, people desire.'
Interbrand 2024

When analysing the values associated with the Hermès brand, one of the words which keeps coming back is *timeless*. It's as if the objects produced by the fashion house are indeed outside of time, as if they were designed and created to last forever.

That 'forever' category also includes special objects which almost never belong to the world of fashion. The defining characteristic of fashion is time: it marks the rhythm of evolution through its cycles of variation and it offers those who follow it the security of being in the here and now, of being 'modern'. Many philosophers and sociologists have expressed ideas about the concept of modernity, including Immanuel Kant and Georg Simmel. The poet Arthur Rimbaud weighed in when he wrote, in *A Season in Hell*: 'One must be absolutely modern.' Even Italian author Giacomo Leopardi at times reflected on topics which were seemingly less central to his poetics, such as fashion, underscoring their transitory nature.[1] As envisioned by these thinkers and poets, modernity is characterised by constant tension between tradition and innovation, stability and change and, while modernity has liberated people from tradition, it has also introduced the new predominant duty of continuous renewal. Novelty for novelty's sake, even, at times, at the expense of good taste.

The semiotician Roland Barthes offers a deep understanding of fashion as a cultural phenomenon and reveals how this isn't just a matter of aesthetics or personal preference, but a complex system of symbols which convey social, cultural and psychological meaning. However, it isn't always as revolutionary and free as might be expected, according to Barthes: 'Clothing is in the fullest sense "a social model", a more or less standardized model of predictable collective behaviours...'[2]

In terms of fashion, time is manifested through the concept of seasonality, with new collections which are regularly launched to meet the demand

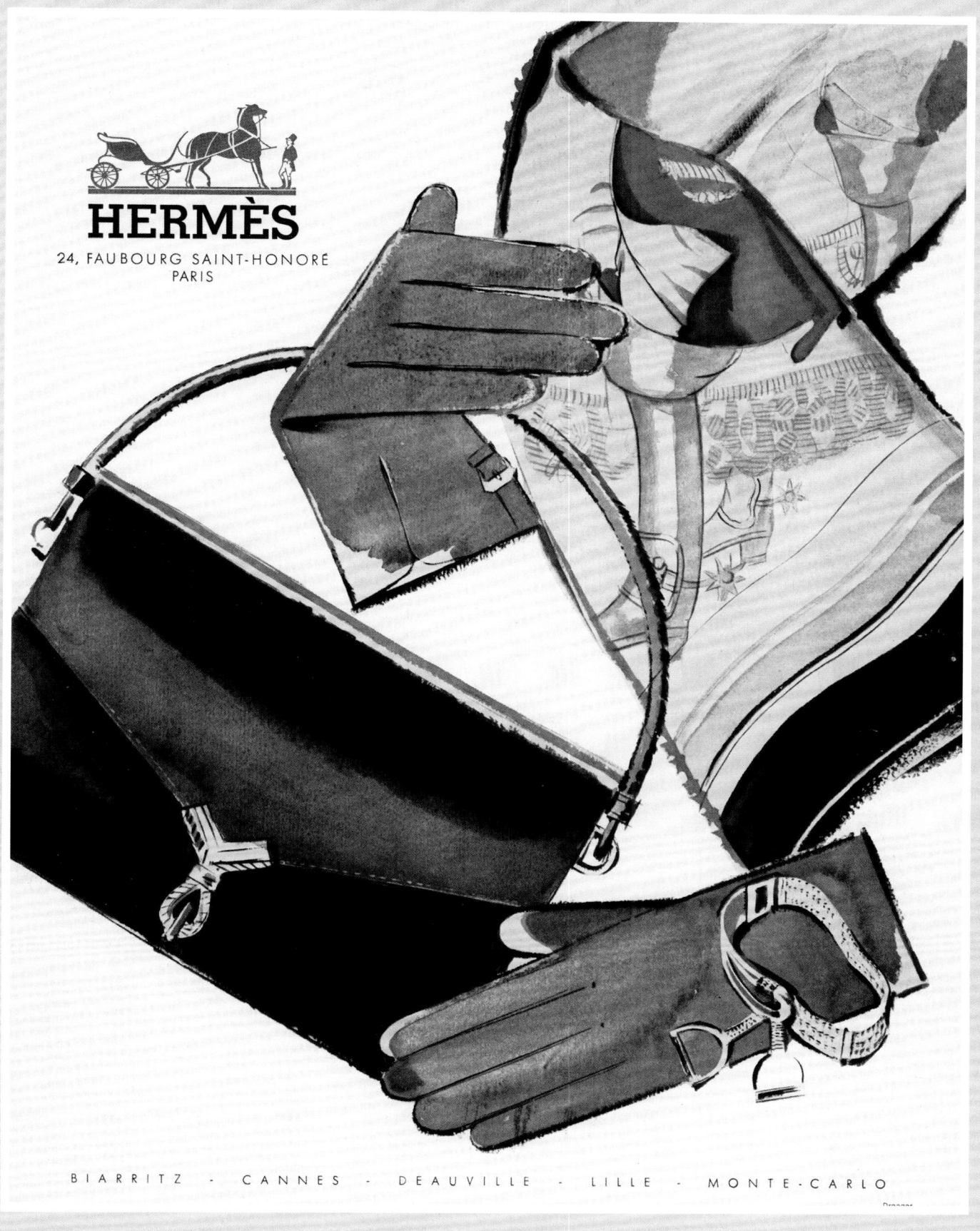

Hermès advert that presents a complete look with a bag, scarf, gloves and a stirrup-detail bracelet, France, 1956.

for new items. Barthes observes how this perpetual cycle of change creates tension between fashion as an individual expression and fashion as a social system, in which the pressure to be 'fashionable' becomes a form of control.

In the context of fashion, 'killing the old' is inevitable to abandon the even-keeled styles of tradition while building always-new identities. In fashion, identity no longer arises from the customary way of dressing, but clothing and its accessories are a crucial component of the ever-renewed social construction of the self. But, to stand out, fashion yells while style speaks softly. And, in the words of Véronique Nichanian, who has designed the brand's menswear for over 20 years, it is precisely the idea of 'quiet luxury' which Hermès harks back to: 'I'm in the business of clothing, not fashion',[3] distancing herself from the forced cycle of 'new at all costs' to attest to the desire for renewal, sure, but while respecting a specific style.

Some objects consistently appear as part of the dress or collective imagination of a given society without being tarnished by the transience that essentially characterises fashion, becoming 'classics' and 'timeless'. This category includes creations by Hermès, especially the bags, silk scarves and jewellery that are contained within the pages of this book.

These appear after a selection process made necessary because the brand's complete catalogue includes tens of thousands of items, including furniture and decorative items, beach accessories, lighting, texts, linens and even toys and tack for horses. A kaleidoscopic, colourful, joyful and vast world – one that would be impossible to grasp entirely. And, in any case, that wasn't the intent of this book, which takes readers on a journey to discover the brand's values and explores the wonder of items which have become luxury icons.

Hermès accessories – liberated from the iron-clad rhythms and constant forced updates of fashion – are presented as objects which have stood the test of time or which have even stepped into the role of works of art. Indeed, they generally don't reflect constantly evolving trends; instead, they have a more intimate and personal relationship to those who choose them. In this sense, they are close to the concept of jewels as seen by Simmel.

The sociologist stated that the social role of jewellery is to be an object which increases and amplifies the impression of a person and their 'radiations'. Moreover, it is 'a synthesis of the individual's having and being'[4]. Moreover, jewellery (just like some accessories, we might add) goes beyond the sphere of bare needs and belongs to the category of the 'superfluous'.

A superfluous that dovetails well with flashy consumption or with 'Veblen goods'[5]: that is, goods for which the demand increases as the price increases, thereby giving the item itself prestige. We can certainly speak of such an effect for the Hermès products with notable price points.

The former CEO of Hermès, Patrick Thomas, once remarked: 'The luxury industry is built on a paradox: the more desirable the brand becomes, the more it sells but the more it sells, the less desirable it becomes.' His comment perfectly summarises the brand's strategy of exclusivity.

Its jewellery, silk scarves and bags are meant to be passed down from one generation to the next, taking on meaning which is both personal and familial. As such, they become symbols of continuity and personal ties. They're objects but not objects of consumption; they're tools through which individuals can express their identity. They offer a form of stability and duration which differentiates them from fashion. They arise by challenging the fast and repetitive rhythms of production, as if in every piece of leather tanned, in every stitch sewn by hand, in every quality control there was a secret code, the unique and personal style which makes every piece recognisable through a series of tangible and intangible elements.

Time returns as a central element of production which requires months of work and which tests the quality of an object and its capacity not to lose value in the long term, and to acquire it instead.

To this end, Hermès emphasises craftsmanship and quality materials. The selection of the leather, fabric and other raw materials used by the brand is done with extreme care, and every step in the manufacturing process is defined by dedication to perfection. This commitment to quality is clear in all the brand's products, from the iconic bags such as the *Birkin* and the *Kelly*, to the silk scarves and the clothing and accessory collections. Craftsmanship isn't just a manufacturing method; it's an essential trademark which defines the aesthetics and intrinsic value of these objects.

In the words of Pierre-Alexis Dumas, Creative Director of Hermès: 'I think that Hermès objects are desirable because they reconnect people to their humanity... Our customer feels the presence of the person who crafted the object, while at the same time the object brings him back to his own sensitivity, because it gives him pleasure through his senses.'[6]

The driving force behind the choices of quality and uniqueness is the intense desire of the brand, as a company, to uphold its exclusivity. The aura of sophistication is important for Hermès, the goal of which is to make 'ultra-premium' luxury goods which maintain their value over time. In some cases, they become true investments.

The stylistic features of Hermès, important and distinct elements, have been built and maintained for over a century, helping to create a visual identity which is also innovative and deeply rooted in tradition. The fashion house has created a brand identity which reflects its founding values, constructing a solid bridge between what the company wants to represent and the way it's perceived by its audience.

As a result, Hermès has maintained its philosophy based on values such as heritage, quality and sophistication, all designed to create with minimalism in mind.

Minimising to maximise sensations and emotions: an incredibly powerful and modern way of doing things which still looks to tradition, and for this reason, is freed from the need to continuously invent new stylistic codes, skilfully reinterpreting its original ones. Archetypes which give rise to objects that unite form and function in timeless quality.

It is there where the element of time, or better yet, timelessness, plays the leading role in the story of Hermès accessories and the brand's philosophy, infusing them with intangible preciousness.

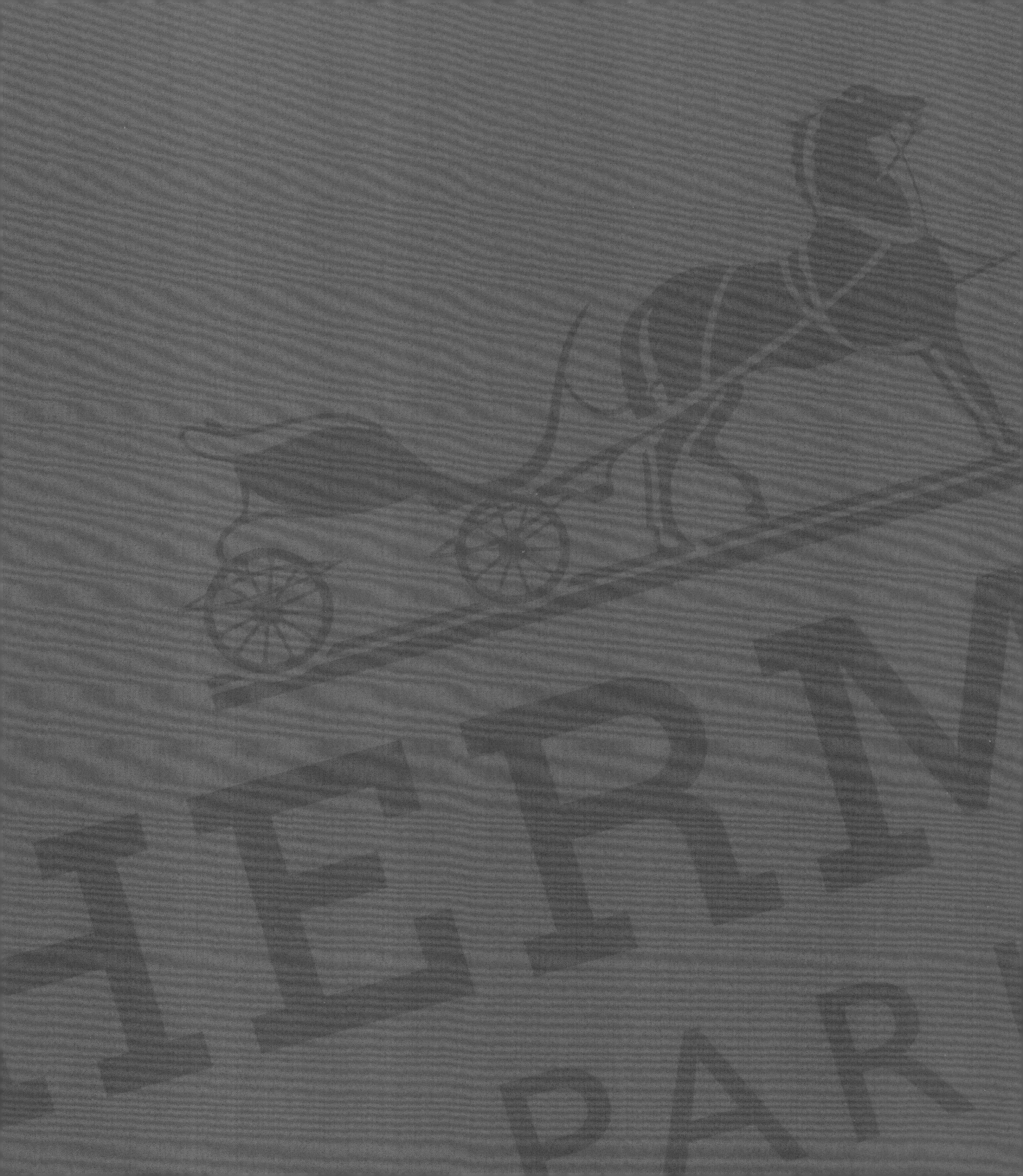

HISTORY

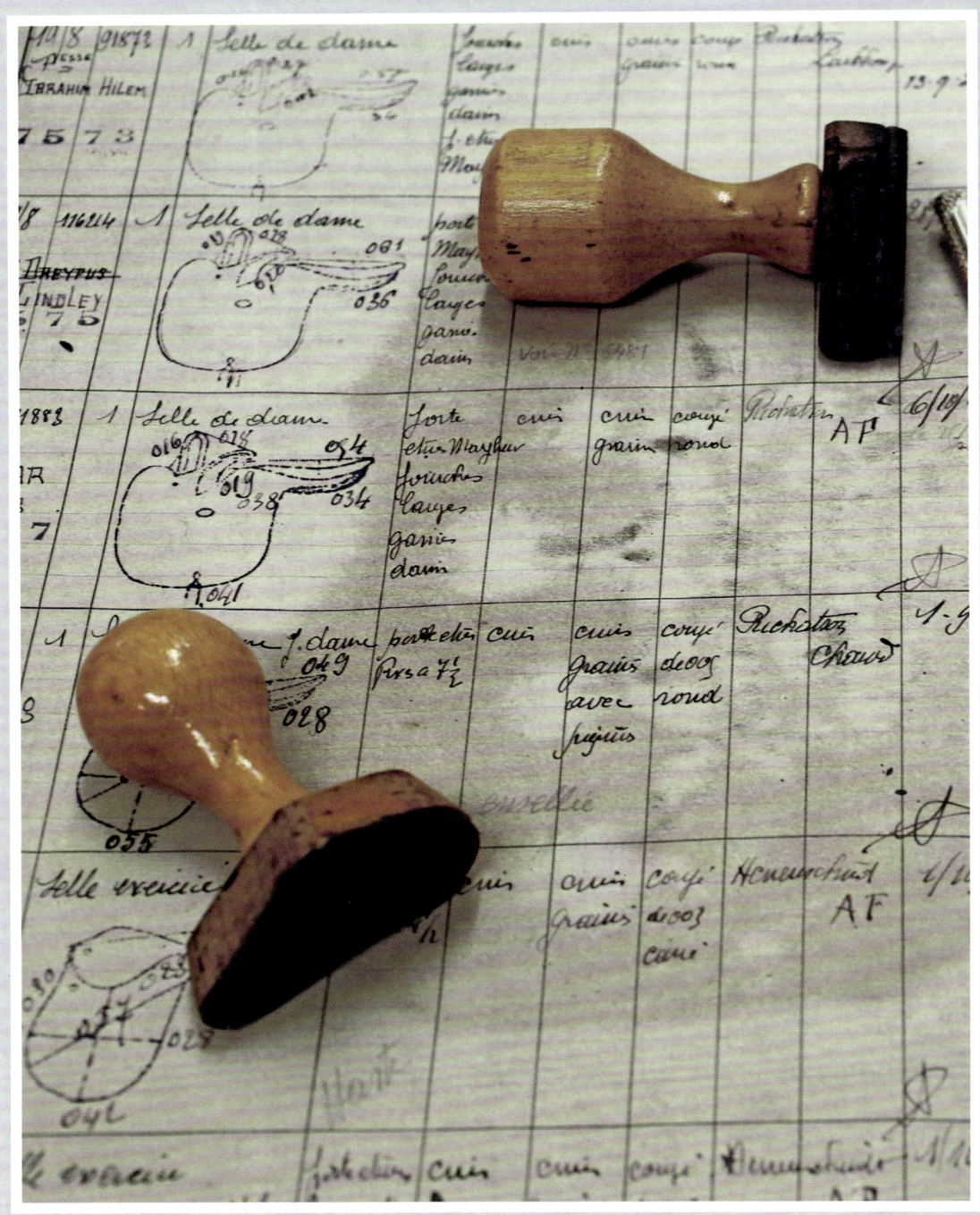

Order book for entirely handmade saddles from the Hermès atelier in France.

HERMÈS: SUCCESS IN VALUES

....

Hermès isn't just a luxury brand: it's a veritable institution in the fashion industry, a symbol of elegance and refinement thanks to the vision and work of Thierry Hermès and his descendants.

Hermès is nothing short of iconic in the world of luxury. According to the brand consultancy Interbrand, Hermès ranked 22nd on its list of Best Global Brands – Top 100 in 2024, worth 37.4 billion USD. That places it as the second luxury brand in the world, behind only Louis Vuitton, which comes in eleventh place, worth 50.9 billion USD.[1]

That success is even more impressive if we consider that Hermès doesn't have a large portfolio of different brands like its main competitors, such as LVMH, Richemont and Kering. Instead, what it has is a range of products, from leather goods, lifestyle accessories and furniture to perfume, watches, jewellery and ready-to-wear, all of which are sold under the Hermès name.[2]

The brand's target customers are generally individuals with abundant spending power who are willing to invest in exclusive products which are crafted with meticulous attention to detail and quality.

The company's product range has expanded over time, despite maintaining an absolute consistency in terms of design, products and communication style, thereby achieving greater and greater success up to today. However, the story of one of the world's leading luxury brands began over a century ago, and is inextricably linked to the Hermès family.

German roots

Thierry Hermès, the founder of Maison Hermès, is a legend in the luxury world, but his story winds its way amid historic events and the mystery which shrouds the lives of those who have created incredible things without being born into wealthy families.

Thierry was born in Krefeld, northern Rhineland, in January 1801. Krefeld is located in Germany today, but was then part of the Confederation of the Rhine, an alliance of German countries established and protected by Napoleon.[3] His family was French in origin and, being of the Protestant faith, his ancestors probably moved to the German side of the border in the 17th century so that they could freely practise a religion which was looked down upon in France. The youngest of six, he was raised in a simple home, though not an impoverished one, permeated by values linked to hard work. In practice, all the youths in the family helped run the small inn which their father, Dietrich, opened in 1780 in central Königstrasse.[4] Krefeld was a small yet booming town thanks to its local fine textile trade. In particular, the silkworks of the von der Leyen family had gained international fame, drawing clients from all over Europe. It was there that Thierry must have learned about the exquisite fabric that would become so important to his brand.

Inns were places where travellers would let their horses rest, and it's possible that young Thierry had the job of welcoming them, learning about these marvellous animals and a world that would have a lasting influence on his future. His entrepreneurial spirit, on the other hand, must have been passed down to him from his father who, son of a forester, had opened a successful business.[5]

Nothing is known for sure about Thierry's life from 1816 until 1821, the year in which he is first documented as living in Paris. There are different hypotheses about what happened in his life, but, as his parents and brothers are no longer mentioned, it can be presumed that he became an orphan and was left to his own devices. The Thierry who reached the French capital certainly was young and eager to create a new life, spurred on by the Protestant work ethic that would remain with him throughout his life.

Despite the conservatism and austerity introduced by the Bourbons after the fall of Napoleon and the economic crisis of the 1820s and 1830s, France, and Paris in particular, would soon undergo a new wave of pomp and splendour thanks to the Second Empire established by Napoleon III in 1852.[6] The city offered unique opportunities to those who had the talent and tenacity to come out on top. In particular, the aristocracy and upper middle class loved horseback riding, a popular pastime which required a wide array of tack and other gear. This was precisely the world in which Thierry decided to open his business. At first he probably worked as a coachman and groom, but in 1837 he opened his first harness workshop in Rue Basse-du-Rempart, near La Madeleine. The location was no accident: not long before the republican conspirator Giuseppe Fieschi had attempted to assassinate King Louis-Philippe of France in that quarter, killing 18 people. Consequently, local real estate prices fell and Thierry, who had a good nose for a bargain, seized the opportunity. Hermès specialised in the manufacture of bridles, saddles and other equestrian tack, realised with fine craftsmanship. His work stood out for attention to detail, quality materials and technical innovation.

An atelier of fine goods

In those years, demand for tack and other equipment for horses was steadily rising. Horseback riding wasn't just a fundamental means of transport for most people; it was also a status symbol and a recreational activity for elites. In the early 1800s, having a passion for all things related to horses was a defining trait of French nobility. Equitation, in particular, was considered a noble and refined art, practised by gentlemen as an essential part of their upbringing. The Equestrian Acade-

my founded in the 17th century at Versailles was a riding school for much of the 19th century, where officials and non-commissioned officers learned the art of controlling a horse, a symbol of elegance and discipline. Being an able horseman meant demonstrating a set of virtues, such as courage, self-control and grace.

The nobility also cultivated its enthusiasm for horses through horse races, which would become popular in the 1820s and 1830s. French nobles began to import English breeds, such as the thoroughbred, which soon would become the stars of

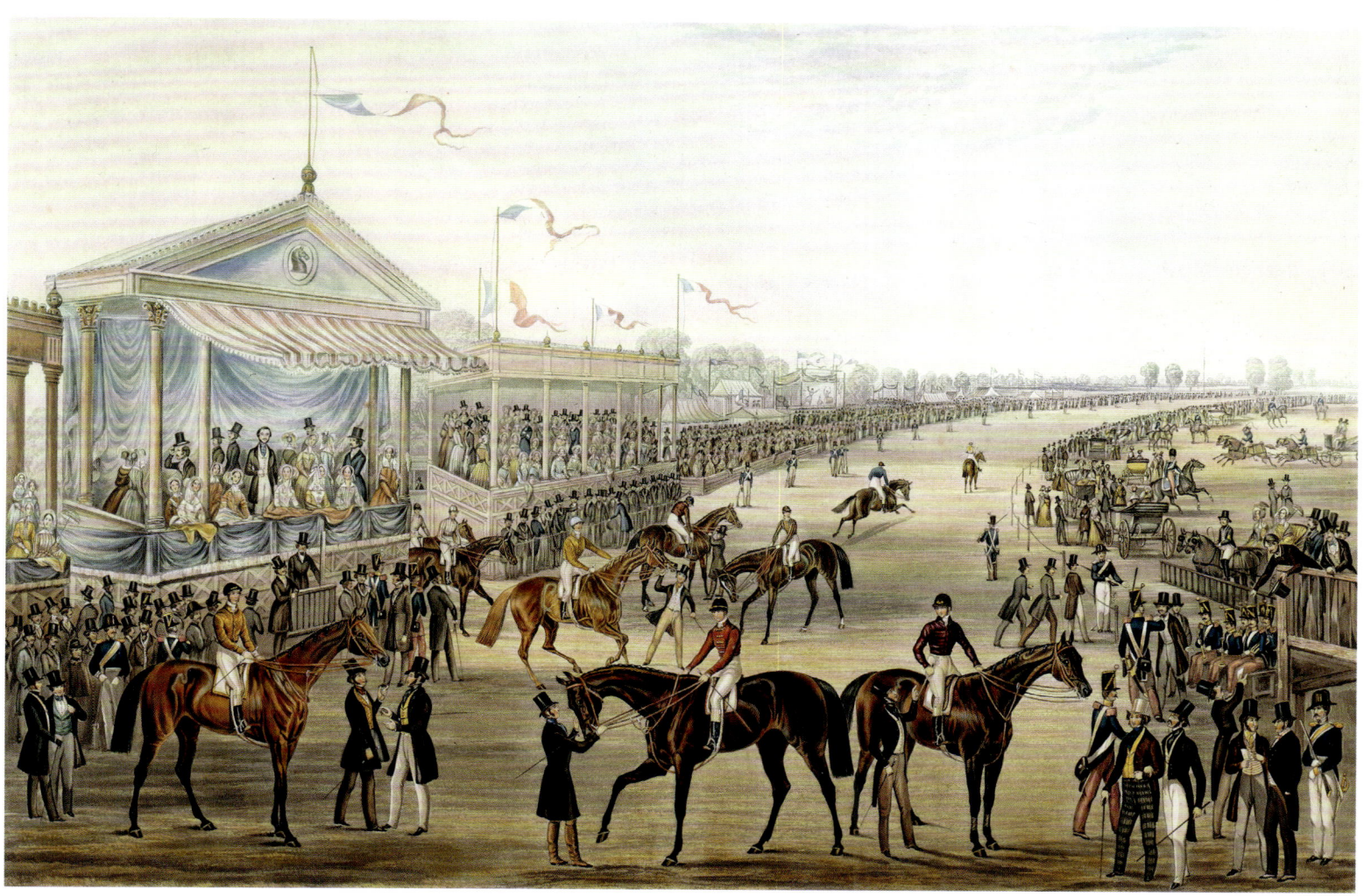

Print of the *Prix du Jockey Club in Chantilly in 1841*. John Frederick Herring Sr, France.

races in large royal and private stables. The first official races were held at the racetrack of Chantilly, and the Prix du Jockey Club, founded in 1836, became one of the most prestigious competitions of the day.

The most well-equipped stables and horse-drawn carriages were tangible expressions of economic power and aristocratic distinction, and a love of horses helped shape the look of clothing and accoutrements, with finely crafted saddles, bridles and harnesses which reflected the taste and refinement of the owner.

Thierry not only created high-quality goods; he offered impeccable service to his customers too. His reputation grew quickly and his clientèle became increasingly exclusive.

The young artisan even received a prize for the quality of the work he showed at the 1855 Paris Exhibition, an event that brought together artisans and entrepreneurs from around the globe to exhibit the best technological and artistic innovations. This success was the start of a long list of recognitions which the Parisian *maison* would receive.

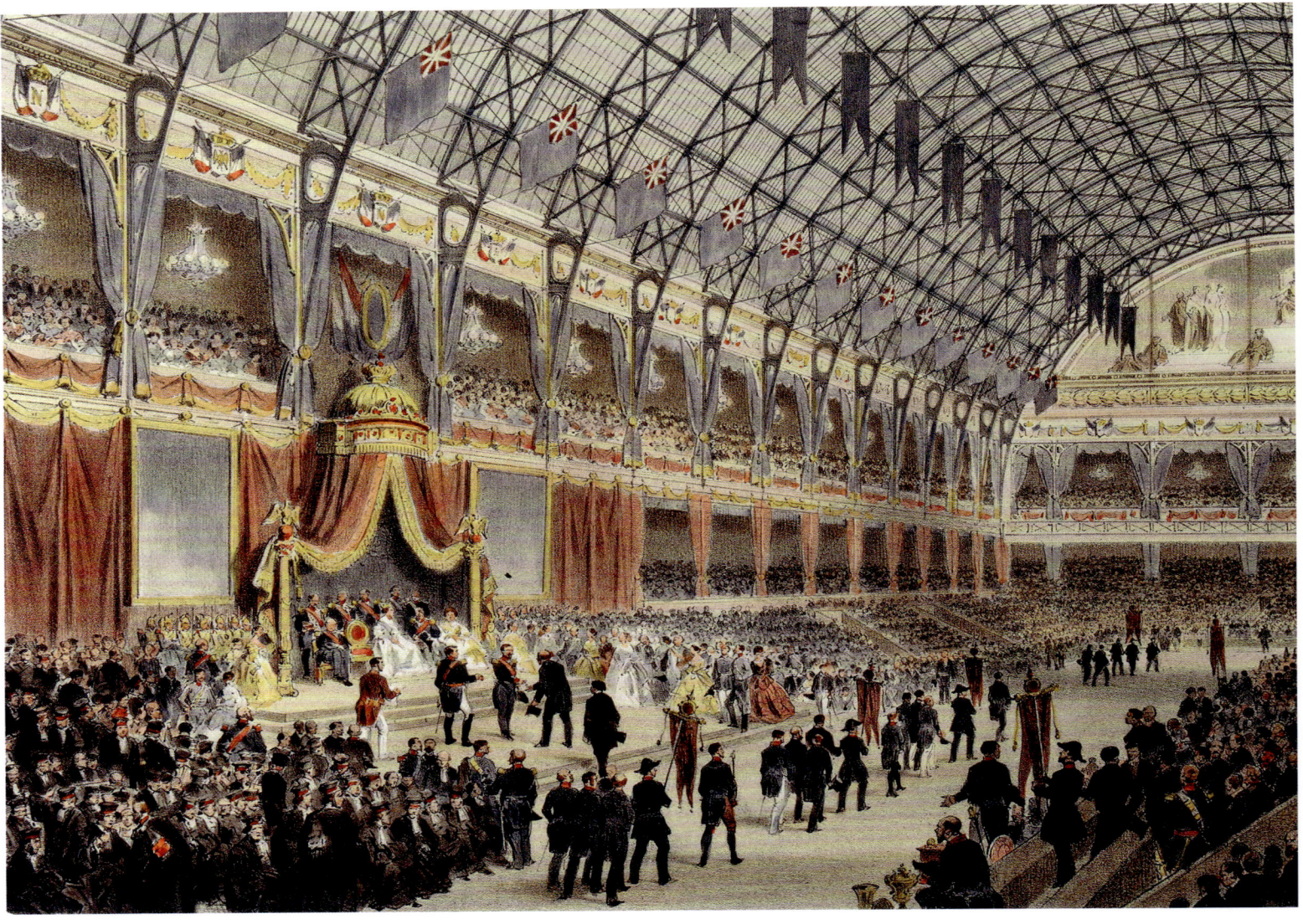

Innovation and diversification

Thierry Hermès died in 1878, leaving the company in the hands of his son Charles-Émile who, while keeping the focus on horse tack, began to diversify the brand's product range. He introduced new items such as luggage, bags and accessories in leather. This expansion marked the start of the transformation of Hermès from a saddler's workshop to a maison that sold many different high-quality products.

In the late 1800s, Paris was in the midst of an urban, industrial and cultural transformation which made the city a symbol of modernity and excellence in fashion, jewellery, fine art and gastronomy.

Led by Baron Georges-Eugène Haussmann, the city was completely reorganised in terms of urban development between 1853 and 1870. The main goal was to make Paris more modern, cleaner and more accessible. Its famous grand boulevards, monumental squares, new parks and elegant buildings created a context that exalted wealth and luxury, a true stage for the social life of the upper classes. This new Paris drew international attention,

becoming not only a cultural and artistic hub, but also an important commercial centre where luxury industries found their perfect habitat.

High fashion was born in Paris thanks to Charles Frederick Worth, an English couturier who opened his atelier in Paris in 1858. He forever shifted the paradigm of the relationship between couturier and client. Many other designers followed in Worth's footsteps, transforming the city into a hub of creativity and sartorial innovation. Among them, in the early 1900s, were Jacques Doucet, Paul Poiret and Jeanne Lanvin, who introduced new styles and techniques and helped make Paris a place where trends took shape. Fashion houses would become veritable temples of luxury popular among the aristocracy and upper middle class of France and beyond, who came to Paris to purchase exclusive clothing.

Alongside the finest dressmakers and tailors, the jewellers of Place Vendôme and Rue de la Paix – from Cartier to Boucheron and Chaumet – became symbols of luxury and fine craftsmanship. Their clientèle included kings, emperors and industry magnates, attracted by the refinement and exclusivity of French creations.

Lithograph of the closing ceremony of the 1855 Universal Expo in Paris and the awarding of prizes to the exhibitors at the Palais de l'Industrie. France, 19th century.

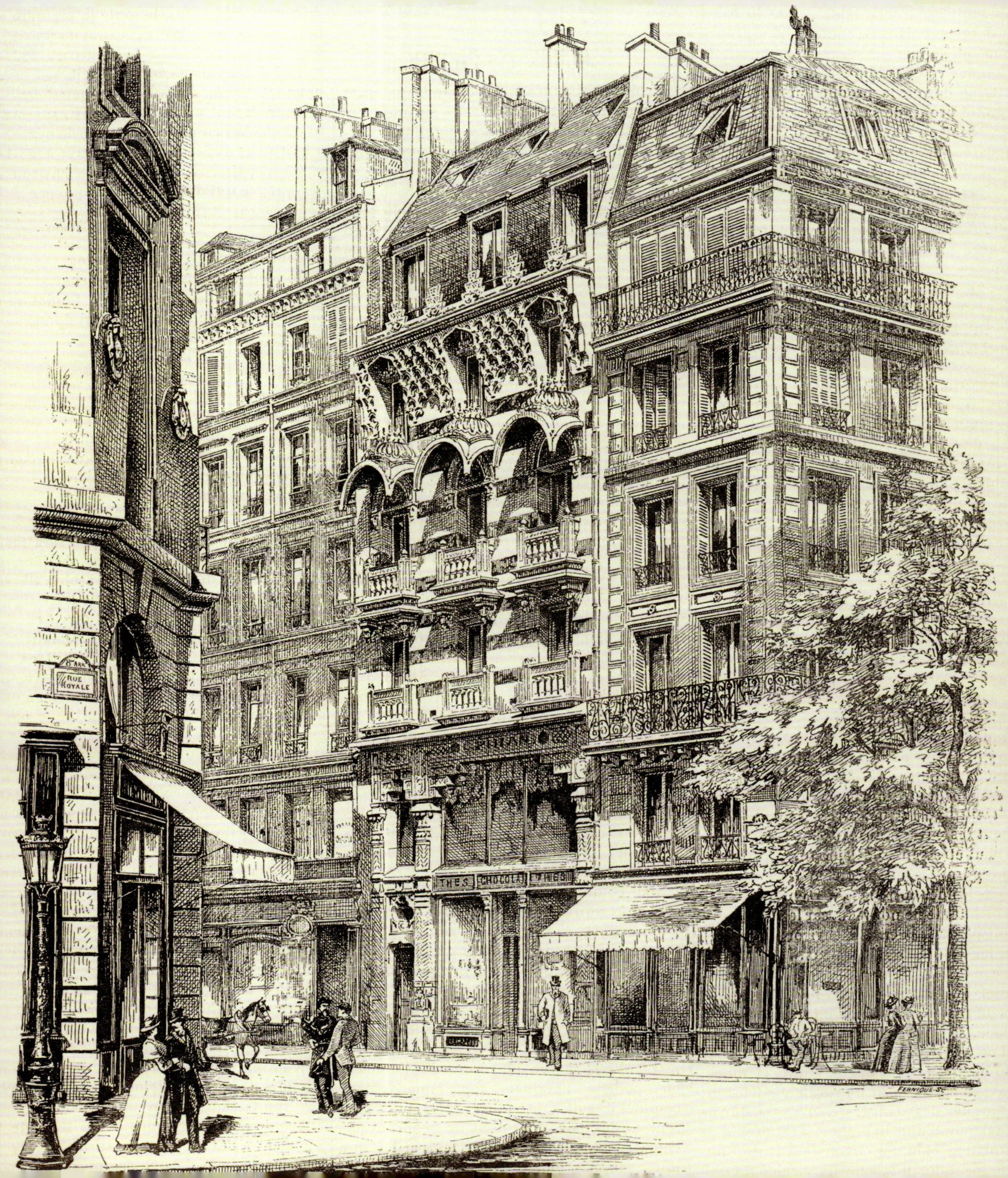

Seeking his place in that gilded world, Charles-Émile Hermès moved the Hermès fashion house to 24 Rue du Faubourg Saint-Honoré in 1880. This new location, in one of the most elegant quarters of Paris, made the brand even more visible and accessible to that exclusive circle of customers.

To carve out a special niche among the many other luxury goods on the market, Hermès decided to focus on the quality of its leather as its defining trait. The maison used only the finest hides, tanned according to traditional handcrafted methods which guaranteed exceptional durability and unrivalled beauty. This rigorous approach to the selection of materials became one of the pillars of the brand's reputation.

In this historic context of industrial and creative buzz, Charles-Émile was assisted by his two sons, Adolphe and Émile-Maurice. The second-born was an aesthete and a passionate traveller, and the *gauchos* of Argentina would be an inspiration to him. Seeing the bags they used to carry their gear, he came up with the *Haut à Courroies* (literally 'high belts'). First produced *c.*1897, the bag is characterised by an ample yet rigid structure, with adjustable straps and durable handles which allowed horseback riders to transport saddles and boots, reflecting the equestrian roots of the brand. Over time, this bag (now called the *HAC*) became a fine design icon and a prestigious accessory. It would also form the base for the design of the Kelly bag.

Etching of the building in Rue du Faubourg Saint-Honoré which became the Hermès headquarters in 1880. Illustration for *La Semaine des Constructeurs*, Huitième Année. France, 1883–1884.

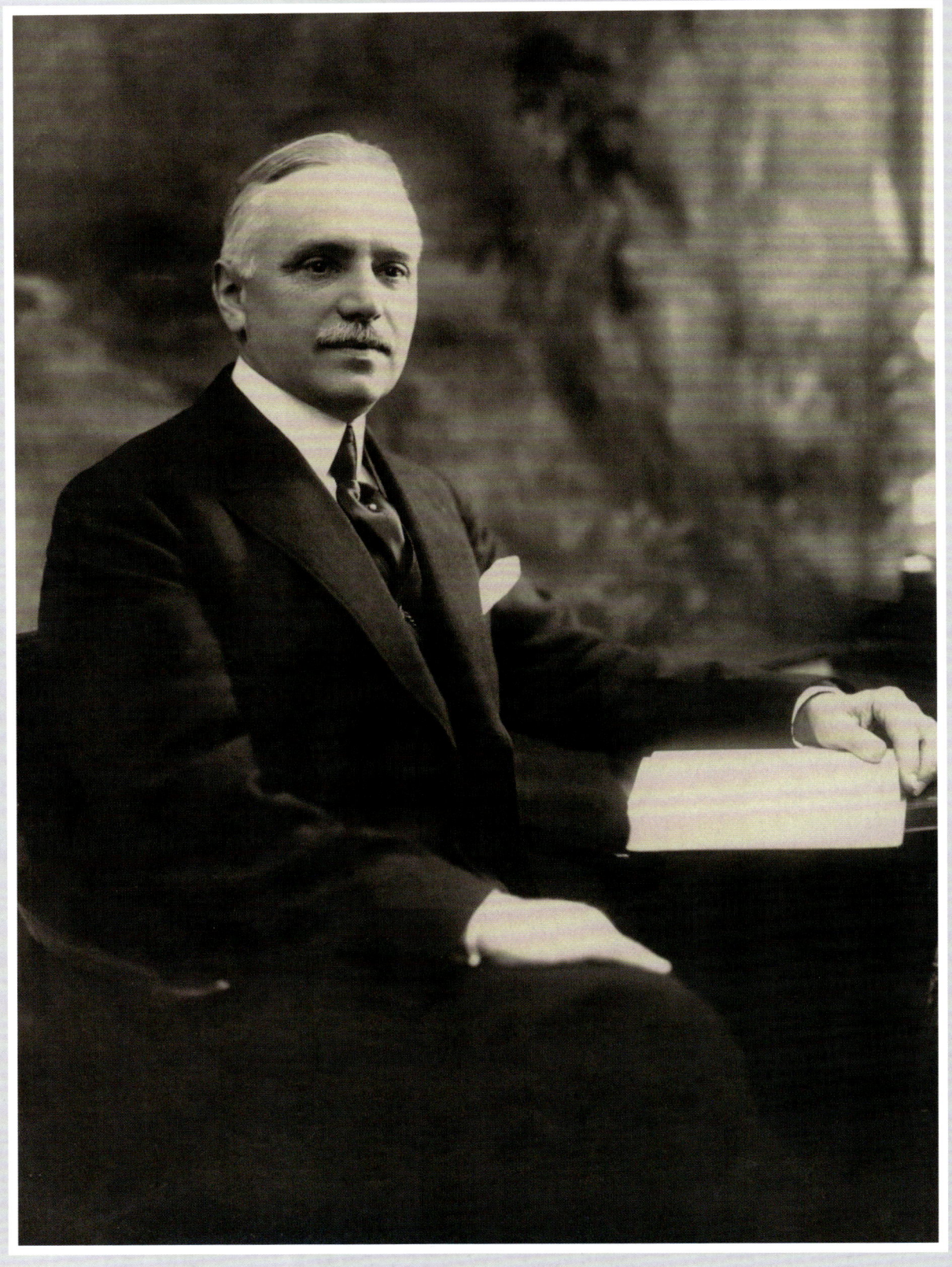

Portrait of Émile-Maurice Hermès. Led by his *flâneur* instinct, he created the 'world of wonders' which is now part of the Hermès Museum. Tuned in to modernity, he turned the company into a luxury brand.

The instinct of a *flâneur*

From a young age, Émile-Maurice was an enthusiastic collector. Travelling the world, he amassed a wide range of objects, from works of art to furniture, old books and items tied to the equestrian world, which reflected the origins of the fashion house. His tastes and interests went beyond the personal: they would deeply influence the aesthetics and identity of the brand too. His private collection, which can still be admired in the original Hermès offices in Paris, has become a source of inspiration for many of the company's creations.

His family members called him a *flâneur*, a term made famous by the poet Charles Baudelaire, who used it to describe a person who loved to roam the city streets and give in to unhurried exploration, free from rigid plans, which would in turn give rise to creativity.

He was the first Hermès scion to want to travel to discover new cultures and, as often happened at many other luxury fashion houses, to establish ties with the representatives of royal houses, European nobility, and the American upper class, who would then become loyal customers of the brand.

For this refined new clientèle, constantly on the hunt for items that were both unique and exclusive, Émile-Maurice wanted to provide a wider range of products. So, under his leadership, the Parisian fashion house began to expand into new categories. A man of his times, he understood that the world was changing and that horses, the magnificent animals which determined his success, would soon be replaced by rumbling motor cars. Starting in the early 1900s, these new vehicles began to be seen on the city's streets, driven by the fortunate few who could afford them. The first car races began around that same time, attracting many motor enthusiasts. The Hermès catalogue expanded to include blankets to protect passengers as they rode in the first open-top cars, and also leather trunks, travel bags, gloves, leather accessories and picnic baskets designed to attract sophisticated and international new customers. Another strand of the maison's DNA was thus created.

The dream of a prosperous and festive life was interrupted in 1914 by the First World War. Émile-Maurice was sent to North America to select the leather to be used for the saddles of the French cavalry. While he was scouting materials in Canada, his attentive and curious eye was drawn to the closure mechanism of the convertible top of the car in which he was travelling. It was a zip. Realising its potential use for bags and jackets, he contacted the owner of the patent and obtained an exclusive licence for France. In 1918, for the first time ever, he used a modern zip, incorporating it into a leather golf jacket to be worn by the Prince of Wales, then a style icon and later Edward VIII. It was a smashing success which marked a turning point in the brand's history, a step towards expansion into the clothing industry. As of 1919, the maison would be managed by Émile-Maurice.[7]

The 1920s brought a breath of fresh air and enthusiasm to the entire world. Known as the Roaring Twenties, this decade saw a sharp break with old mores regarding clothing and fashion. Travel on modern transatlantic ocean liners made it possible to dream of a life lived to the rhythm of dancing and cocktails. Fashion reflected this free spirit, especially for women, who abandoned their corsets in favour of shorter, more linear dresses, like the famous little black dress by Coco Chanel. For men, on the other hand, three-piece suits were in vogue. In particular, spending time outdoors, the game of golf, tennis matches, kayaking, sailing and car racing were activities loved by young men and women, who hadn't ever had so much freedom. Sporty style thus influenced clothing too.

Once again able to interpret the zeitgeist and an enthusiastic innovator and trailblazer, Émile-Maurice understood the new role women played in society and the new opportunities this created. He began to produce new lines of objects made just for them, a market which was never abandoned and which would become central to the fashion house. Advertisements from the time demonstrate that Hermès had become a brand with a wide product range.[8] Saddles and hunting accessories were complemented by large sporty bags, suitcases, vanity cases, cigarette cases, golf bags and women's bags.

....

Hermès bags were ideal for women who travelled on the *La France* ocean liner. Advertisement by Léon Bénigni, France, 1927.

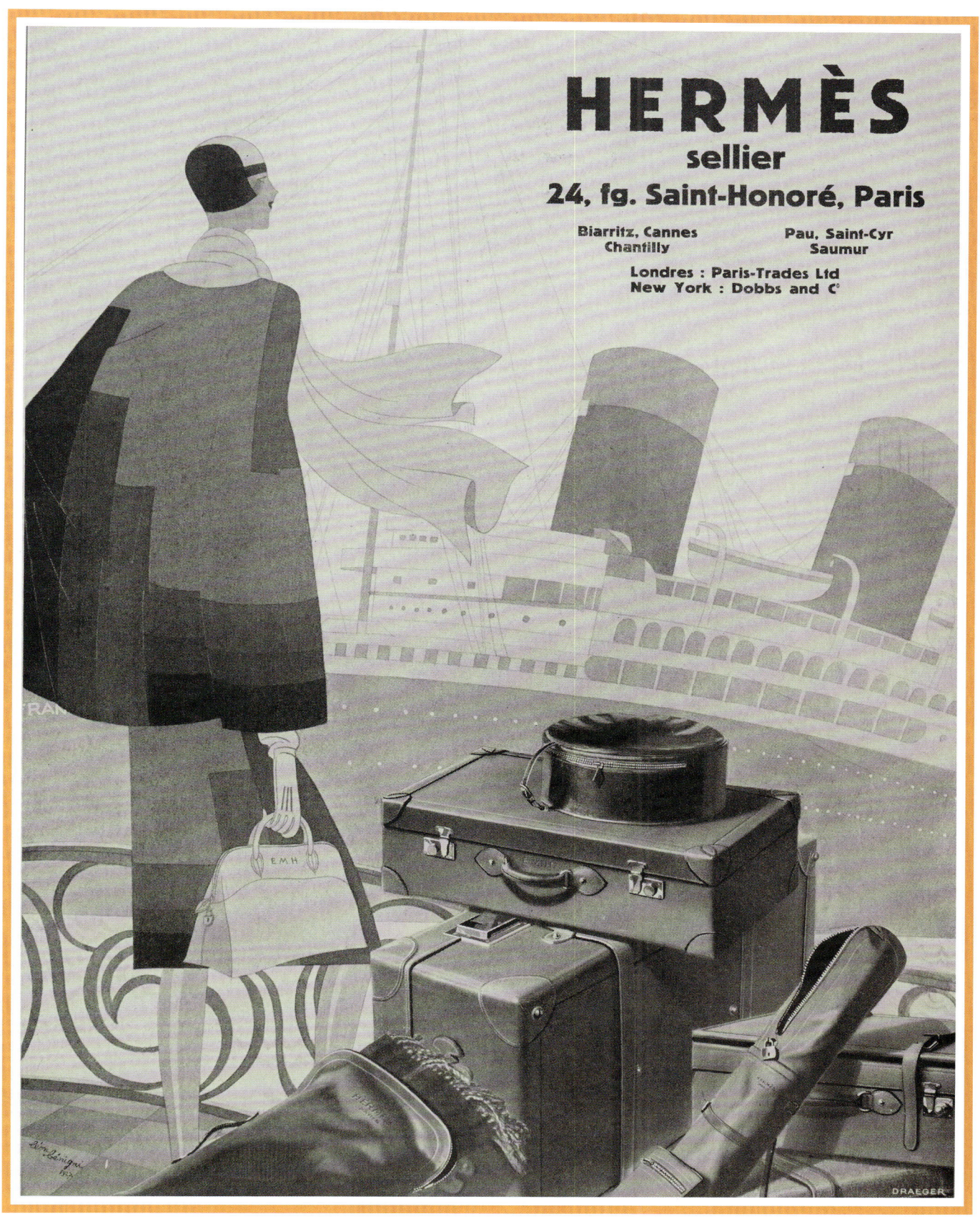

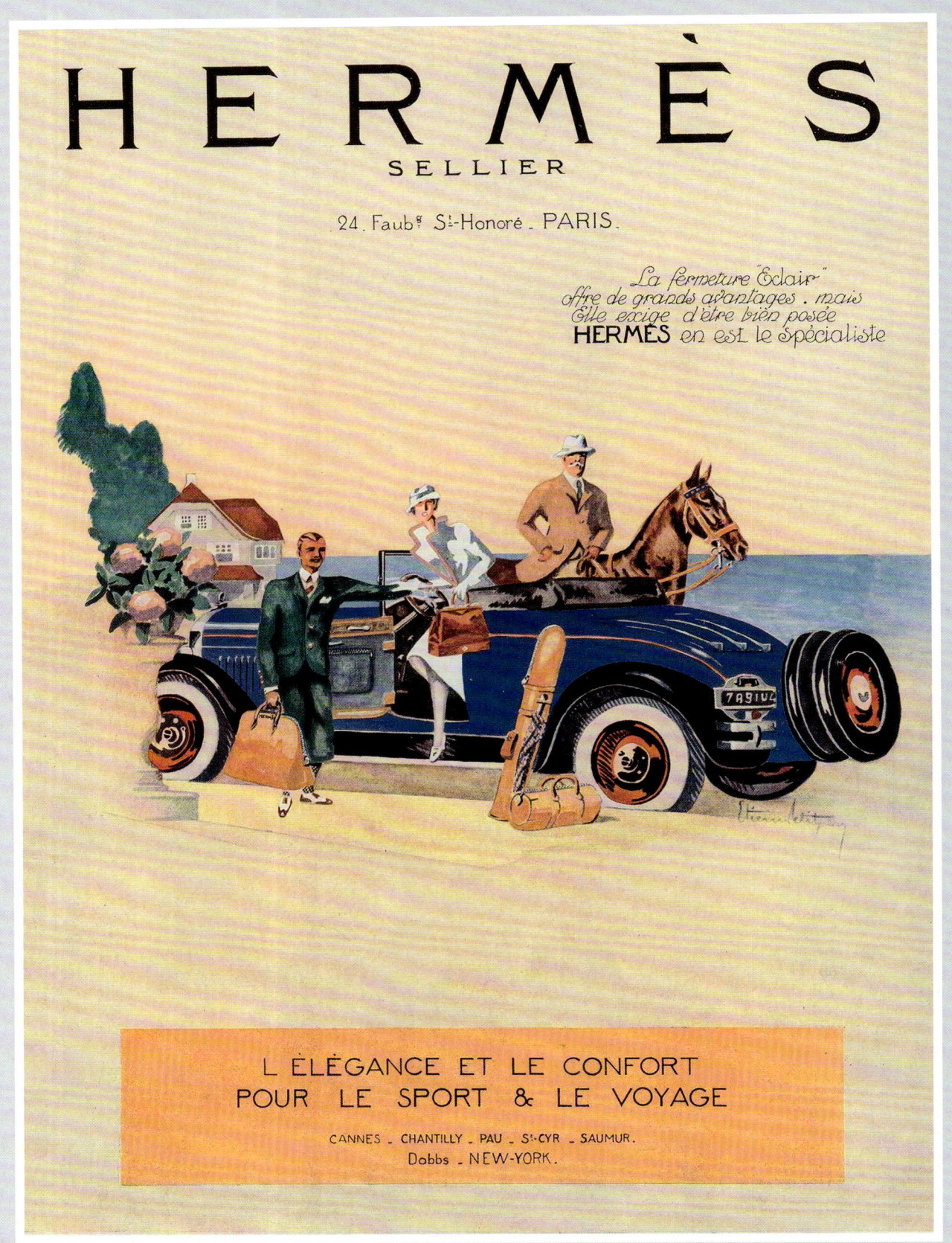

Advertisement for sport and travel bags highlighting the advantages of the *Éclair* (zip) closure which was the speciality of Hermès. Designed by Etienne Petitjean, France, 1926.

In 1923, the collaboration between Ettore Bugatti and Hermès gave rise to the *Bugatti* bag, an ode to its drivers. Later on, the bag would be renamed *Bolide*, 'racing car' in French and a reference to a passion for speed, and it would become one of the styles that has been produced for over a century. Designed for car trips, the Bolide was the first bag to be equipped with a zip. It united functionality and luxury with an understated practical design which met the needs of modern life.

Another bag worth special mention in the Hermès universe is the *Sac à Dépêches*, which was created in 1930. This work bag was designed to be an elegant and secure way to carry paperwork and personal items. It stood out for its rigid and clean structure, and it was finished with a metal closure. An understated and essential silhouette made it a symbol of refinement, ideal for businessmen and other professionals.

Bags for women were made too, ranging from casual styles such as cross-body bags to more formal options, such as the pouches seen in other advertisements, designed to accompany their *mises* on different occasions and times of the day. Of the particularly innovative ones, the *365* bag stands out. Its name reflects the concept of a bag which is suitable for every day of the year and, thanks to bellows construction, it could expand as needed in a combination of practicality and luxury.

During this vibrant time, Hermès began to produce clothing lines, starting with menswear in 1925 and followed by women's haute couture in 1929.

In hindsight, making a fashion début the same year the stock market crashed, leading to a global recession, may seem like madness. But this Parisian maison, the same one which got its start in a different market entirely, was adept at interpreting women's fashion of the 1930s. Stylist Lola Prusac, who designed these new collections, played a leading role in the creation of an innovative and distinct Hermès aesthetic. Polish in origin, Prusac introduced bold elements such as geometric motifs and bright colours which were inspired by modern art, especially the De Stijl movement. Her designs united the handcrafted style of Hermès with avant-garde artistic influences. Her bags and scarves with abstract prints became emblematic, ahead of the curve in the taste for modernism. They also brought a bold touch to the world of luxury. The clothing which Hermès produced for women also included outfits designed to wear in the era's new sports cars.

Accessories remained central to the fashion house, and a few objects destined to become classics were created at this time.

In 1927, Marie Gerber (one of the four sisters of the famous French design house Callot Soeurs) was looking for a belt to embellish her creations. She asked Hermès to create one, drawing inspiration from her elegant dog collars with square studs and pendant rings used to attach a lead. The *Collier de Chien* belt was born. Over the years, the fashion house would turn it into countless versions of chokers and bracelets, still sold today.

That same year, Hermès introduced silver jewellery for the first time. The collection was launched with the *Filet de Selle* bracelet in silver and leather, the form of which is borrowed from saddlery.

Another piece of jewellery destined to become a brand icon was created in 1938, based on an idea by Robert Dumas, who had begun to help his father-in-law Émile-Maurice run the business. It's the *Chaîne d'Ancre* bracelet, with a design that was inspired by sailing: the interconnected oval links in silver recall the large chains attached to boat anchors.

New perspectives

Émile-Maurice Hermès had four daughters, one of whom died young. However, the other three reached adulthood and got married. None of them joined the family business: it was their husbands who did, starting in the 1930s. First was Robert Dumas, the husband of Jacqueline, then Francis Puech, who married Yvonne, and Jean-René Guerrand, who wed the third sister, Aline.

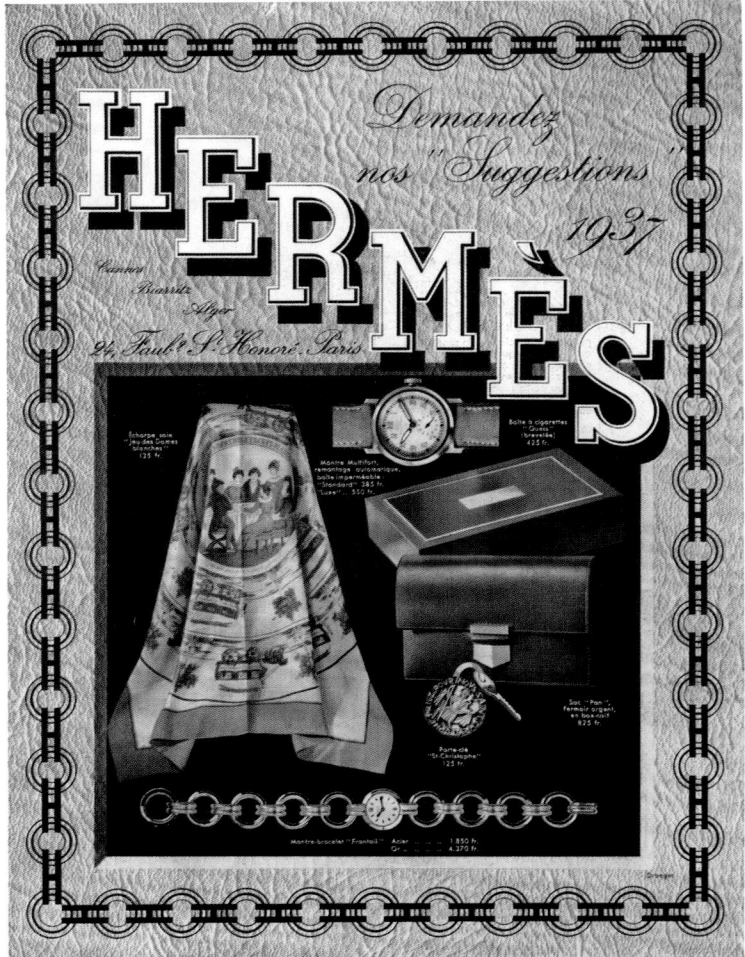

Dumas was a creative and he mostly oversaw the artistic direction of the brand. Puech and Guerrand joined the business management side, bringing their strategic executive vision. Guerrand in particular was known for his discipline and his attention to detail, which ensured consistent quality for Hermès – and the ability to conquer new global markets.

Together, these three leaders helped transform Hermès from a family-run business into a global luxury brand without altering its handcrafted roots and tradition of excellence.

In addition to the *Chaîne d'Ancre* bracelet, Dumas can be credited with the invention of another of the brand's iconic products. In 1935 he designed the *Sac de Dames à Courroies*, reworking the *Haut à Courroies* from the end of the previous century to make it better suited to women. This bag was destined for a glorious future. All it took was one photograph to turn it into a legend: in 1956, a pregnant Grace Kelly carried it to conceal her bump. It was later renamed the *Kelly* in honour of the princess.

The 1930s also gave rise to the first silk scarf, called the *Jeu des Omnibus et Dames Blanches*: it was created in 1937 to celebrate the fashion house's 100th anniversary. The print on its surface was inspired by a French board game that was popular in the late 1800s. With this accessory, which the brand called a *carré*, Hermès sparked a renaissance for the silk square, which women found more comfortable to wear than a hat, especially when travelling by car.

This page – Advert depicting a set of men's accessories such as the *Multifort* watch, the *St. Christophe* keychain and the *Guess* cigarette case, and women's accessories, including a *Jeu des Dames blanches* silk scarf, a feminine *Frontail* bracelet-watch and the *Pan* bag. France, 1936.

Opposite – Grace Kelly with the Hermès bag, which was called the *Sac de Dames à Courroies* at the time. Taken in 1956, the image travelled the world and the bag was renamed the *Kelly* in honour of the Princess of Monaco in 1977.

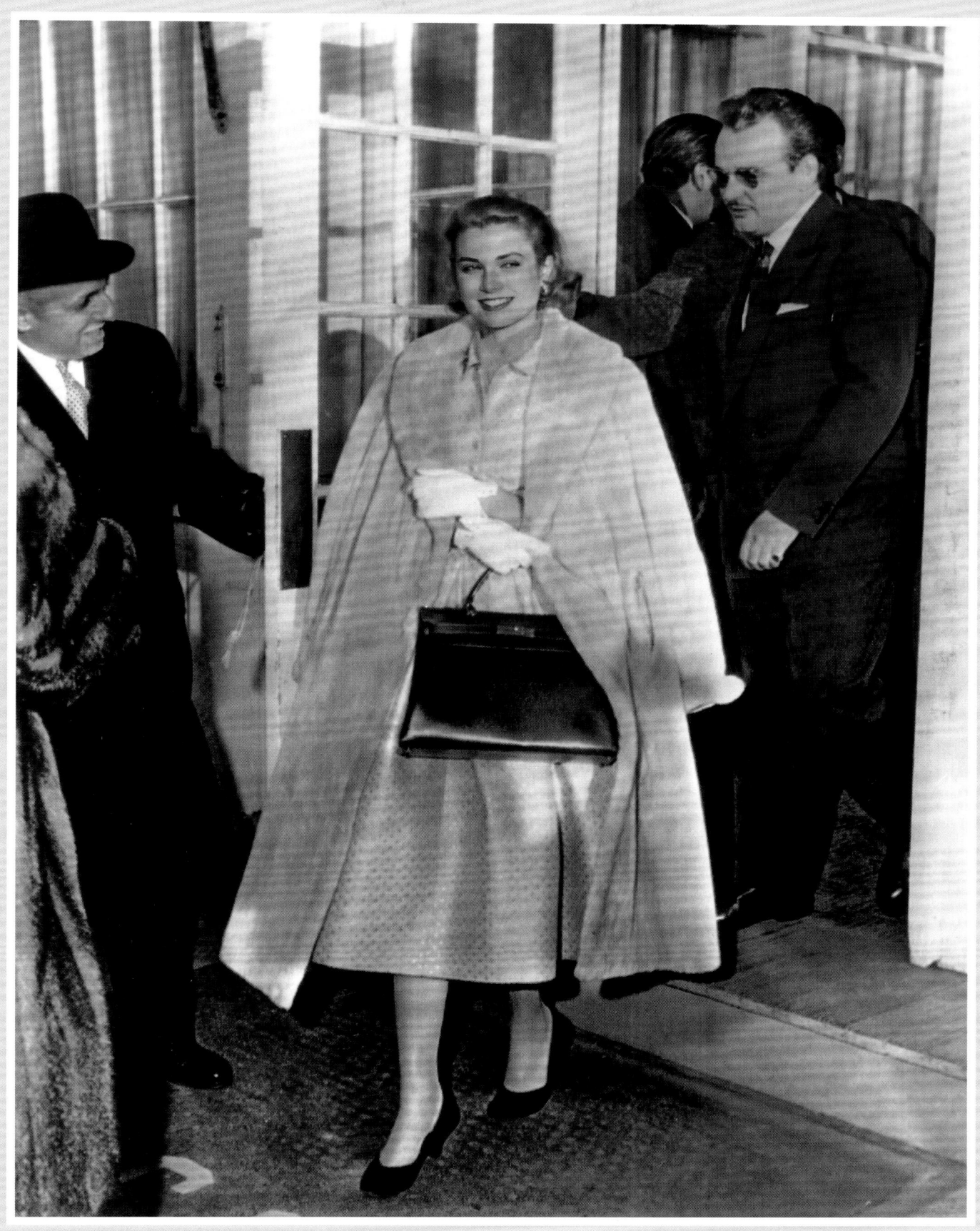

In the 1930s, Hermès became a coveted brand not only in Europe, but also in the United States, where it began to export its products, signing sales agreements with large department stores such as Neiman Marcus in New York.

Unfortunately, the Second World War brought the work of French fashion houses like Hermès to a grinding halt, although its Paris boutique would stay open even during the conflict.[9]

The desire to start again was strong in the post-war period and Hermès returned to the drawing board with a creative impetus, proposing an increasingly vast array of garments, accessories and adornments.

During that same period, after having created their wonderful silk scarves for women, the three brothers-in-law who had taken the reins of the business turned once again to the companies of Lyon, famous for the production of silk, and asked them to produce the menswear accessory par excellence: the neck tie.

The first Hermès neck ties were released in 1949, thanks to the intuition of Bobby Breward, an Englishman who was the manager of the Cannes boutique. A neck tie was obligatory attire for men wanting to enter the local casino, and many came to the nearby Hermès shop in search of one. Aiming to meet the demand, the brand began to produce this accessory in silk. The first featured prints referencing the equestrian world, and those were followed by intricate and original motifs, from naval themes to horse racing, from geometric designs to the animal kingdom. Since then, thousands of versions and variants have been sold. This product quickly became a must-have for refined gentlemen, continuing to expand the prestige of the brand into the world of men's clothing.

The theme of travel returns in this advertisement shot in front of a Wagons-Lits train: the woman wears an elegant head-to-toe look complete with luggage, gloves, a silk scarf, bag, skirt-suit and jacket, all by Hermès. France, 1952.

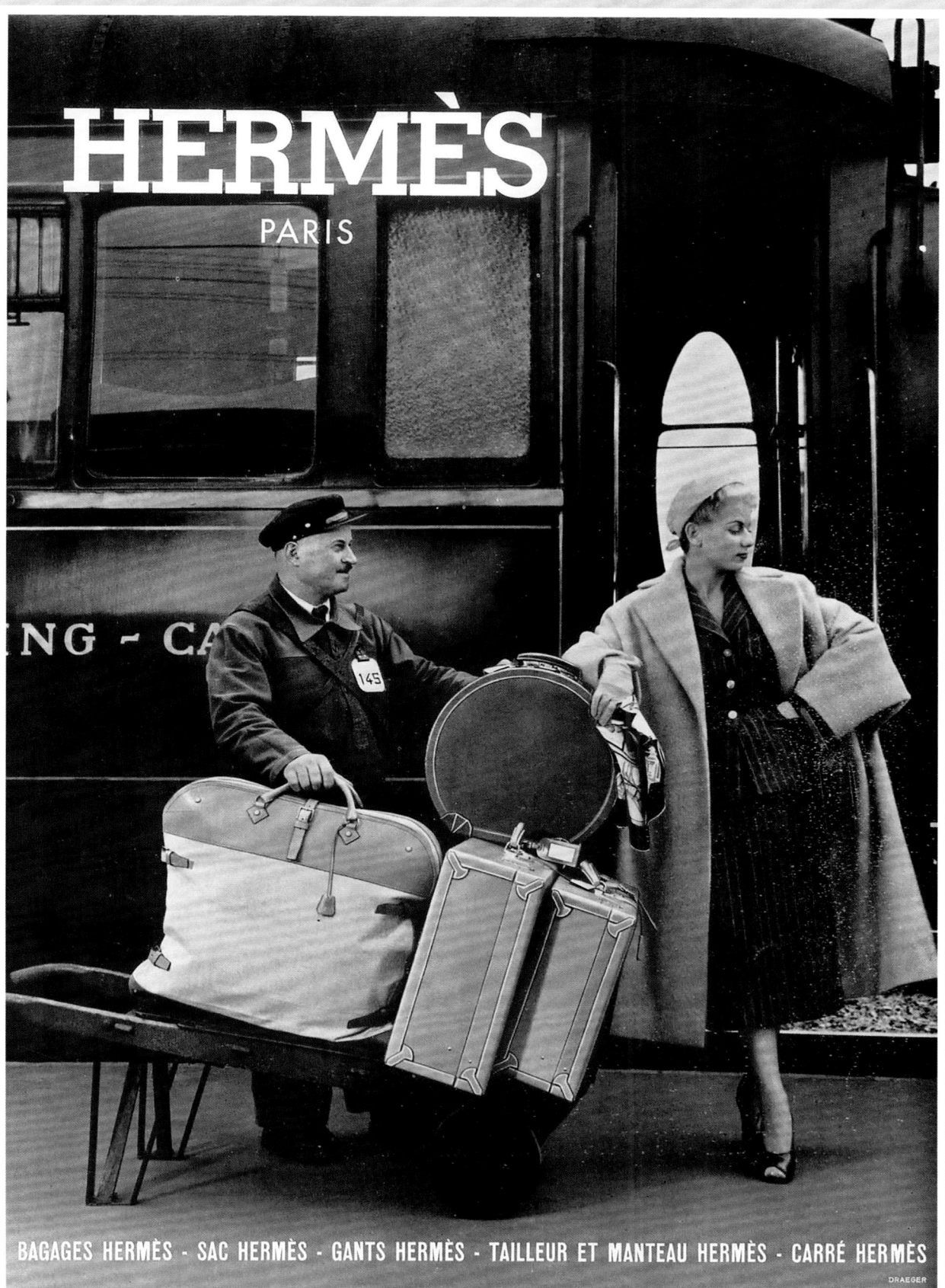

Distinctive features of the brand

The war, however, was an event that left Hermès with one of its most distinguishing elements: its boxes. Recognisable for their iconic orange colour, they have become a distinguishing characteristic which is on par with the luxury products they contain. It must be said that the orange hue wasn't the brand's original choice for its packaging. Up until the 1940s, Hermès used boxes in different colours, such as cream and gold. But, due to the scarcity of dye during the Second World War, it began to use orange, the only hue available in large quantities at the time.

The orange hue came to be so closely associated with the brand that in 1994 it was registered as the official Hermès colour, while the boxes would eventually come in almost 200 different shapes to hold various products. Even the brown cotton ribbon which closes the boxes has become emblematic of the brand. On-tone with the trim of the boxes, those ribbons feature 'HERMÈS PARIS' across their surface and saddle stitching along their edges. They've even been given a name: *Bolduc*, in honour of the Netherlandish town of Bois-le-Duc ('s Hertogenbosch) where they are produced.

Also in the post-war period, Robert Dumas created the logo that has since distinguished the maison. He was inspired by a drawing made in the mid 19th century by the painter Alfred de Dreux, and called *Duc attelé, groom à l'attente*, which was part of the art collection of Émile-Maurice. The Duc Attelé symbol is characterised by a buggy drawn by horses and a nobleman facing them, and it has become iconic, reflecting the historical roots of the company and its heritage of fine craftsmanship in the production of horse tack.

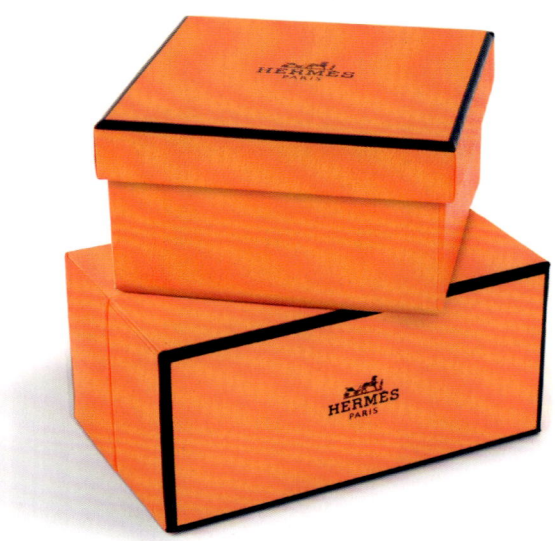

In the post-war period, Hermès packaging got its characteristically vibrant and energy-packed bright orange hue.

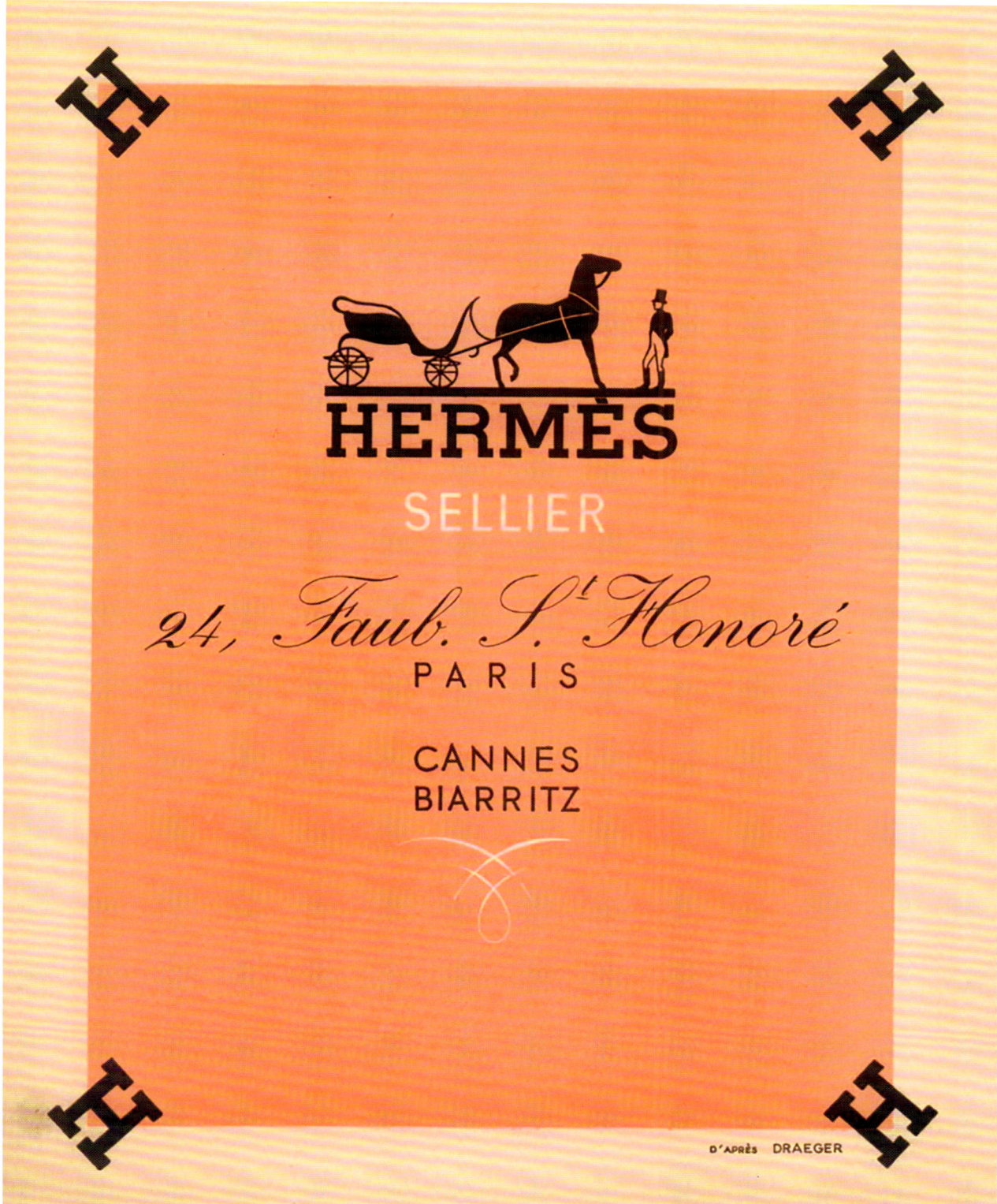

Hermès advert listing its branches. France, 1944.

Growth and expansion

After Émile-Maurice died in 1951, Robert Dumas took on the creative direction of the brand, managing it jointly with his two brothers-in-law. Under his leadership, the brand continued to expand and experiment, strengthening its position as one of the world's most prestigious and iconic luxury fashion houses.

In the 1950s, Hermès continued its diversification, which had started in the previous decades. Its silk scarves became seminal accessories thanks to new prints and bright colours, adored and flaunted by the style icons of the era, from Grace Kelly to Jacqueline Kennedy and Audrey Hepburn.

The success of its silk scarves sparked the introduction of other lines of accessories, such as gloves, belts and wool scarves, all characterised by impeccable quality and sophisticated and innovative designs.

Leather-working traditions, fundamental to Hermès since it was founded, continued to evolve in the 1950s. Bags were updated and even became famous, such as the *Kelly* and the *Haut à Courroies*, while new styles were also introduced, such as the *Mangeoire* (1954), a bucket bag in soft leather suitable for casual looks.

In terms of fashion, the brand followed the style dictates of the post-war period: dresses with ample skirts and cinched waists in pastel hues and floral prints with *mises*, to be worn during the day, as well as dresses for cocktail hours, for formal evenings and even grand soirées, all indispensable in a woman's wardrobe. At Hermès, the fashion department was entrusted to a group of creatives who brought elegance though not necessarily innovation to the style of the decade.

In the early 1950s, like many other fashion brands, Hermès decided to offer its customers a signature olfactory experience. As such, in 1951, *Eau d'Hermès* was introduced, created by Edmond Roudnitska, the *parfumeur* celebrated as the father of modern perfumery. His intention was to evoke 'the interior of a Hermès bag, enveloped in the scent of a perfume'. Following a path similar to that of Chanel, which sought an abstract note for its N°5, far from that of traditional florals, Hermès wanted a fragrance that was evocative and closely linked to its identity.

Eau d'Hermès was one of the maison's first explorations of a market other than leather goods and fashion accessories, anticipating what would become a key industry for the brand in the years to come.

Opposite page – Advert for a trouser suit with a Mangeoire bag, all by Hermès. Illustrated by Pierre Simon. France, 1953.

Following pages – Christmas advert featuring a bag, gloves, a watch and a bottle of *Calèche* perfume, all by Hermès. Advert by French watercolourist and engraver Pierre Pagès. France, 1962.

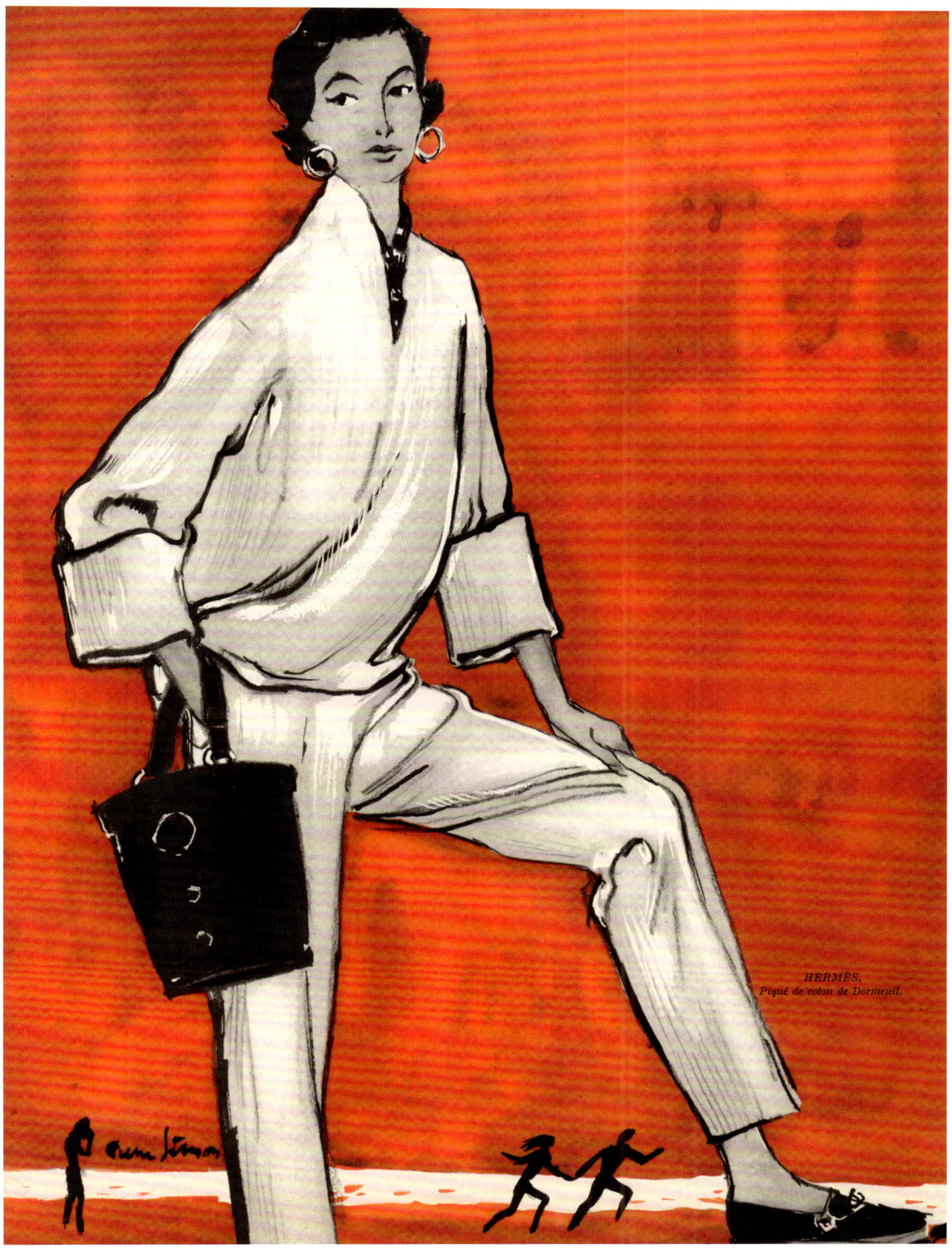

HERMÈS.
Piqué de coton de Dormeuil.

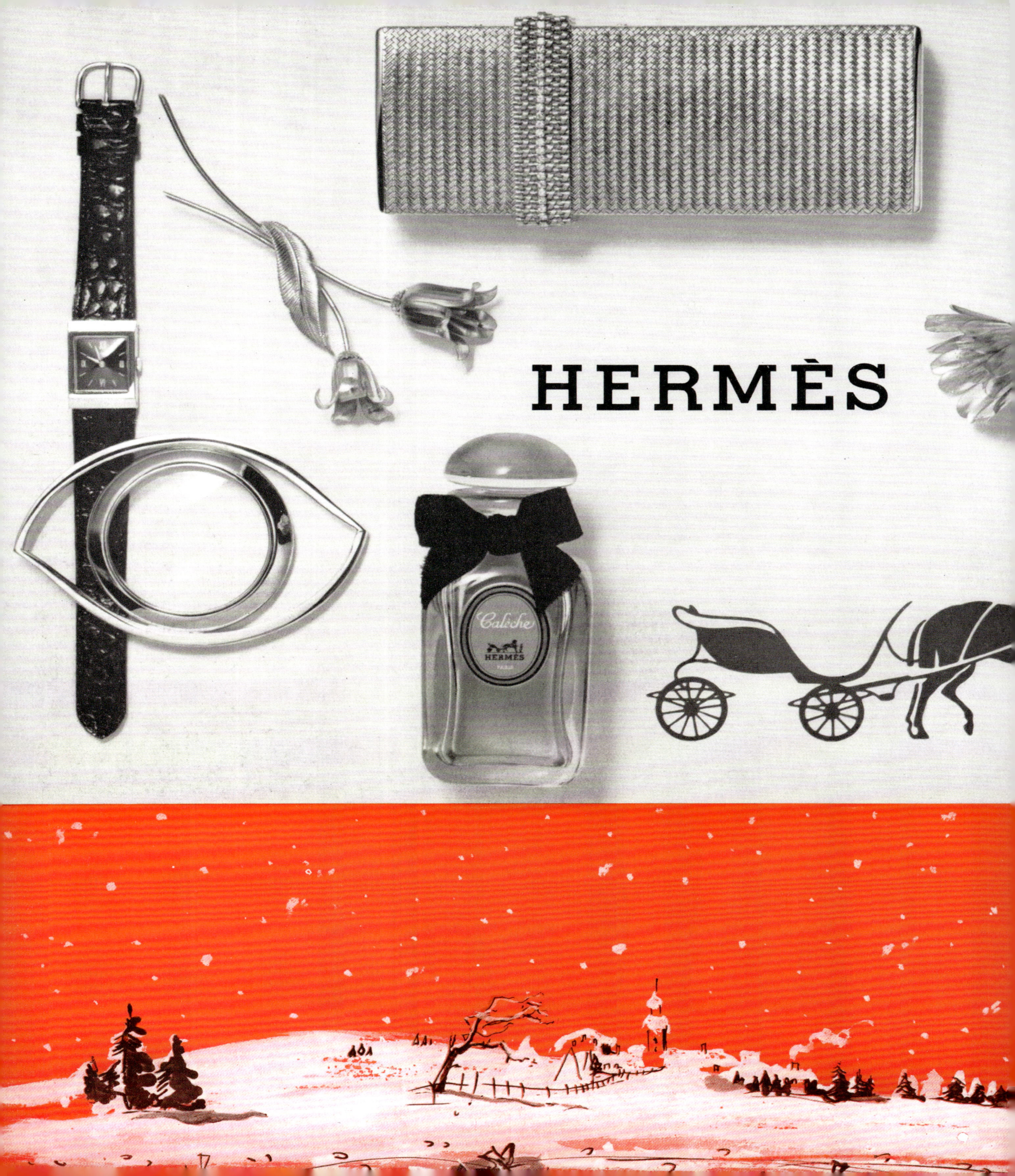

HERMÈS

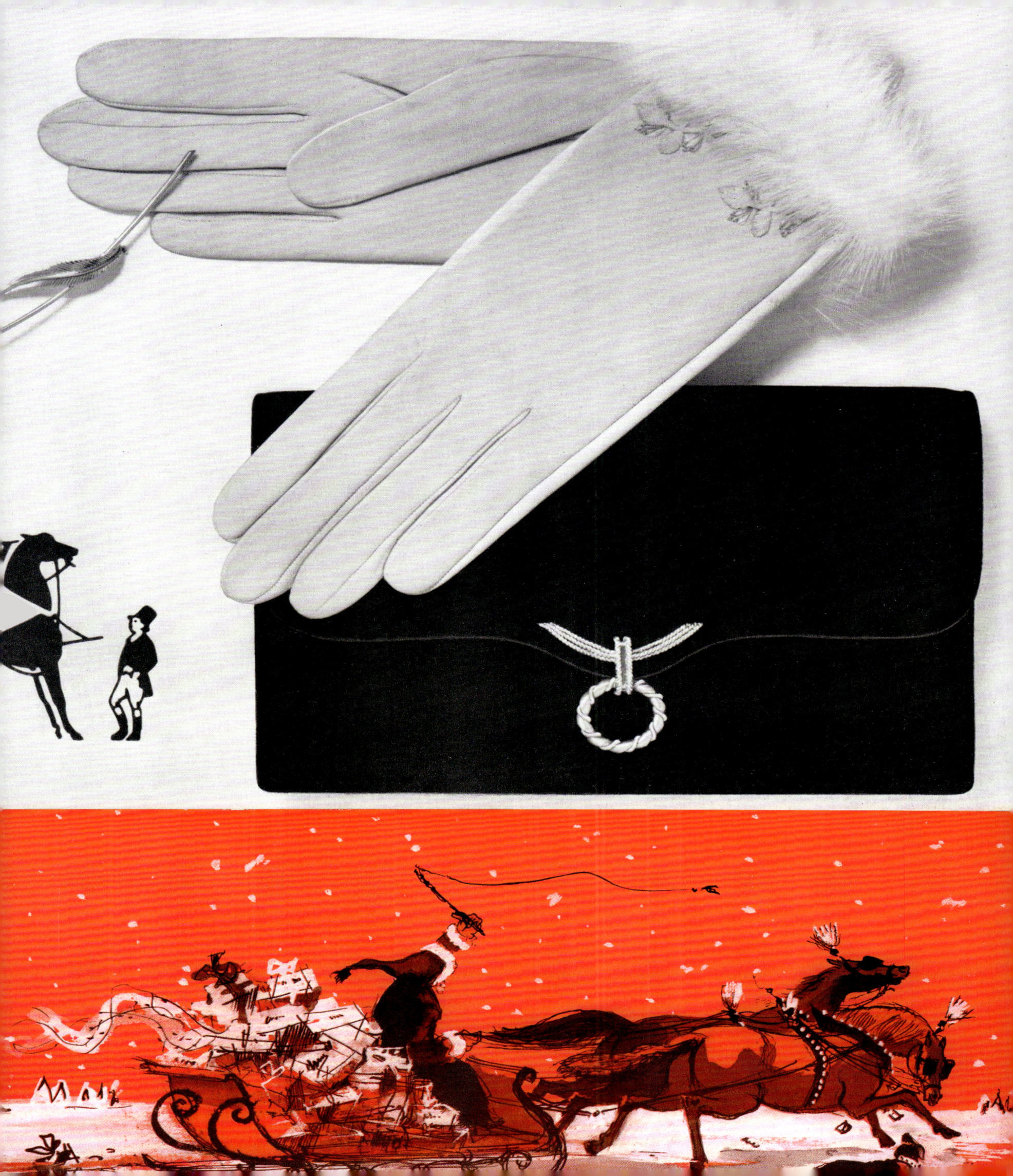

This was also the decade in which Hermès further reinforced its presence in Europe and the US. It opened boutiques and points of sale in the main fashion capitals, introducing its style and luxury craftsmanship philosophy to an increasingly broad and sophisticated clientèle. Hermès creations would become an integral part of the collective imagination, tied to the idea of luxury and sophistication.

In the 1960s, the brand introduced new stylistic elements and broadened its collections, trying to give luxury an innovative interpretation. A symbol of the brand since the 1950s, the silk scarves were refreshed with new motifs that reflected the vibrant and dynamic aesthetics of the decade. At the same time, Hermès continued to promote the luxury leather goods industry, focusing on iconic styles such as the *Kelly*, which shot to fame thanks to Grace Kelly, later Princess of Monaco, and the *Constance*, introduced in 1969. This style, characterised by the H-shaped closure, was and still is one of the fashion house's bestsellers.

In 1967, the first ready-to-wear collection for women was created, entrusted to Hungarian-French stylist Catherine de Karolyi. From then until 1980, she was the one designing the women's clothing and accessory collections, and she can be credited with the famous H-shaped buckle used on belts, bags, shoes and many other accessories.

In this decade, Hermès introduced new products that went beyond leather goods, such as jewellery and home goods, which enriched its product range and met the growing demand for luxury accessories in all areas of daily life. Even the perfume segment grew further, reinforcing the link between Hermès and the beauty and lifestyle worlds.

Around this time, Hermès began to collaborate with famous artists and designers to make its products even more exclusive. The connection with art not only enhanced the uniqueness of Hermès creations, it also strengthened the image of the brand as a cultural reference point and as a fashion house.

Even the shop windows of the boutique became artistic expressions. In the early 1960s, Leïla Menchari, a graduate of the Beaux-Arts Academies of Tunis and Paris, began to assist in the decoration of the window displays of the shop in Faubourg Saint-Honoré. From 1978 to 2013, she was promoted to Director of Decoration, continuing this creative, flamboyant and bold work. After her, stage and film decorator and set designer Antoine Platteau was given control of the shop windows, which took on the look of small elegant theatres.

Hermès continued its international expansion, opening new sales points in the world's main capital cities, such as New York and Tokyo. This expansion strategy reflected the desire of the maison to position itself as a global luxury leader. At the same time, every Hermès boutique was designed to reflect the brand's philosophy, with meticulous attention to aesthetics and the customer experience.

....

Hermès window displays are intended to evoke curiosity, awe and surprise in passers-by, and also to transport them to a colourful and exotic world. This window display, featuring a painting by Thierry Bruet as the backdrop, is by Leïla Menchari, who for years was the artistic director of the shop in Faubourg Saint-Honoré. Hermès Boutique Opéra, 1985.

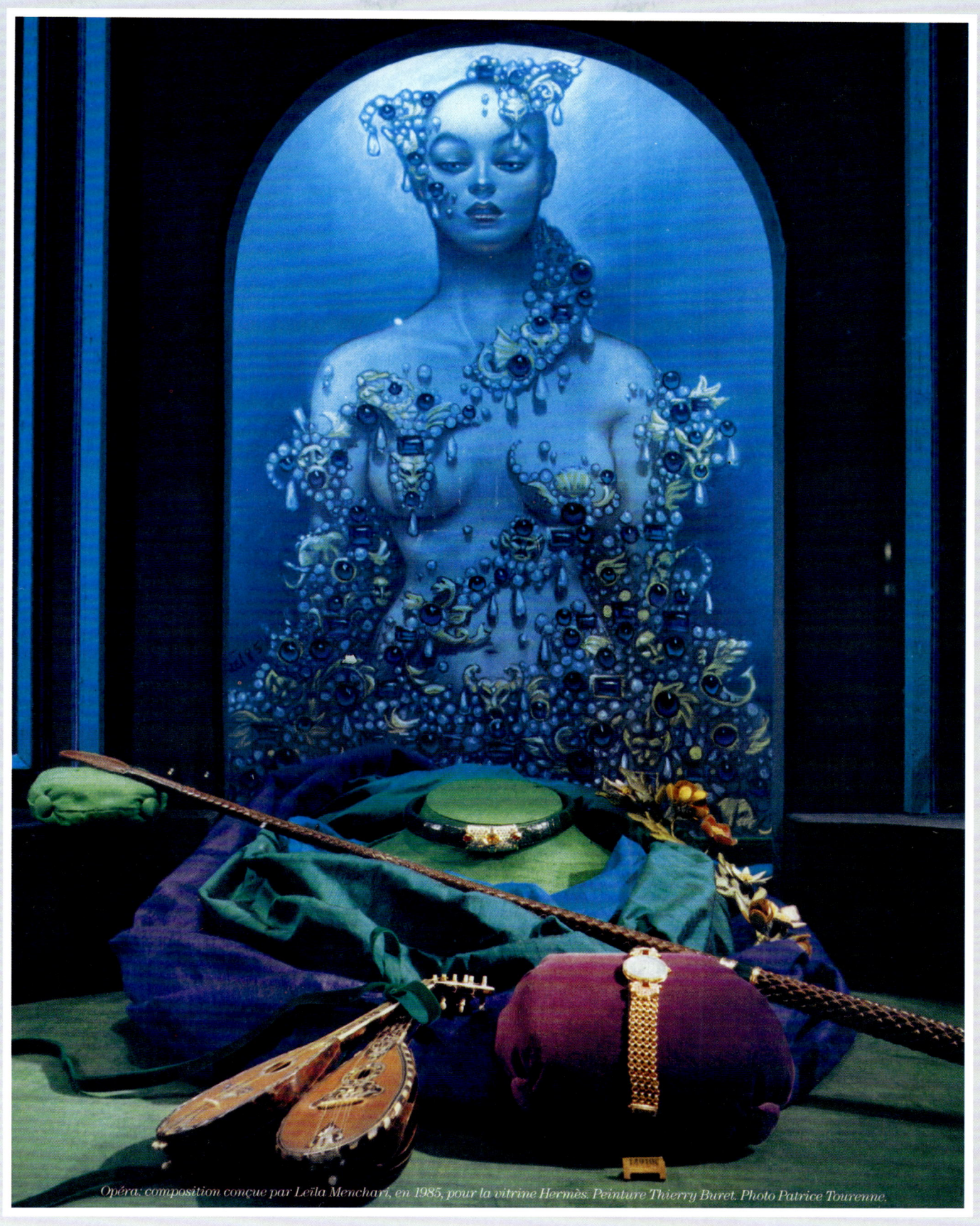

Opéra; composition conçue par Leïla Menchari, en 1985, pour la vitrine Hermès. Peinture Thierry Buret. Photo Patrice Tourenne.

Reinventing luxury

As was tradition, the Hermès family heirs began to prepare for succession, getting the younger generation involved. Jean-Louis Dumas, Robert's son, began working for the company in 1964.

After having studied law and political science, then gone on adventures around the world and lived and worked in New York at Bloomingdale's, young Dumas proved to be passionate about beauty and artisan processes, updated with a modern twist. He was appointed general manager in 1971 at just 33 years old. In 1978, after his father's passing, he became chairman.

He can be credited with a gradual revolution which made it possible for Hermès to reinvent itself, re-examining the concept of luxury. A visionary who was curious about everything and all cultures, he diversified the maison and catapulted it onto the global stage, adapting its products to the tastes and trends of the decade, characterised by greater stylistic experimentation and social change. Even if Hermès was already well-established as a symbol of refinement and high-quality craftsmanship, this period was an opportunity to explore new directions in terms of materials, design and marketing strategies, while staying true to its distinct DNA.[10]

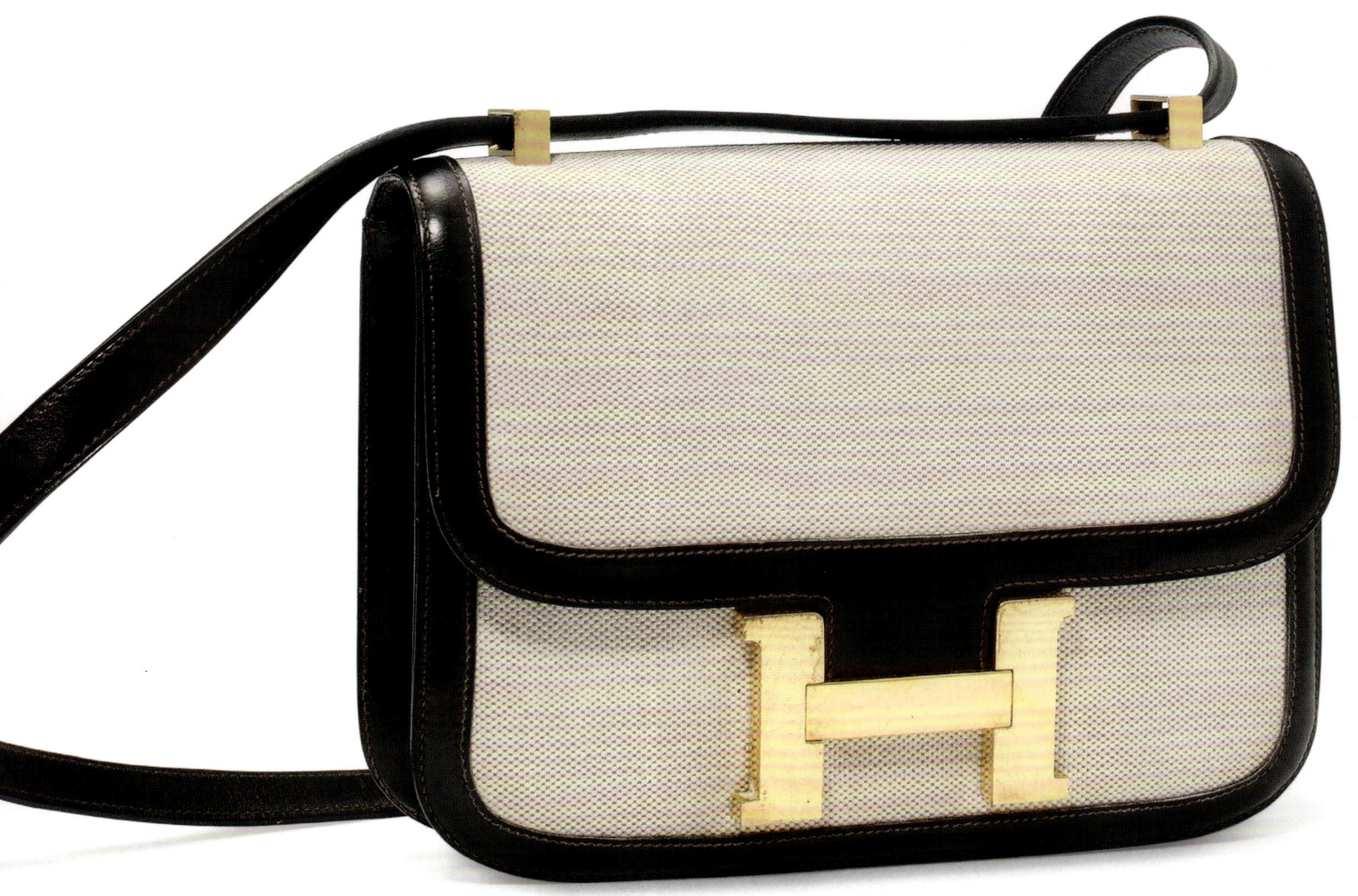

Under the creative oversight of Jean-Louis Dumas, Hermès engaged designers such as Eric Bergère[11] and introduced garments with a more casual and practical touch, which easily adapted to the new needs of a decade in which fashion was becoming more practical, while remaining elegant and refined. This evolution allowed the fashion house to reach a broader consumer base and to strengthen its presence in the world of luxury clothing.

The 1970s were also important years for the evolution of Hermès' leather goods, and special attention was paid to the quality of its materials and innovation in its designs. Moreover, that same decade saw the introduction of new accessories including belts, wallets and small leather goods, all characterised by iconic details such as the H-buckle, which became a highly recognisable symbol.

During these years, silk scarves also continued to be one of the most iconic accessories produced by Hermès. The prints, which were inspired by equestrian, floral and historical themes, embodied the essence of the fashion house. Now reinterpreted by cutting-edge designers and artists, these became a true stylistic signature for celebrities and sophisticated women around the globe.

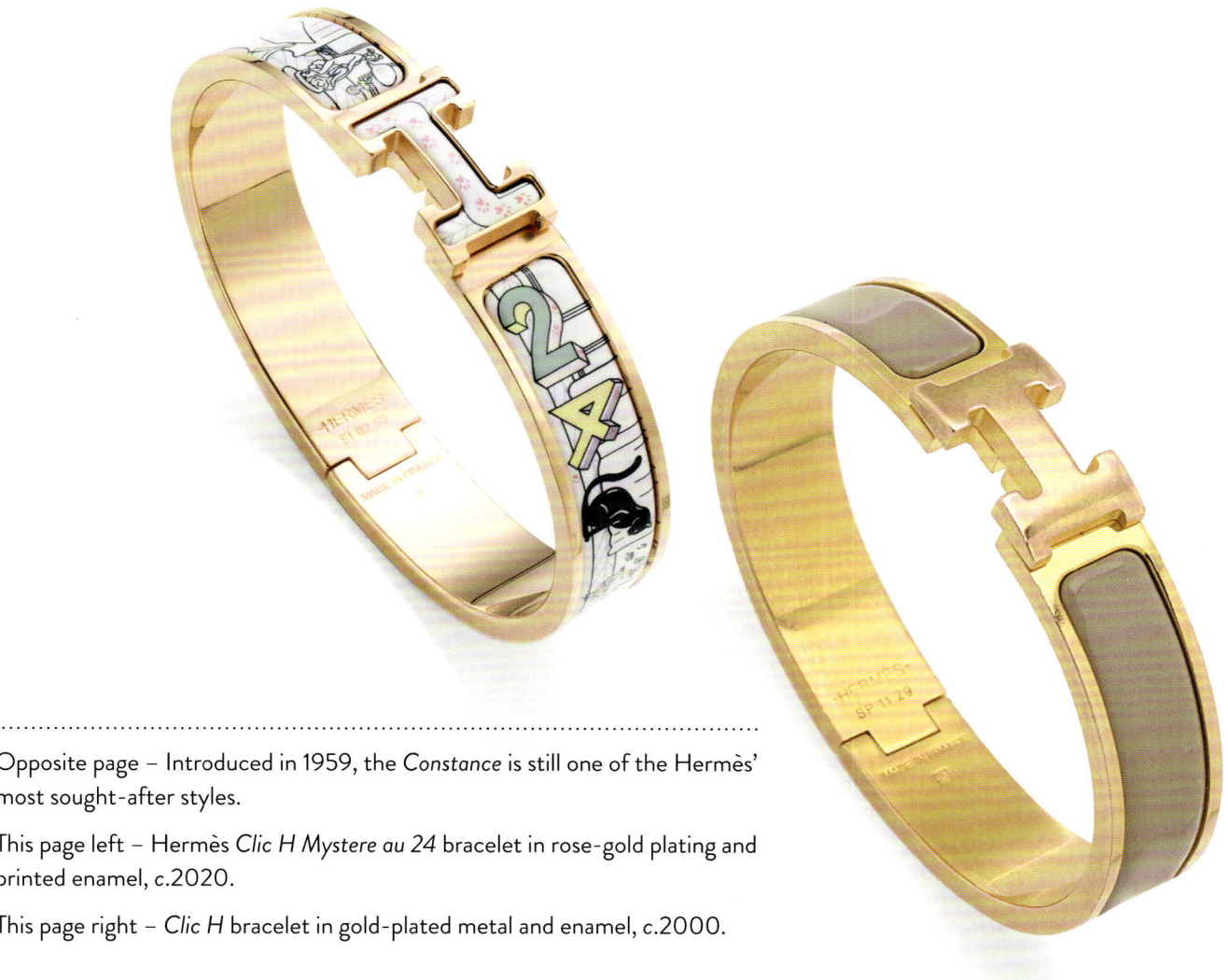

Opposite page – Introduced in 1959, the *Constance* is still one of the Hermès' most sought-after styles.

This page left – Hermès *Clic H Mystere au 24* bracelet in rose-gold plating and printed enamel, *c.*2020.

This page right – *Clic H* bracelet in gold-plated metal and enamel, *c.*2000.

At this time, Hermès also introduced new fragrances that reflected the luxury and elegance which defined its aesthetic. In parallel, it developed a line of items for the home, presenting decorative objects which were elegant yet also functional.[12] A collection complete with furniture and home furnishing fabric would be ready only in the early 2000s, partnering with important designers such as Enzo Mari and Antonio Citterio.

In 1975, the *Kelly* watch was introduced and, the following year, the enamelled bracelets began to be sold. Both of these objects would become signature pieces for the company.

In this context of renewal, the collaboration between Rena Dumas and Hermès was particularly valuable.[13] Starting in 1976, it resulted in over 300 of the brand's boutiques being renovated according to her refined aesthetic vision, which included the use of prized natural materials. One of the last to receive her artistic touch was the famous boutique in Rue du Faubourg Saint-Honoré in Paris, given a new look in 2007.

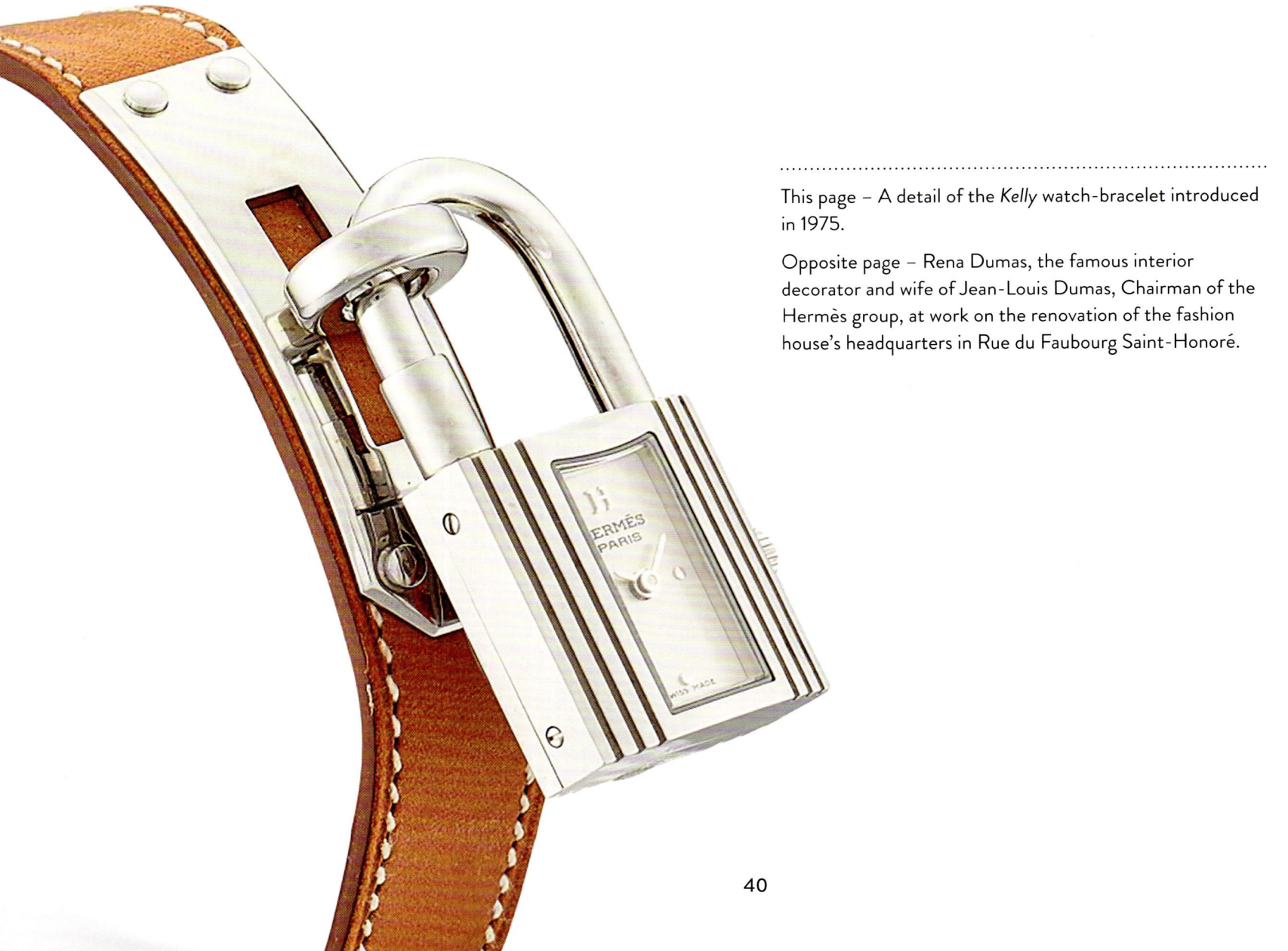

This page – A detail of the *Kelly* watch-bracelet introduced in 1975.

Opposite page – Rena Dumas, the famous interior decorator and wife of Jean-Louis Dumas, Chairman of the Hermès group, at work on the renovation of the fashion house's headquarters in Rue du Faubourg Saint-Honoré.

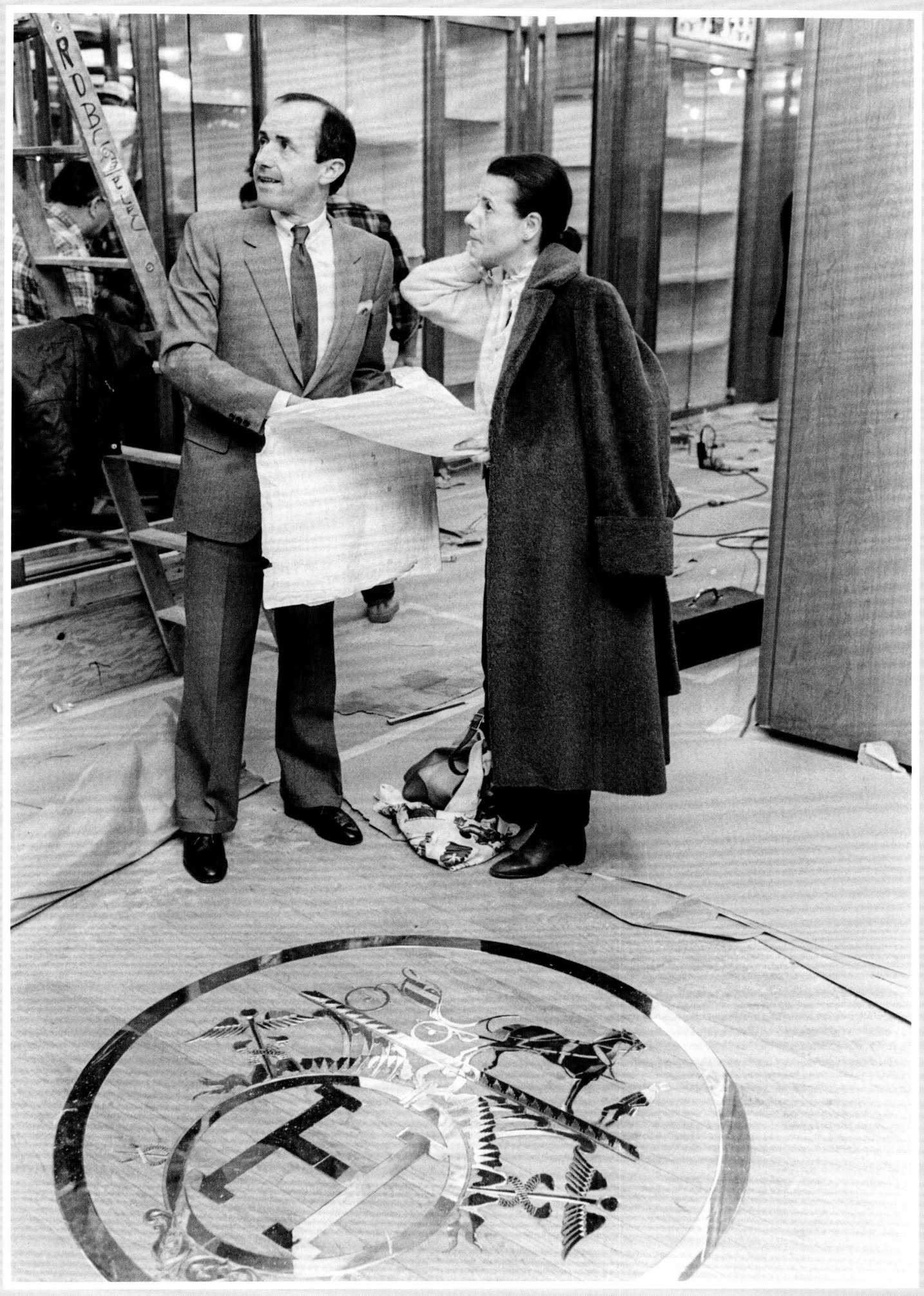

Plan well and take risks

While Jean-Louis Dumas was at the helm, Hermès increased its presence abroad, opening new boutiques and partnering with important retailers in the world's main fashion capitals. This strategy allowed the fashion brand to build a global distribution network and to strengthen its position in the international luxury market.

Partly by luck and partly by the ability to quickly seize the opportunities that life presents, Hermès created another icon in the 1980s: the *Birkin* bag, which was released in 1984.

The *Birkin* is the result of a chance encounter on a Paris–London flight between Jean-Louis Dumas and artist Jane Birkin, who complained that there were no comfortable, lightweight and roomy bags which could carry all the items and accessories a travelling woman needed to bring with her. Upon his return to Paris, the director of

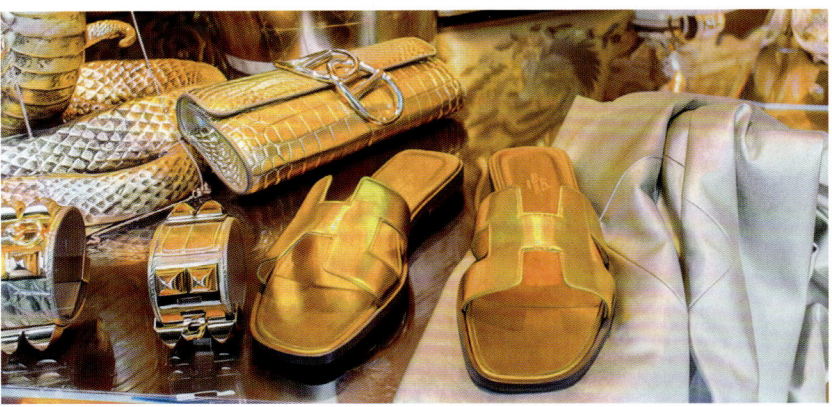

....

This page – Various accessories by Hermès, including *Oran* sandals and *Collier de Chien* bracelets.

Opposite page – Jane Birkin loved to customise her Hermès bag with stickers, Buddhist prayer beads and colourful charms.

Hermès designed the bag of her dreams for her. Elegant and capacious, it was ideal for day and evening alike. Its success was global and destined to last.

In 1987, Hermès celebrated 150 years in business. In Paris, memorable fireworks over the Pont Neuf celebrated the milestone. This festive moment would be transformed into a theme, the first in a series that, since then, has been perpetuated each year, united by one inspiration: all the creations of the brand.

From the 1970s to the 1980s, Hermès began a phase of acquisitions which brought unique know-how to the maison. In 1976, Hermès began to open up to the art of footwear production via an agreement with the English house John Lobb; in 1978, it began to develop timepieces with the name *La Montre Hermès*, followed by cutlery and table accessories with the silversmiths Puiforcat which it acquired in 1993, and glassware with Saint-Louis, integrated in 1995.

Significant collaborations also arose around this time, such as that with designer Pierre Hardy for shoes and accessories, improving its appeal in modern luxury. In 1997, Hardy designed the *Oran* sandals, inspired by the city of Oran, Algeria: a minimalist style with the symbolic 'H' motif. Collection after collection, this icon would come in an ample range of colours and materials.

It wasn't until the end of the 20th century, however, that the company began to head down a bold and innovative new path in the fashion industry, appointing Belgian stylist Martin Margiela Creative Director of *ready-to-wear* in 1998.[14]

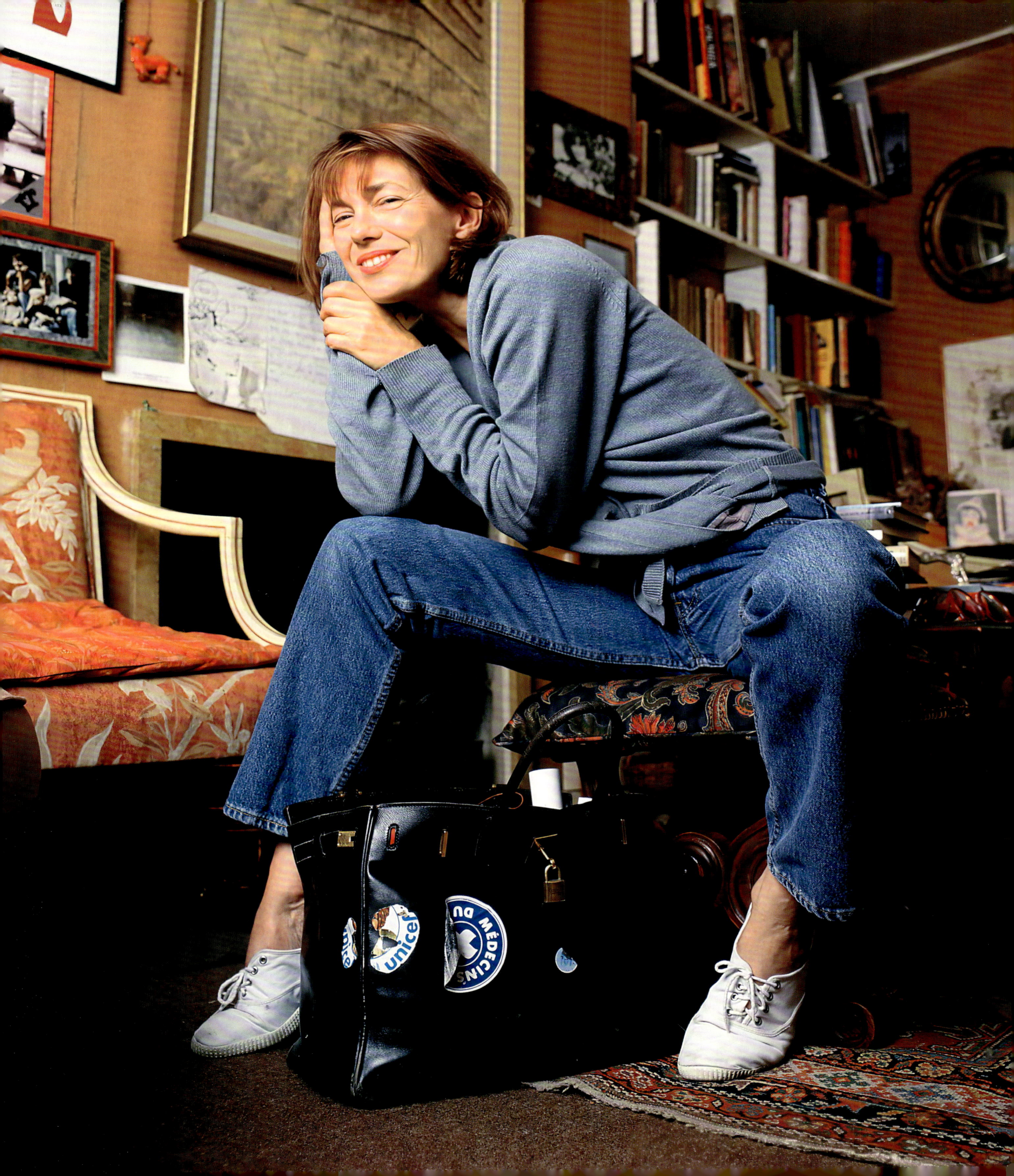

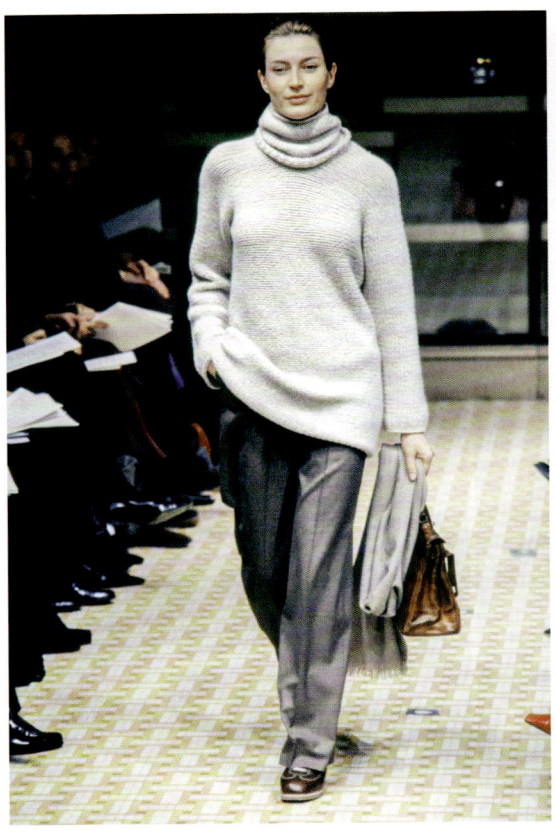
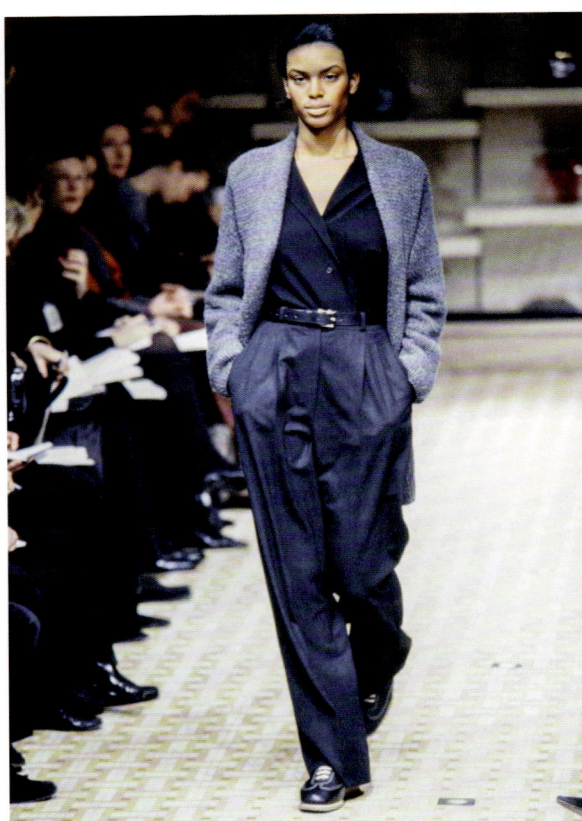
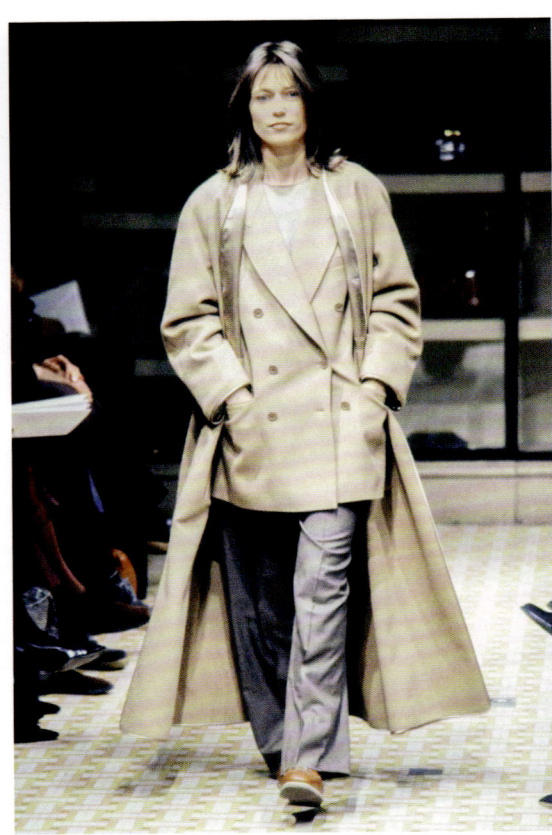

Fashion, reinterpreted

The collaboration between Hermès, the historic luxury brand, and Margiela, the visionary designer, was one of the most interesting and revolutionary in the world of fashion. The latter was known for his conceptual and minimalist approach, which was diametrically opposed to the traditional luxury of the maison.

This partnership, which would last six years, managed to define an age and bring Hermès into a new modern era, all thanks to Margiela's distinct and unconventional approach. While upholding the identity of Hermès as a symbol of timeless elegance, Margiela managed to redefine it with his unique style, pushing fashion to a balance between subtle luxury and radical innovation and making it possible to attract new customers who were younger and more modern.

One of the first challenges which Margiela faced at the helm of Hermès was that of combining his aesthetic sensibility with the brand's identity, without completely distorting it. While Hermès collections were traditionally characterised by vibrant colours, fine textiles and sophisticated cuts, Margiela opted for a more understated approach focused on simplicity and practicality. Instead of focusing on bright colours, he introduced a palette of neutrals – beiges, greys, blacks and whites – and designed clean silhouettes and essential lines.

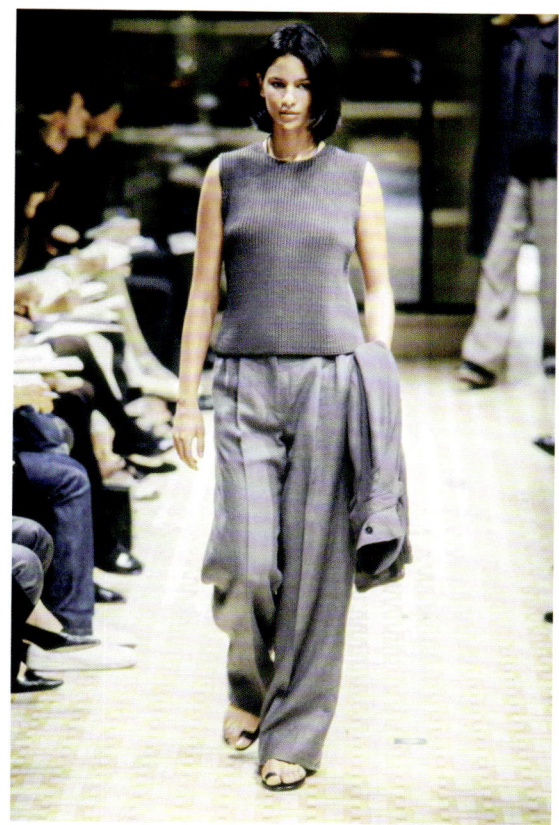 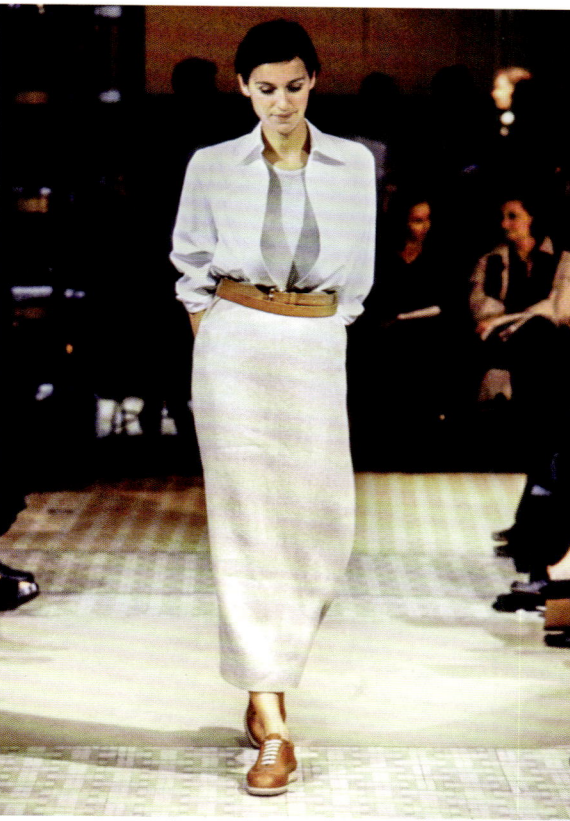 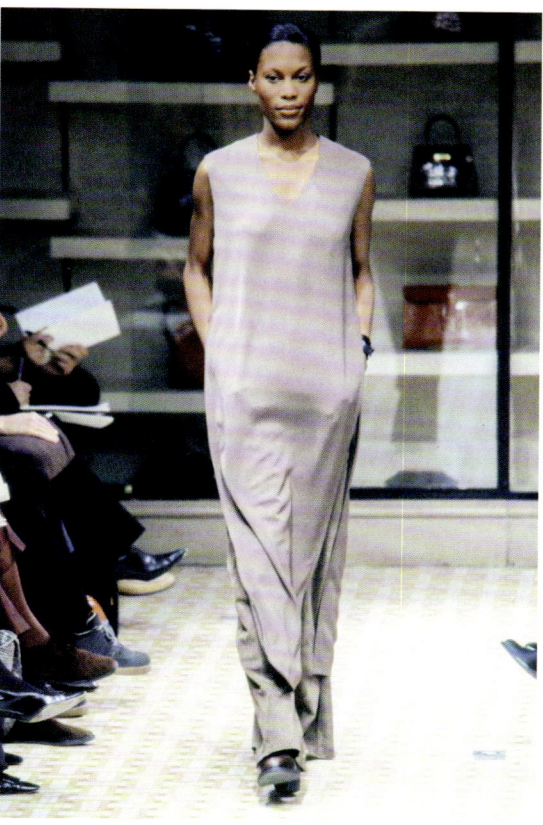

Images from the 1998 S/S and A/W runway shows designed by Martin Margiela.

Margiela proved to have a profound vision of contemporary luxury, able to adapt to the values of Hermès. He managed to fuse his concept of 'invisible luxury' with Hermès craftsmanship, emphasising the quality of the materials and attention to detail without having to resort of excessive decoration or large logos. His creations for Hermès were designed for sophisticated, confident women who appreciated quiet luxury and timeless elegance. This approach marked a meaningful change in the perception of the brand, leading it to become a symbol not just of luxury, but also modernity and refinement.

Margiela's most significant innovation was his ability to reimagine classic garments from the Hermès archive through a contemporary lens. For example, his reinterpretations of the trench coat, pencil skirts and cashmere pullovers exemplify his modus operandi: every piece was characterised by meticulous construction and an impeccable fit, but pared back to the essential.[15]

In an era in which consumers sought out authenticity and craftsmanship, Margiela offered them exactly what they were looking for while staying true to the Hermès aesthetic. Today, many of the garments created at that time are considered iconic and they are still remembered for their sophistication. Margiela's influence marked the start of a new chapter for Hermès, allowing the brand to evolve and to stay in step with the times, without sacrificing its identity.

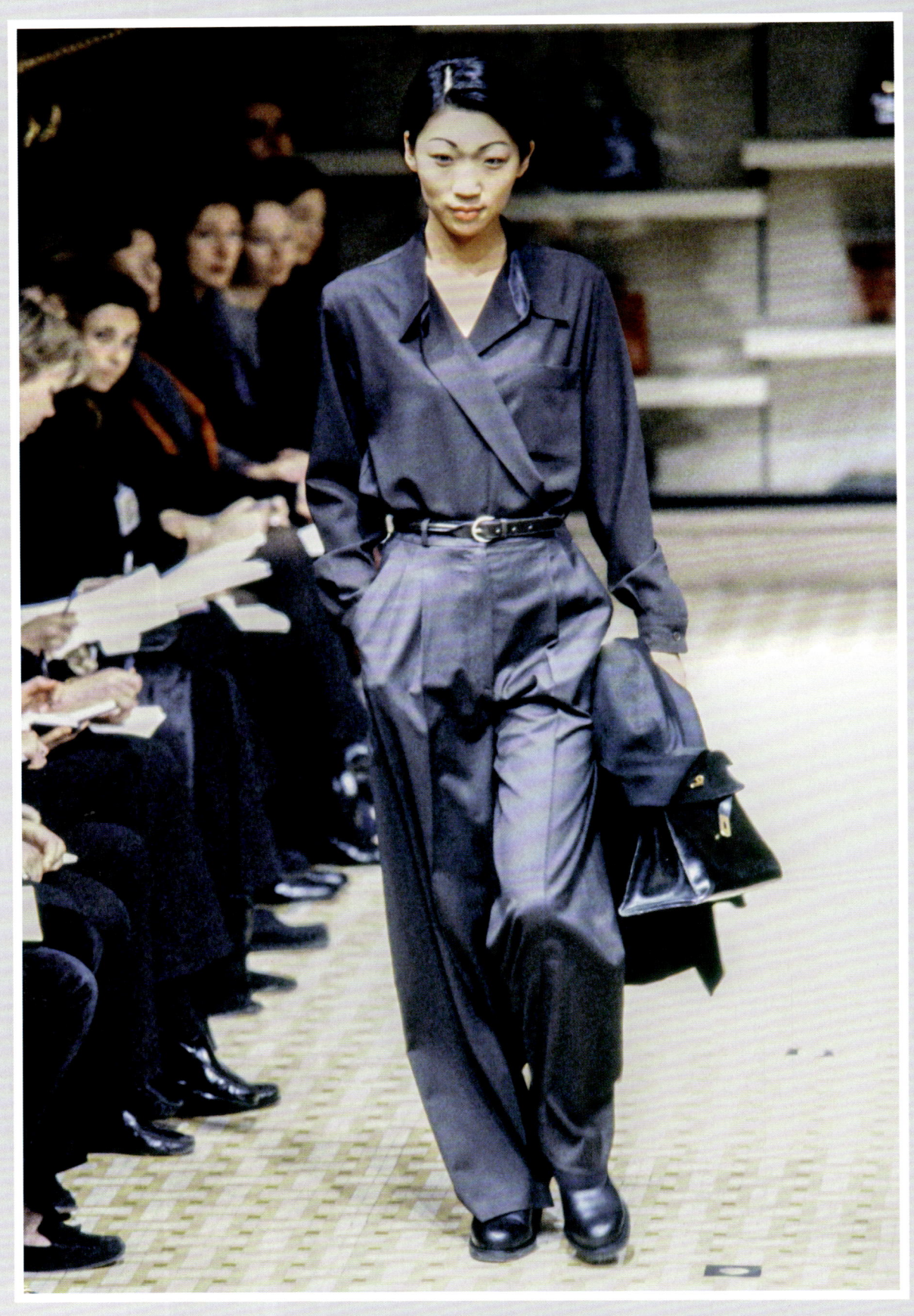

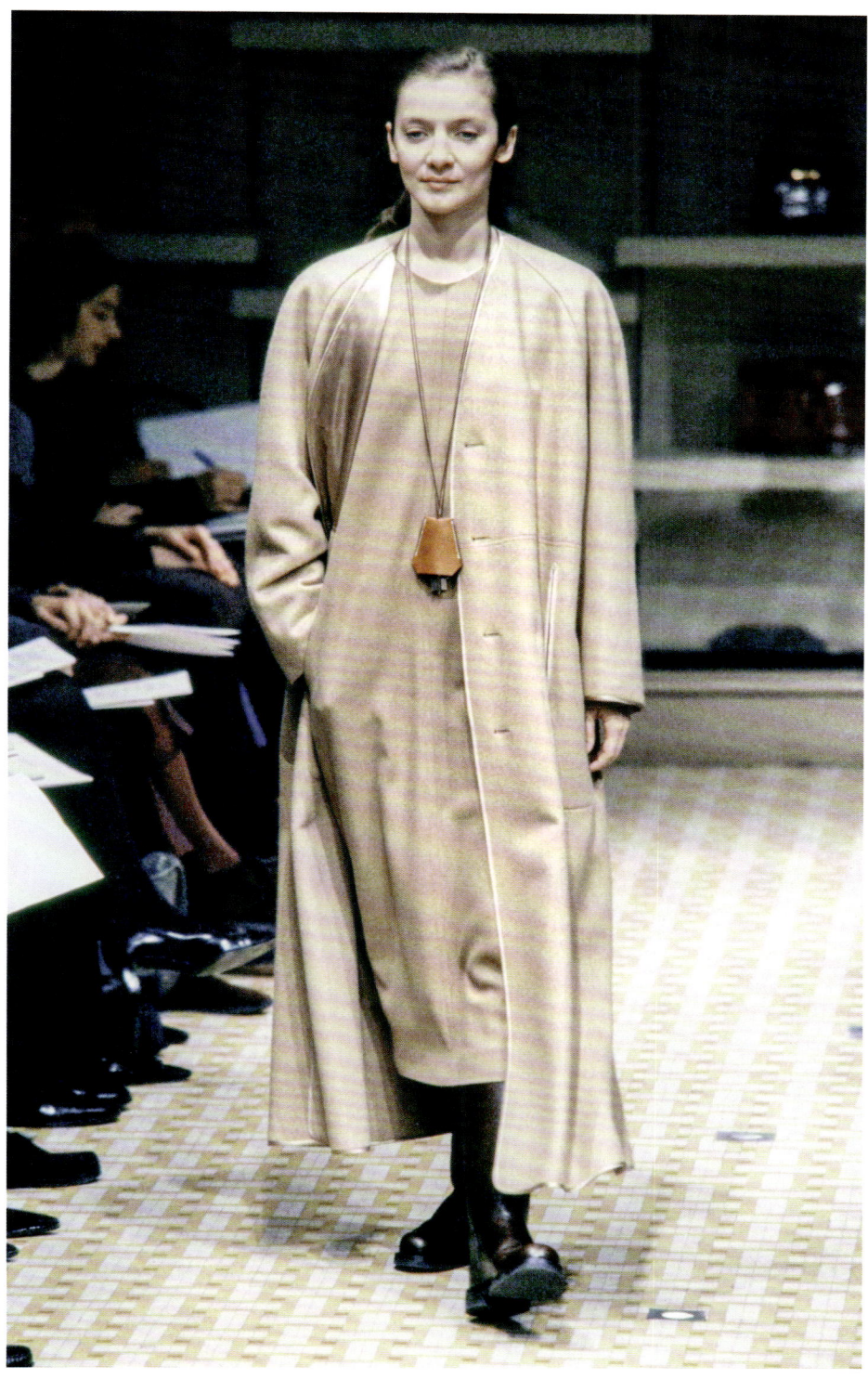

From the 1998 A/W ready-to-wear collection designed by Martin Margiela for Hermès.

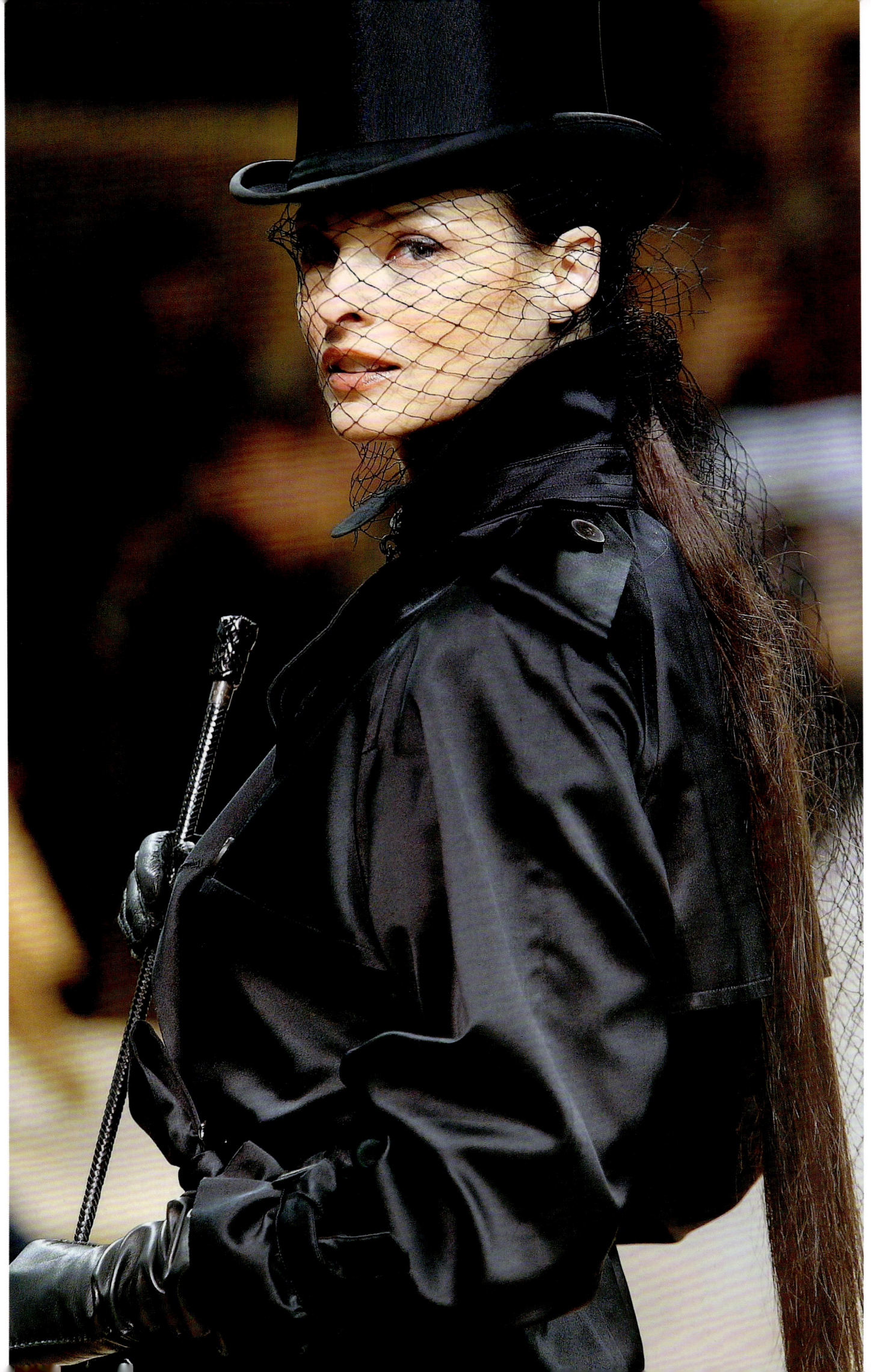

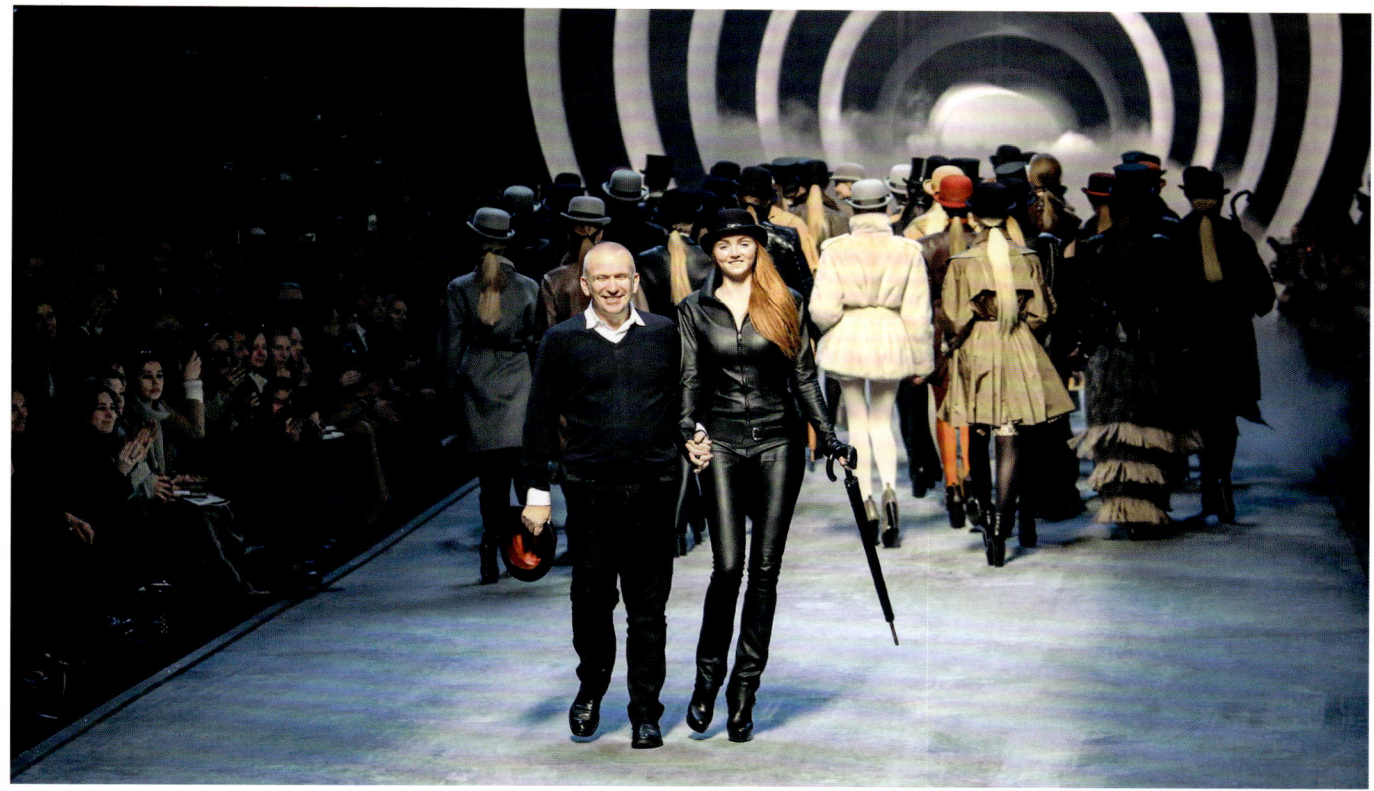

Opposite page – Linda Evangelista dressed in sexy equestrian wear for Hermès in 2004.

This page – The finale of the presentation of the Hermès 2006–2007 A/W collection designed by Jean Paul Gaultier.

Another famous collaboration, which began in 2003 and ended in 2010, was with Jean-Paul Gaultier, who brought new aesthetic codes to the maison's fashion products. When Gaultier took on the role of Creative Director of Women's ready-to-wear at Hermès, many wondered how a designer so well known for his rebellious and theatrical style would adapt to the image of the fashion house, which was founded upon tradition, discreet elegance and understated garments. Nevertheless, Hermès was looking for someone who could update its line of clothing, giving it a contemporary touch without sacrificing the values of luxury and craftsmanship which distinguished the brand.

This designer, known for his bold, irreverent style rich in cultural references, brought a breath of fresh air and provocation to the classic, sophisticated elegance of Hermès.[16] He united two seemingly opposite worlds with an innovative balance of luxury and experimentation.

Working with prized materials and classic forms, he managed to introduce more structured cuts and details which evoked the equestrian world – a central element in the Hermès aesthetic – fusing it with his personal style.[17]

Even the iconic silk scarf was transformed: Gaultier used it in unusual ways, as a top or a skirt, demonstrating that this is an accessory with a versatile and timeless spirit.

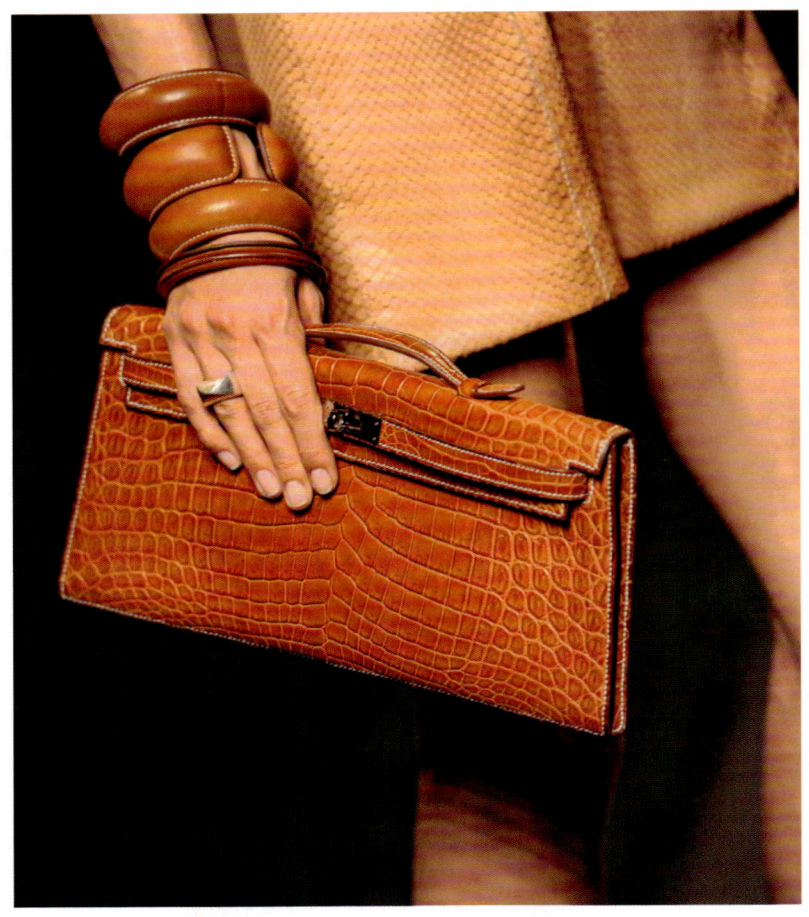

This page – An example of the *Kelly Cut* introduced by Jean Paul Gaultier in 2007, here in a crocodile clutch version.

Opposite page – For Jean Paul Gaultier, the *Kelly* bag could transform into a soft belt bag or even as a top.

Gaultier also reinterpreted some of the brand's most iconic bags, giving them a bold and innovative touch and introducing the *shoulder* versions of the classic *Kelly* and *Birkin*.[18] One of the most famous styles designed by Gaultier is the *Birkin Shadow*, a playful interpretation of the classic *Birkin*. In this version, Gaultier drew the pockets and buckles of the bag directly on the leather itself. Another iconic Gaultier creation for Hermès was the *Flat Kelly*, a foldable and more casual version of the classic *Kelly*, which can be folded and bound with a leather belt, making it easy to transport and perfect for travel.

During his tenure, Gaultier also played with different materials, including crocodile, Togo leather and soft leather, experimenting with brighter colours and bold combinations.

Gaultier's role as creative director brought more than fresh ideas to Hermès; it also increased the brand's visibility on an international scale. His collections, characterised by an aesthetic originality that united the timeless luxury of Hermès with his provocative style, drew the attention of a younger, more varied audience, and reinforced the link between the fashion house and the world of contemporary fashion.

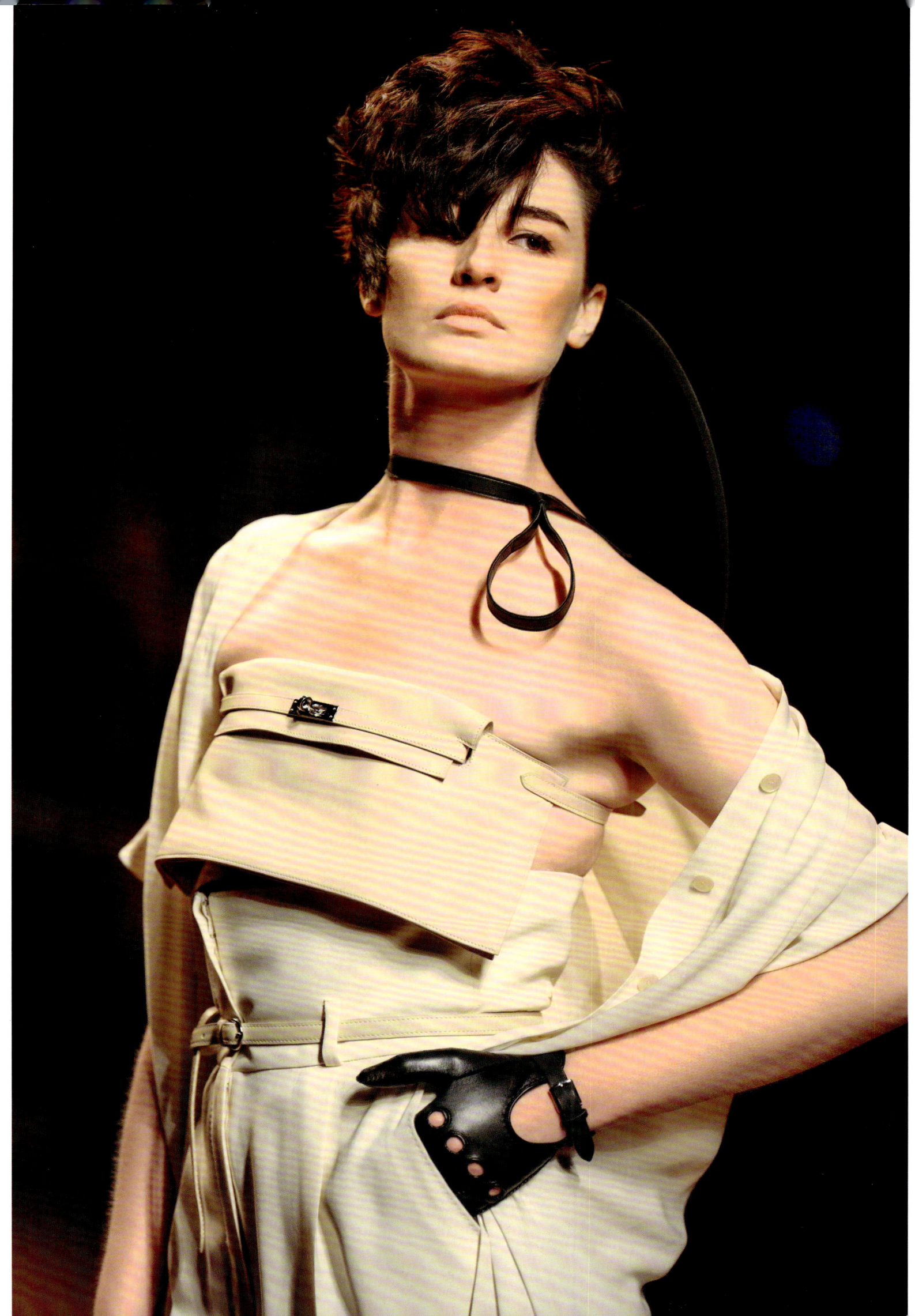

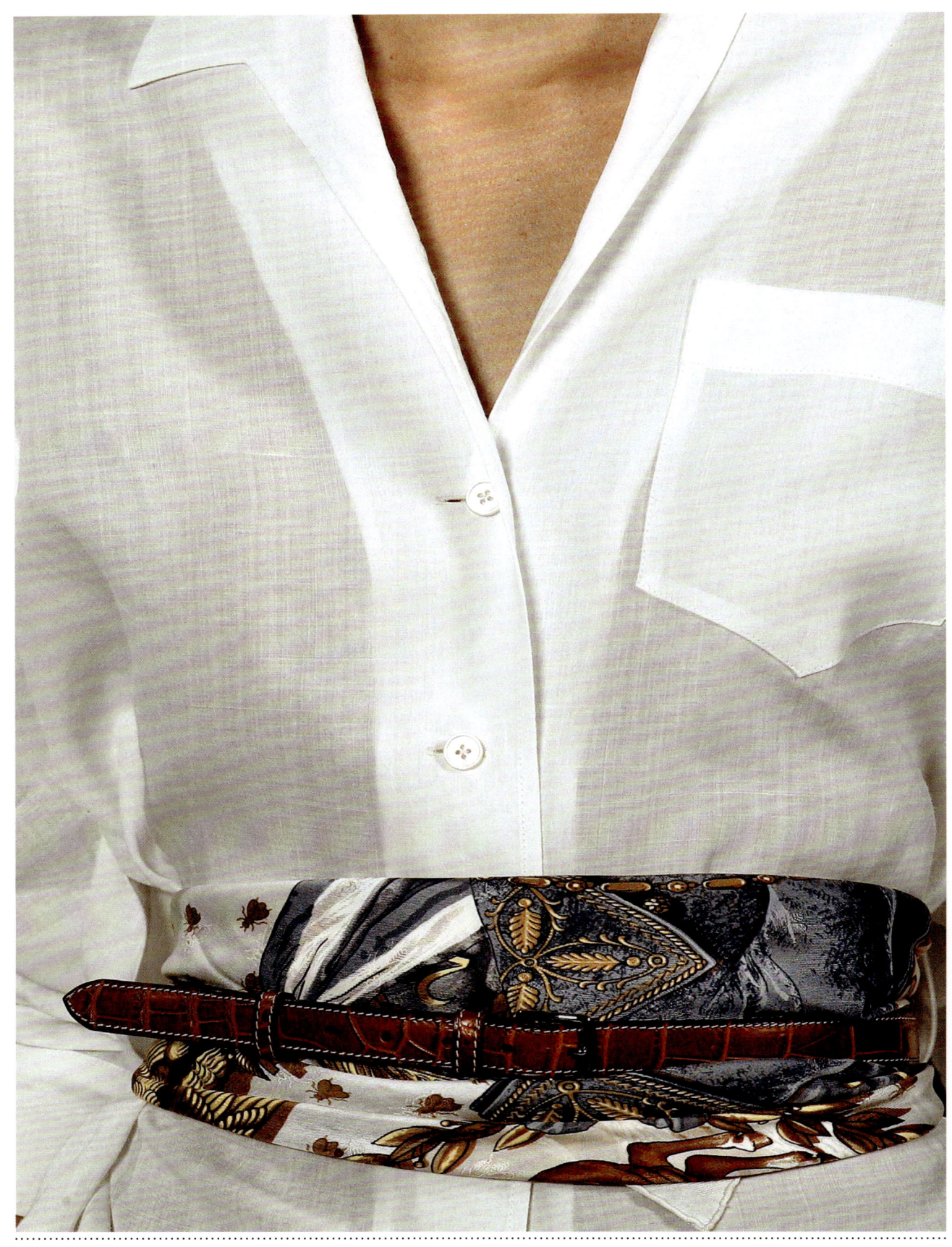

This page – Wearing a silk scarf as a belt was another one of the provocations of the *enfant terrible* of fashion for Hermès.

Opposite page – Detail of a leather corset from the A/W 2004 collection by Hermès under Jean Paul Gaultier's creative direction.

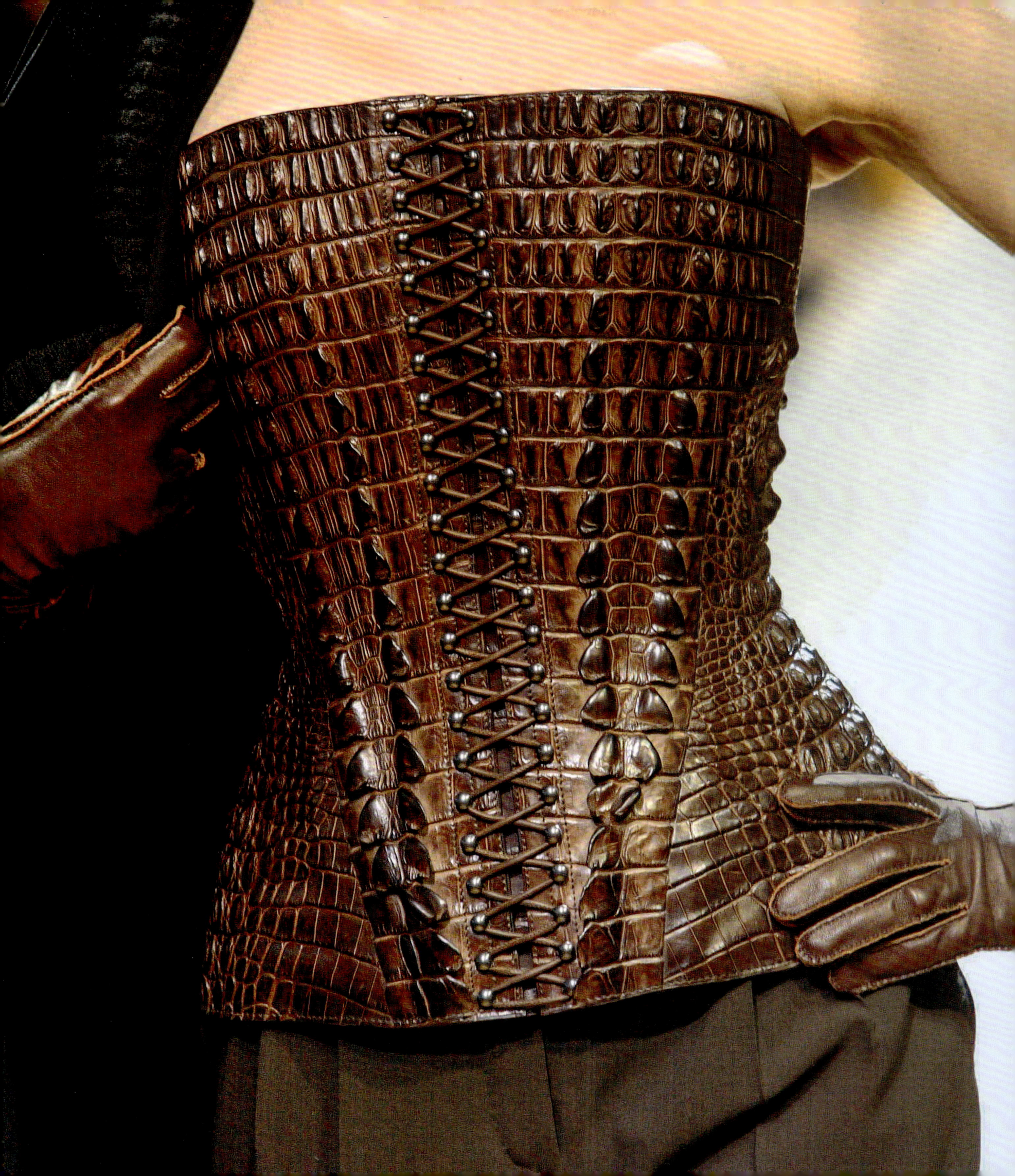

Entrepreneurial growth and risk

Driven by Jean-Louis Dumas, Hermès expanded around the entire globe, with the opening of numerous boutiques, each one of which elegantly combined the brand's identity with the local culture.[19] As such, different international Maison Hermès locations were opened, such as that in Madison Avenue, New York in 2000, a treasure chest made of brick and glass designed by Renzo Piano, followed by Dosan Park, Seoul in 2006. Moreover, Hermès opened its online boutique in the US starting in 2002, followed by France three years later.

In 1992, the brand's leather workshop left the first floor of 24 Faubourg Saint-Honoré to be relocated to Pantin, just outside of Paris. The new workspace for the brand's artisans is a bright, spacious building. The site was expanded in 2013 with the *Cité des métiers*, a vast project which grouped various buildings connected by themed gardens.

Jean-Louis Dumas had led Hermès through a period of extraordinary growth and success, bringing the company to its initial public offering in 1993.

A member of the fifth generation, Pierre-Alexis Dumas, son of Jean-Louis Dumas, was appointed Creative Director of Hermès in 2005. Under his guidance, the brand would expand its range of know-how. In 2010, parallel to the jewellery line, he presented the first collection of *haute bijouterie* (high jewellery). The following year, the maison introduced home textiles and wallpaper for the first time. That was followed by the Hermès Apple Watch, a bold collaboration with Apple, which launched in 2015.

At the behest of Pierre-Alexis Dumas, the brand gave new impetus to its patronage policy and philanthropic dedication with the launch of the *Fondation d'entreprise Hermès* in 2008.

The Hermès Foundation finances many projects in various fields, including contemporary art, education, traditional craftsmanship and environmental protection. Through these programmes, Hermès helps promote the culture and support the growth of local communities, strengthening the bond between company and society.

In 2010, *L'atelier Petit h* was opened under the guidance of Pascale Mussard, niece of Jean-Louis Dumas, implementing an unusual initiative within the maison: that of 'backwards' creation. Starting from unused materials left over from Hermès' production, artisans and designers unleash their creativity as they craft items that are unique and unexpected, supported by the fine workmanship of the brand.

2010 was also the year that saw change in the fashion department, when Christophe Lemarie became Creative Director, while in 2014, management of the women's collections went to Nadège Vanhee-Cybulski. Much less turnover has occurred in men's fashion: Véronique Nichanian has headed this department since 1988.

Management of the company, on the other hand, went to the right-hand man of Jean-Louis Dumas, Patrick Thomas. The latter has devised a strategic decentralised organisation, and also restructured Hermès' global presence according to geographical area. Thomas also ensured the transition between the two generations up to the appointment of Axel Dumas, nephew of Jean-Louis Dumas, as CEO in 2013.

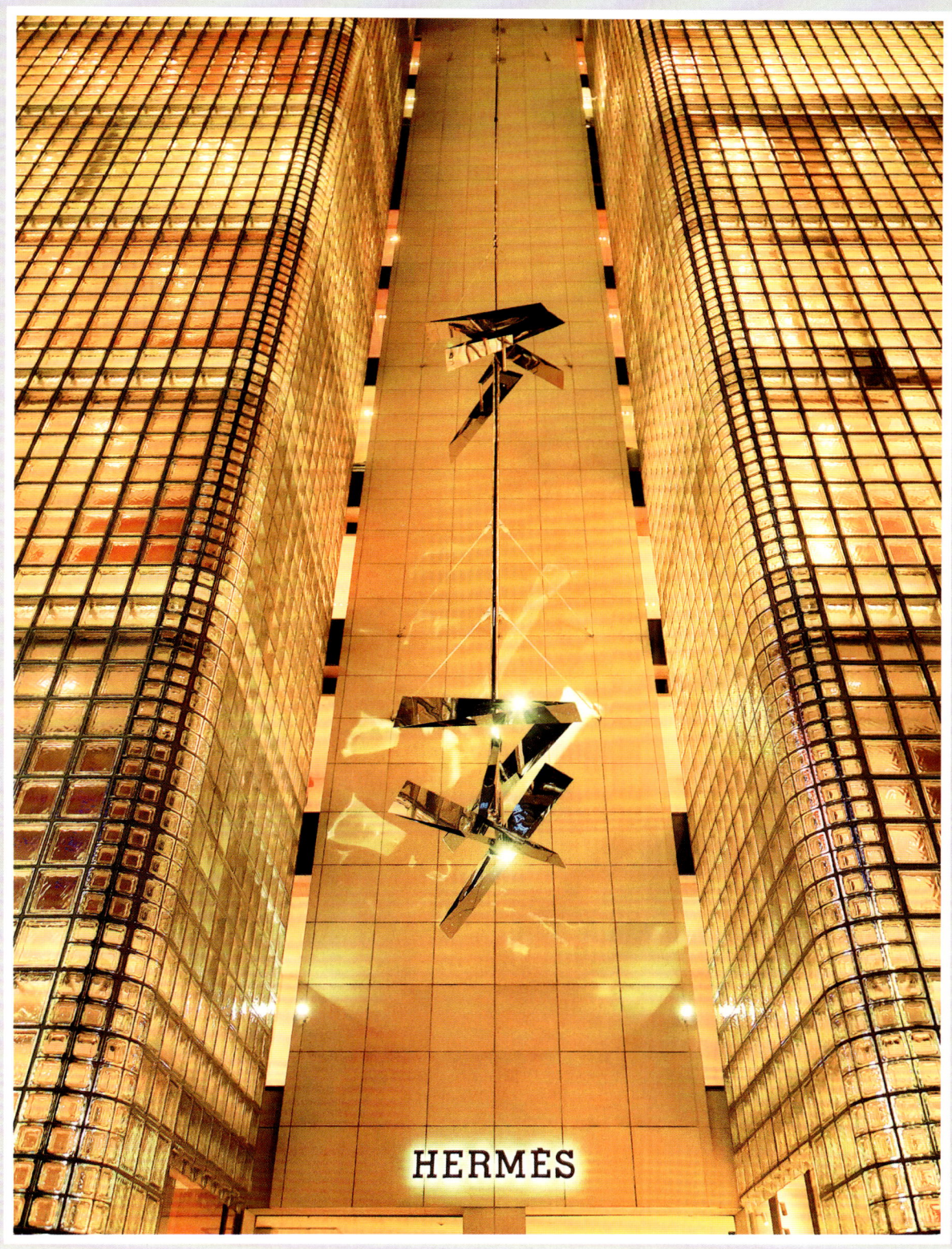

Opened in 2001, the Hermès headquarters in Tokyo was designed by Italian architect Renzo Piano.

'Friendly' fire

Legend has it that, one morning in October 2010, Bertrand Puech, one of the heirs of the Hermès family, and Patrick Thomas, CEO of the brand, received a call from Bernard Arnault, founder of the luxury giant LVMH. Arnault told them that LVMH had acquired a significant number of shares in Hermès; the investment was presented as friendly and aimed at offering the brand strategic and operational assistance, Arnault later said.

Known for a number of luxury brand acquisitions such as Dior, Fendi and Bulgari, LVMH was on the hunt for new brands to expand its portfolio, and Hermès was a special opportunity: an exclusive brand which stood for discreet luxury and high-quality craftsmanship, with a loyal customer base. However, Hermès saw the buyout attempt as a threat to its identity and independence, fearing that becoming part of LVMH would compromise its values and long-term vision.[20]

When the battle with Arnault began, the Dumas, Guerrand and Puech branches of the Hermès family held about 73% of the company. But LVMH had managed to secretly buy up about 23% of the company's shares, which, given the corporate structure of the Hermès group, would have given it a good amount of influence in terms of strategic decisions.

In response, the Hermès descendants took action to defend the brand's independence, creating a family-owned holding company which united over 50% of the company stock and thereby making any outside acquisition extremely difficult. In 2014, after years of tension and legal battles, LVMH agreed that it would slowly sell its stock in Hermès, thereby bringing an end to the planned acquisition.

This event reinforced the image of Hermès as a brand loyal to tradition and craftsmanship, able to withstand market pressures to preserve its independence. Moreover, it was a rare case in which a luxury giant had been rejected, strengthening Hermès' role as a symbol of autonomy in the world of premium fashion.[21]

The sixth generation

Today, Hermès is one of the most recognisable and respected luxury brands, with a global presence which includes boutiques in all of the world's fashion capitals. The company remains family-managed, with the descendants of Thierry Hermès still involved with the company. This continuity has made it possible for Hermès to maintain its identity and original values, despite the company's exponential growth.

Once he became CEO in 2013, Axel Dumas, the nephew of Jean-Louis Dumas, reinforced the growth of the group with the opening of the fifth Maison Hermès in Shanghai in 2024, and the opening of various flagships around the world. In 2019, Hermès landed in a new country, Poland, opening a boutique in Warsaw. Axel Dumas also strongly supports the digital growth of the group which, in 2017, overhauled the hermes.com website. This project represented the technological evolution of Hermès, in line with the expectations of customers, who are increasingly connected. Under his leadership, the group has even accelerated the multi-channel evolution of the organisation.

Axel Dumas is focused on sustainability and innovation, promoting initiatives to reduce the company's environmental impact and to support traditional craftsmanship.

Hermès continues to keep most of its production in France and to perpetuate its know-how to benefit creativity.

'We don't look too much at the competition, because we might be influenced,' joked Dumas during the presentation of the company's financial report in July 2023. When he listed the four fundamental values of the brand, the first one was 'independence'.

The company continues to be a leader in leather goods, but it is consistently expanding its portfolio, which includes ready-to-wear, watches, perfume, jewellery and home goods. Every new line of products has been launched with the same dedication to quality and craftsmanship, the values which have characterised Hermès since it was founded. All of the 16 'crafts' at Hermès are allowed creative freedom, inspired each year by a theme, shared by the entire maison.

The company created its 16th *métier* in 2020. The result of planning, research and development launched five years prior, the *Beauty* department has revealed its first collection of lipstick: *Rouge Hermès*.

The Hermès family sees the company not only as a business, but also as the guardian of artisan and cultural traditions. In 2021, Hermès created the *École Hermès des Savoir-Faire* (CFP). The school provides professional training which results in a nationally recognised diploma in the leatherworking industry.

The company which Thierry Hermès founded almost two centuries ago has gone through numerous transformations, but it has always stayed true to its fundamental values: quality, craftsmanship and attention to detail. Its story is evidence of how sharp vision and unwavering dedication to quality can create something long-lasting, able to withstand the passing of time and fashions.

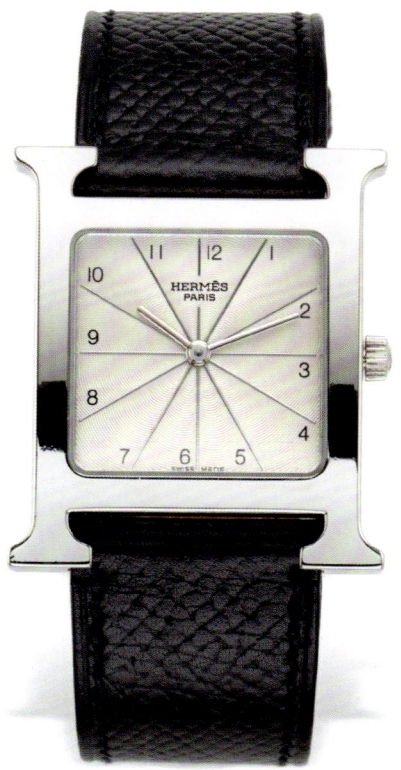

Hermès *Heure H*, 2000s. Steel case with a black leather band and a hook buckle. A classic piece among Hermès watches.

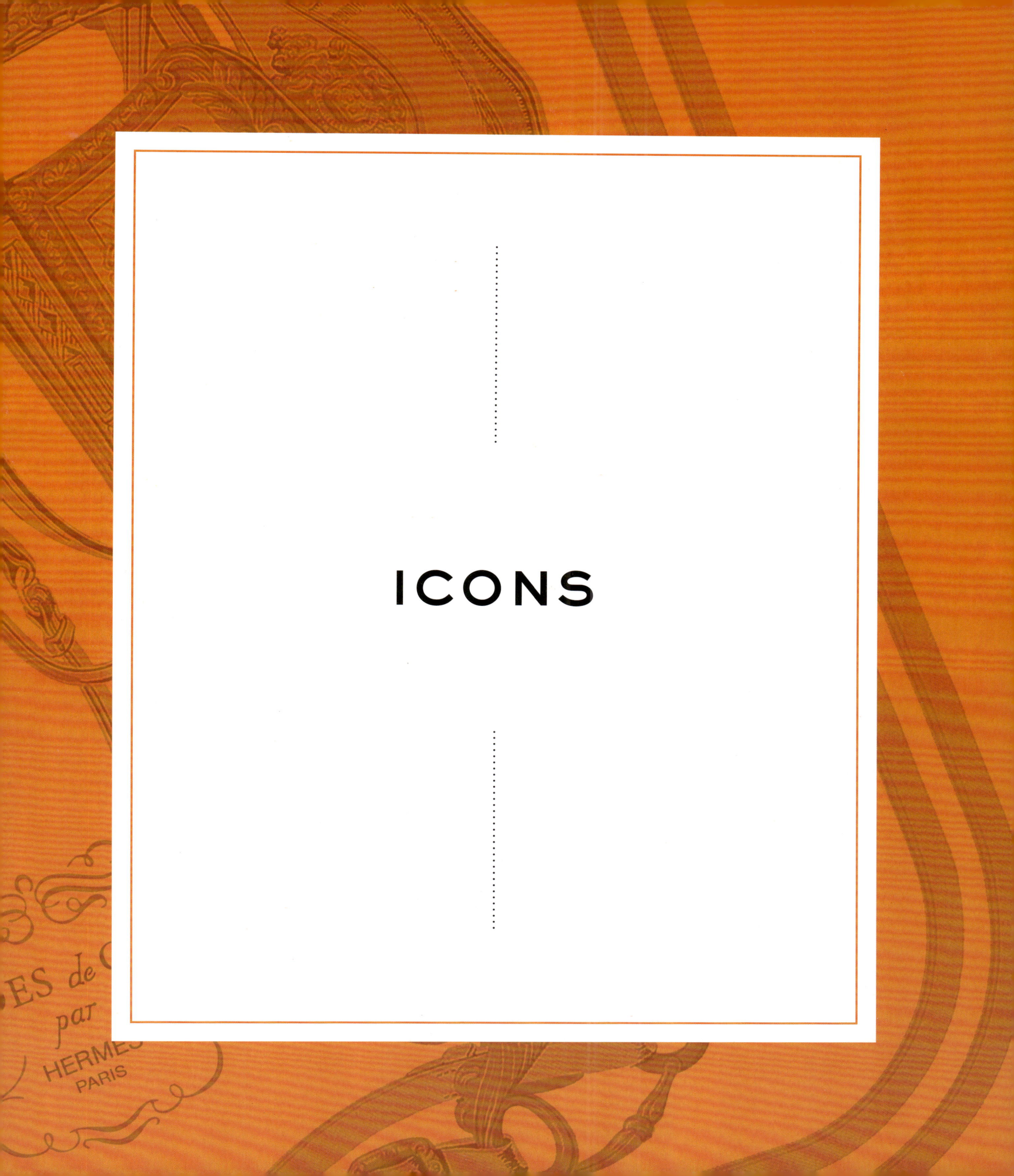

ICONS

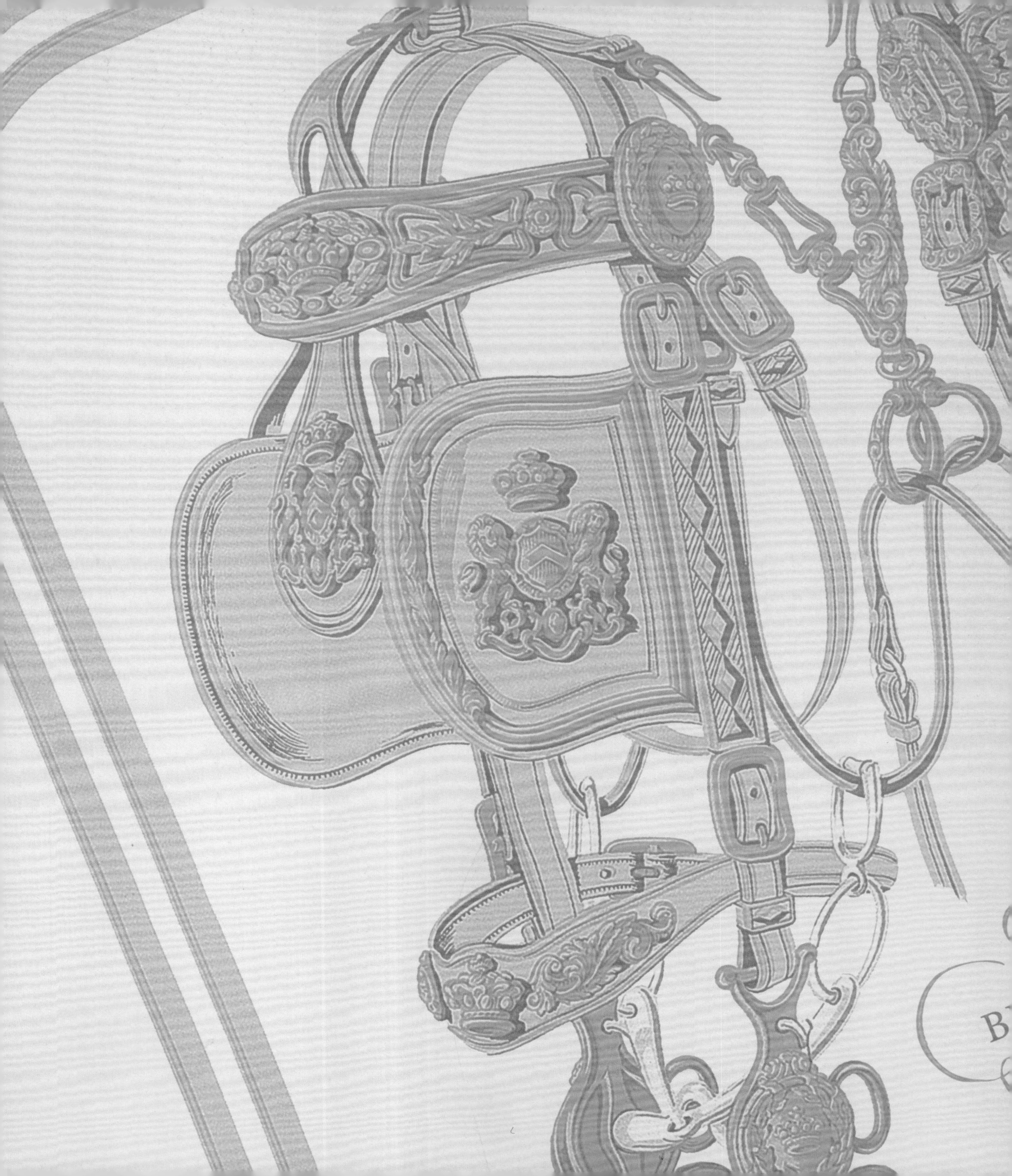

Silk scarves

·················

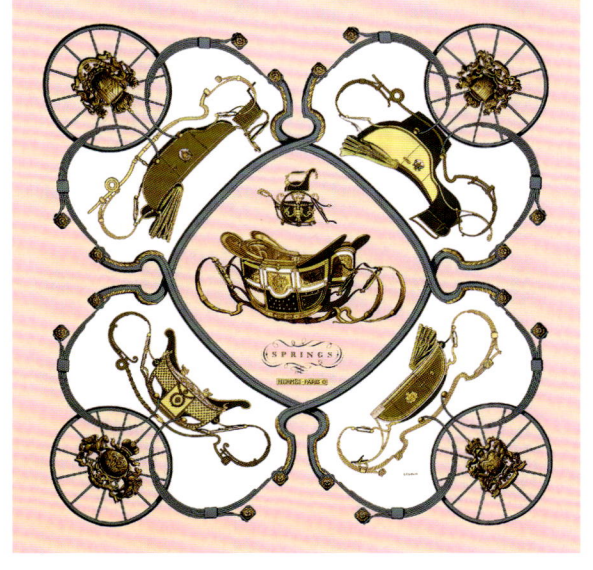

A STORY OF CREATIVITY AND SILK

· · · · · · · · · · · · · · ·

Silk scarves envelop, embrace, cover and contain, yet they are eternally sophisticated, an accessory that can define an outfit. And those by Hermès are part of a consistent, alluring narrative.

Silk scarves have ancient origins. They arose out of the need to protect the head from the sun, though they were soon imbued with social and religious meaning. Over the centuries, they gradually became symbols of elegance, adapting to trends and fashions.

Although they are mainly worn by women today, silk scarves were once accessories principally used by men. In the Middle Ages, knights paraded the silk scarves given to them by their wives (dames) during tournaments or even in battle. In the 17th century, Croatian soldiers wore scarves for practical reasons: made in silk for nobles and cotton for the lower classes, scarves indicated the

rank they held. The soldiers of Napoleon's *Grande Armée* used them to protect their necks and throats from inclement weather and also to identify the military corps to which they belonged.

Starting in the 18th century, handkerchiefs which were embroidered and embellished with lace began to appear in the wardrobes of nobility, while the *fichu* was used to cover the deep necklines of women's clothing.

In the 19th century, headscarves were worn by peasant women, though they became elegant and fashionable thanks to Queen Victoria, who liked to wear large silk shawls.

During the age of aviation (the early 20th cen-

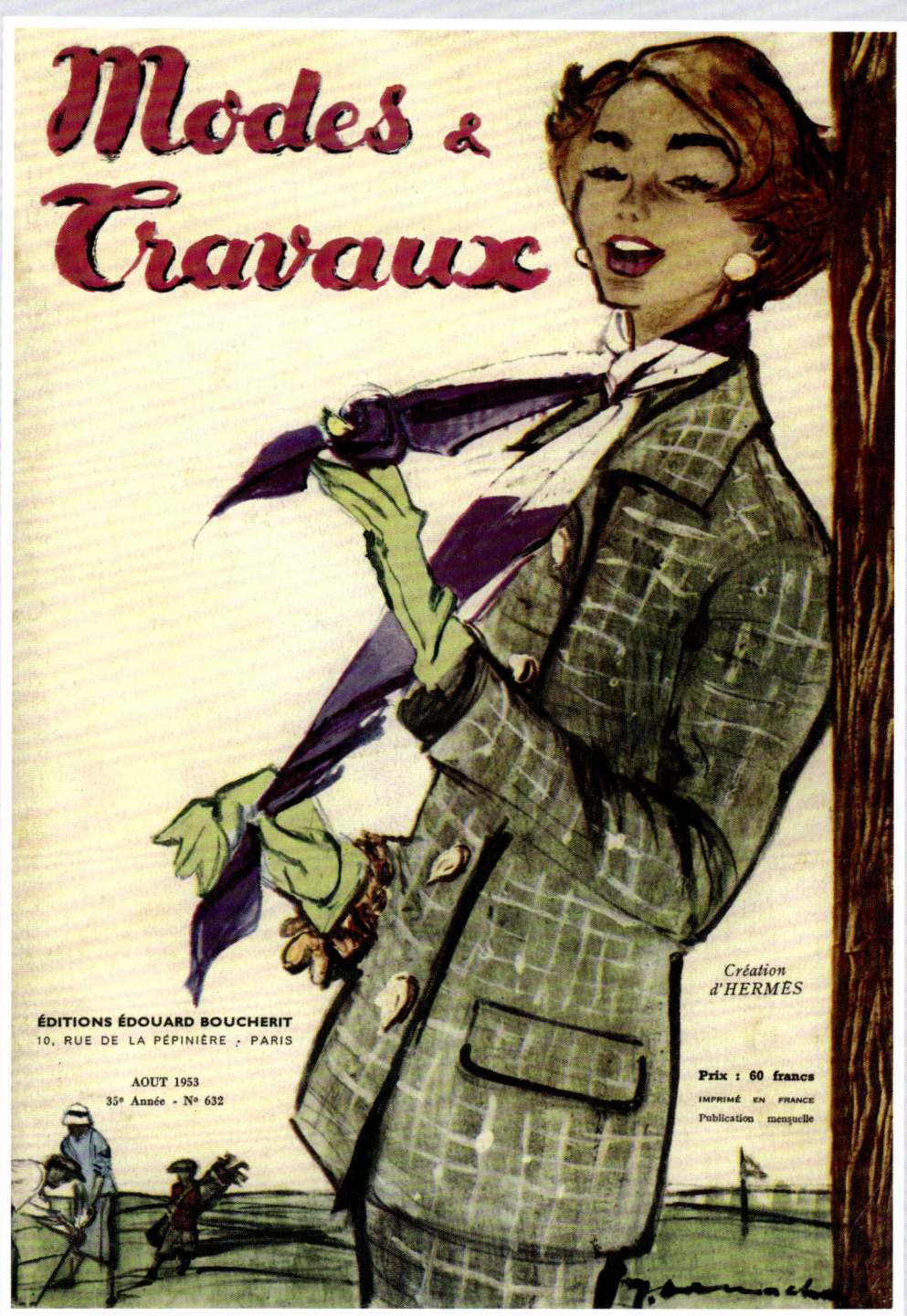

Cover of *Modes et Travaux* magazine from August 1953 with a model wearing a suit and a silk scarf by Hermès. Illustration by Jaques Demachy.

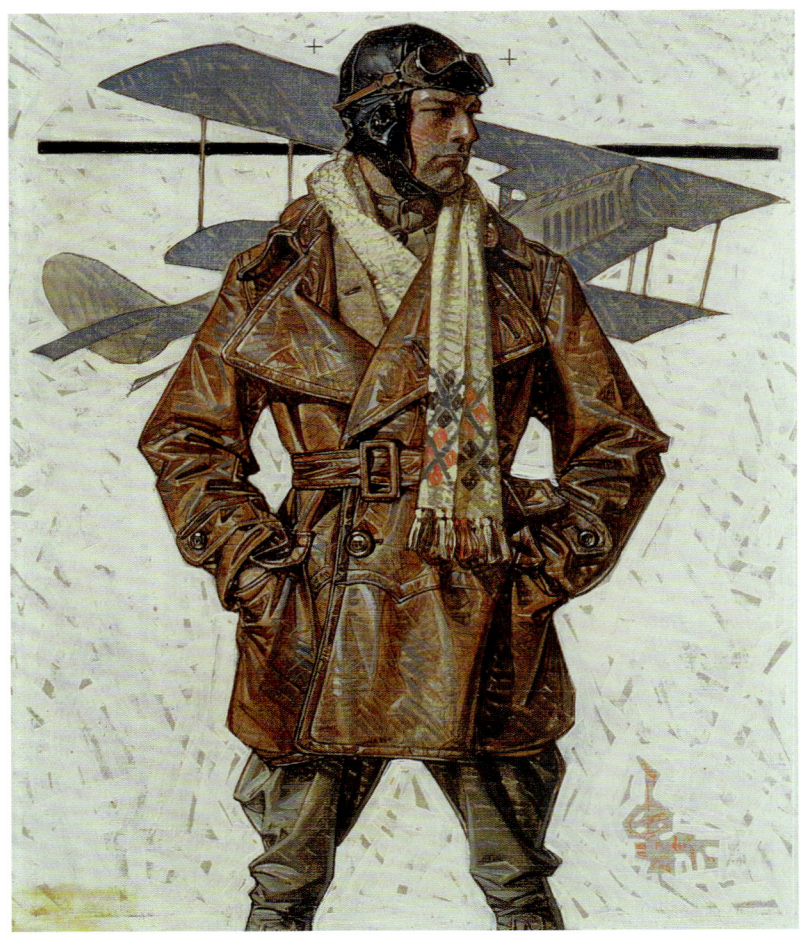

Pilots wore scarves as elegant accessories around the neck in the 1920s and 1930s.

tury), scarves in this precious material were used by pilots to cover the neck, becoming part of their uniforms. During the Belle Époque, silk scarves finally earned their place in the history of women's clothing. Chic couturiers of the time, such as France's Paul Poiret, created silk scarves with bold prints which fashionable women of the day wore as sophisticated shawls, tied at the front or wrapped around the head like turbans. In the 1920s, during the Jazz Age, women wore short dresses and silk scarves wrapped around their boyish coiffures; while in the 1930s, silk scarves were more practical to wear than a hat during open-top car rides.

This accessory was also the emblem of female factory workers during the Second World War. However, it wasn't until the 1950s and 1960s that silk scarves became a true must-have: countless film stars and celebrities of the day were frequently seen wearing this accessory, which the Parisian fashion house Hermès had elegantly reinvented in the previous decade.

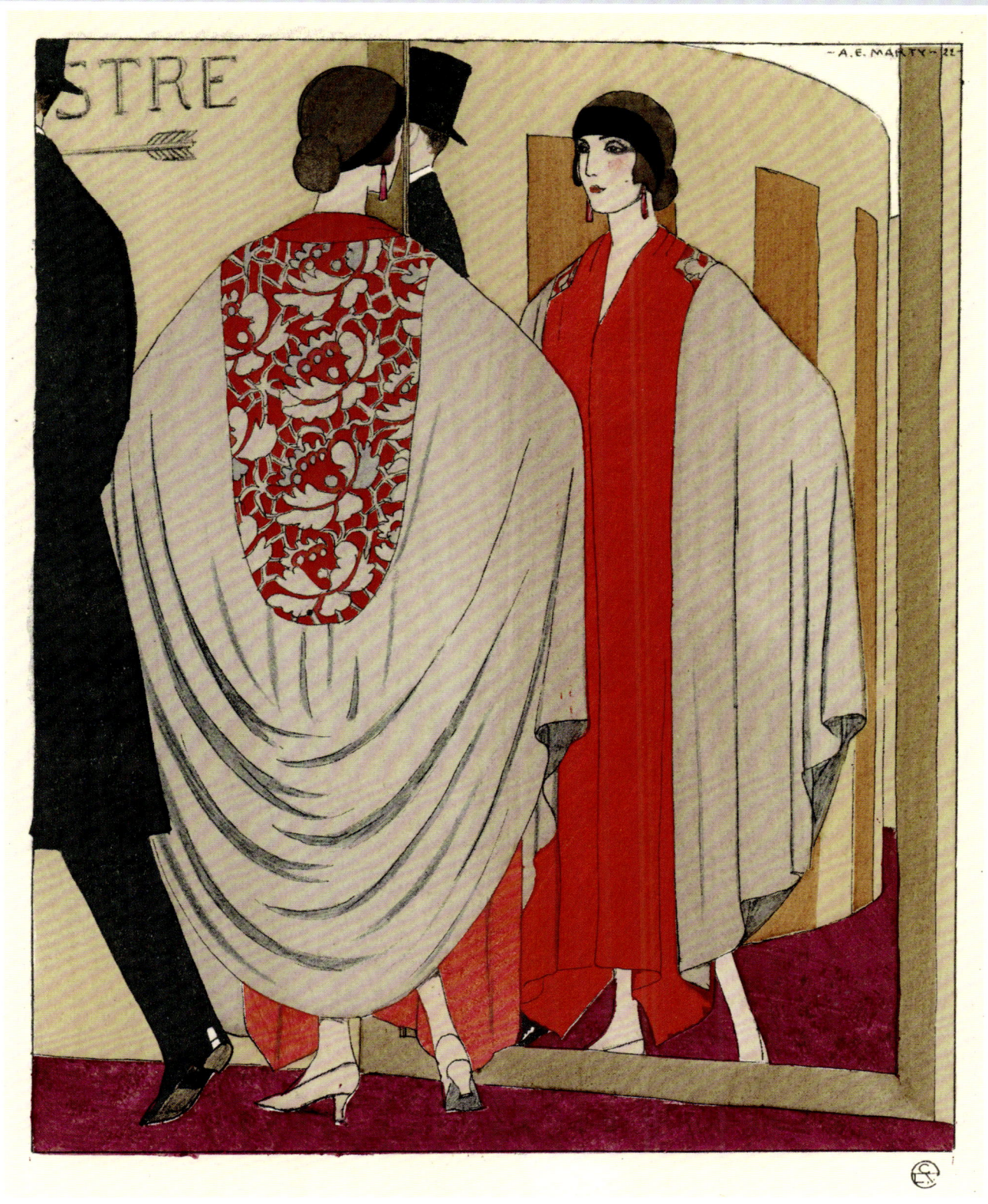

In the 1920s, women wore silk scarves as head wraps, creating a new style.

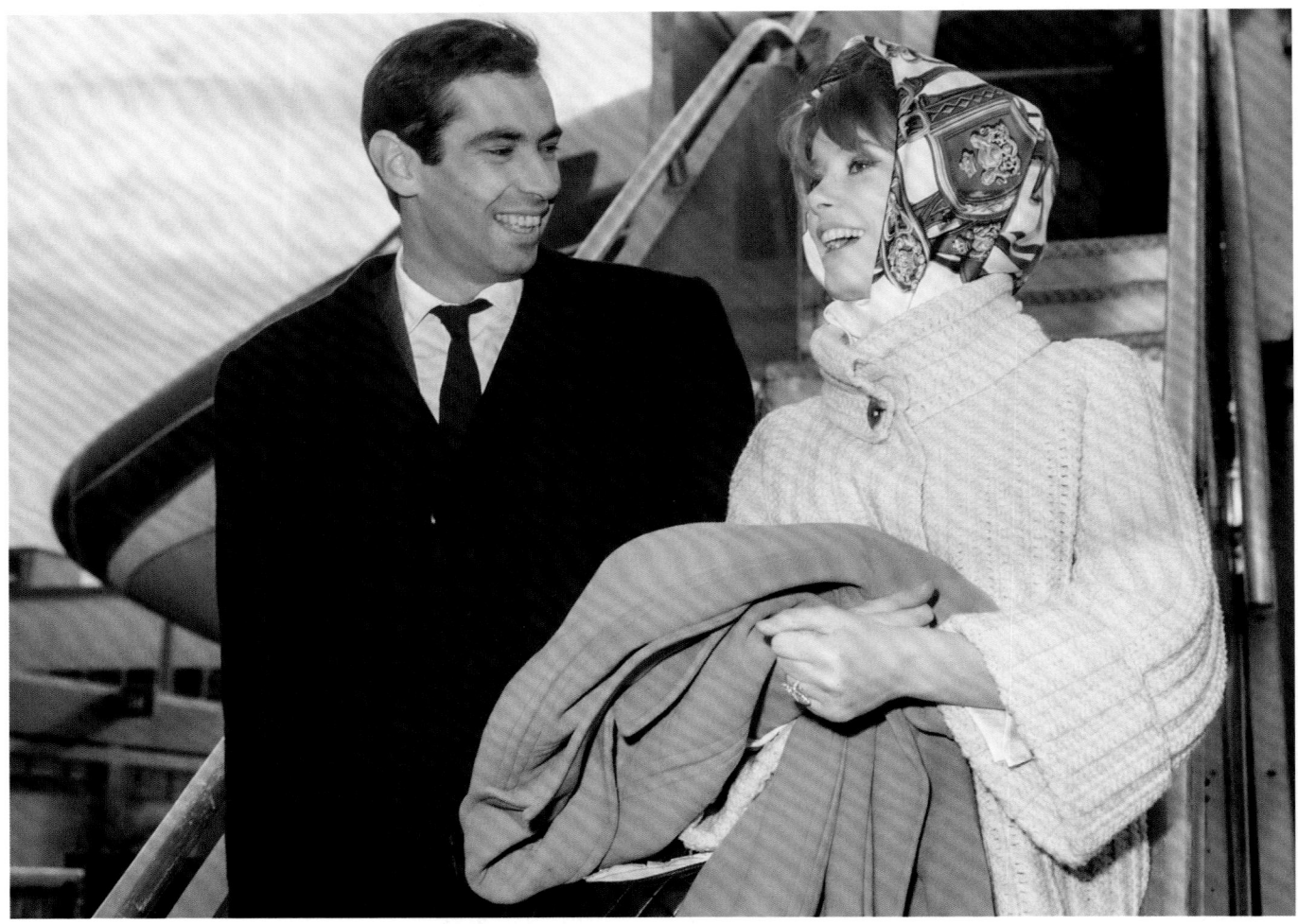

This page – A scarf was in fashion on every occasion in the 1950s and 1960s. For example, women often wore one as a head covering, knotted below the chin, as shown by Brigitte Bardot here. The scarf is the *Bride de Gala* style.

Opposite page – Jacqueline Kennedy Onassis wearing a scarf styled with a pair of oversize sunglasses in the 1970s.

Style icons such as Audrey Hepburn, Catherine Deneuve and First Lady Jacqueline Kennedy flaunted silk scarves tied under the chin, de rigueur with oversize sunglasses, while Brigitte Bardot wore silk scarves as headbands. Elizabeth Taylor preferred to wear them with the ends wrapped around her neck, or tied behind the nape of her neck and dangling down her back. Chic even when injured, Grace of Monaco was photographed with a silk scarf as a sling for her broken arm.

In the 1970s, divas such as Bianca Jagger and Lauren Bacall, and celebrities such as Jacqueline Kennedy Onassis, wore them as headbands which covered their foreheads, intertwined like a turban, under hats or around the neck. In the following decade, silk scarves were updated once again and seen on the new stars. Grace Jones wore hers as a sort of veil to complement her androgynous looks and Madonna knotted them around her rebellious hairstyles.

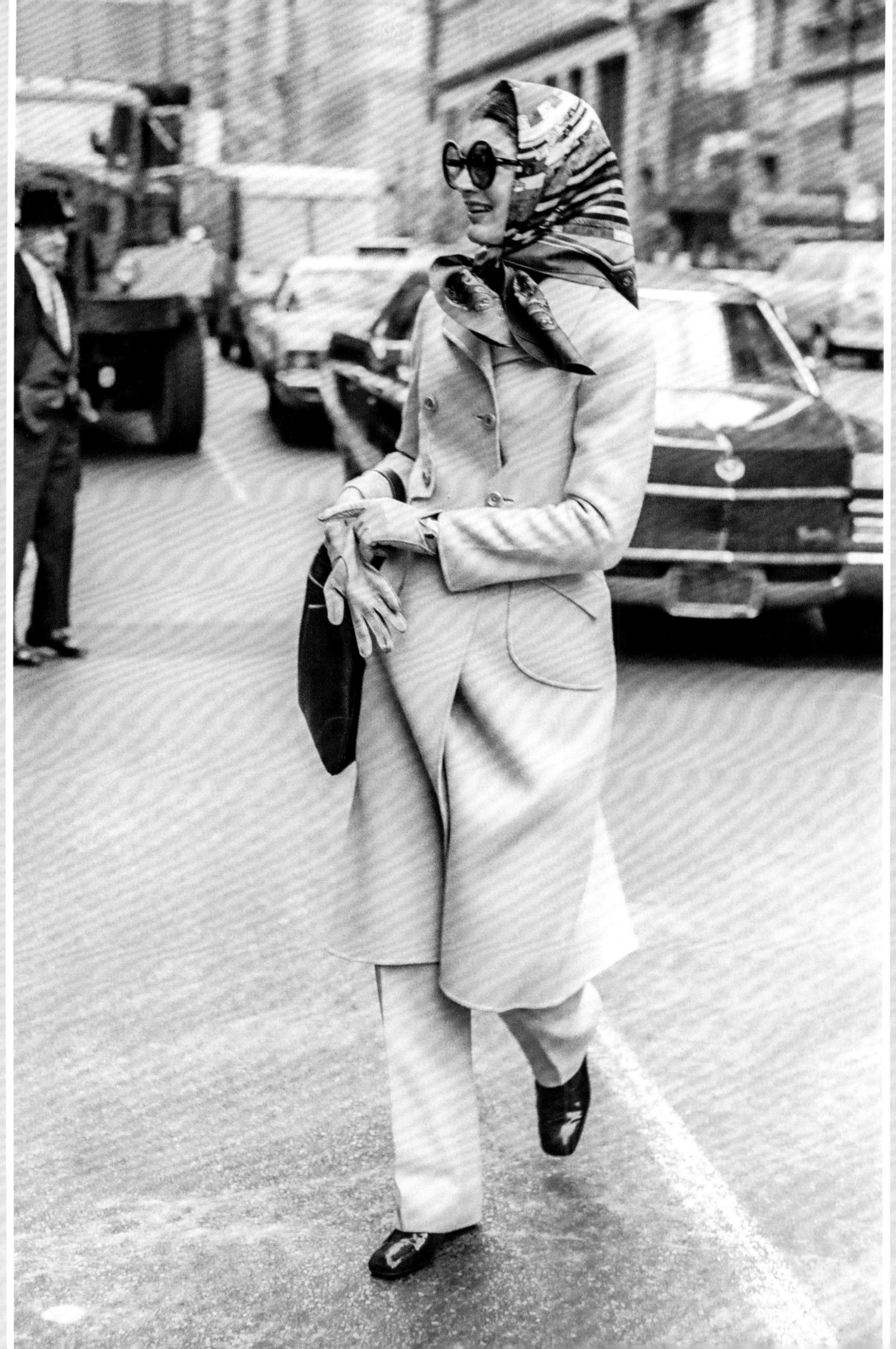

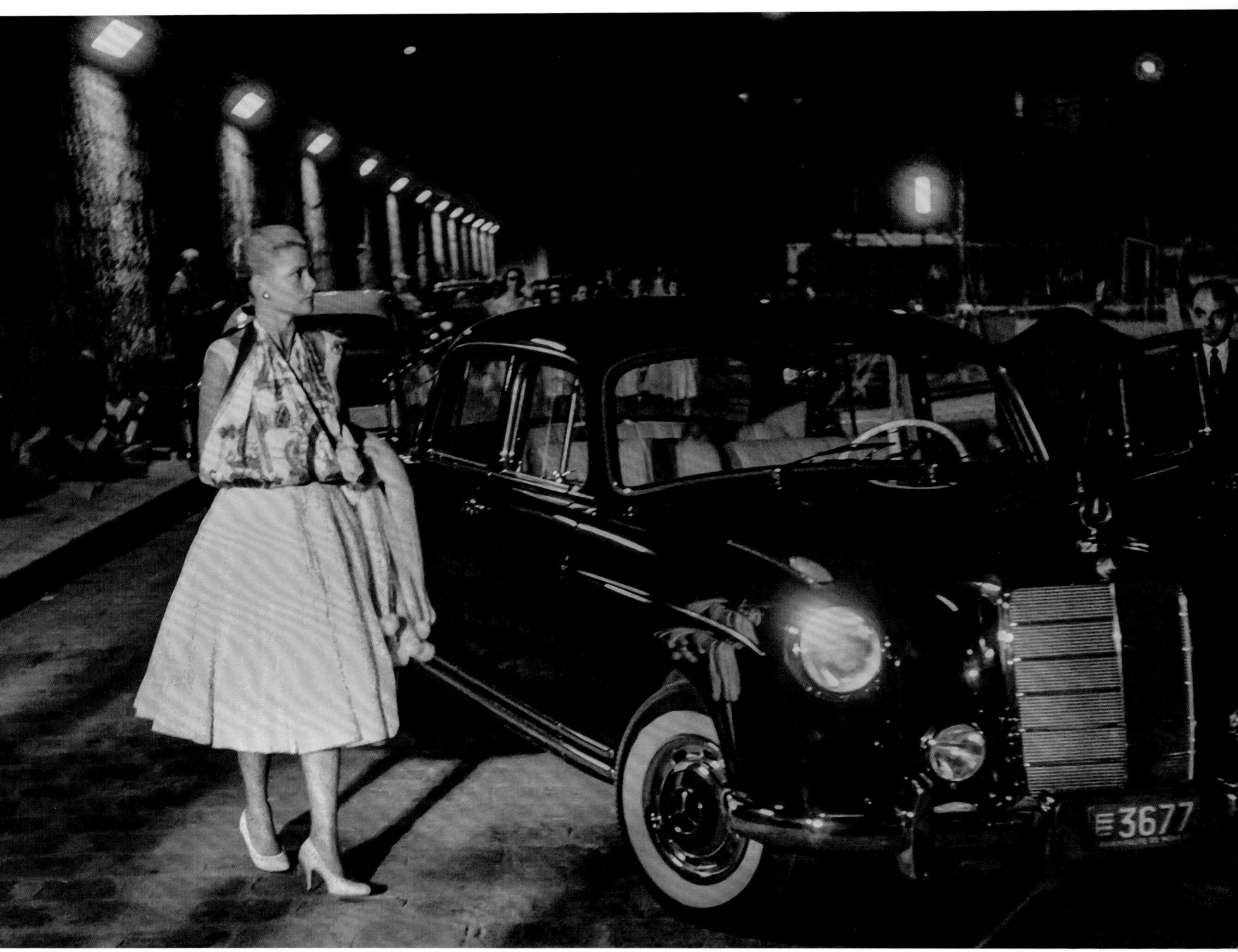

Grace of Monaco using a silk scarf as an arm sling. The design is the *Deo Juvante* (1957/58), which celebrates the heritage of the principality with its colours, coat of arms and motto, *Deo Juvante*, which means 'With the help of God'.

In that same decade, silk scarves continued to be symbols of formal elegance: they were the accessory of choice for the British Prime Minister Margaret Thatcher. In 1986, Hermès could count on a very special spokeswoman, Queen Elizabeth, who had worn an Hermès silk scarf in one of the photographs chosen for the stamp issued to celebrate her 60th birthday. (The photograph had been taken in 1973.)

In the 1990s, silk scarves were worn as bandannas by hip-hop and R&B stars like Jennifer Lopez and the members of Destiny's Child, or styled elegantly by the tenor Luciano Pavarotti, who had an extensive collection.

In the early 2000s, an Hermès silk scarf was chosen as the essential accessory for the looks worn by the terrible main character of *The Devil Wears Prada*, becoming one of the recurrent themes of the film.

From Kendall Jenner to actress Eva Mendes and singer Rihanna, today's celebrities continue to use silk scarves in ways which run the gamut from dapper to pirate-inspired, reflecting individual style.

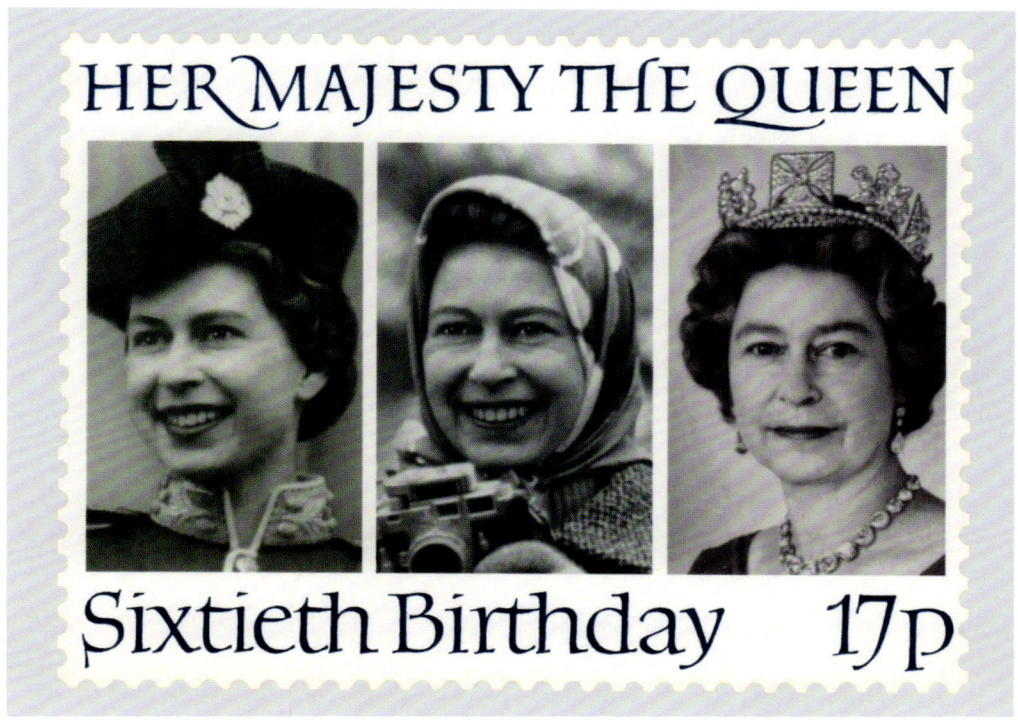

Elizabeth II, Queen of the United Kingdom, was another fan and collector of Hermès scarves. In one of the three portraits for the stamp celebrating her 60th birthday, she is seen wearing a scarf knotted under her chin.

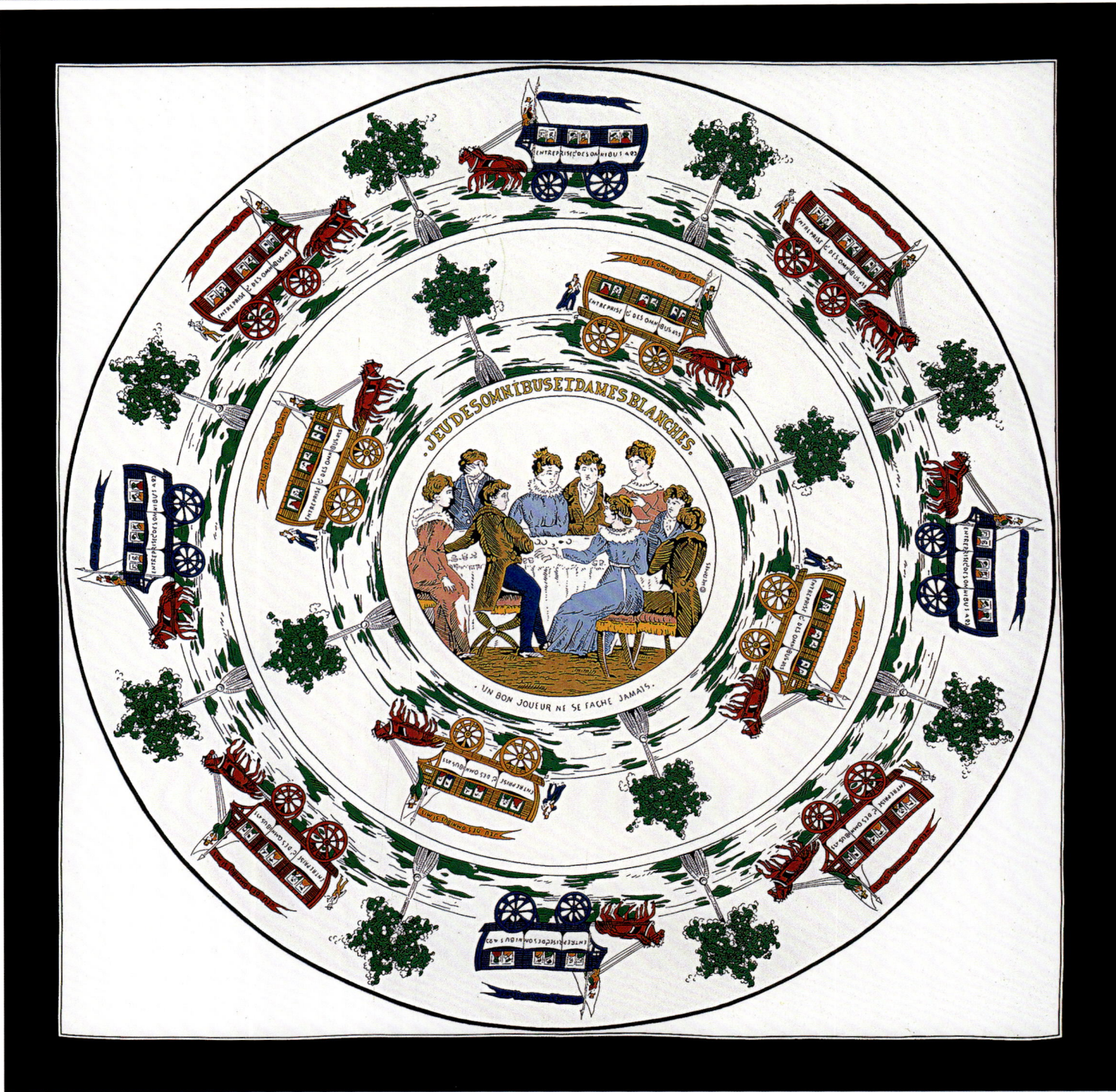

This page – The *Jeu des Omnibus et Dames Blanches* silk scarf which Hugo Grygkar designed for Hermès, 1937. The composition captures the dynamism of the city with elegance and a nostalgic spirit, illustrating details of the vehicles, passengers and the urban landscape with flowing lines and refined style.

Opposite page – The *Ex-Libris* scarf by Hermès, designed by Hugo Grygkar in 1946. It references the bookplate by Émile-Maurice Hermès which in turn echoed Alfred de Dreux's *Duc attelé, groom à l'attente*, overlapped with his initials: EMH. On two sides a caduceus can be seen, the staff of the Greek god Hermes and a symbol of peace and trade. Around the medallion are four elegant carriages inspired by vintage designs kept in the Hermès private collection.

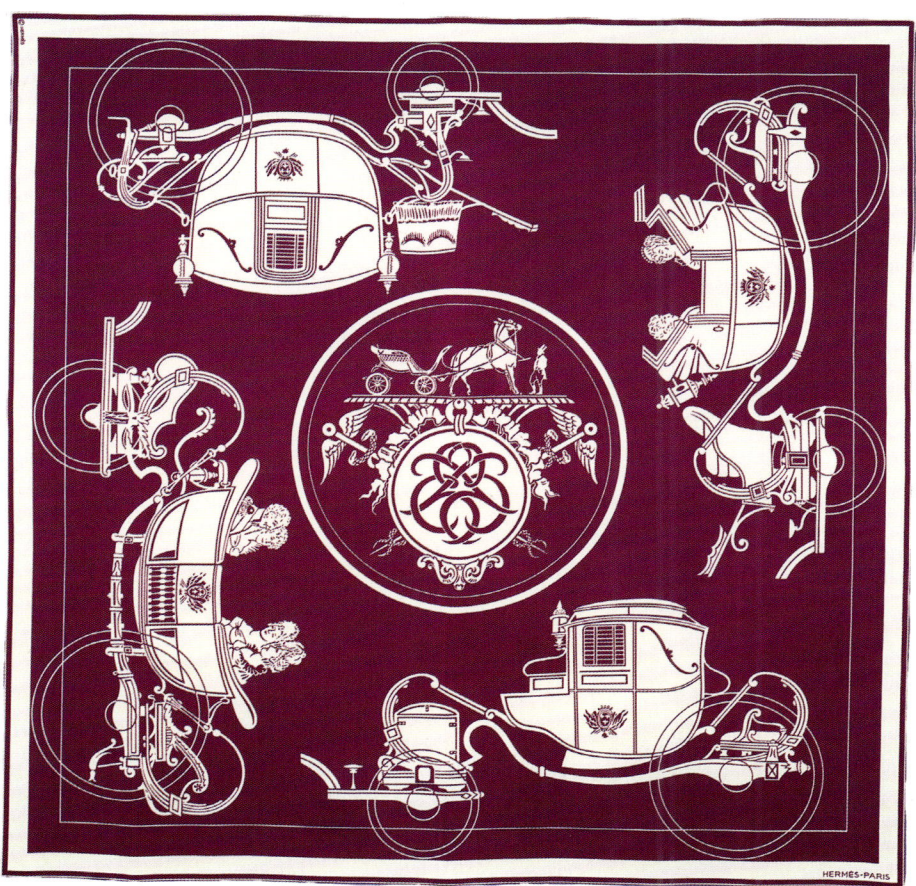

Creative collaborations

In 1937, Émile-Maurice Hermès and his son-in-law Robert Dumas decided to make large scarves with unique prints from the fabric which was used for the jockey silks produced by the fashion house. They went to Lyon, the city of silk, and they produced the first sample of a series which was destined for success.

The original Hermès *carrè* (the term used by the fashion house to distinguish their silk scarves) was *Jeu des Omnibus et Dames Blanches*, inspired by a tabletop game from the 19th century. It portrays *omnibuses* and *dames blanches* (carriages pulled by white horses) which at the time were a popular form of transport in Paris. In a playful touch, Dumas added the phrase: 'A good player never gets angry.'

Hermès hired the best illustrators to work on their scarves from the start. The first was Hugo Grygkar.[1] Inspired by the objects in the large Hermès collection and mixing them with his talent and his creativity, he managed to make this small accessory even more alluring, blurring the line between fashion and art. For example, the *Ex-Libris* scarf (1946) was inspired by a drawing from a bookplate which Émile-Maurice Hermès had created in 1923.

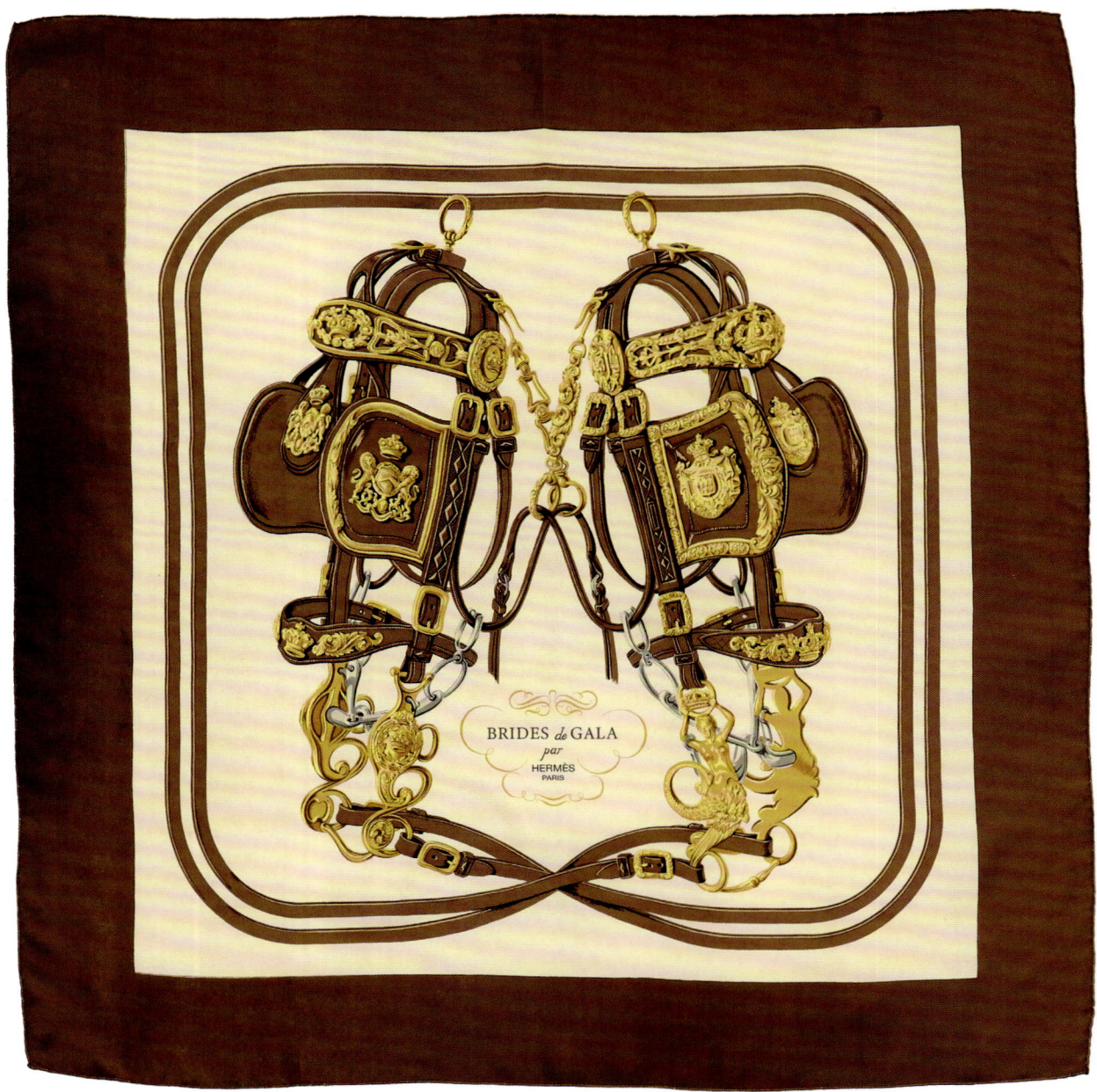

Grykar designed over 100 silk scarves, creating styles still admired today. One of his most famous is *Brides de Gala*, created in 1957, which portrays two parade bridles decorated by noble crests in an elegant interplay of symmetry and clean lines. Often inspired by the equestrian world, Grygkar also explored other themes, including florals and motifs inspired by the Far East. His last collection was *Floralies* (1959).

Hermès *Brides de Gala* silk scarf designed by Hugo Grygkar, 1957. One of the bridles in this composition was part of the collection of Émile-Maurice Hermès and it was originally created for Emperor Maximilian I of Mexico. The bit is decorated with graceful mermaids. The other bridle features the crests of the Ferronays Counts. *Brides de Gala* has been revisited and reprinted countless times over the years.

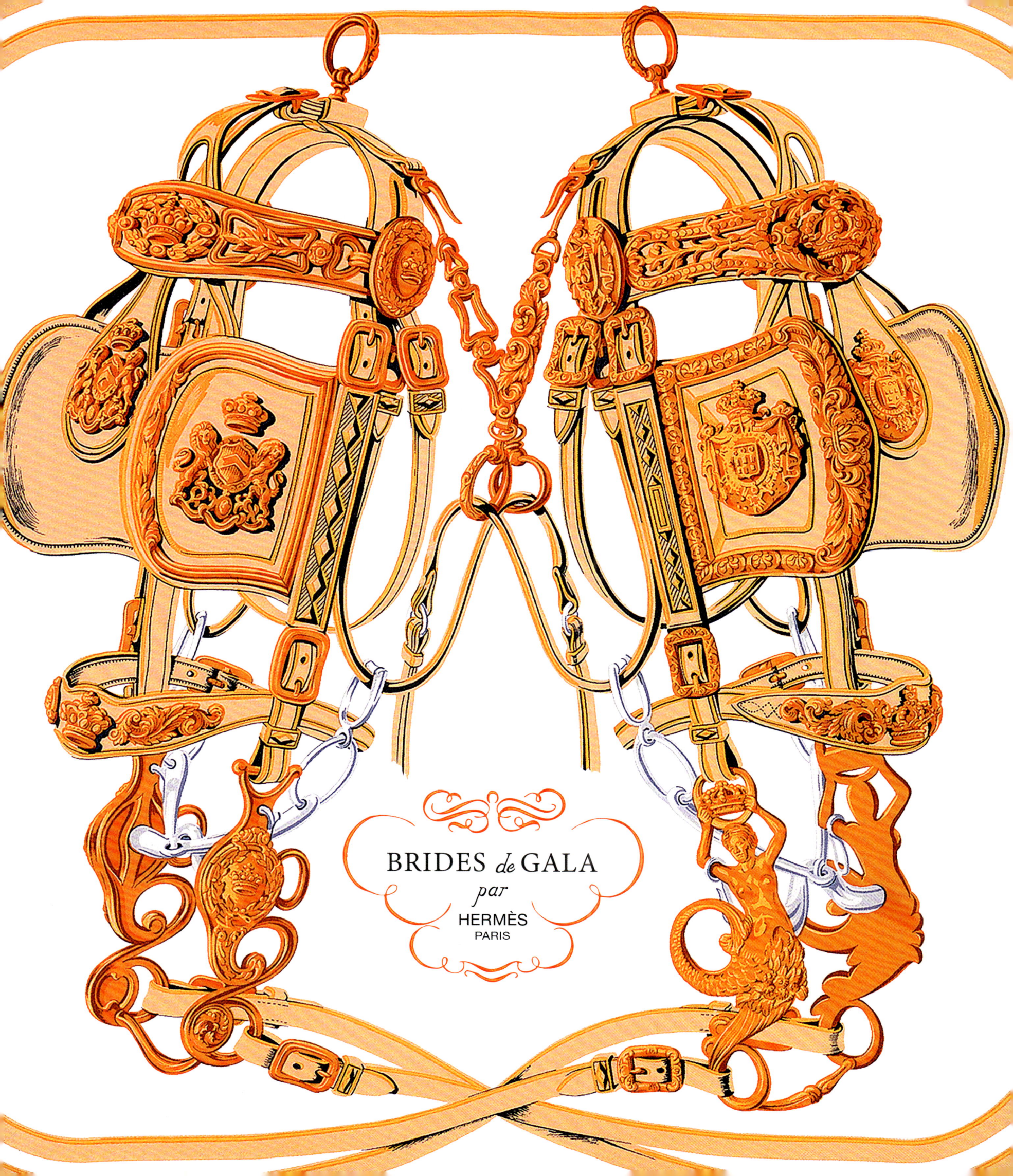

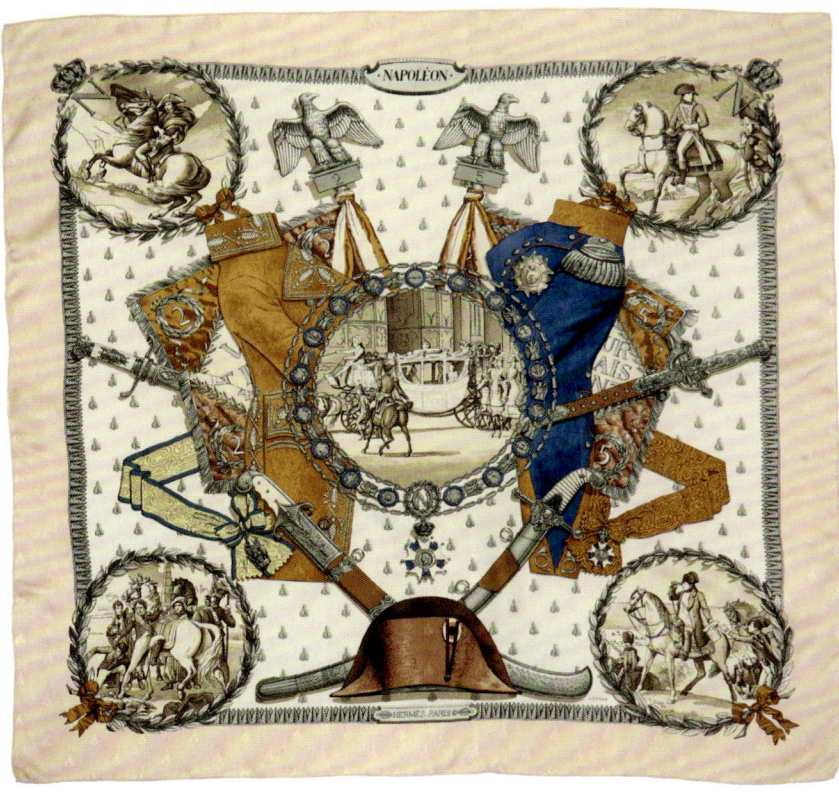

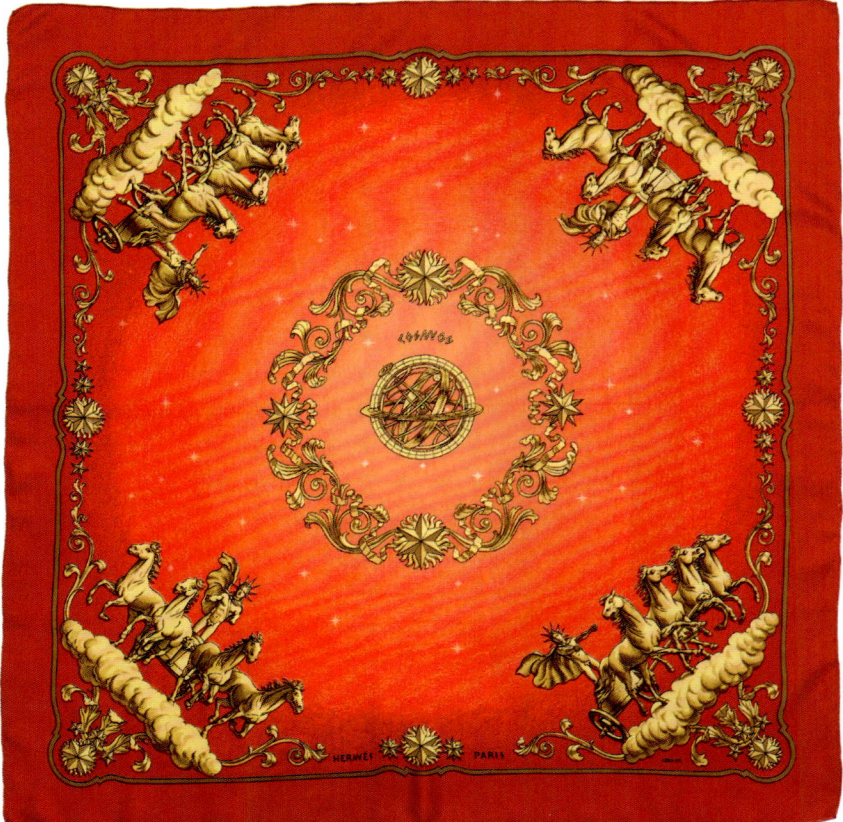

The Grykar style is distinguished by vivid designs, harmonious colours and balanced forms.

Another important name in the history of *carrès* is Philippe Ledoux, who designed some of the fashion house's most iconic silk scarves in the 1950s for a total of over 90 creations.[2]

His designs celebrate the equestrian world, history and nature, and they are famous for their details and narrative complexity. Some of his most famous pieces are *La Comédie Italienne* (1962), *Napoleon* (1963), *Cosmos* (1964) and *La Promenade de Longchamps* (1965). Ledoux's style helped define the identity of Hermès, transforming each silk scarf into a small masterpiece which evokes exciting distant lands, always with a refined nostalgic touch.

Since then, the brand has had hundreds of stylists, graphic designers, illustrators and artists use their creativity to overcome skilfully the limits that the shape and material imposes, in the realisation of a vast range of fascinating works, each one assigned a name which evokes a story or a narrative world.

....

Top – *Napoleon* silk scarf by Hermès, designed by Philippe Ledoux, 1964. This silk scarf features symbols, objects and important moments in the life of Napoleon: uniforms, insignia and drawings. The background is dotted by bees, symbols of the empire.

Bottom – *Cosmos* silk scarf by Hermès, designed by Philippe Ledoux, 1964. This silk scarf features Apollo, the sun god, driving his precious four-horse chariot on each corner of the composition. An armillary sphere sits to the centre.

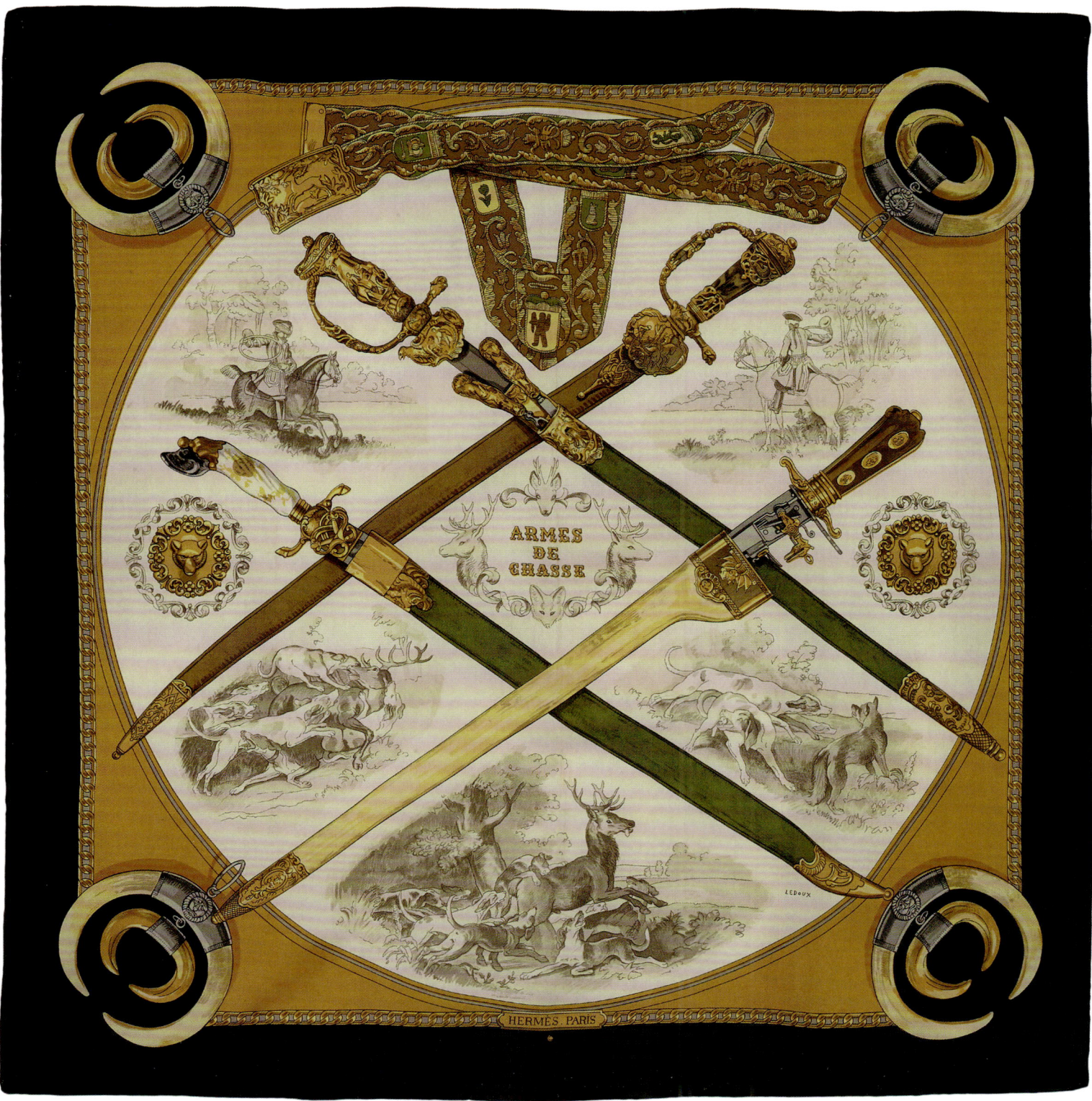

Hermès *Armes de Chasse* silk scarf designed by Philippe Ledoux, 1970. This scarf features two men on horseback, dogs and hunted deer in the background, while criss-crossed swords appear in the foreground.

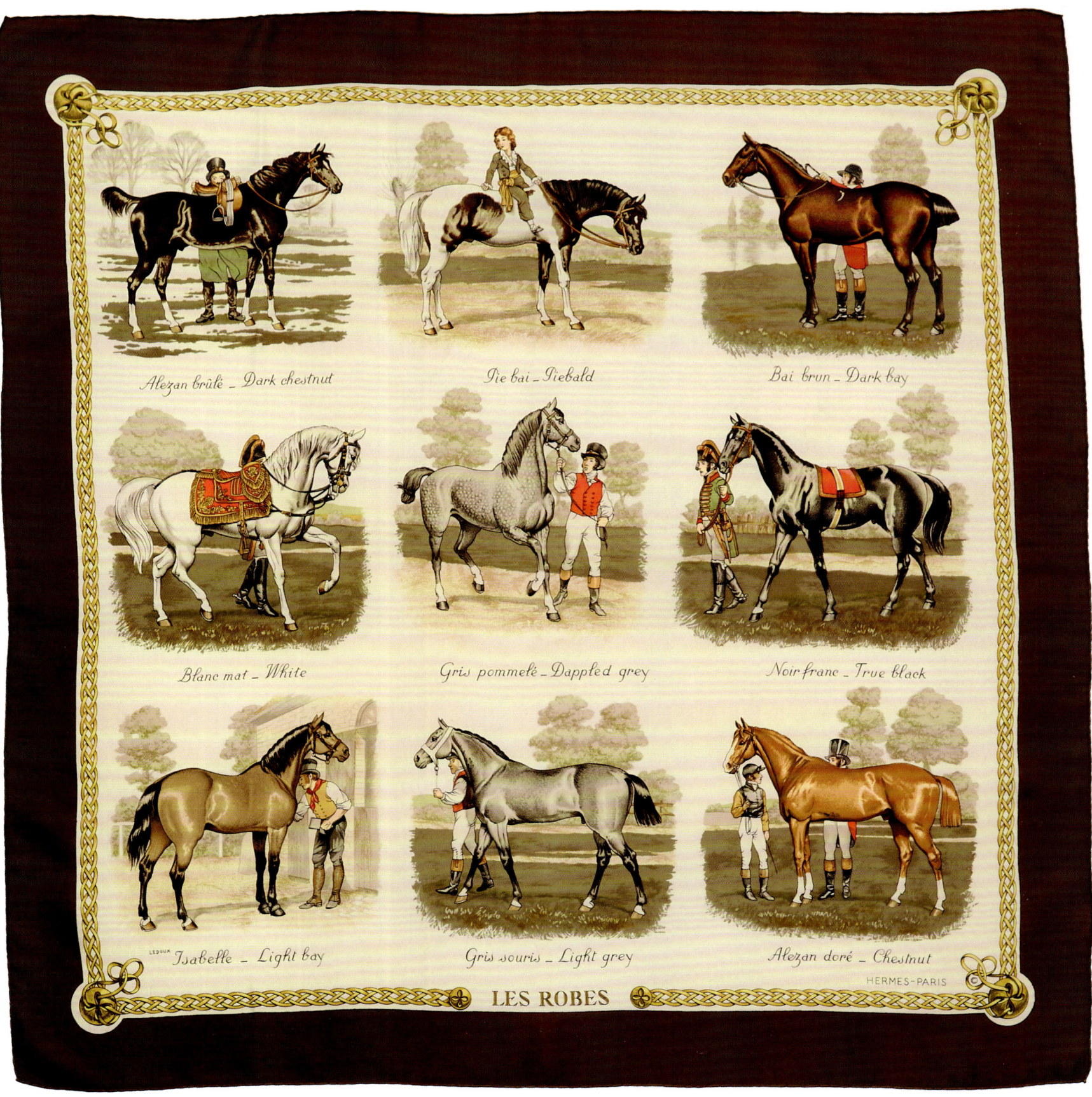

Alezan brûlé – Dark chestnut

Pie bai – Piebald

Bai brun – Dark bay

Blanc mat – White

Gris pommelé – Dappled grey

Noir franc – True black

Isabelle – Light bay

Gris souris – Light grey

Alezan doré – Chestnut

LES ROBES

HERMES-PARIS

Hermès *Les Robes* silk scarf designed by Philippe Ledoux, 1968. Horses with different coloured coats are portrayed in figurative style, set onto a grid.

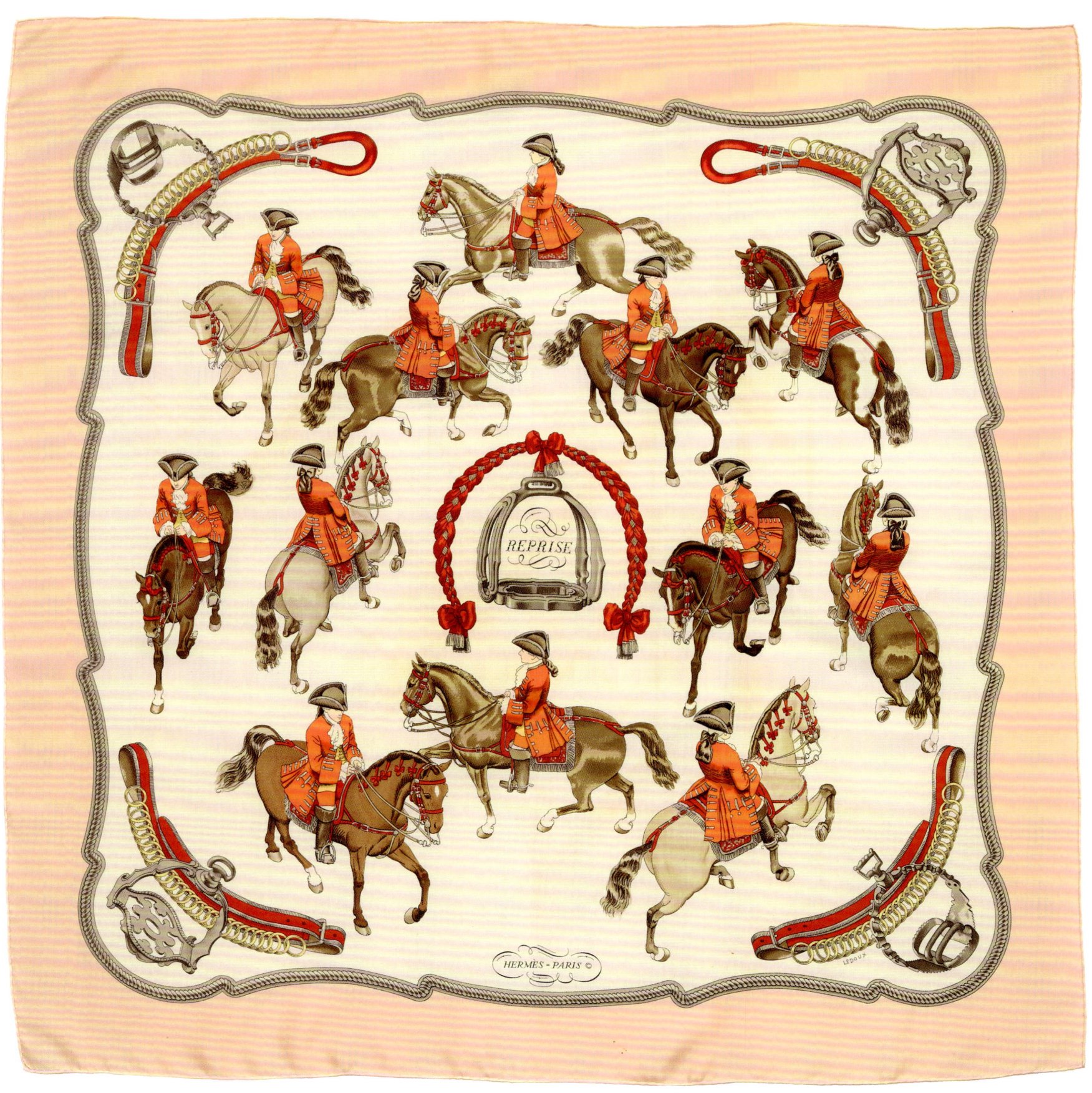

Hermès *Reprise* silk scarf designed by Philippe Ledoux, 1970. The scarf portrays different 18th-century horses and riders as they execute a reprise, which is a sequence of different moves, presented in a dressage riding ring.

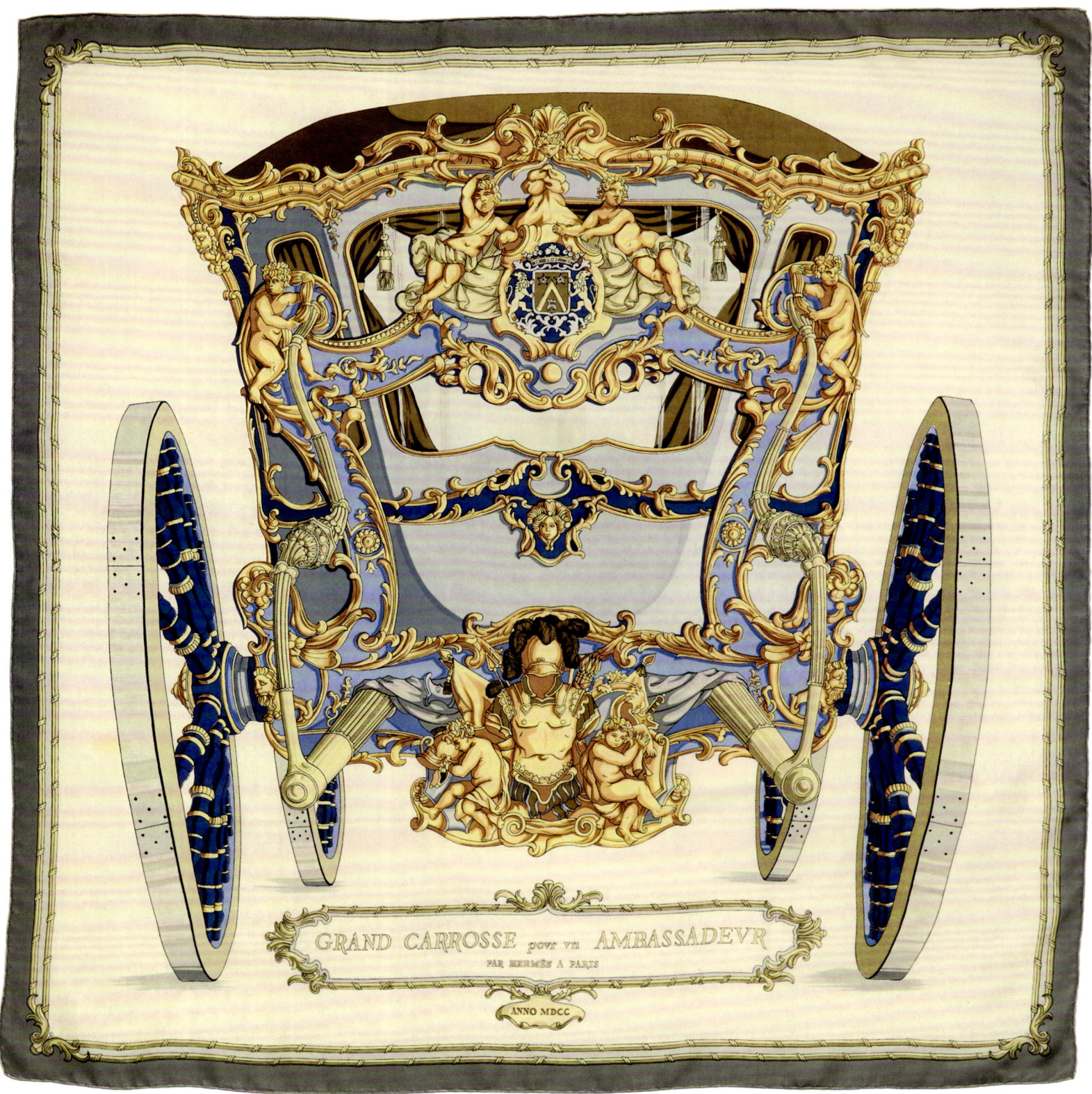

Hermès *Grand Carrosse pour un Ambassadeur* silk scarf designed by Lise Coutin, 1961. An 18th-century carriage with important golden friezes and noble coats of arms designed to carry an important person, such as an ambassador, is the subject of this composition.

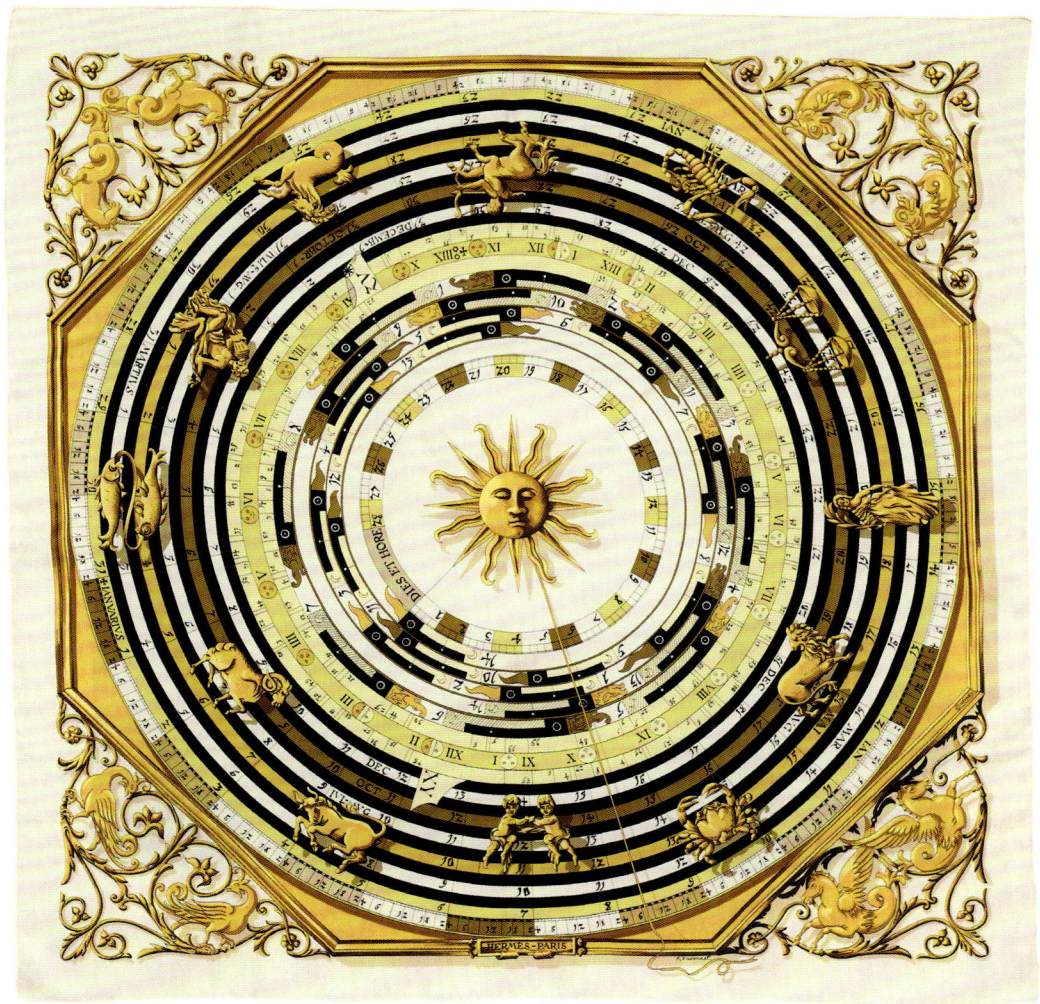

Hermès *Astrologie – Dies et Hore*, silk scarf designed by Françoise Façonnet, 1963. An astrological chart from the Renaissance, found in the collection of the Paris Observatory Museum, was the inspiration for this silk scarf.

Narration with recurring themes, and images with continuous references, is precisely what makes this enigmatic universe so interesting and open to interpretation.

Some themes appear frequently on Hermès silk scarves, such as those related to the world of horseback riding. However, there are others too; themes such as carriages, cars and boats recur often, as do historical motifs, especially those referring to the Napoleonic era, and designs featuring flora and fauna. Yet others are the pure products of the imagination and vision of the creatives who designed them.

Today, the Hermès archive includes about 2,500 designs, a number that increases considerably given the different colourways which are available for each style. It's impossible to list them all; instead, the following is a selection that, aside from a few bestsellers, is almost inevitably personal.

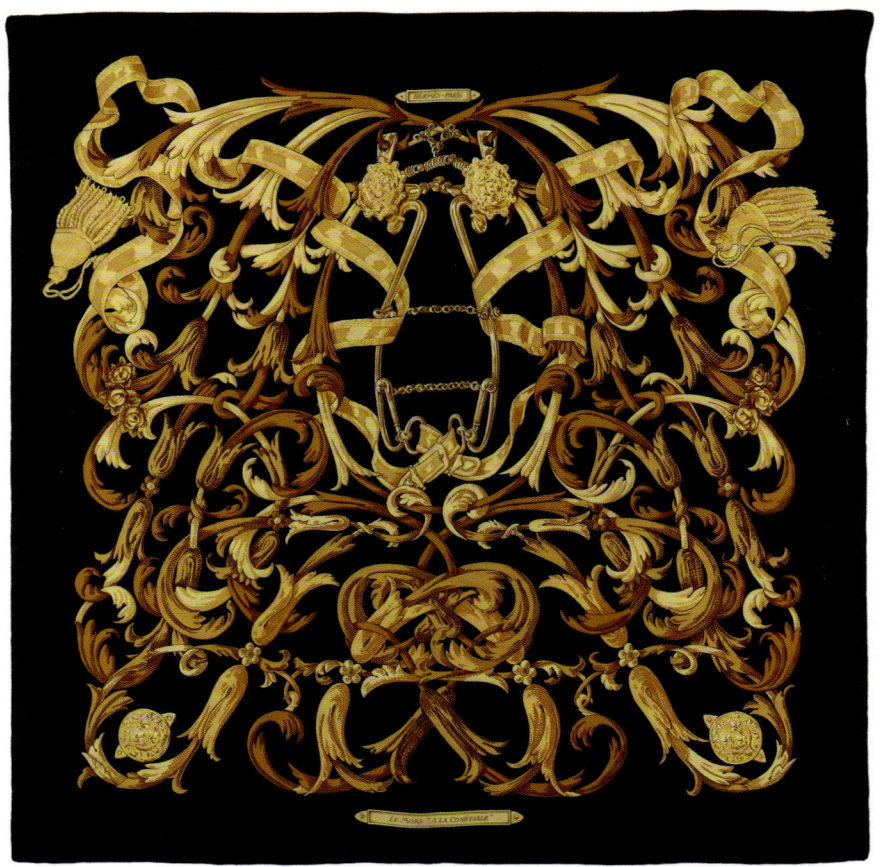

This page – Hermès *Les Mors a La Conétable*, silk scarf designed by Henri d'Origny, 1970. This scarf celebrates the horse bit as an essential part of the equestrian command in an intricate composition of objects and leaves with tassels and crests.

Opposite page – Hermès *Les Mors a La Conétable*, silk scarf designed by Henri d'Origny, 2000. Placed in a horse's mouth and connected to the reins, bits make it possible to guide the direction of a horse. They're called *jouets* in French when they contain a few small metal tear-drops which cause the animal to salivate and help him accept the bit. One detail in this composition is enlarged until it becomes an entire scarf.

The French-Ukrainian graphic designer Adolphe Mouron (pseudonym 'Cassandre') was the one to come up with the *Perspective* designs (1951), which portray an architectural motif, and *Literature* (1952), which is a tribute to his love and mastery of graphic design and typography. The first plays with optical illusions and depth, creating a sense of dynamic movement on the silk surface; the latter, on the other hand, celebrates the beauty of letters and words, transforming words into visual art.

The collaboration between the painter Henri de Linarès and Hermès gave rise to creations full of natural details inspired by hunting and the animal kingdom. His designs reflect classic elegance. Some of the most sought-after by collectors are *Plumes* (1953) and *Chasse à Vol* (1962).

The illustrator Henri d'Origny began working with Hermès in 1958, introducing elegant and playful motifs, inspired mainly by the equestrian world.

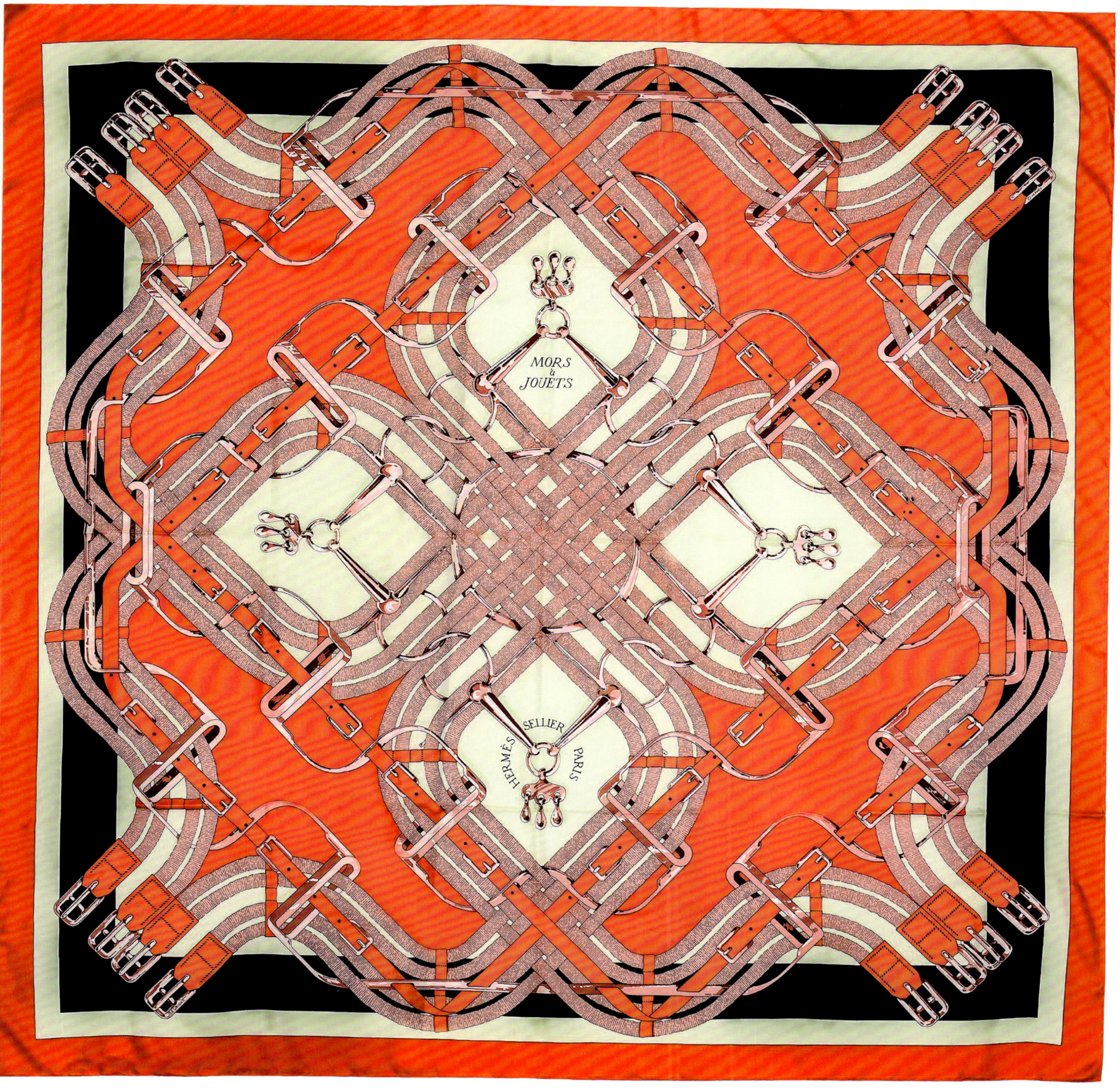

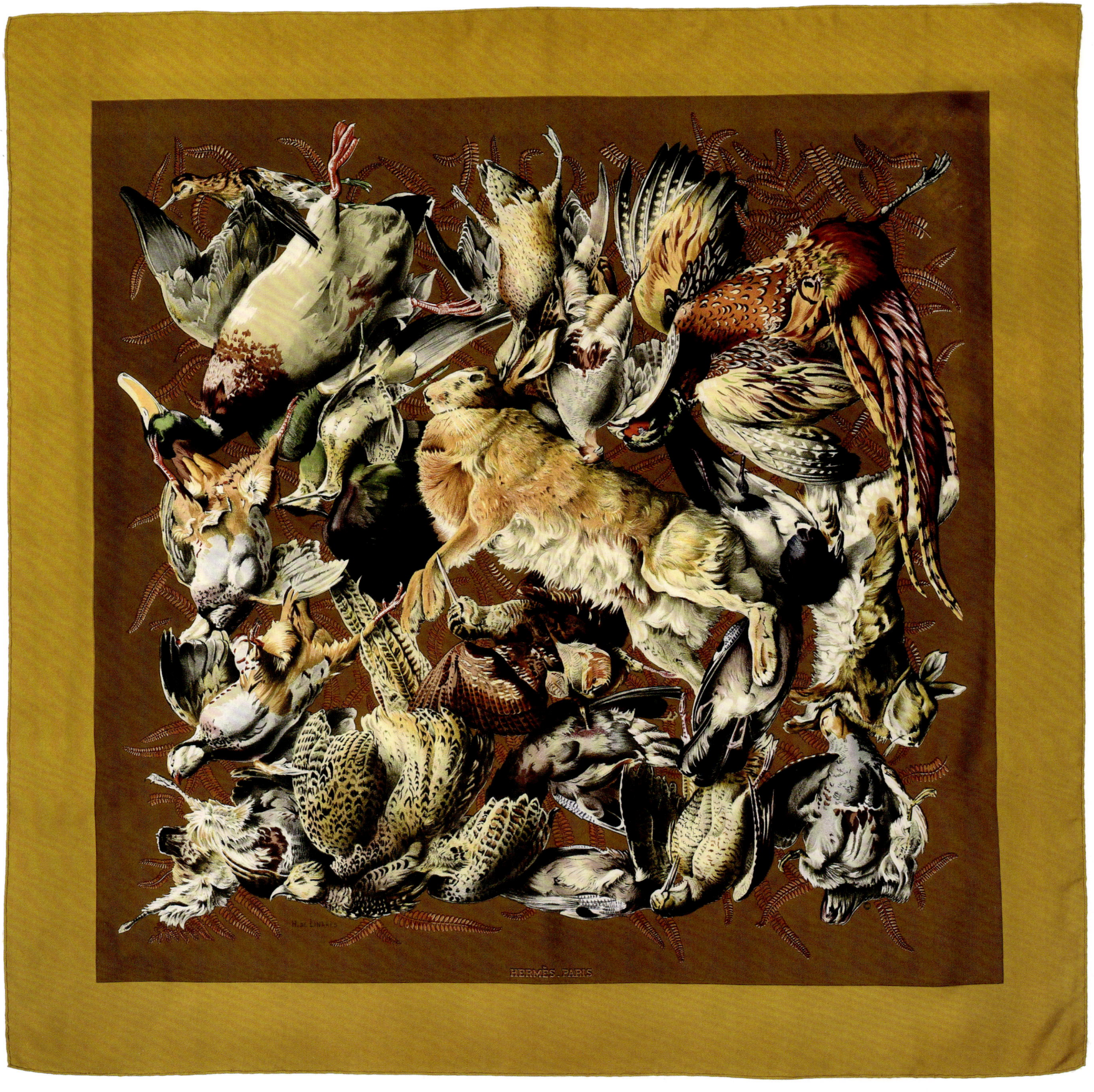

Hermès *Gibiers* silk scarf designed by Henri de Linarès, 1966. The world of birds and hunting inspired the designs of de Linarès.

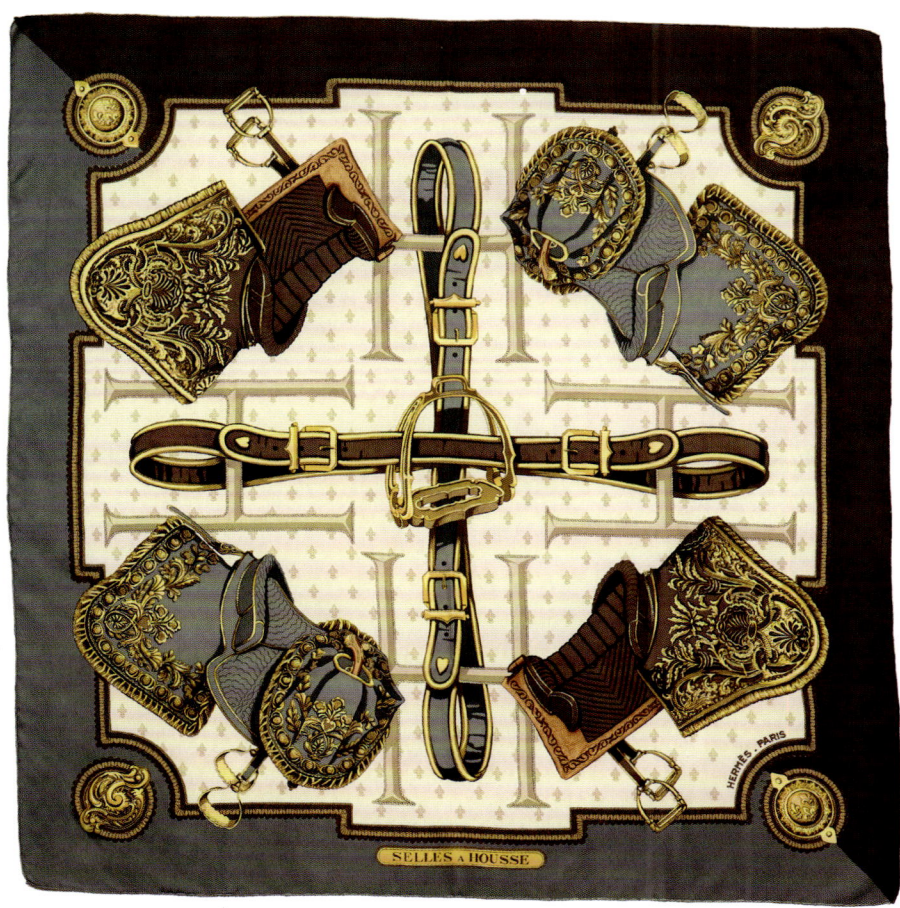

Hermès *Selles a Housse* silk scarf designed by Christiane Vauzelles, 1967. This scarf portrays a splendid four-saddle motif divided into four quarters by Hs looped into crossed straps.

Other famous silk scarves are *Les Bassets* (1956) with portraits of dachshunds painted by Xavier de Pont, and the four felines in *Les Leopards* as imagined by Christiane Vauzelles in 1967. The latter became one of the motifs repeated by the house over the years, seen on objects such as beach towels and home goods.

In the 1950s, Hermès began working with English artist Caty Latham, who enriched its collections with especially poetic designs characterised by delicate graphics. Latham's creations are often inspired by plants and animals, and also imaginary worlds in which realism intertwines with fantasy. Some of Latham's[3] most notable creations are *Les Clefs* (1956), in which old keys radiate outward into a geometric yet flowing design. It was one of the designs which was reprinted over the years.

The nephew of Philippe Ledoux, Vladimir Rybaltchenko, known as 'Rybal', began his collaboration with Hermès in the 1970s, bringing visionary style and a rich use of colour. Rybaltchenko's works perfectly balance fantasy and tradition, imbuing Hermès with unique artistry. One of his most famous designs is *Les Cavaliers d'Or* (1975).

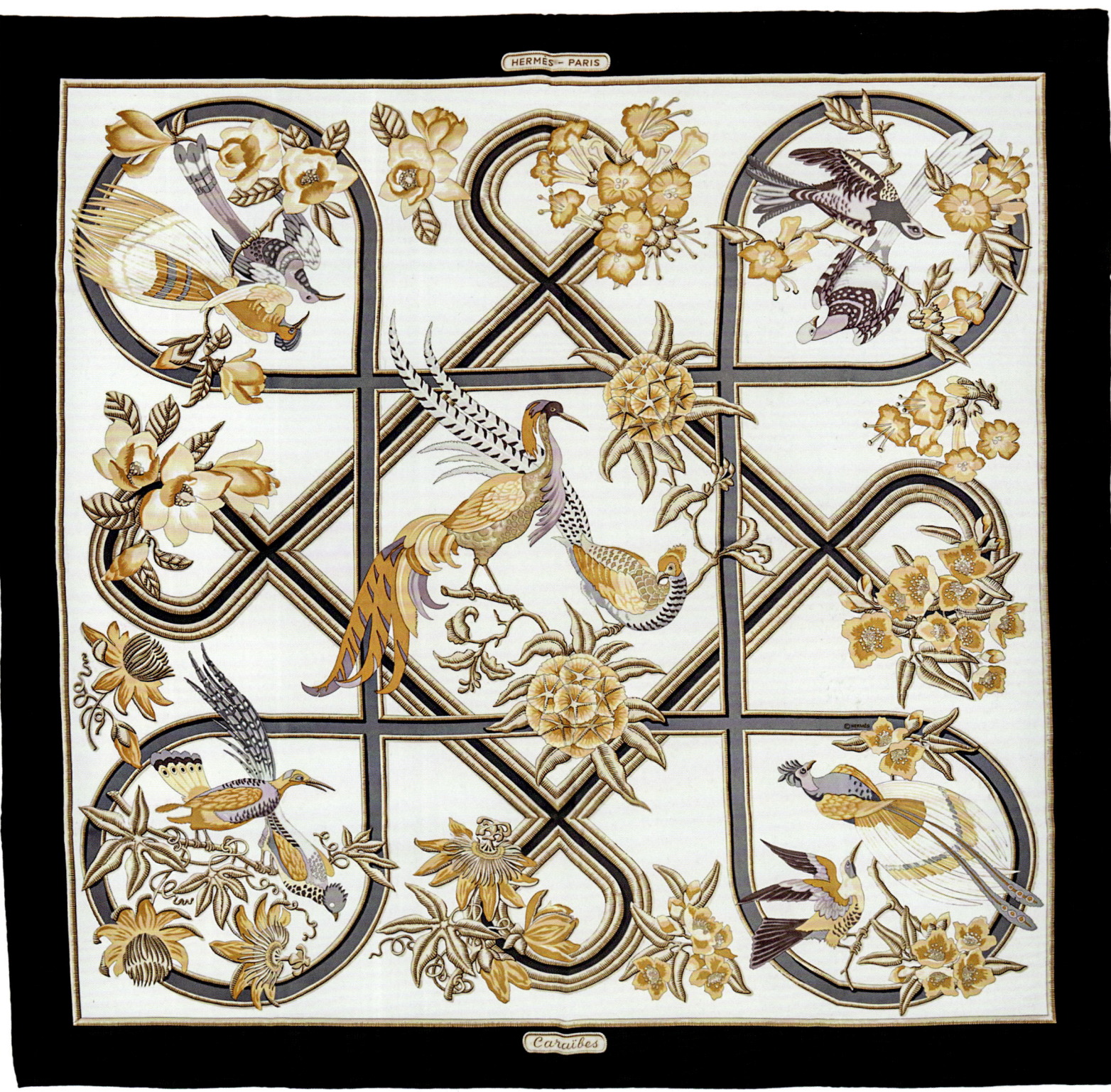

Hermès *Caraïbes* silk scarf designed by Christiane Vauzelles, 1970. A tropical-inspired silk scarf which illustrates an intricate composition of birds and flowers.

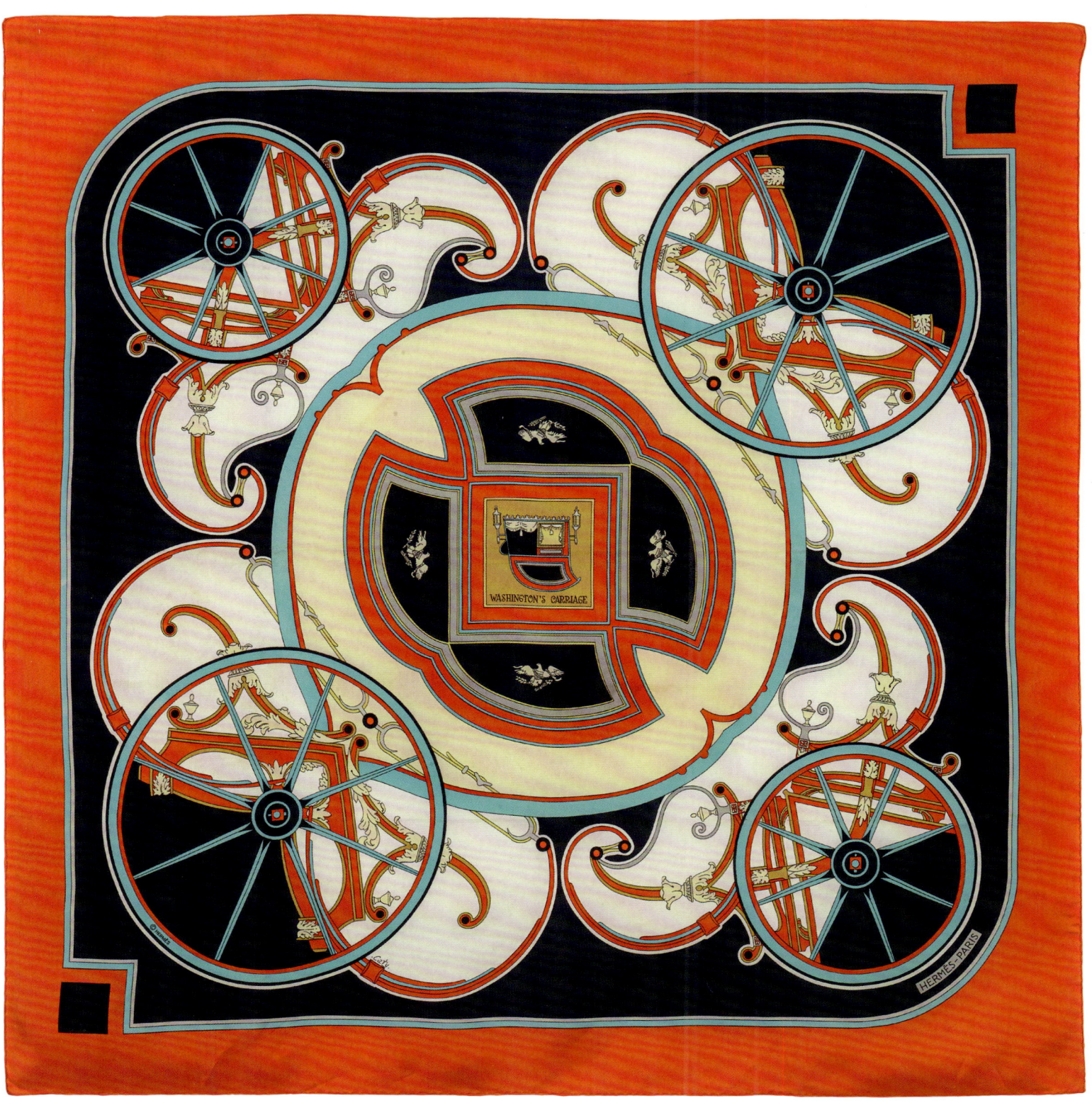

Hermès *Washington's Carriage* silk scarf designed by Caty Latham, 1978. The wheels of the carriage are the stars of this composition, in which red, white and blue are combined with gold.

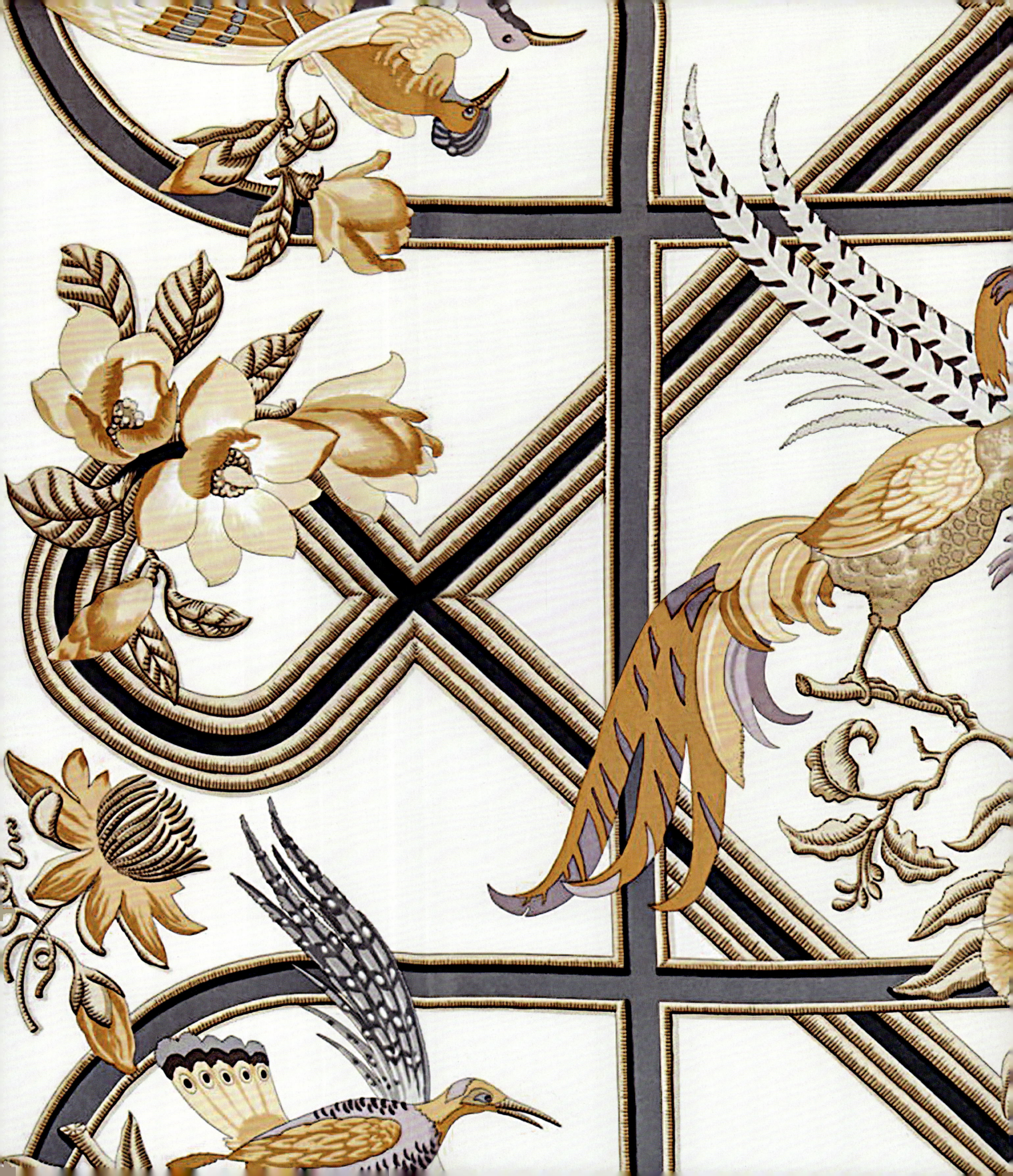

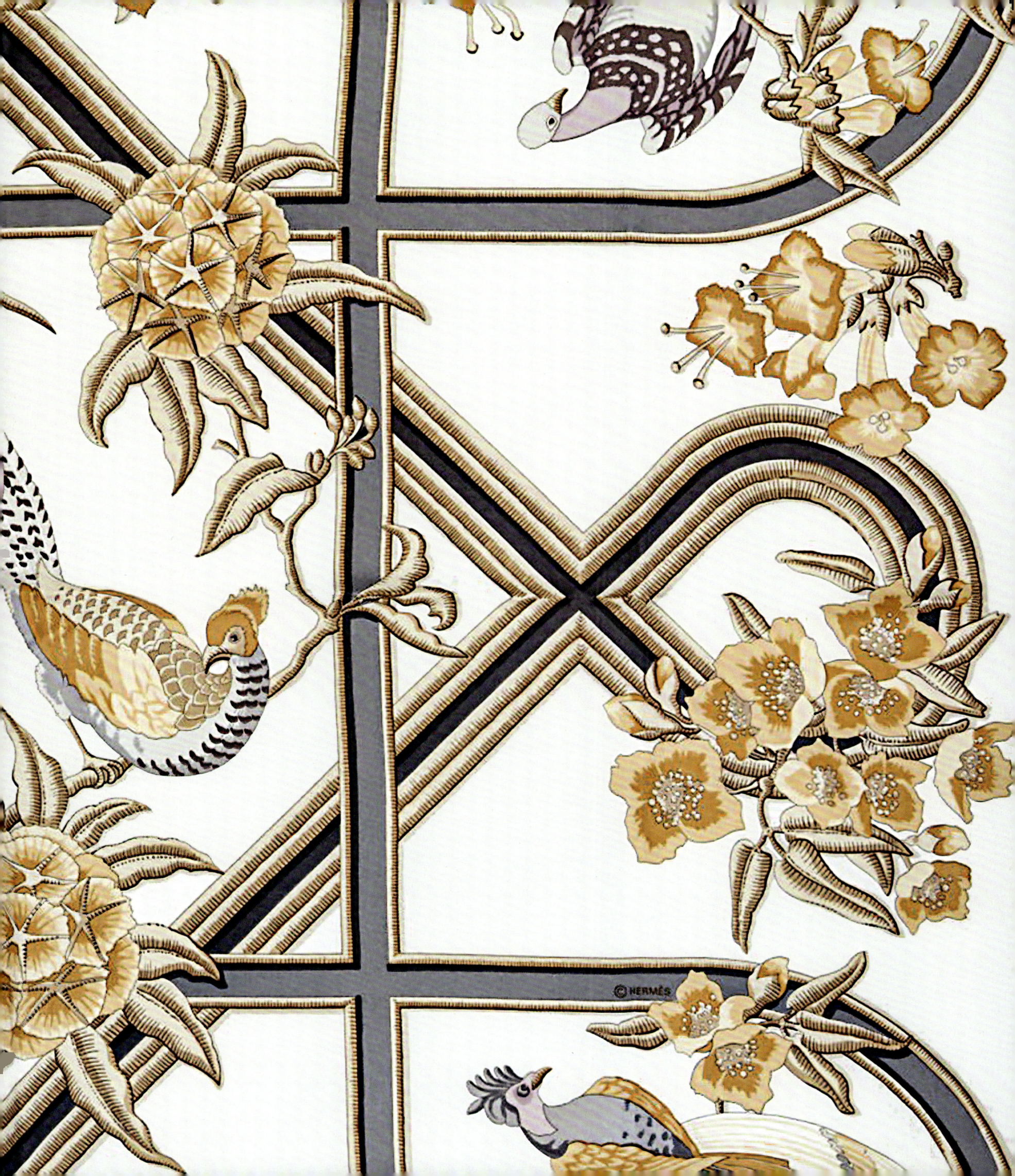

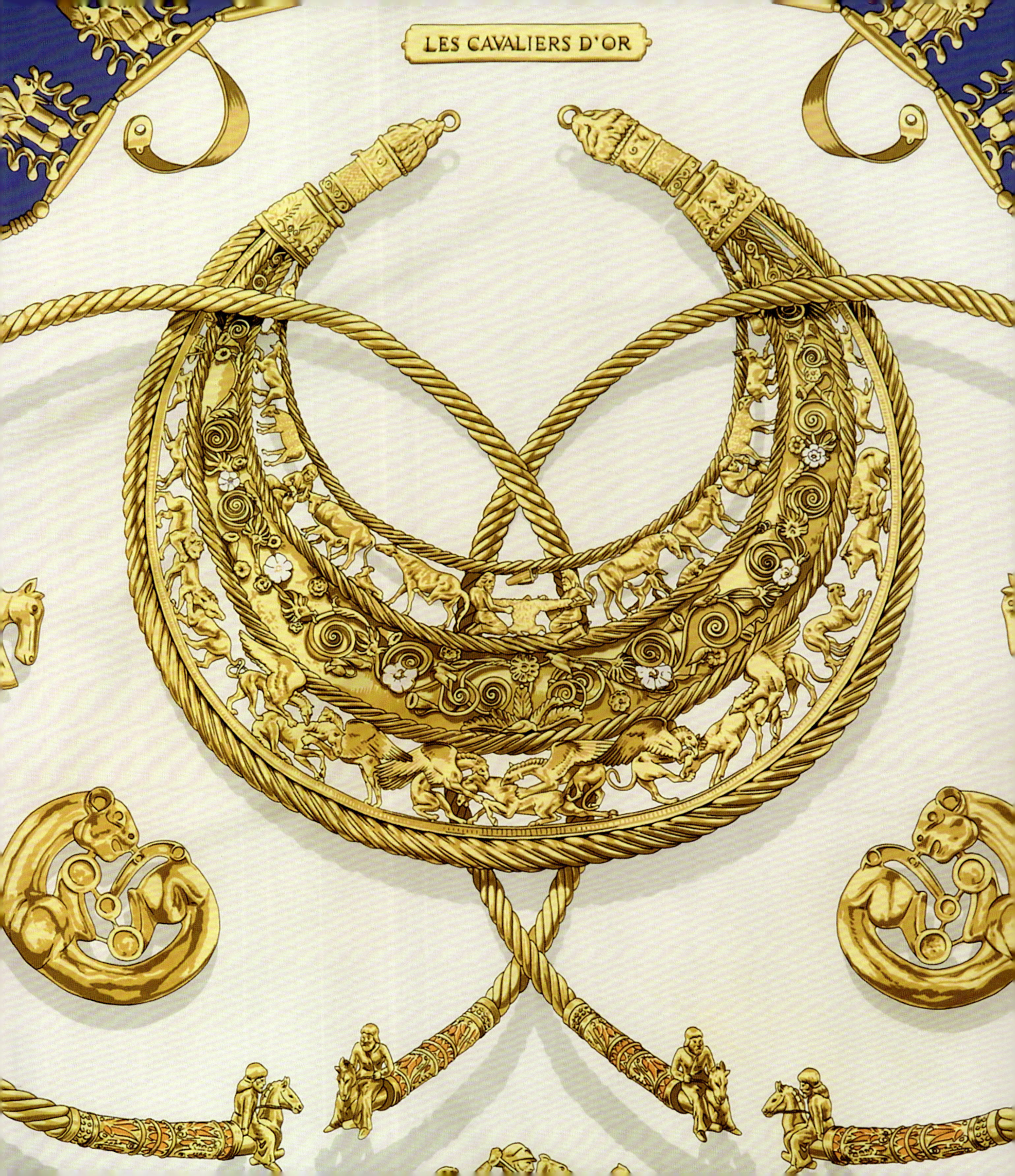

LES CAVALIERS D'OR

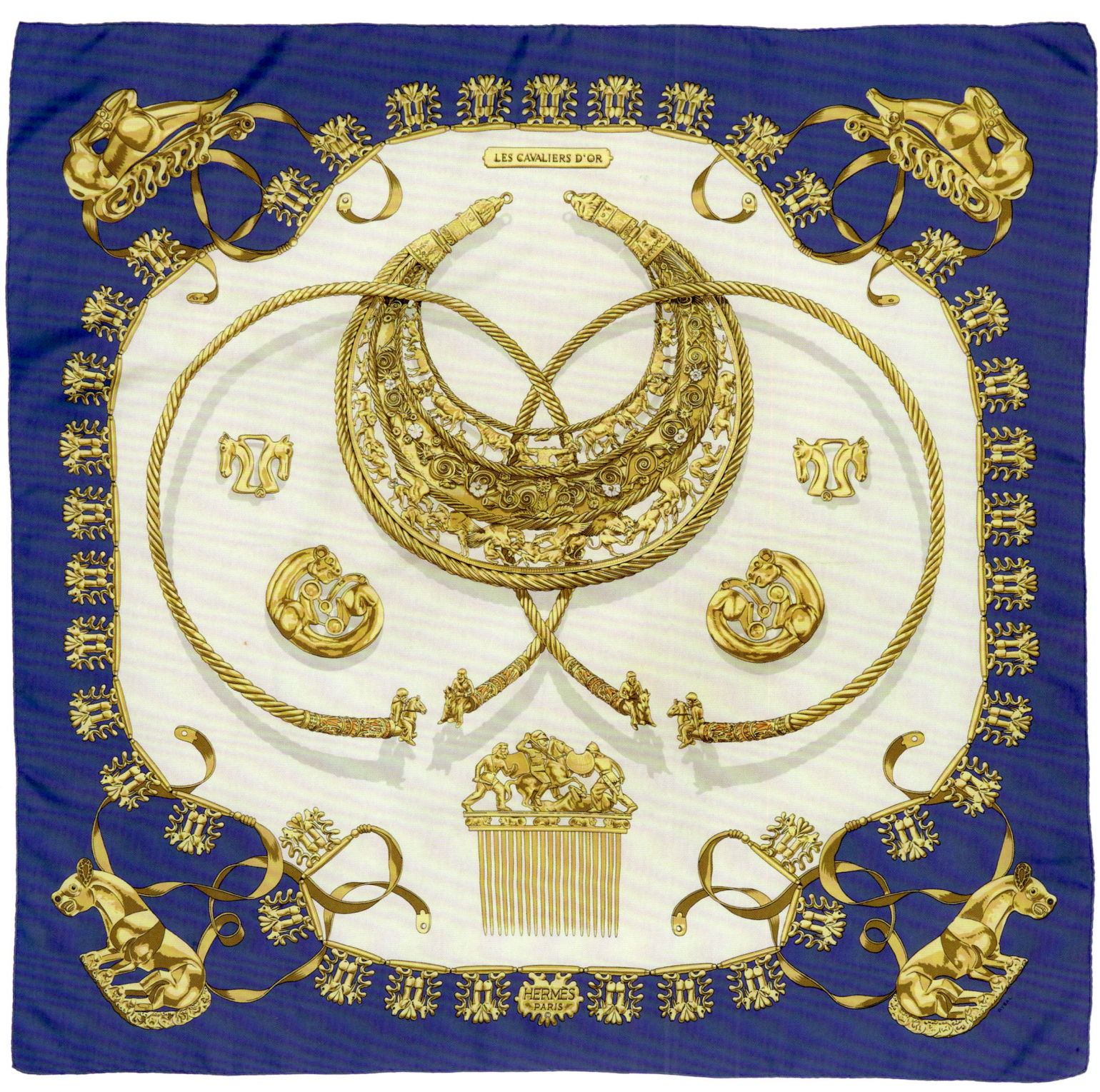

Hermès *Les Cavaliers d'Or* silk scarf designed by Vladimir Rybaltchenko, 1975. This silk scarf portrays a Scythian breastplate in gold from the fourth century BCE and other antiquities found in Ukraine in the 1970s.

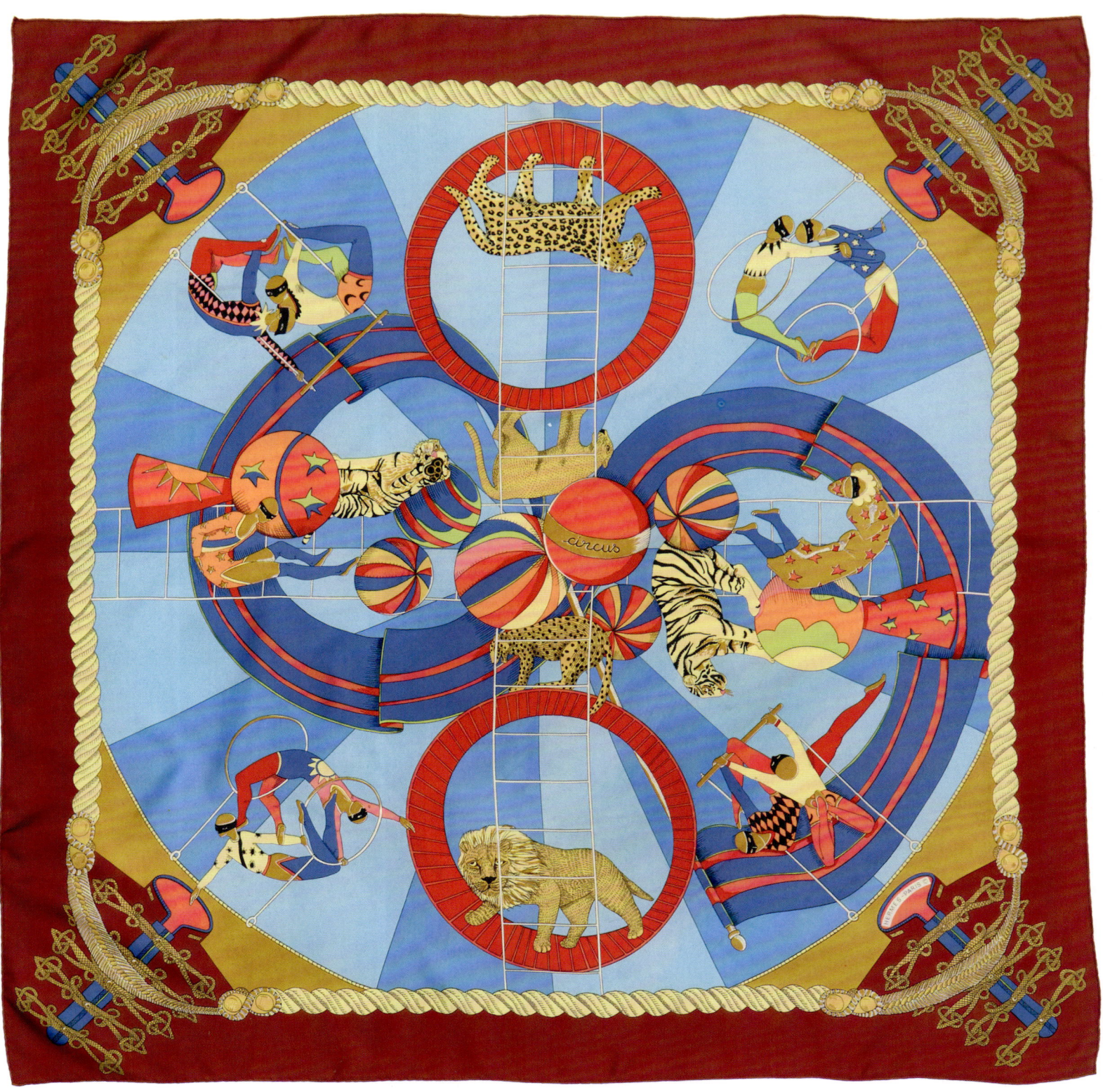

Vintage Hermès *Circus* silk scarf designed by Annie Faivre, 1982. A circus enlivened by felines and acrobats populates this composition by Faivre, who used bright colours and flat shapes for an Art Deco-inspired design.

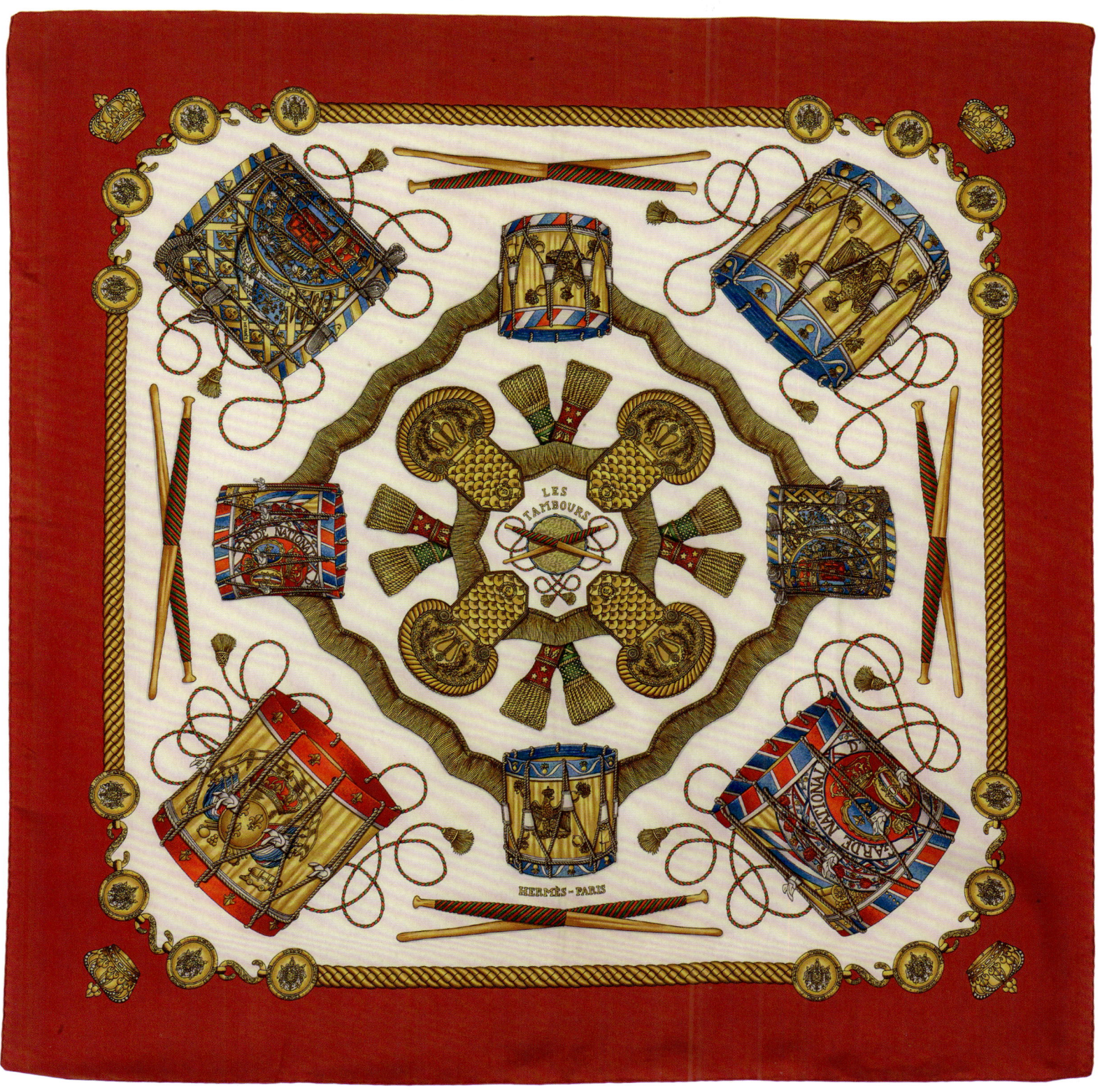

Hermès *Les Tambours* silk scarf designed by Joachim Metz, 1989. The print on this scarf portrays different military drums.

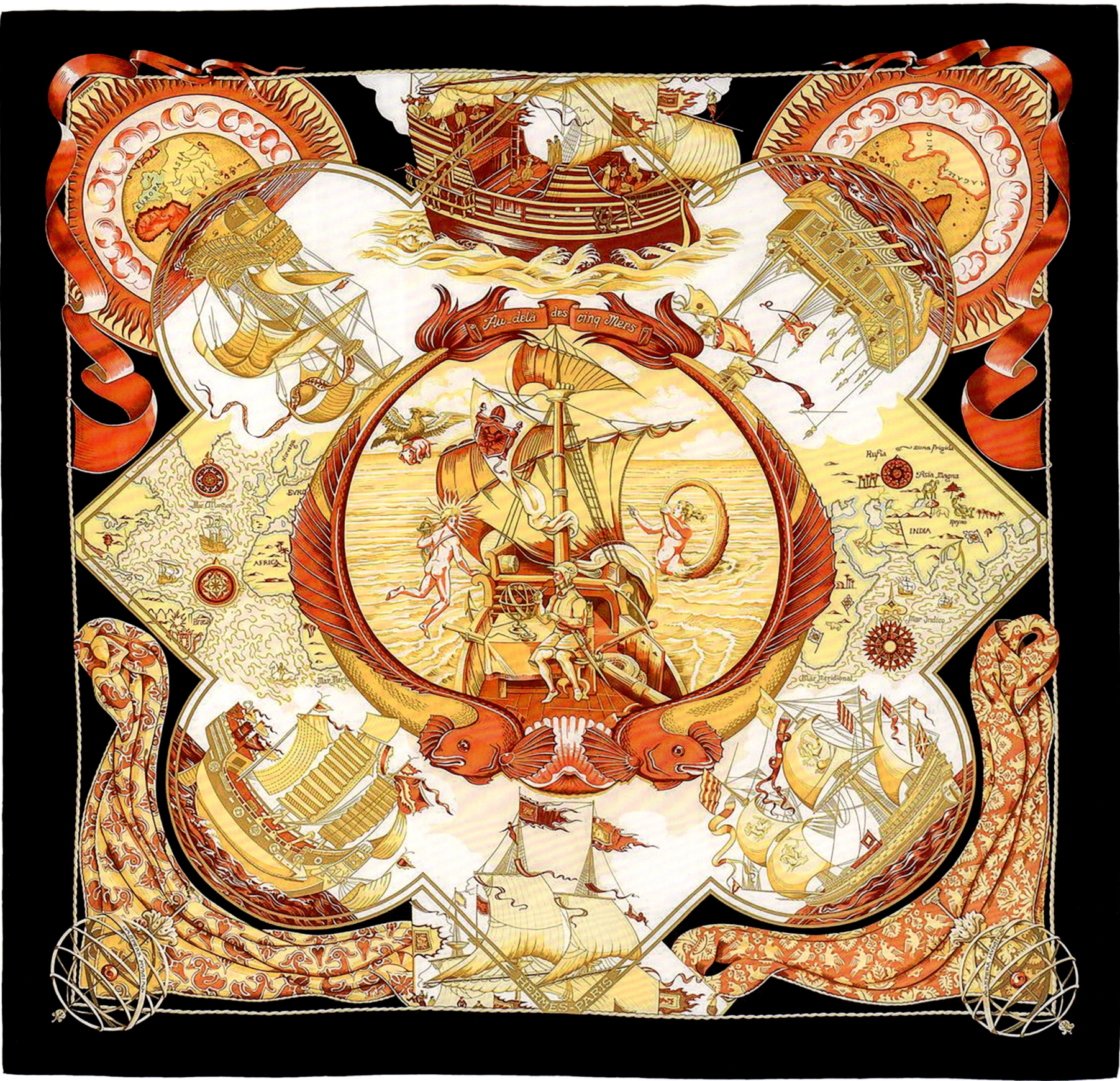

Fantastic worlds

In the 1980s and 1990s, Hermès silk scarves would become veritable status symbols. Celebrities and influential figures regularly wore them, helping consolidate their role as an indispensable luxury accessory.

In 1979 – the same year in which Jean-Louis Hermès launched an advertising campaign in which a model elevated a simple denim jacket thanks to a silk scarf around her neck – the first silk scarf by Annie Faivre was released. Known for her extraordinary graphic sensibility, the artist gave life to a set of prints characterised by abstract geometric shapes inspired by Art Deco. She went on to design 40 silk scarves for the fashion house, such as *Sur un Tapis Volant* (2006), whose composition echoes the entwined motifs of a Persian carpet, or *Chemin de Corail* (2016), which enigmatically and symbolically portrays a fragile sea coral in its tonal nuances.

In 1984, the artist Kermit Oliver was the first American to work with the fashion house. His pieces are known for their narrative complexity and extraordinary attention to detail, with motifs which often celebrate the history of the United States of America, its wildlife and the symbols of American traditions. His first scarf, *Pani La Shar Pawnee* (1984), is a tribute to the Pawnee Indian tribe, deported from Kansas and Nebraska to Oklahoma in the late 19th century. The composition of the *Flore et Faune du Texas* silk scarf, designed to celebrate the 150th anniversary of the state, includes over 50 animals.

Hermès *Au-Dela des cinq Mers* silk scarf designed by Laurence 'Toutsy' Bourthoumieux, 1998. With a composition full of fantastical images and details, the theme of this silk scarf is maritime exploration. Caravels, astrolabes and nautical maps surround the ship with the captain guided by angels and mythological creatures.

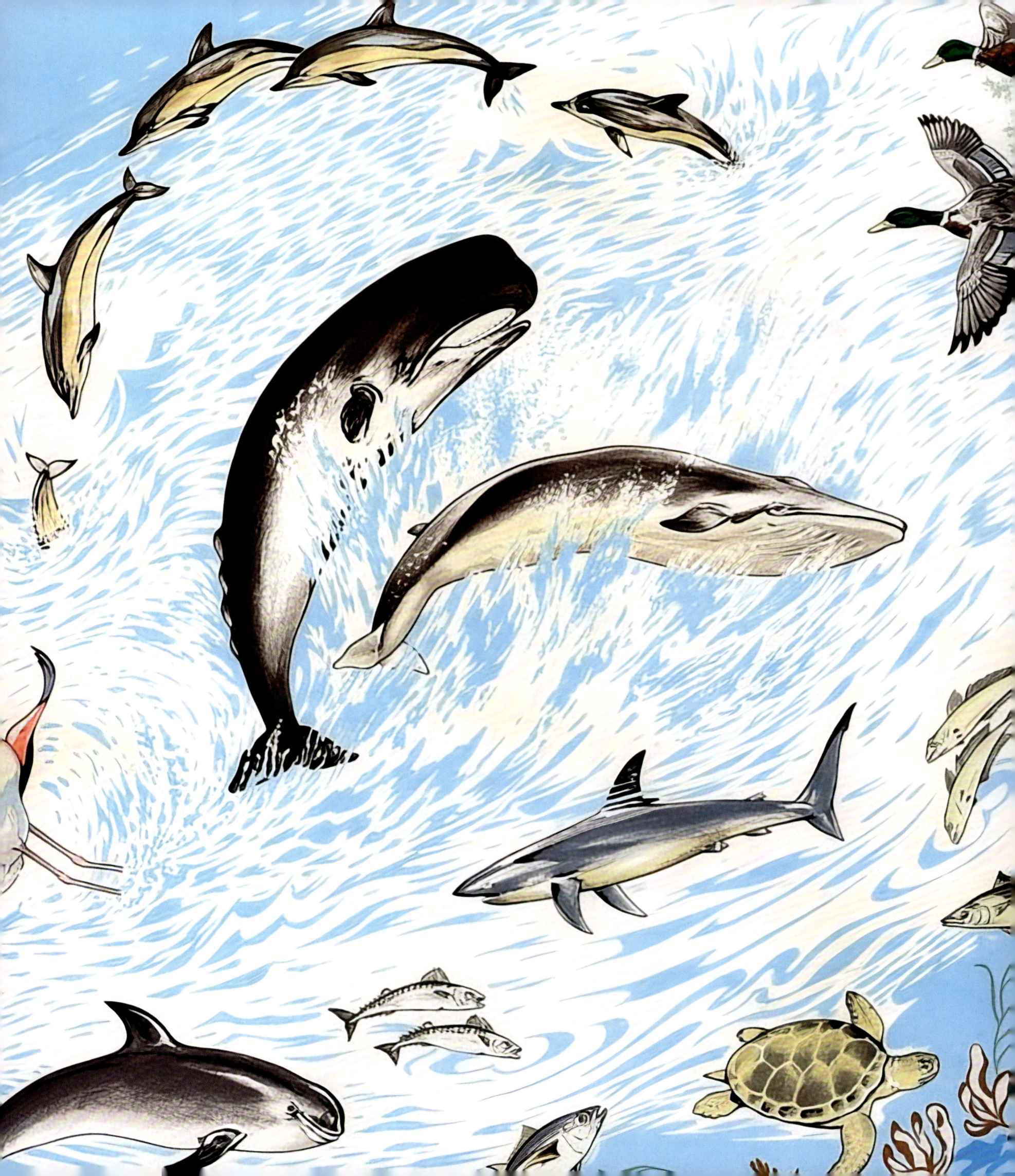

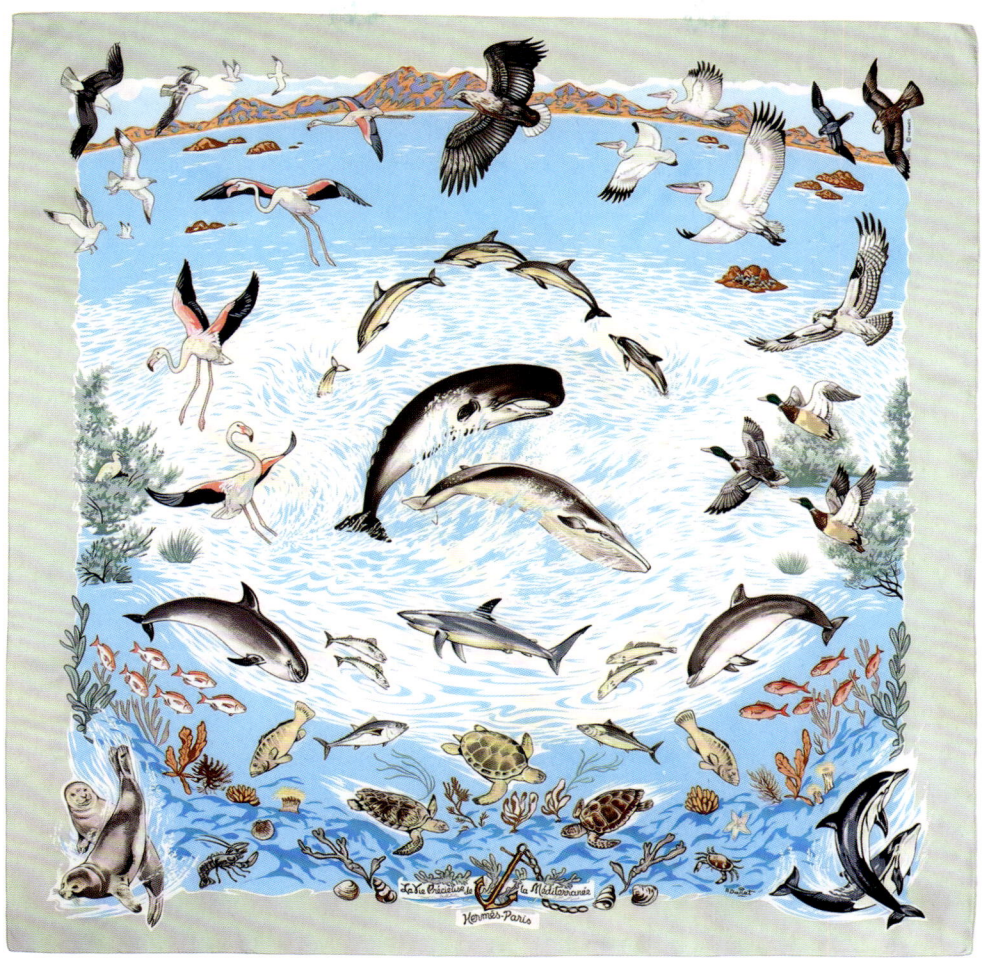

Hermès *La Vie Précieuse de la Méditerranée*, silk scarf first designed by Robert Dallet in 1992 and reissued in 2001. It portrays the fish and birds of the Mediterranean in an evocative way.

Tropical worlds, and their flora and fauna are some of the subjects chosen by Robert Dallet, who dedicated his life to studying the fascinating animal kingdom. He designed *Equateur* in 1988, and *La Vie Précieuse de la Méditerranée* in 1992.

Dimitri Rybaltchenko, son of Vladimir and grand-nephew of Philippe Ledoux, continued on in the family tradition as a designer for Hermès, bringing a dreamlike and contemporary touch to the maison's silk scarves. His designs are known for their balanced compositions, subtle details and bold use of colour. His most famous creations include *Noel au 24 Faubourg* (2004), which portrays the headquarters of Hermès in a festive Christmas snow globe surrounded by decorative motifs, created in eleven different colourways, and *Prieres au Vent*, in which Buddhist pilgrims, anchored by prayer wheels in the four corners, walk in a circle around a stupa, a monument sacred to Buddhists as a place of meditation. Another less poetic and rather ironic piece is *Please, Check-in* from 2009, re-released in 2020.

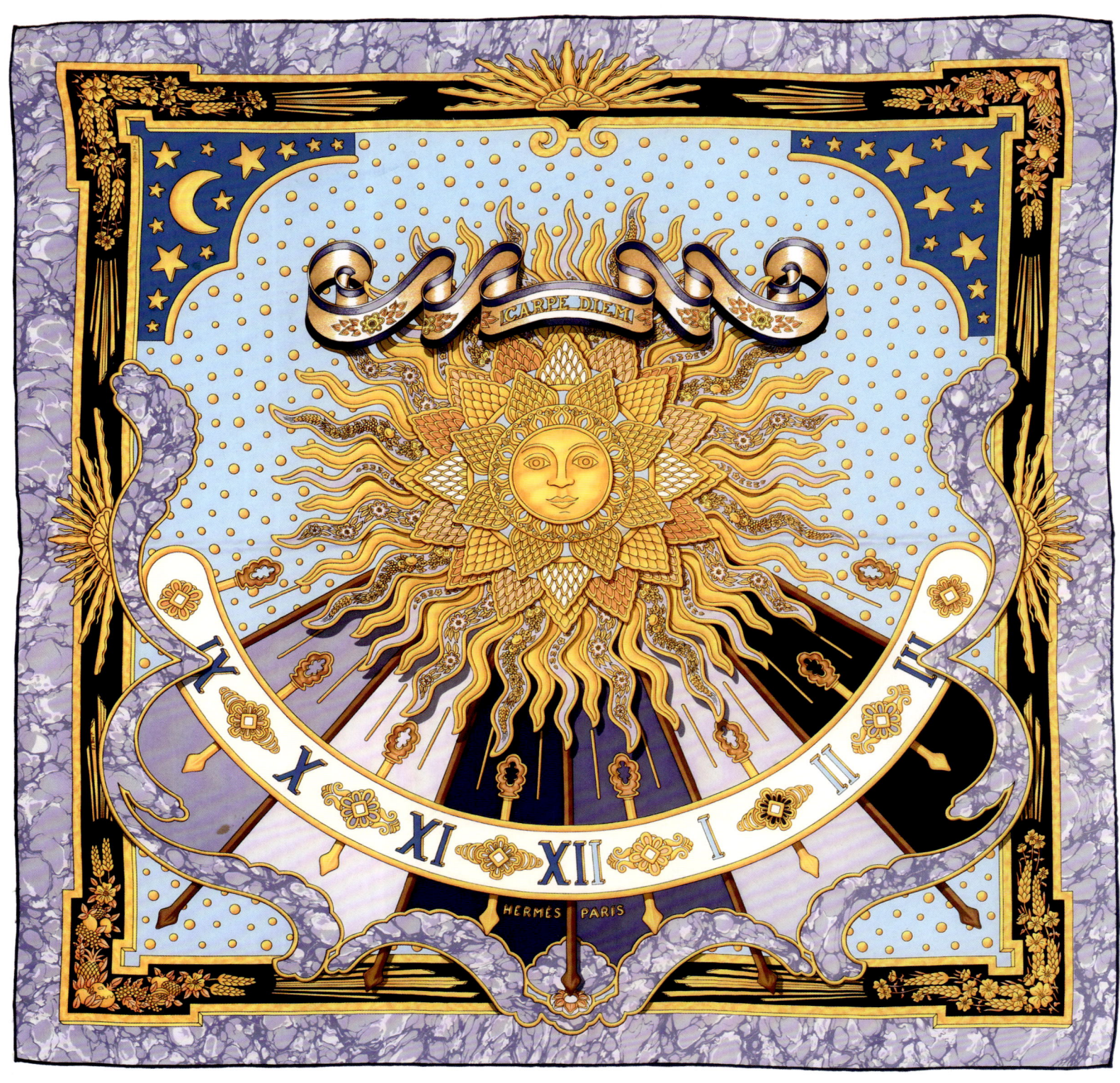

Carpe Diem silk scarf designed by Joachim Metz, 1994. Referring to the idea of time passing, this silk scarf portrays the sun, moon and stars.

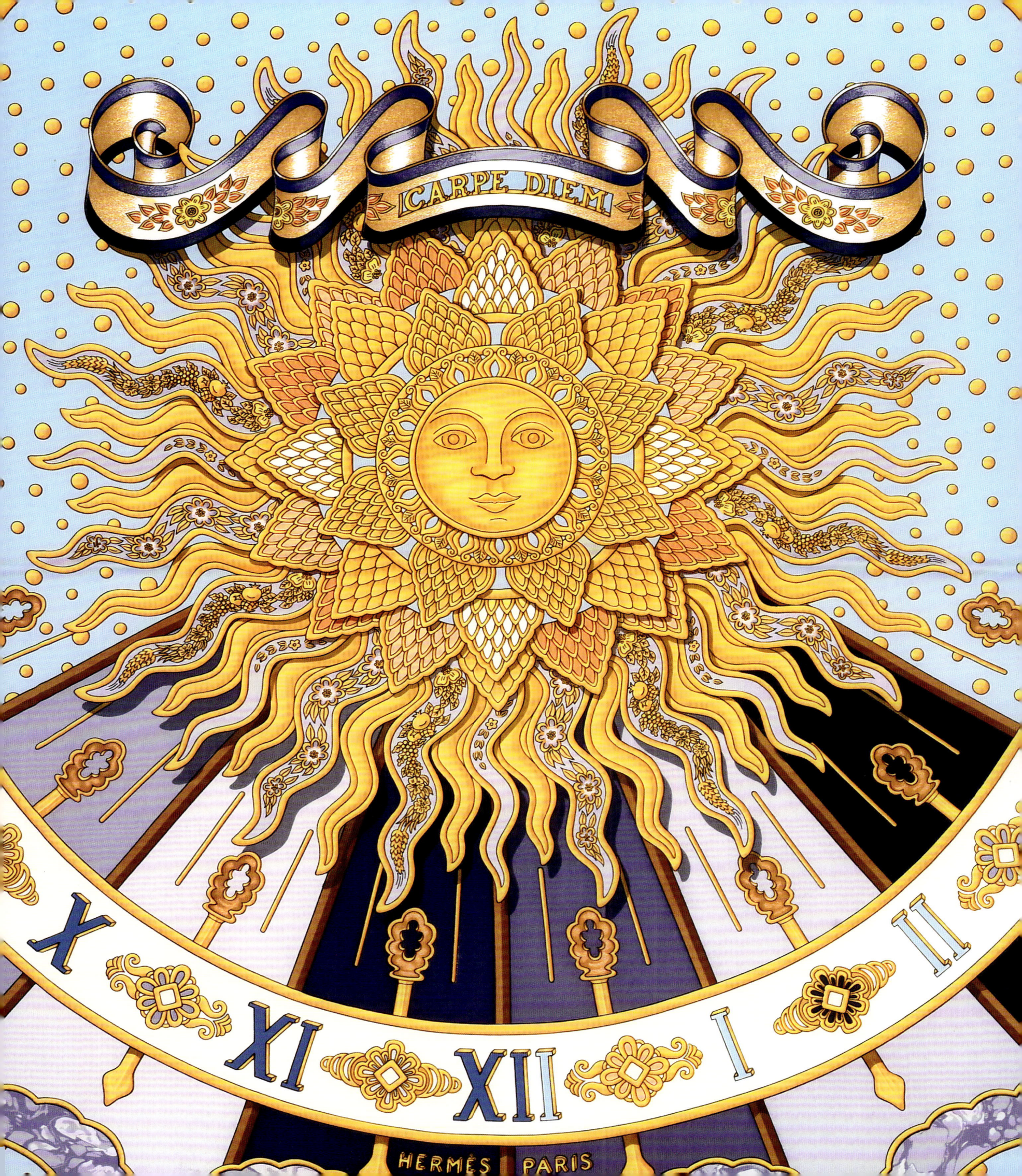

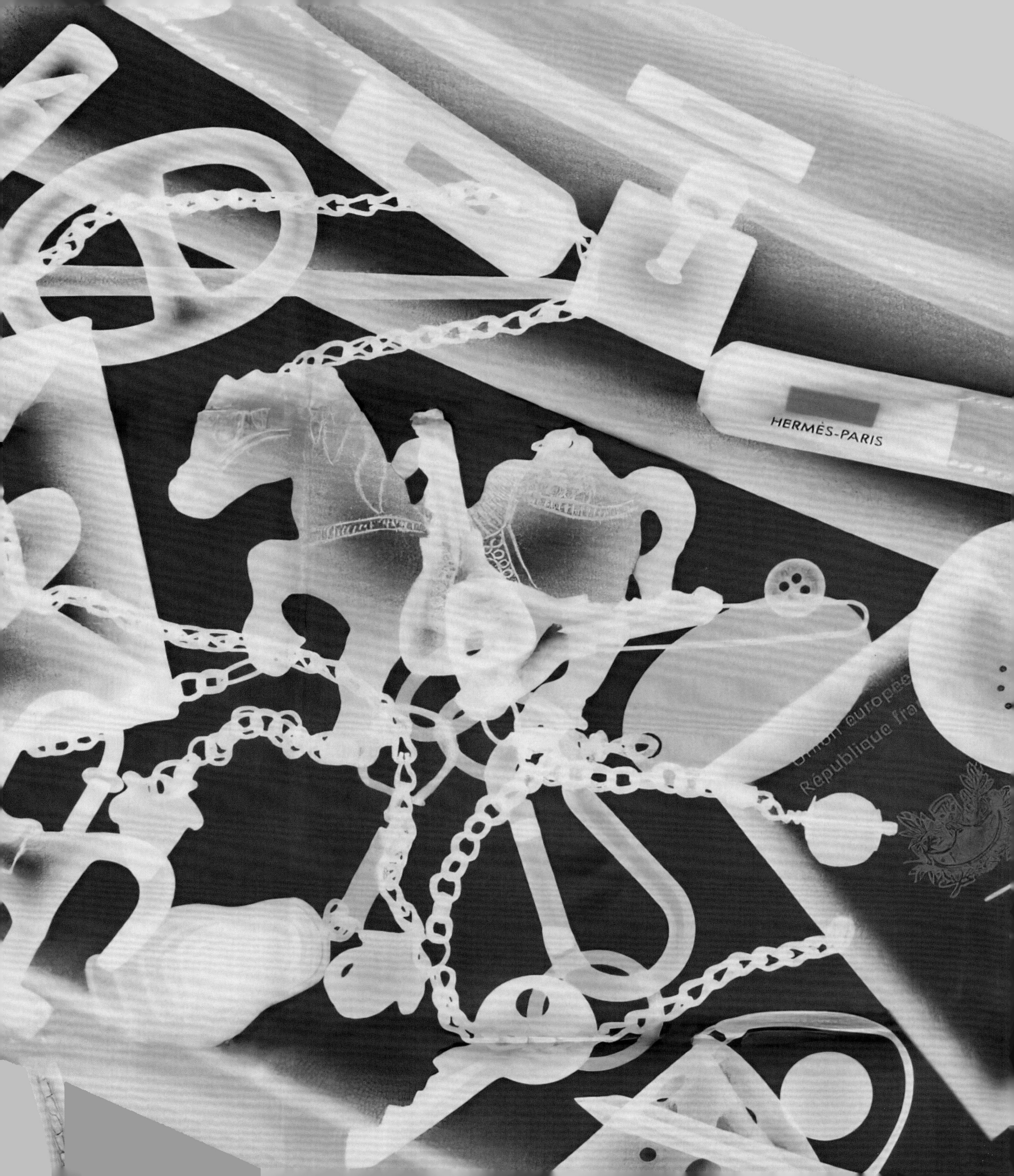

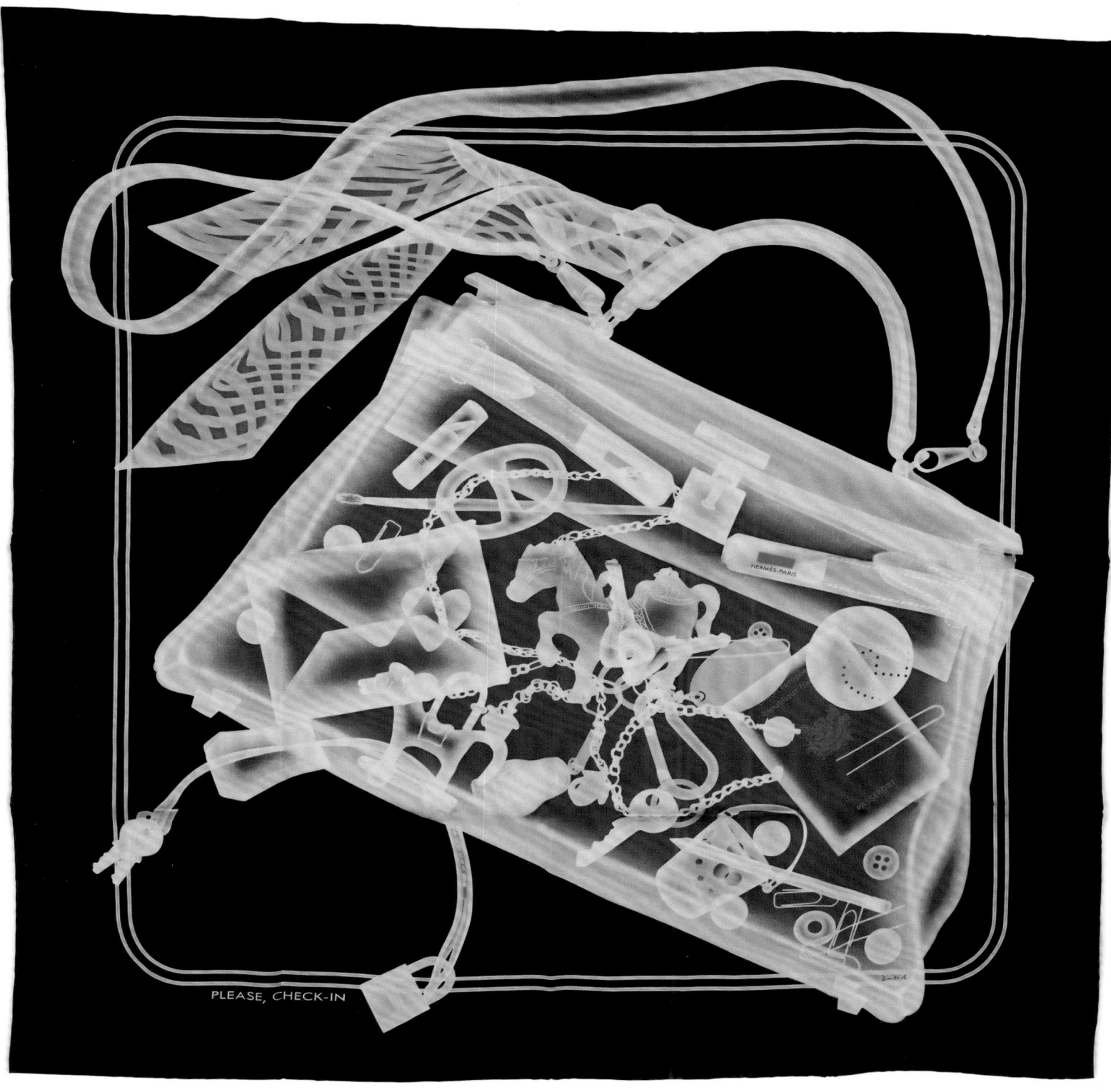

Hermès *Please, Check-In* silk scarf designed by Dimitri Rybaltchenko, 2020. The *Please, Check-In* scarf is a tongue-in-cheek X-ray of a passenger's *Kelly* bag, revealing its contents: souvenirs, a key chain, a good luck charm, a passport and lipstick. The X-ray also reveals the bag's structure: its closure, lock and key chain, its metal feet and even the outline of a small Twilly tied to the handle.

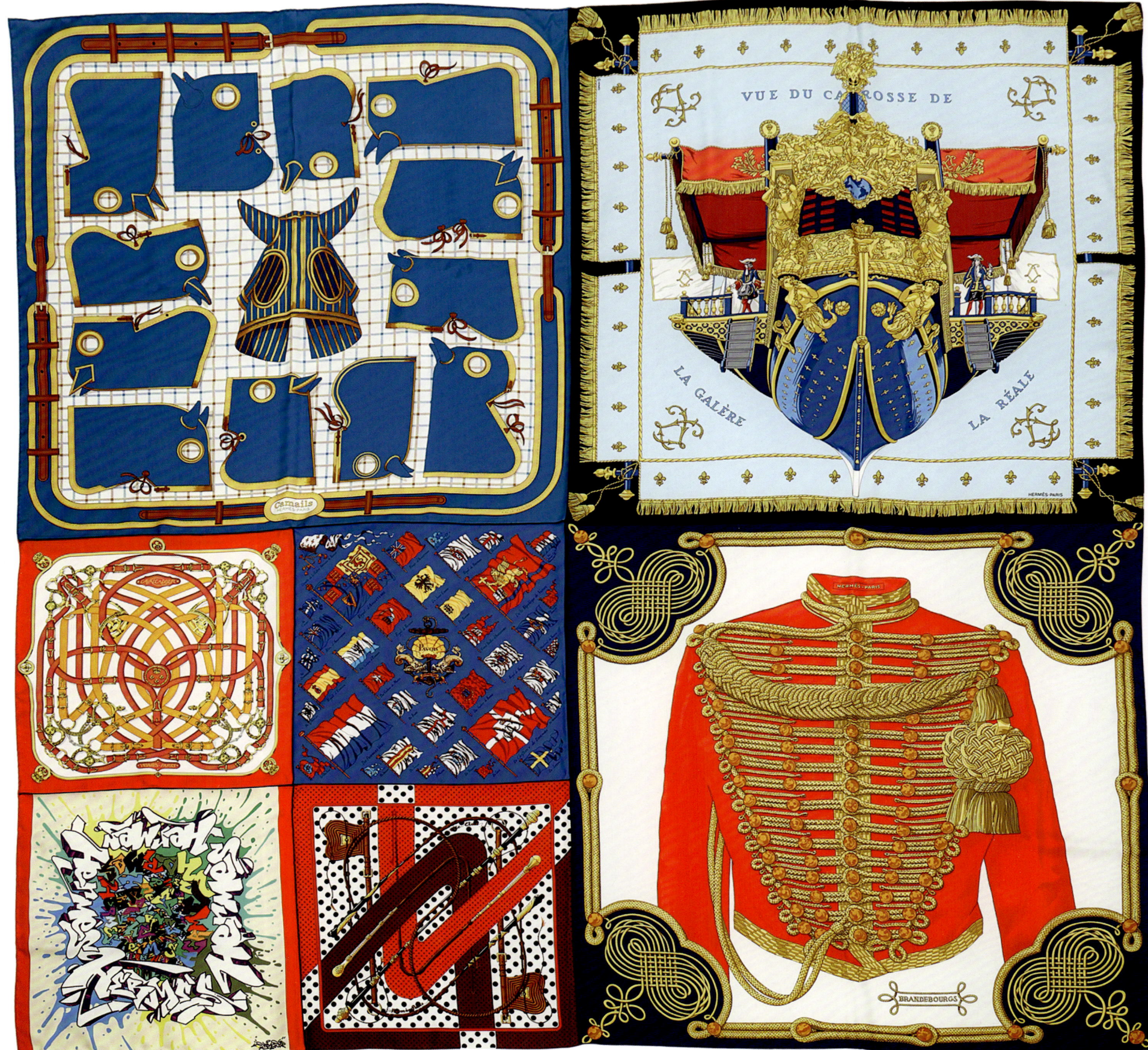

The value of heritage

From 2009 to 2020, Bali Barret was artistic director of women's products at Hermès. The French designer and all-around creative had a sharp sense of fashion and contemporary visual culture, becoming a fundamental asset for the modernisation of Hermès. Barret also helped reinterpret the brand's aesthetic codes through her innovative vision. Starting from the company archives, Barret knowingly mixed classic and contemporary. Under her direction, different collaborations were launched which boosted the popularity of the brand's silk scarves among younger generations. The one with Liberty of London (2009) led to the creation of a scarf that combines Hugo Grygkar's archival *Ex Libris* design with a floral pattern characteristic of the English department store.

The work done with Parisian boutique Colette gave rise to a number of limited-edition silk scarves in 2010, each one with surprising colourways and motifs which tell stories rich in symbolism.

Barret also established an important partnership with Rei Kawakubo, the legendary designer of Commes des Garçons. With it, the *Comme des Carrés* capsule collection of silk scarves was born. Presented in 2013, it was made up of two families: the *Couleur* collection, composed of six different colour designs and characterised by playful abstract motifs, which were sold exclusively in London and Tokyo; and the *Noir et Blanc* collection, composed of five silk scarves in black and white, which were sold exclusively in Comme des Garçons shops.

....

Hermès *Comme des Carrés* silk scarf designed by Comme des Garçons, 2013. In a 200-piece limited edition, this scarf came in a 180 × 180 cm size, double that of a traditional silk scarf.

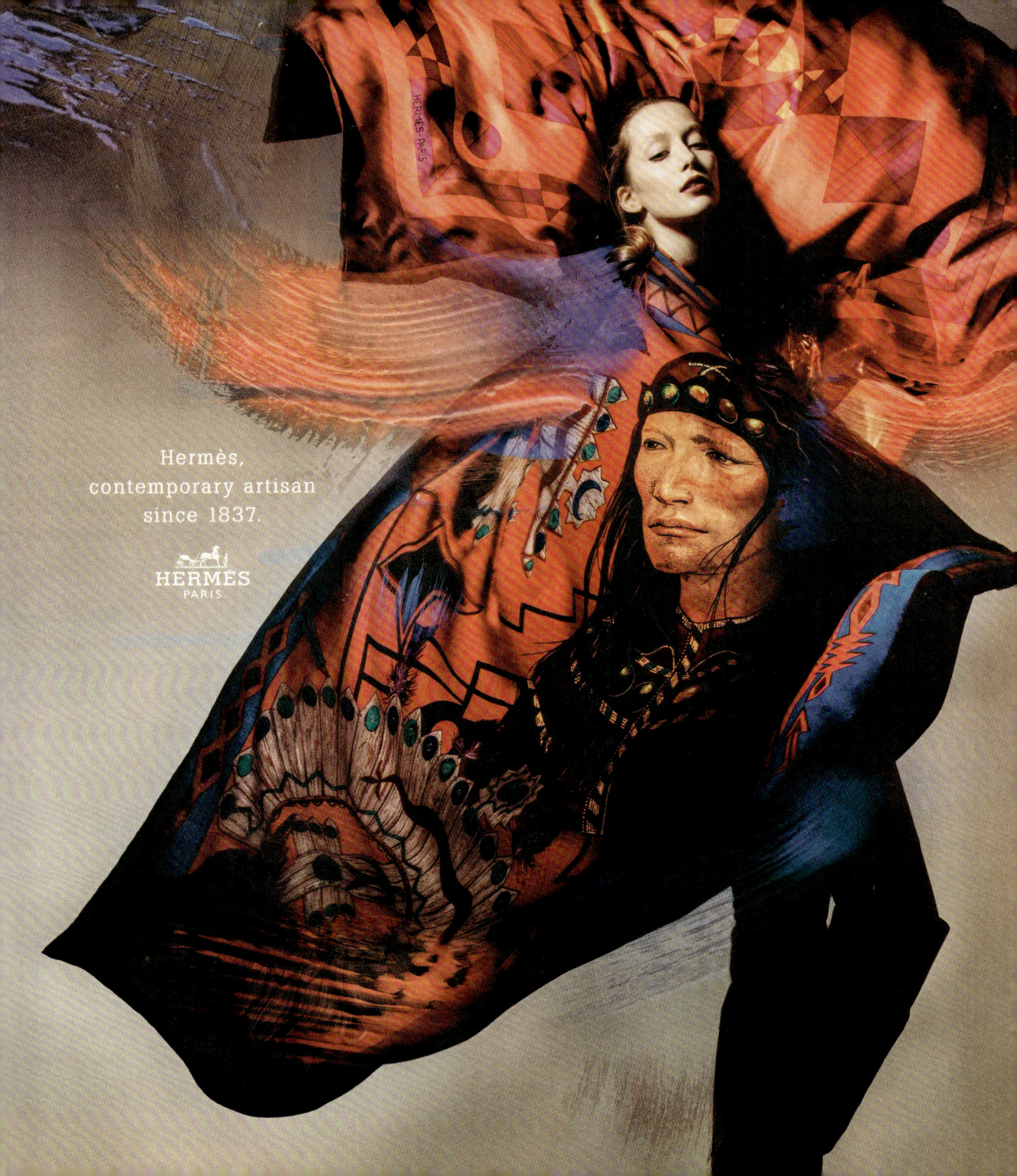

Hermès,
contemporary artisan
since 1837.

HERMÈS
PARIS

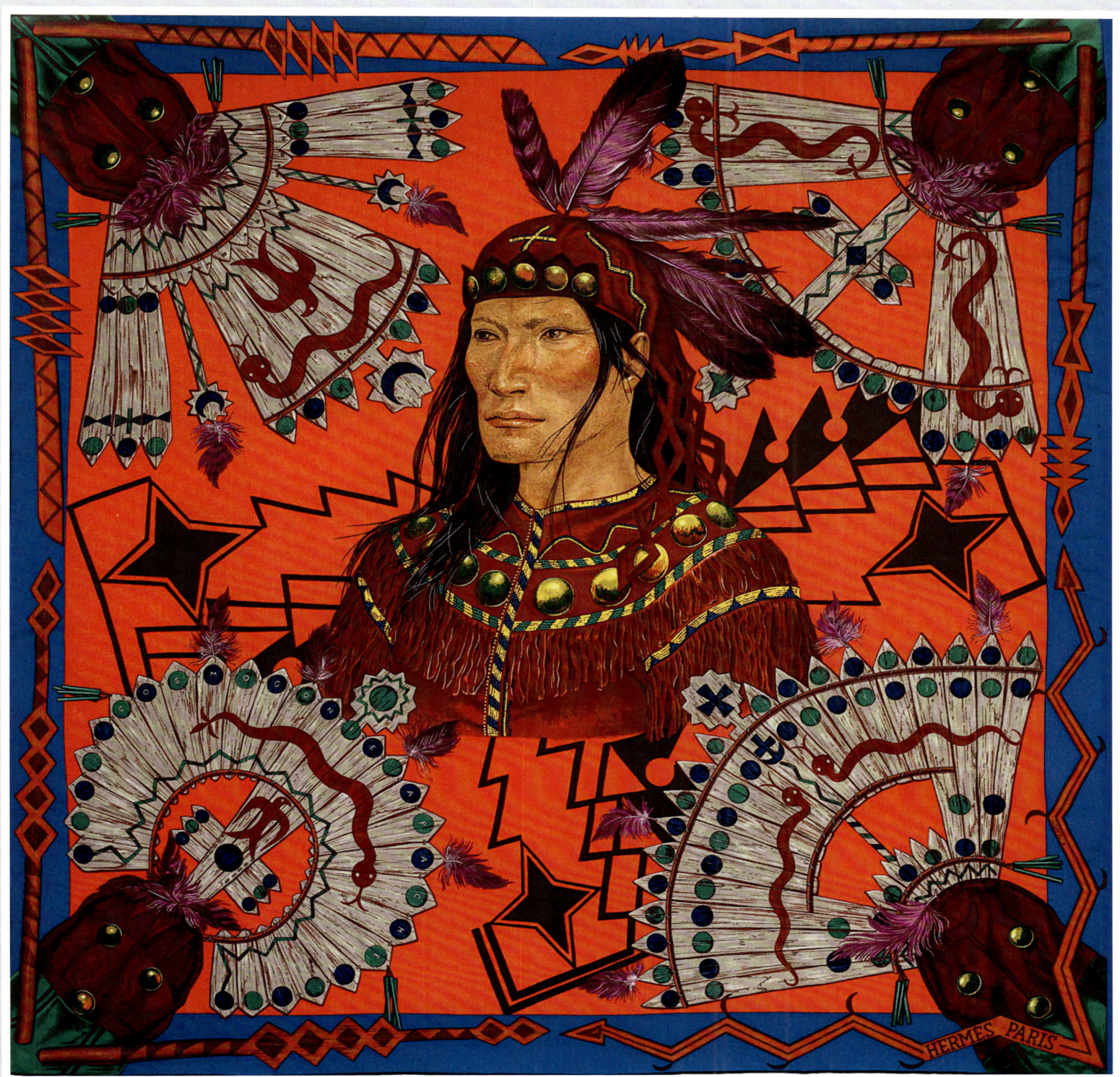

Cosmogonie Apache silk scarf designed by Antoine Tzapoff, 2011. A proud warrior from the White Mountains is portrayed on this scarf, surrounded by traditional Apache symbols. Composed of over 45 colours, it is one of the most complex printed scarves made by Hermès.

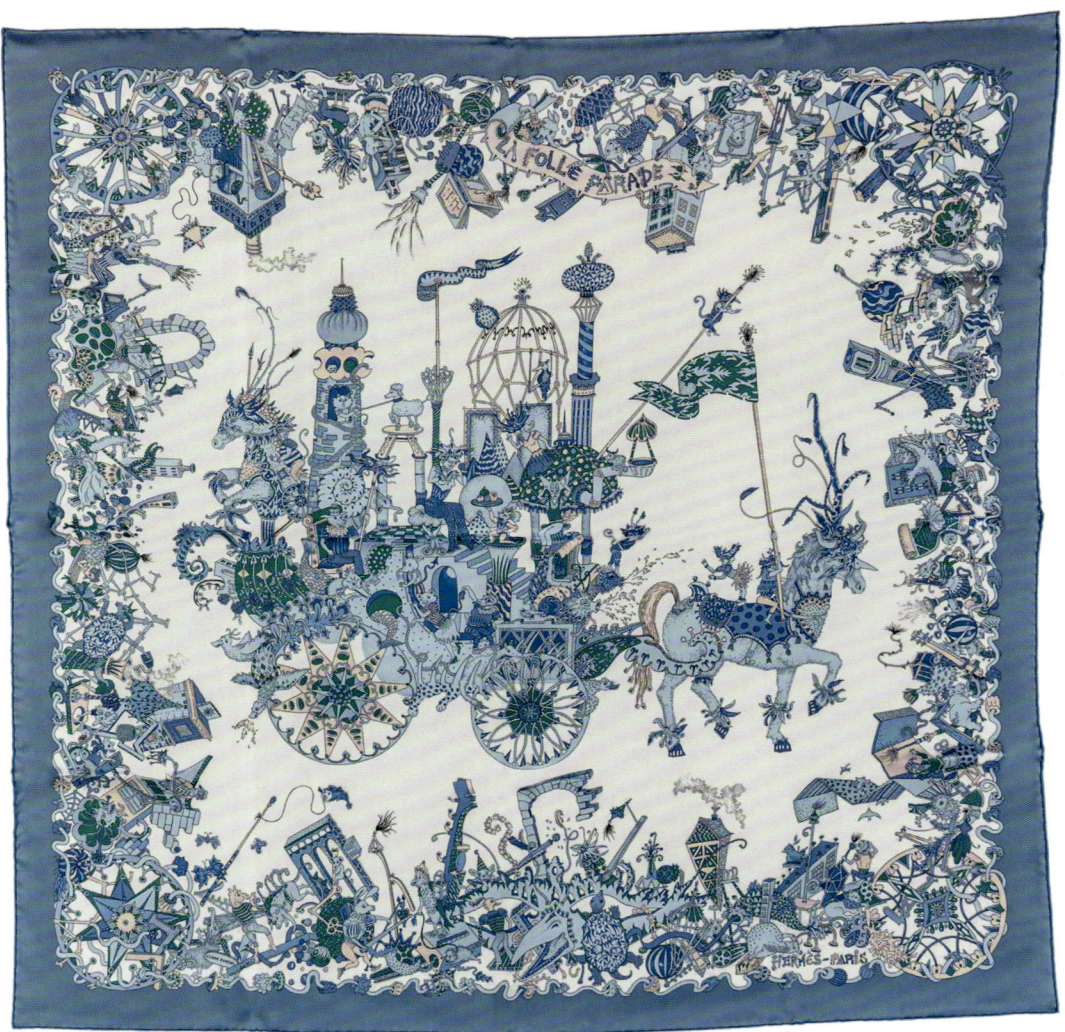

In 2020, Cécile Pesce took the reins as creative director of women's silk.[4]

Her work with Hermès stands out for the ability to evoke emotions through a vibrant colour palette and meticulous attention to composition. Pesce really loved the style of graphic designer and illustrator Virginie Jamin. Her colourful silk scarves are often inspired by legends or present visions like fairy tales which are slowly revealed to the viewer, such as *Belle du Mexique* with the skirts of dancers in movement, or *Zouaves et Dragons*, which presents military uniforms from the 18th century.

For Pesce, the illustrator Katie Scott, who was passionate about biology and known for her botanical canvases, created luminous and colourful worlds which mix fantasy and reality in their portrayal of plants and animals.

....

Hermès *La Folle Parade* silk scarf designed by Claire Fanjul, 2020. Fanjul was inspired by an 18th-century engraving of a Roman carnivalesque cart when she made this scarf. At the centre, a cart is mounted with towers and pulled by a horse in costume.

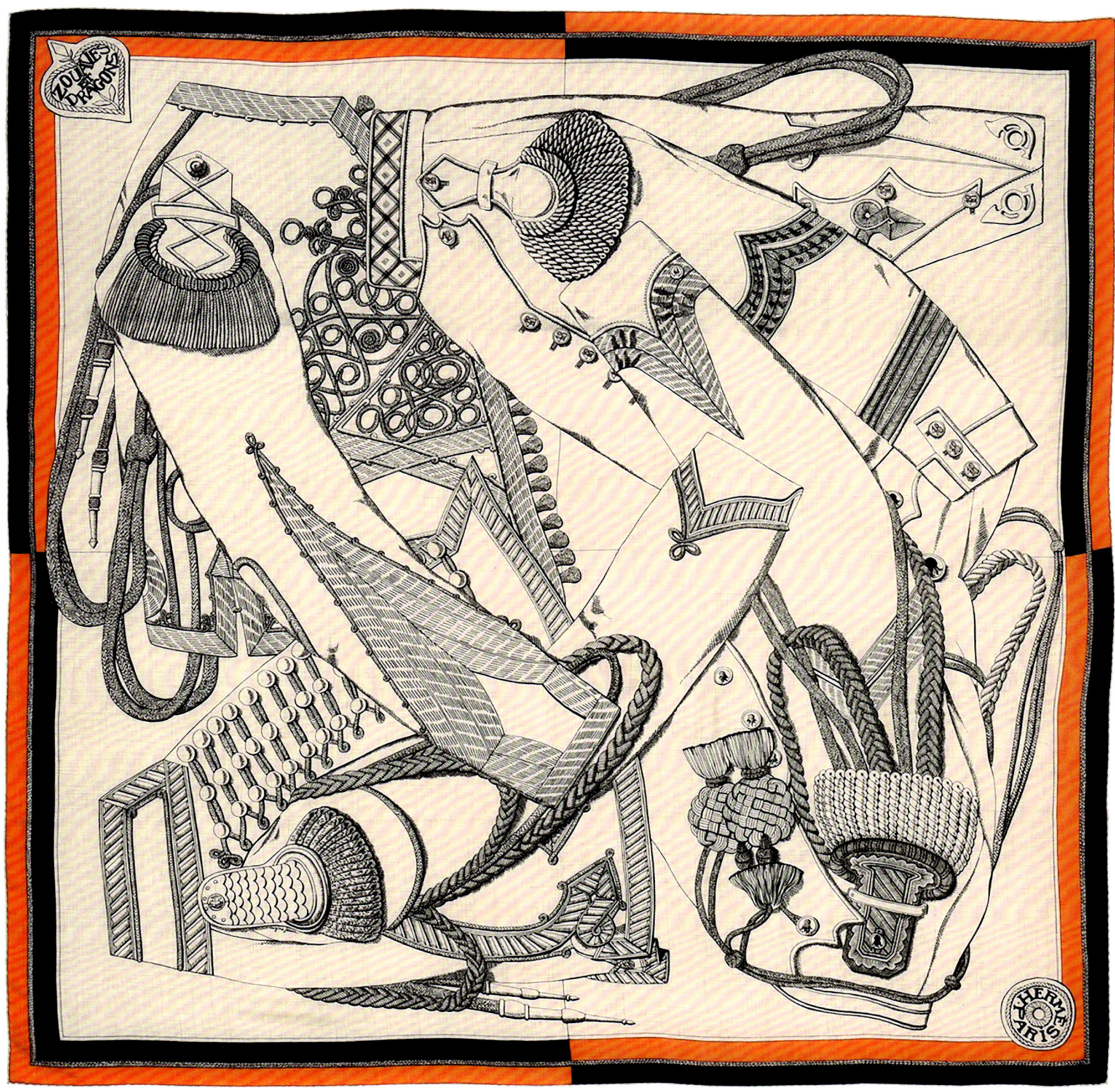

Hermès *Zouaves et Dragons* stole in cashmere and silk designed by Virginie Jamin, 2020. The uniforms of the Zouaves, a light infantry corps from North Africa, and the dragoons, the cavalry soldiers who fought on foot and horseback, inspired this silk scarf.

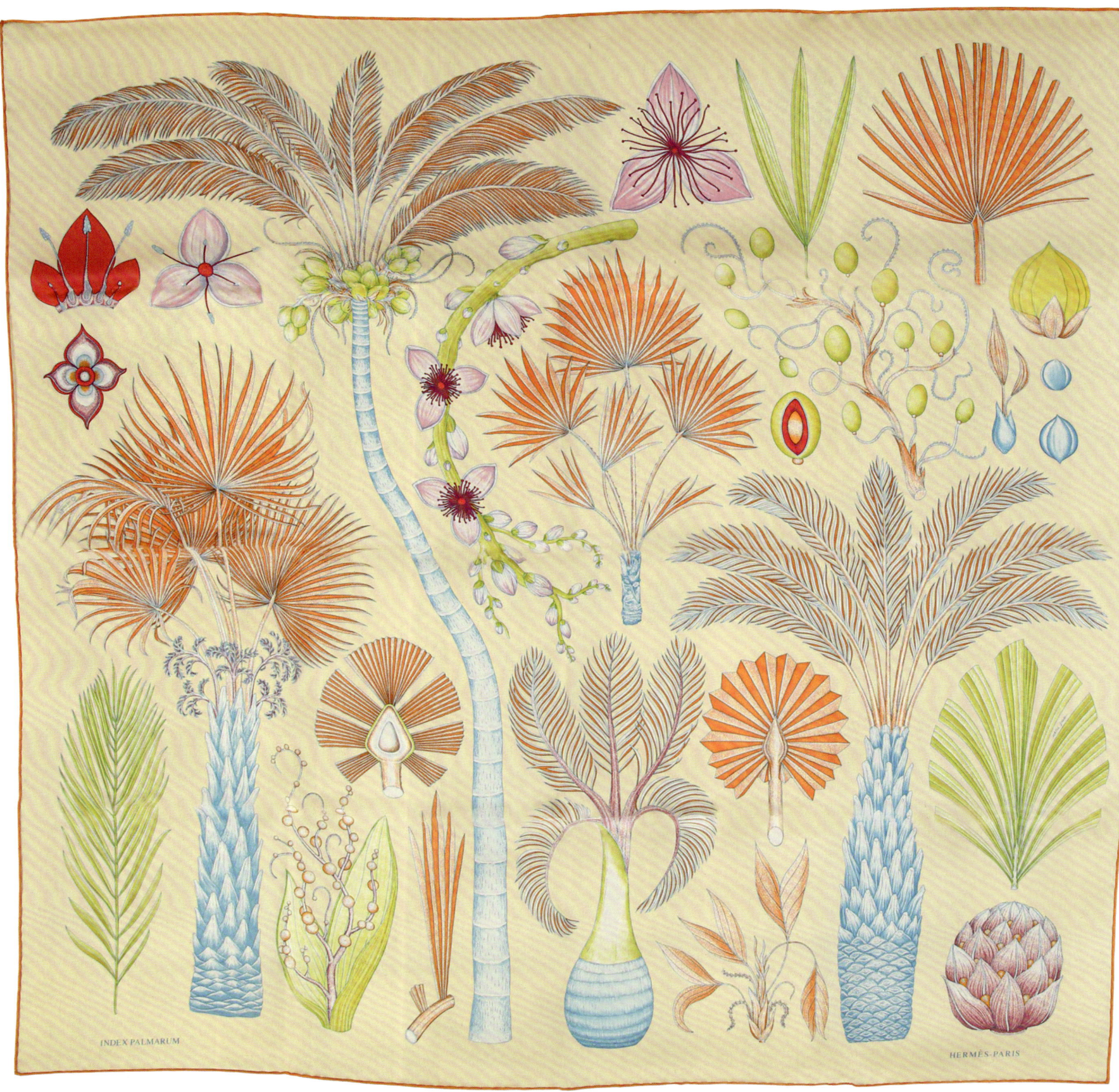

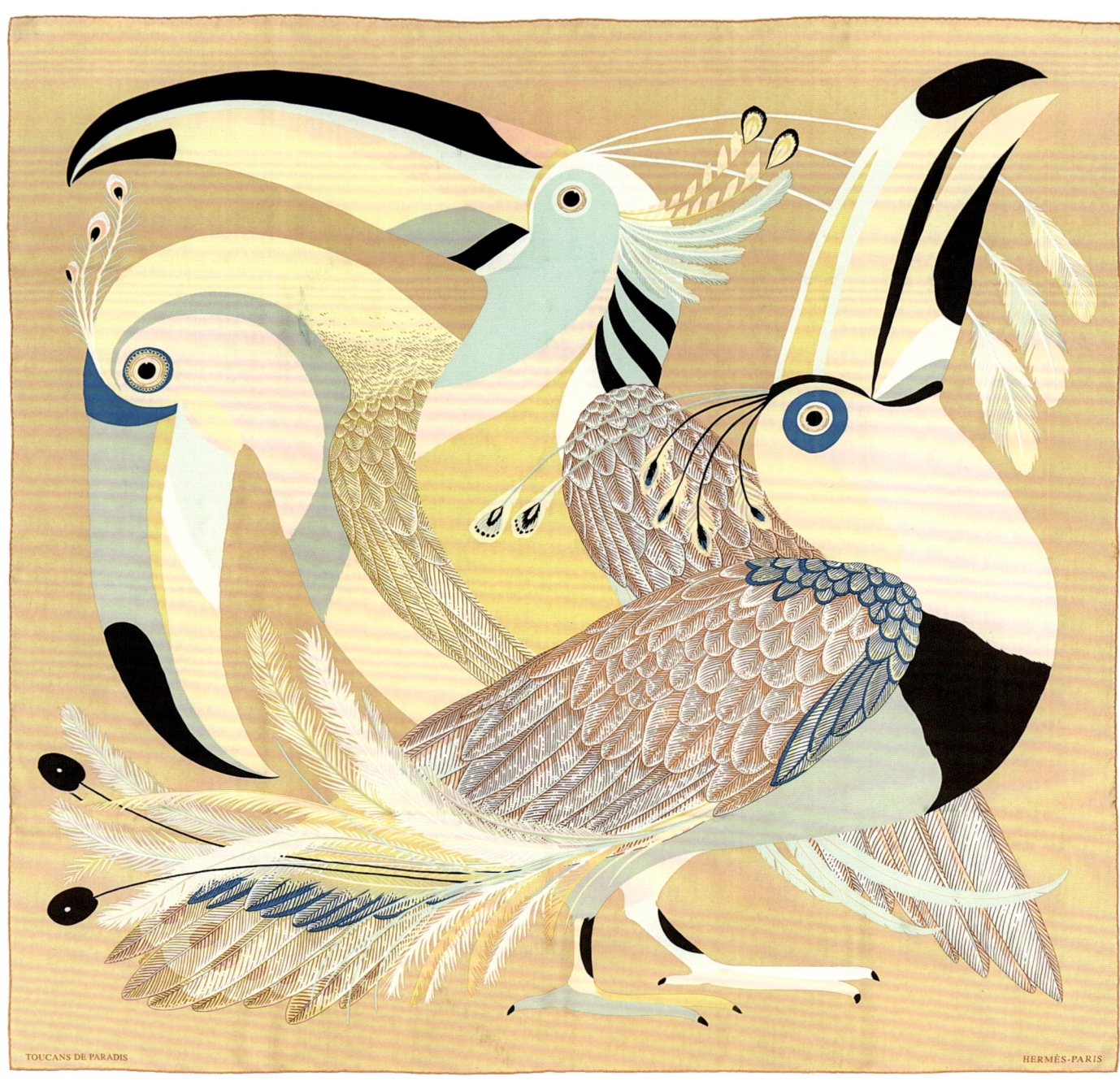

Opposite page – Hermès *Index Palmarum* silk scarf designed by Katie Scott, 2019. Scott was inspired by the *Historia Naturalis Palmarum*, a book by the German botanist, ethnographer and explorer Carl Friedrich Philipp von Martius, dating back to the 19th century. Exploring the palm family in the tradition of botanical plants, Scott has portrayed some species of this plant which she considers to be the 'incarnation of exoticism'.

This page – Hermès *Toucans de Paradis* silk scarf designed by Katie Scott, 2020. This scarf measures 140 × 140 cm. The toucan, a bird identified with tropical forests, is particularly widespread in the Amazon. In this composition, toucans become an imaginary species with decorative plumage similar to birds of paradise or peacocks.

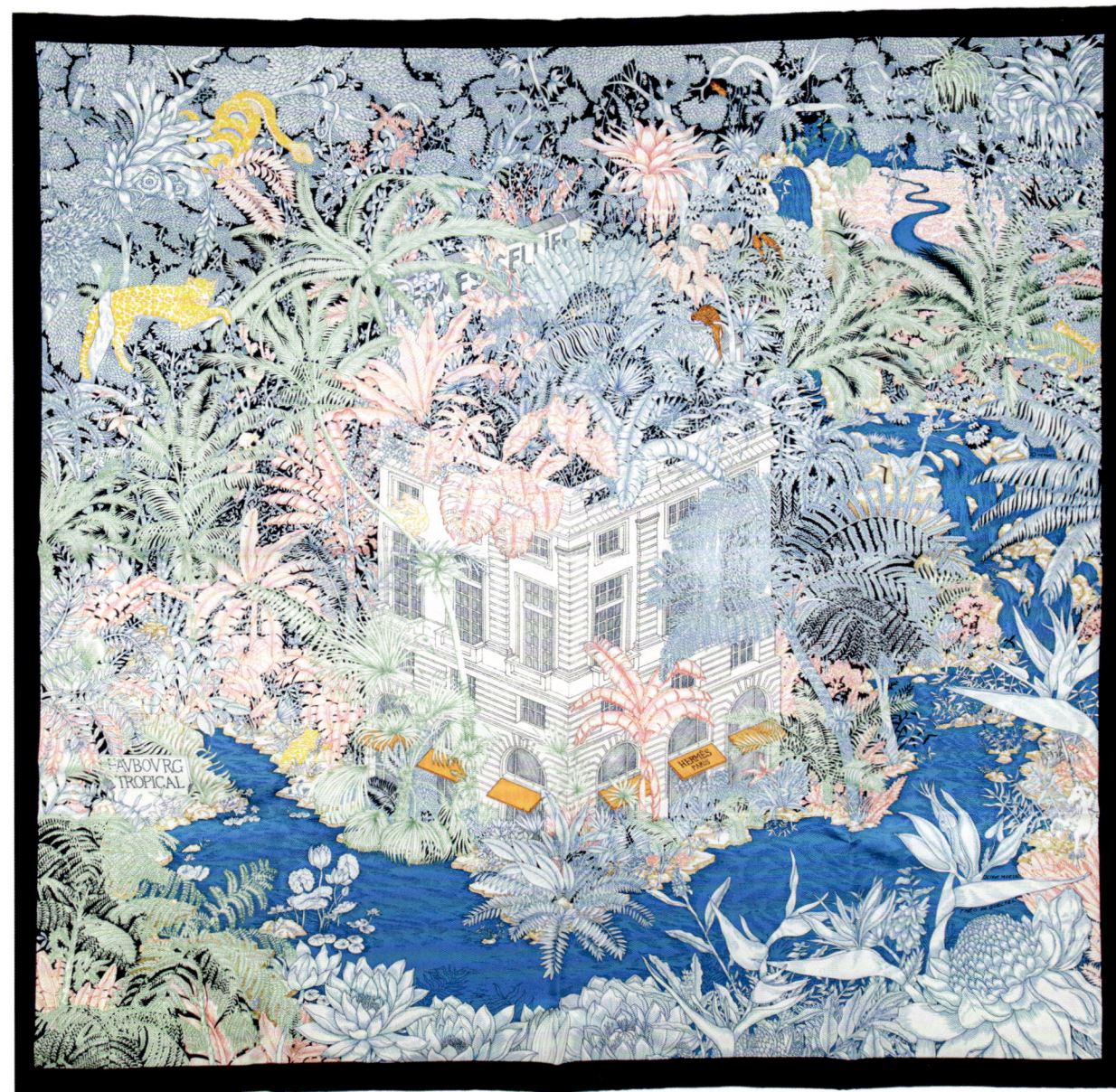

Since 2012, one of the most popular designers at the fashion house has been Alice Shirley, who celebrates the natural world with a paintbrush and bright colours.

The designs by Ardmore Artists for Hermès are an explosion of colour and vitality, inspired by the rich fauna and flora of Africa. *La Marche du Zambèse* (2016) and *Flowers of South Africa*, made in a large format, are particularly famous.[5]

Working as a duo, Octave Marsal and Théo de Gueltzl have made silk scarves which capture the eye with graphic motifs and surprising details. Their creations explore geometric forms and natural worlds, fusing precise lines and organic forms in unique visual harmony. Their *L'Ombre de Pivoines* (2019) is described as 'the city invaded by flowers'.

Each one of these creatives has brought their individual mark to the silk scarves of Hermès, a square canvas on which to express their artistic vision.

Art and new technology

In the ample, diversified world of Hermès creativity, the *Hermès Editeur* programme (launched in 2005) has given rise to a number of collaborations with contemporary artists. It also has opened up new ways of seeing the world of silk scarves.

Josef Albers, the master of abstract painting and colour theory, was the first artist whose work featured in a collection. For the *Hommage au Carré* collection, 6 designs were printed in a limited run of 200 each.[6] His geometric compositions and chromatic explorations were transferred with extreme precision on silk, creating scarves which play with visual perception through contrasts and varying colours.

The second most important chapter of *Hermès Éditeur* was co-written by Daniel Buren, known for his colourful striped compositions and his site-specific installations.[7] The result was the *Photo-souvenirs au Carré* collection, a series of 365 unique pieces on silk. For this project, 22 photo-souvenirs were selected and framed in 2 to 4 ways each, with 18 potential framing options depending on the photo chosen. The colourful striped outlines, characteristic of the artist's work, are a visual constant which unites yet which also marks differences. Buren transformed silk into a visual field of interaction, one in which lines and forms create fascinating optical effects.[8]

In 2012, for the third edition of its *Hermès Éditeur* programme, the maison introduced a new limited edition of scarves by the artist Hiroshi Sugimoto, named *Couleurs de l'Ombre*.[9] For 10 years, Sugimoto used a giant prism to create an extraordinary chromatic display which he captured via Polaroid camera. He and Pierre-Alexis Dumas then selected 20 prismatic images to transfer to silk. The result was a limited edition of 20 silk scarves issued in 7 units each – that is, 140 silk scarves measuring 140 × 140 cm. Making those silk scarves and paying tribute to their infinite shades of colour led to a technical challenge: transferring these expertly captured and immaterial hues to lightweight silk twill via inkjet printing.

In 2016, Hermès collaborated with the painter Julio Le Parc, a pioneer of kinetic art.[10] His designs for *Hermès Éditeur* gave rise to a vibrant new interpretation of silk scarves, playing with movement and optical illusions. Titled *Variations Autour de La Longue Marche*, the result was in an edition of 10 series of 6 unique silk scarves, for a total of 60 pieces measuring 90 × 90 cm. Some were the colours of the prism; others just black, white and grey. Le Parc's creations express energy and vitality, thanks to designs that seem to dance and change when looked at from different angles.

Hermès Éditeur is an example of how the fashion house continues to reinvent itself, creating constant dialogue between art and fashion.

Opposite and following pages – Colourful Hermès *Faubourg Tropical* silk scarf designed by Octave Marsal and Théo de Gueltzl, 2021. This silk scarf celebrates exotic, vibrant nature. With detail-rich motifs and a multicolour palette, it evokes an imaginary tropical garden rising within the Hermès headquarters.

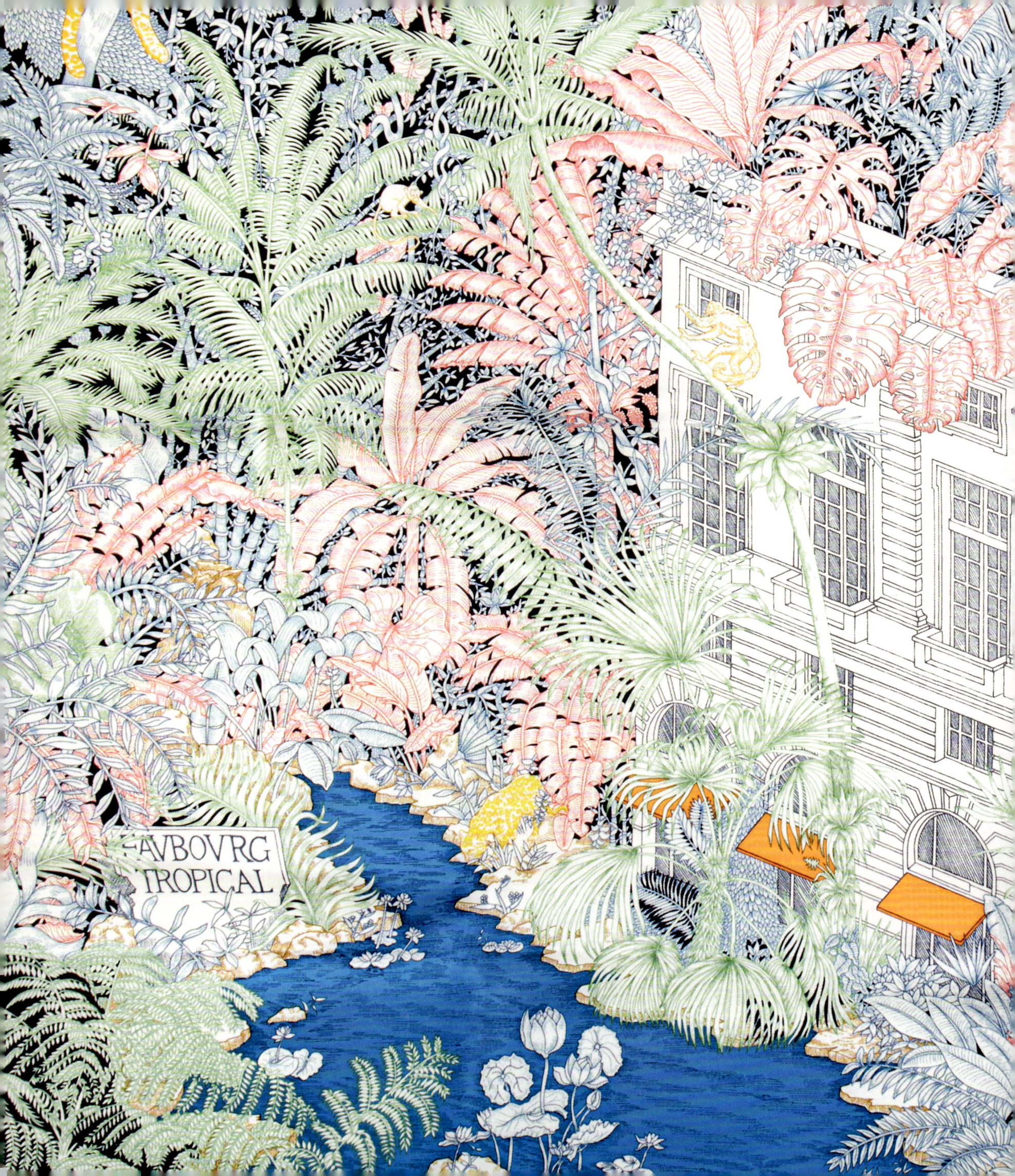

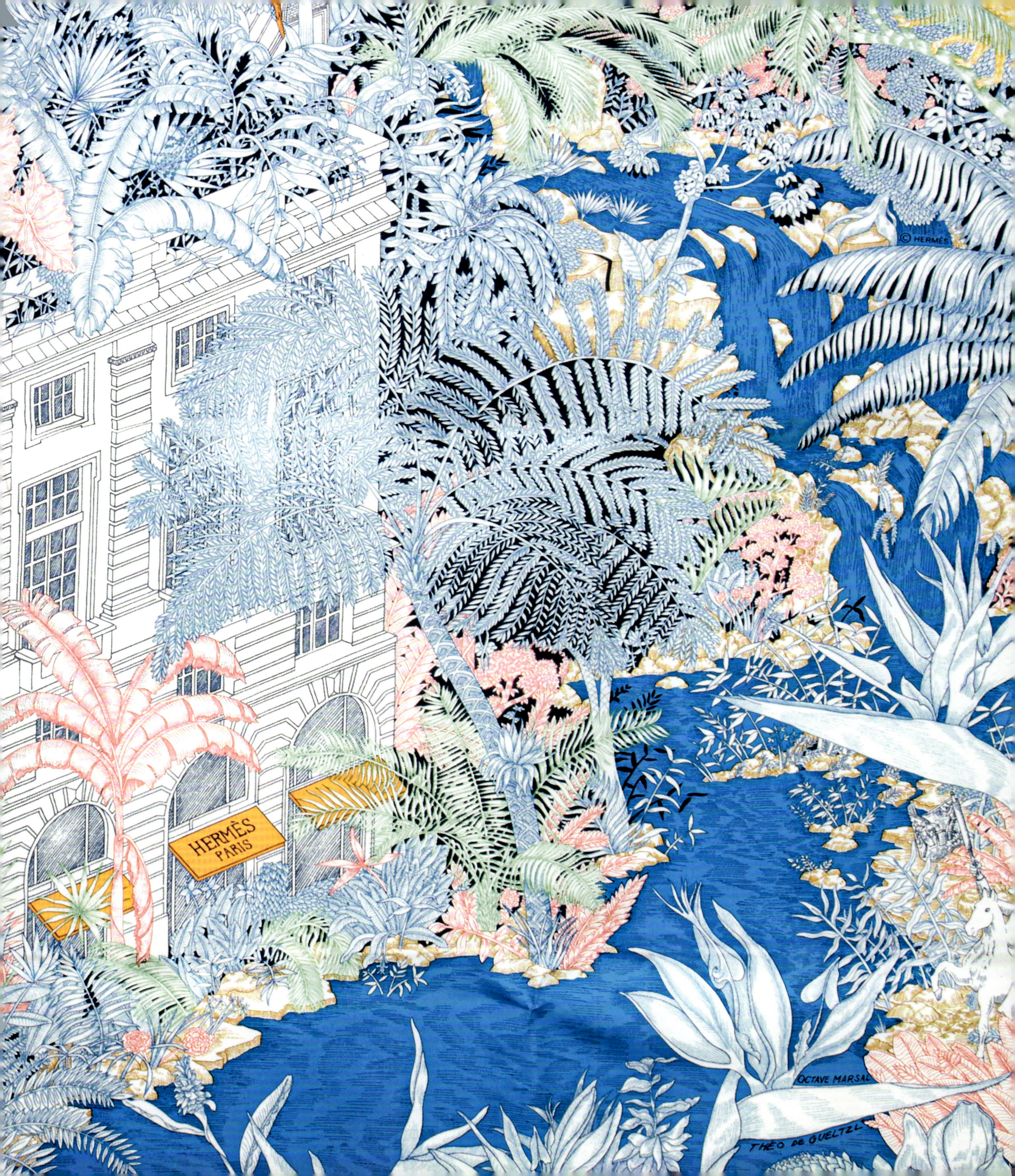

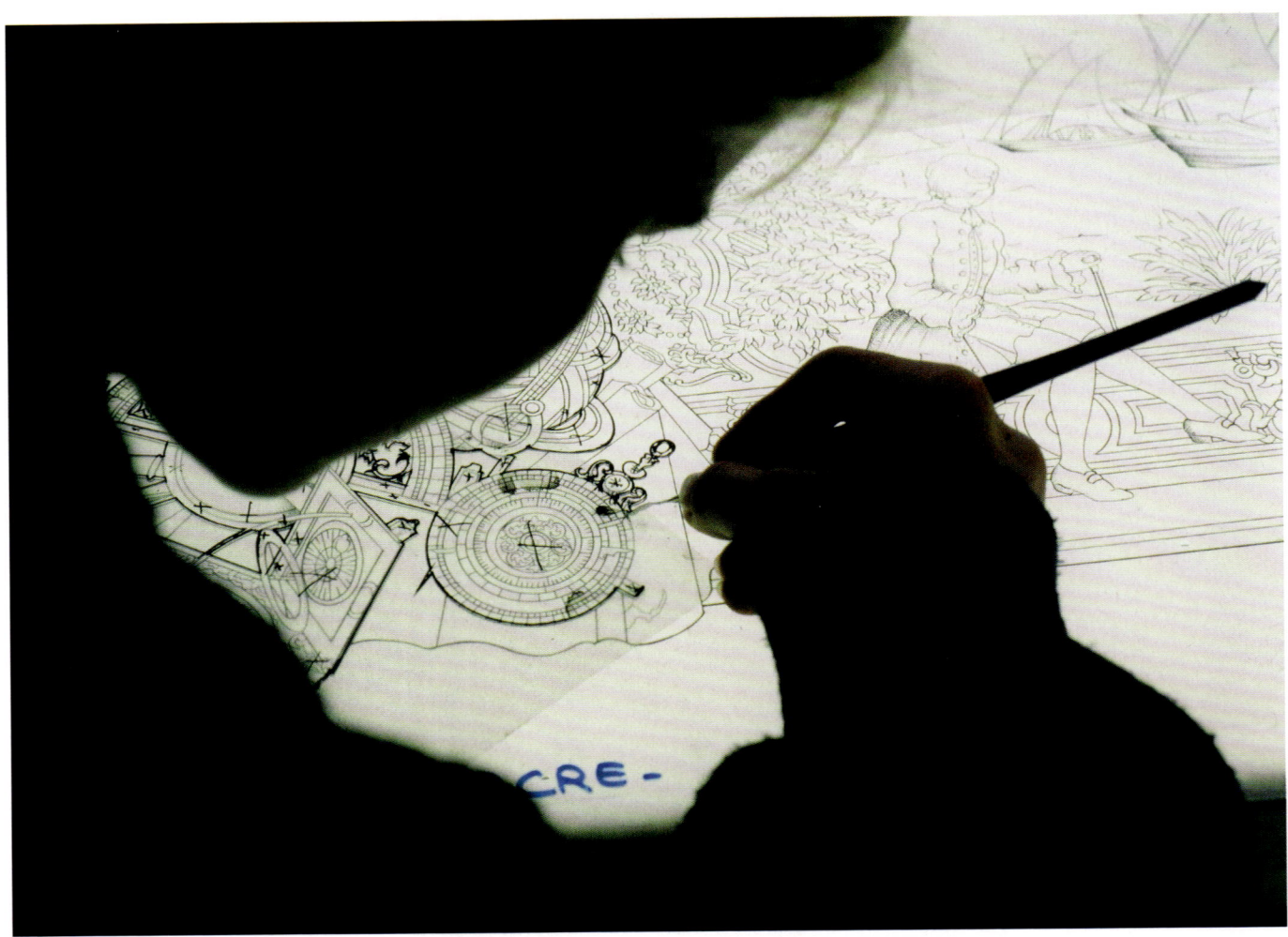

The design of every silk scarf is handled by artists and illustrators who often take months or years to develop a single design.

A refined technique

One fundamental aspect of Hermès silk scarves is the exceptional craftsmanship which goes into each piece. Every silk scarf requires about eighteen months to two years of work, from concept to production.

The drawing and designing phase takes anywhere from three to six months, from a blank sheet of paper to the final colourways. Then it takes six months to a year for what the fashion house calls 'engraving' – that is, separating out all the colours in the image, layer after layer, to create a film for each hue. Master printers in Lyon redraw it all by hand so as to correctly associate all the colours. They then create the multiple screens required, and a team of colourists transfers the image to the fabric, one layer at a time, a process requiring another six months. They test, rehash, correct and improve, working with a palette which ranges from 10 to 12 colour variations for every silk scarf.[11]

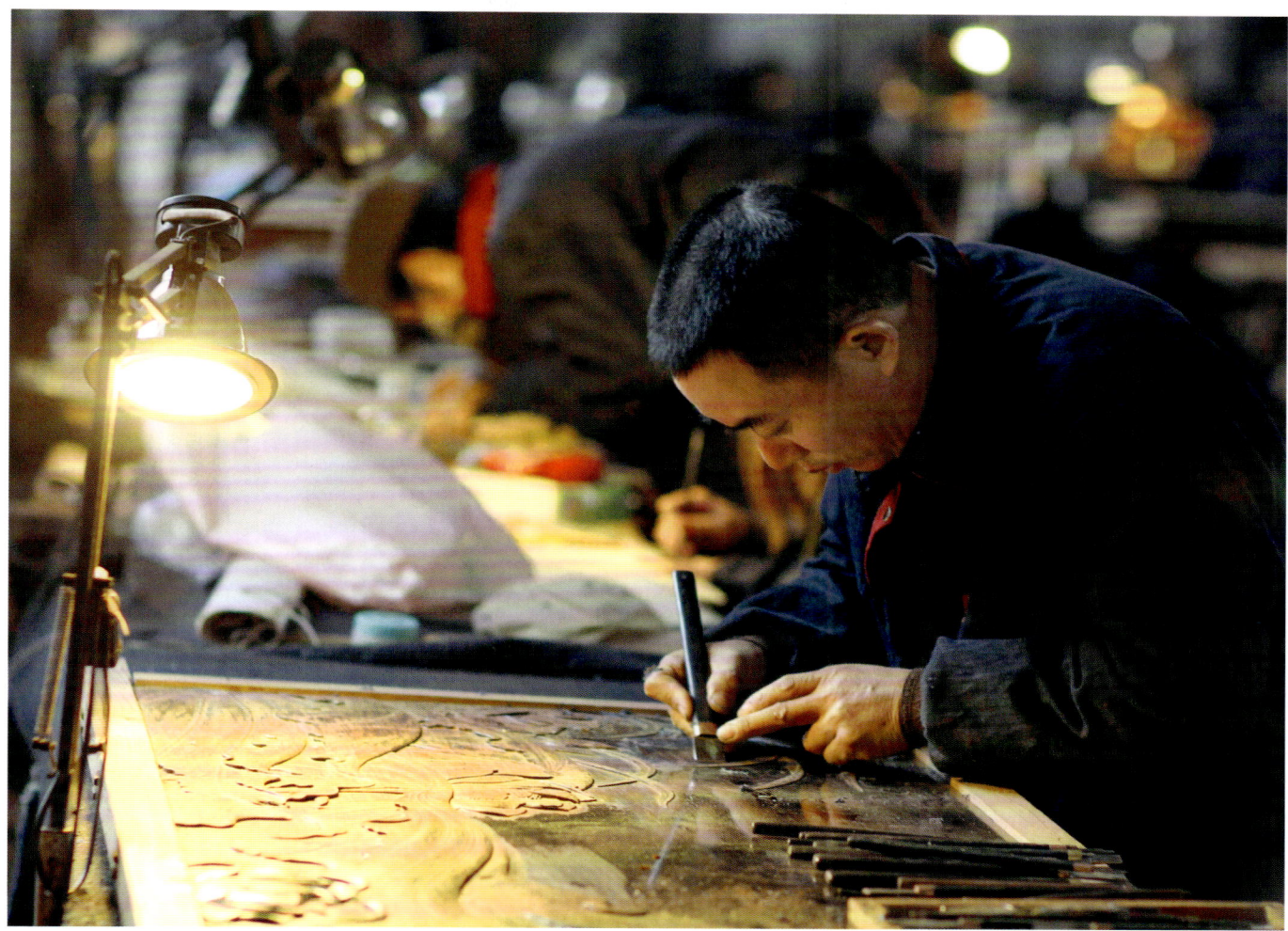

Every silk scarf is the product of meticulous craftsmanship, which includes manual silk-screen printing, a process that can take weeks for each colour used.

The silk used is of highest quality, and it takes 300 silkworms to produce the 4 kilometres of thread that goes into every single scarf, weighing only 65 grams.

The first silk scarf by Hermès measured 90 × 90 cm, a size that has become the standard for the brand's scarves, even if other measurements have been added since then.[12] The square shape, however, does present challenges in its production. One of the most iconic accessories in the world of fashion relies on a tool specially created by a textile maker from Lyon. In 1948, Marcel Gandit patented a square printing system which made it possible to perfectly recreate every single detail of the original design.

The art of silk-screen printing – known in France as *méthode lyonnaise* and used for applying the images to the scarves – is a technique that requires extreme precision and attention to detail. Each colour must be applied separately, and a single silk scarf can require up to 40 screens to complete the entire design.

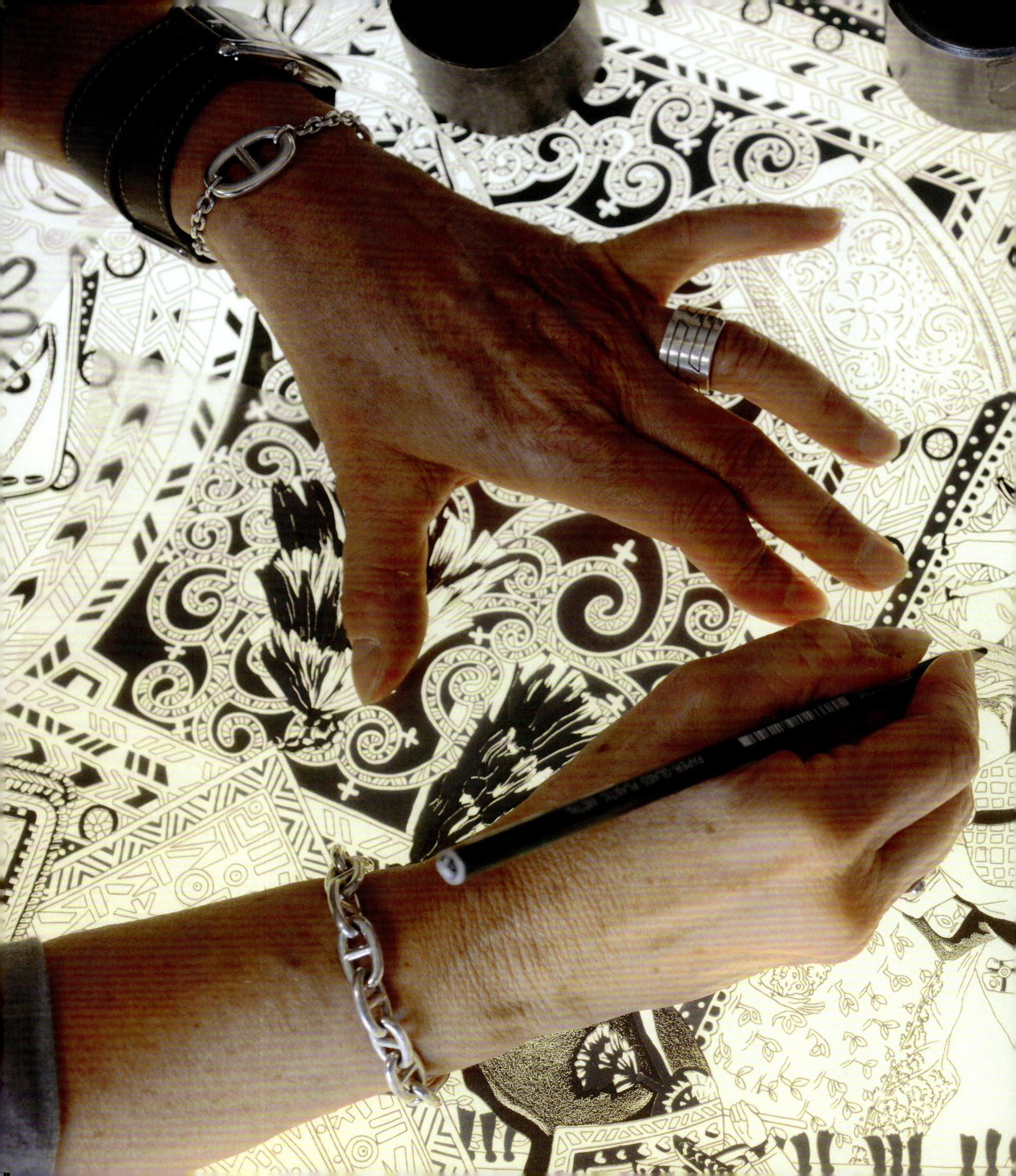

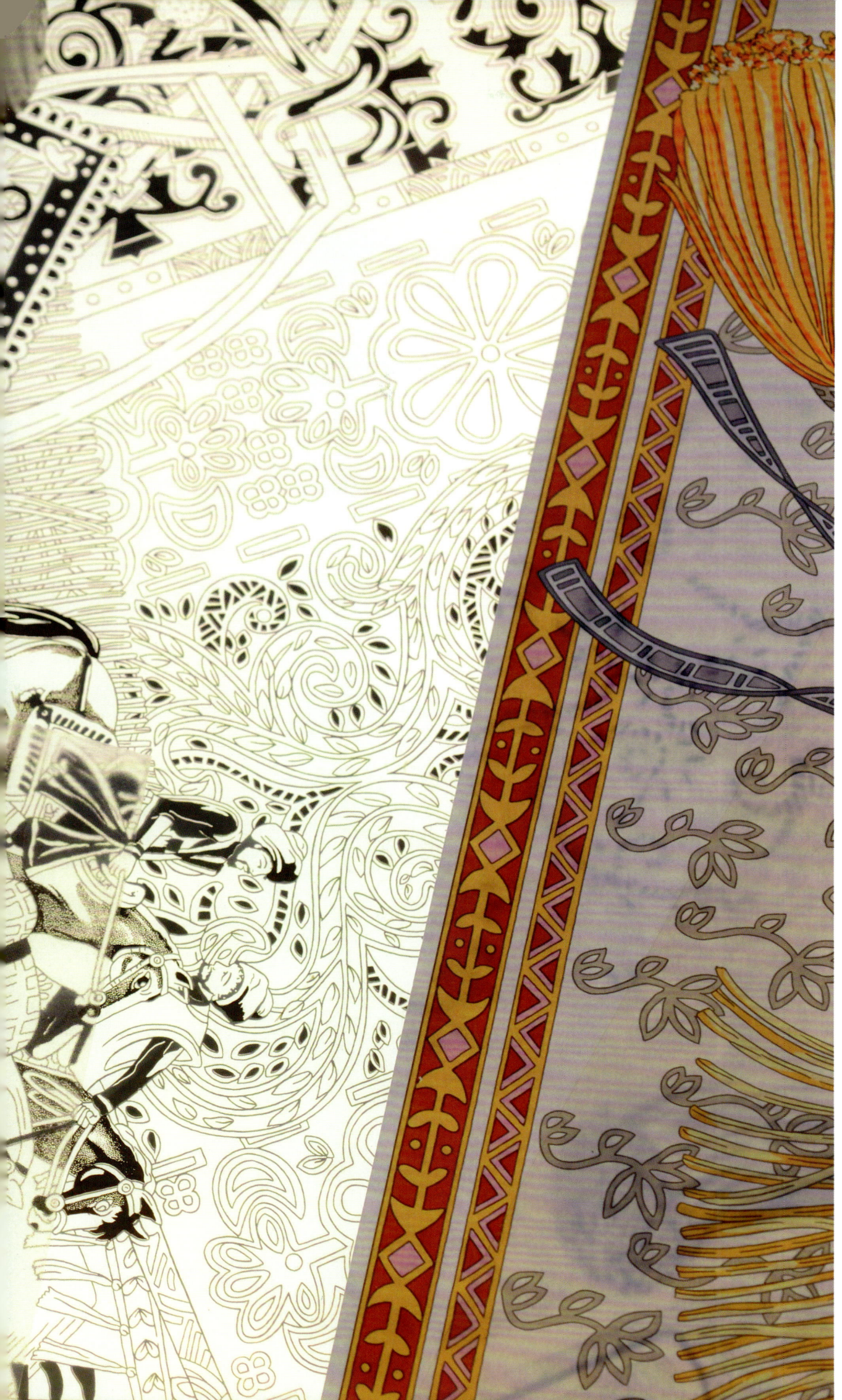

Starting from the artist's creation, the drawing is prepared for silk-screen printing.

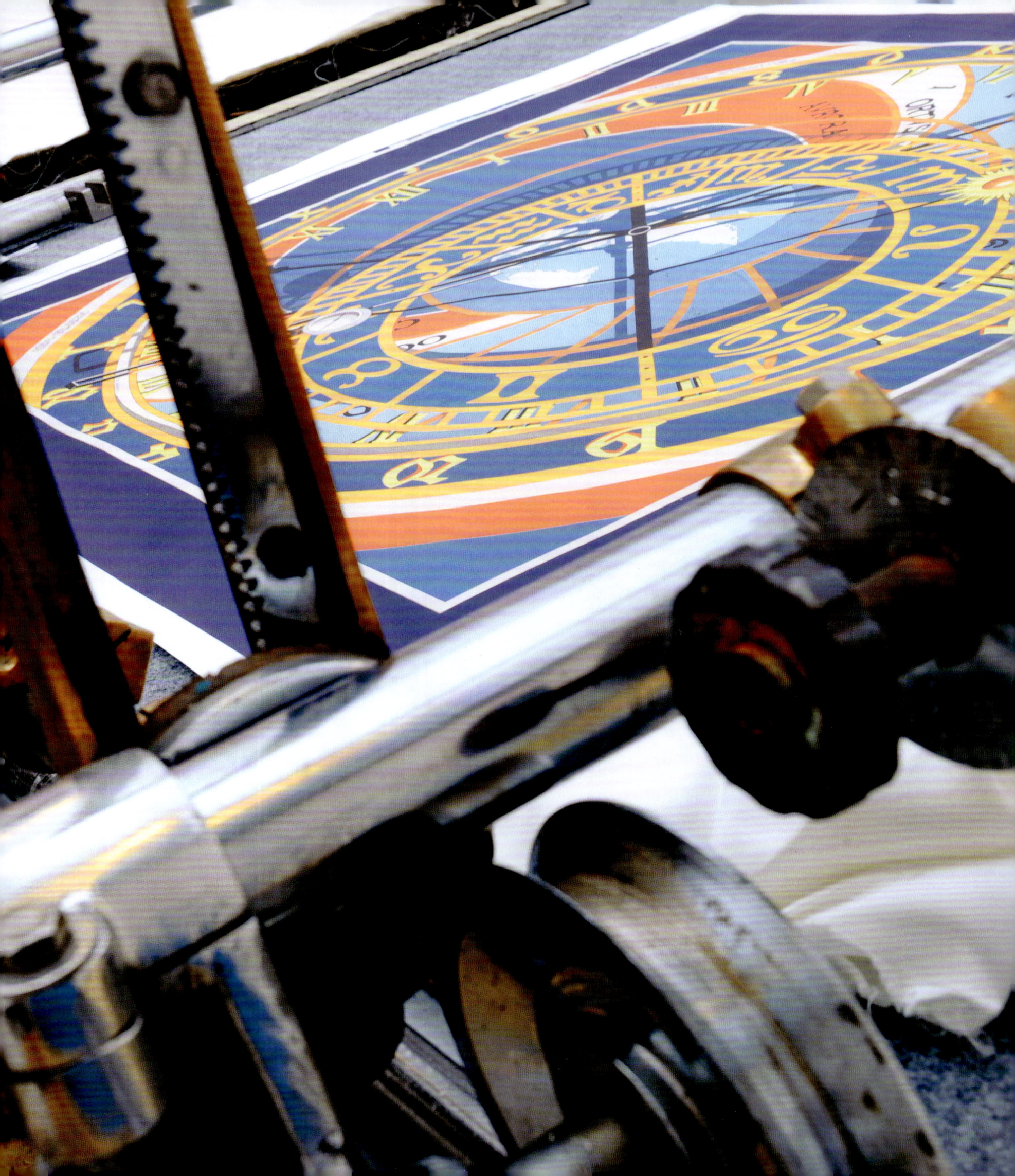

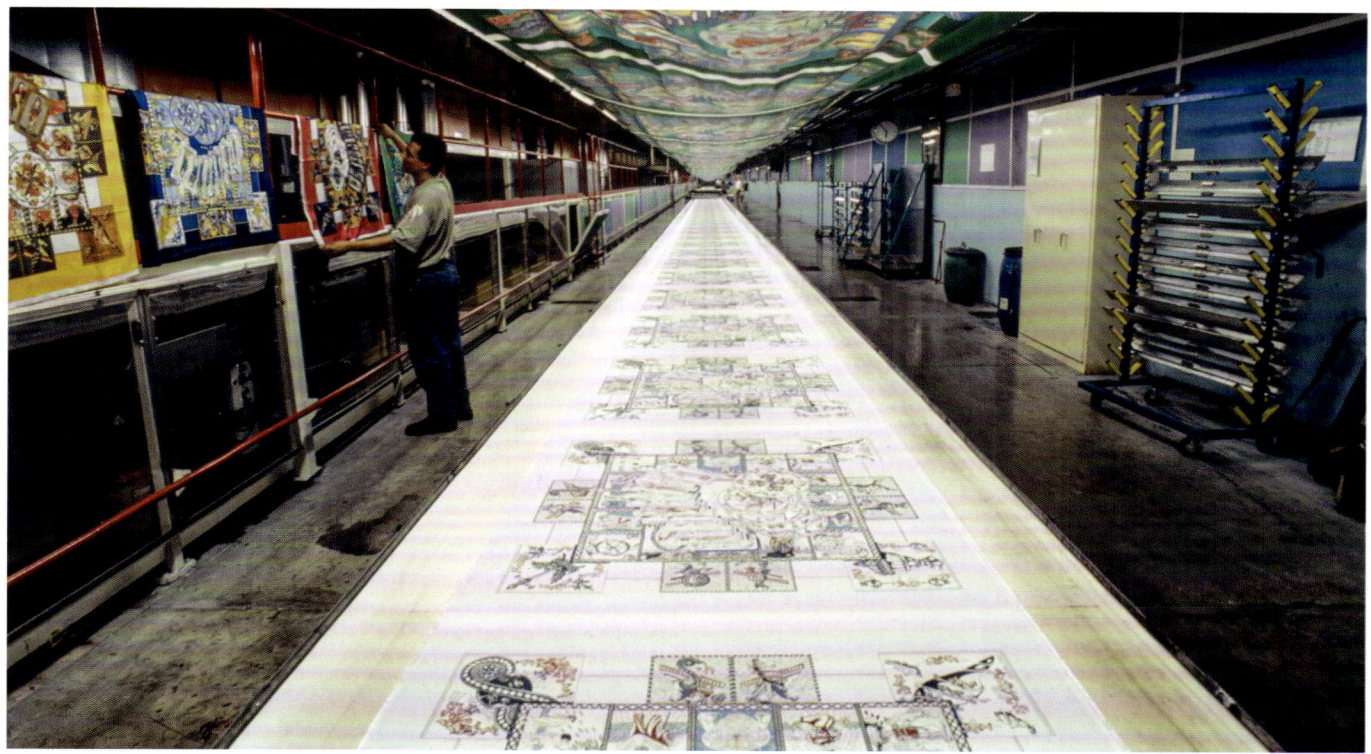

Opposite – The technique requires the use of a scraper to force ink through the mesh; it is a skill that combines art and science. The pressure, angle and speed of the scraper are critical variables that the screen printer must manage with extreme precision to ensure even coverage and sharp detail.

This page – Screen printing or silk-screen printing is a technique which takes its name from the screen traditionally made of silk which is drawn taut over a frame. Parts of the screen are blocked off, allowing ink to pass through only certain parts to create the image on the surface of the scarf placed below it. Each screen is used for one colour, meaning that as many screens as there are colours must be created.

This process not only guarantees the vibrancy of the colours, but also ensures they last over time.

The final touch is the *roulottage*, the exquisite art of hand rolling and stitching the hem of the silk scarf, a refined feature which distinguishes each *carré* made by Hermès.

Over the years, the fashion house has made silk scarves which are printed on both sides, and even tattoo scarves, where pieces of lightweight, colourful cotton voile are sewn onto the silk scarf, and there are those decorated by fringes or flounces.[13] Every year, Hermès presents ten to twelve new silk scarf designs, in two seasonal collections. These new creations are combined with reissues of classic designs, thereby upholding the balance between innovation and tradition.

The history of Hermès silk scarves is rooted in the past, but it still has many worlds yet to explore.

Today, the company proposes many ways to wear its silk scarves: tied around the neck, as a headband, as a hair tie, on the arm or wrist, knotted on a bag, or as a belt – each one defining the wearer's personal style. Or, as Diana Vreeland, another admirer of the brand, once said: 'Put it on without so much as looking in the mirror', giving that act and accompanying accessory the kind of value which blurs the line between beauty and well-being.

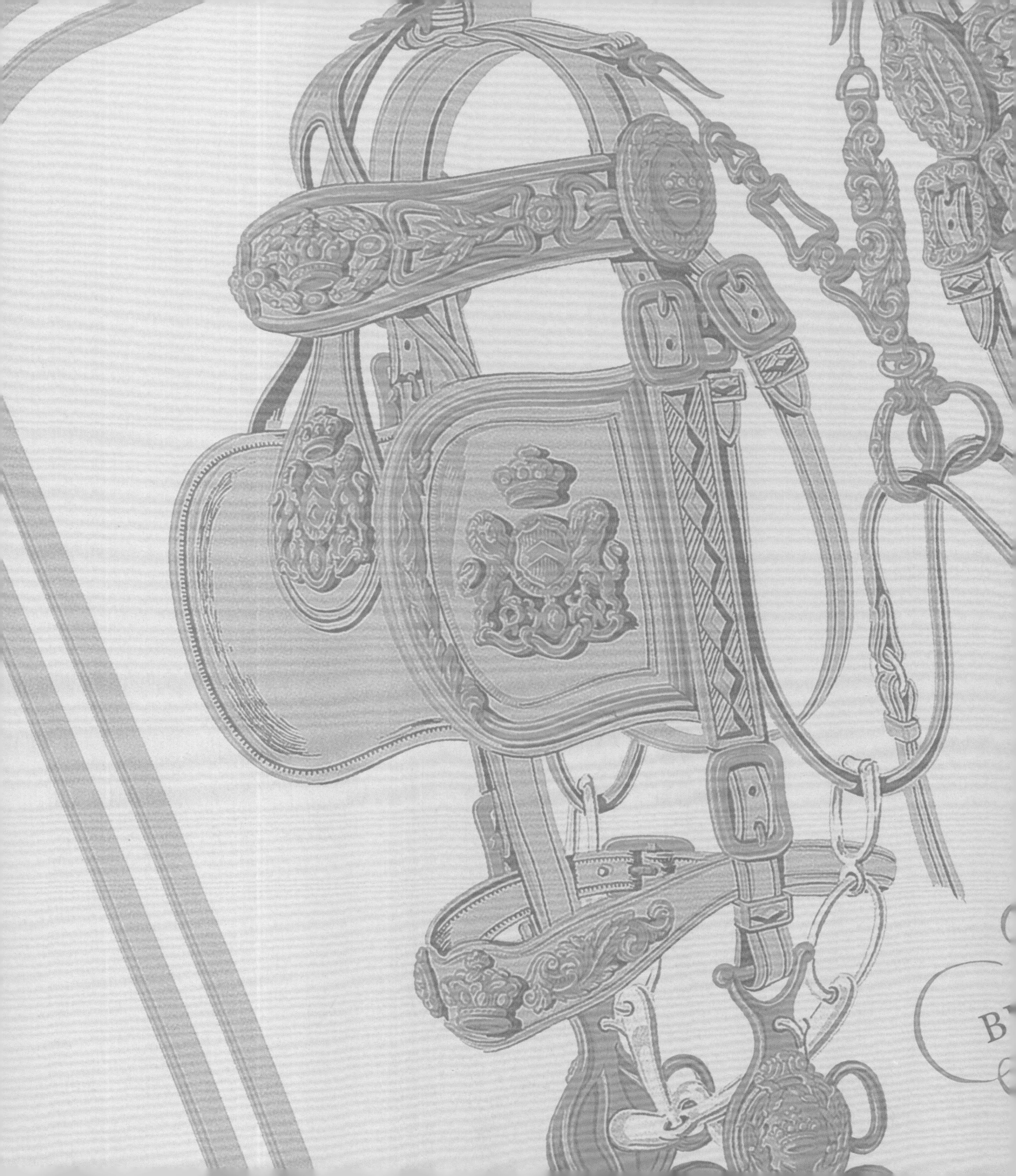

Bags

·················

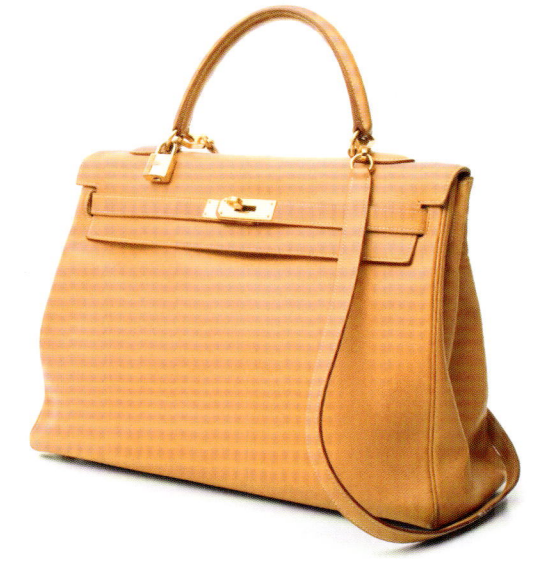

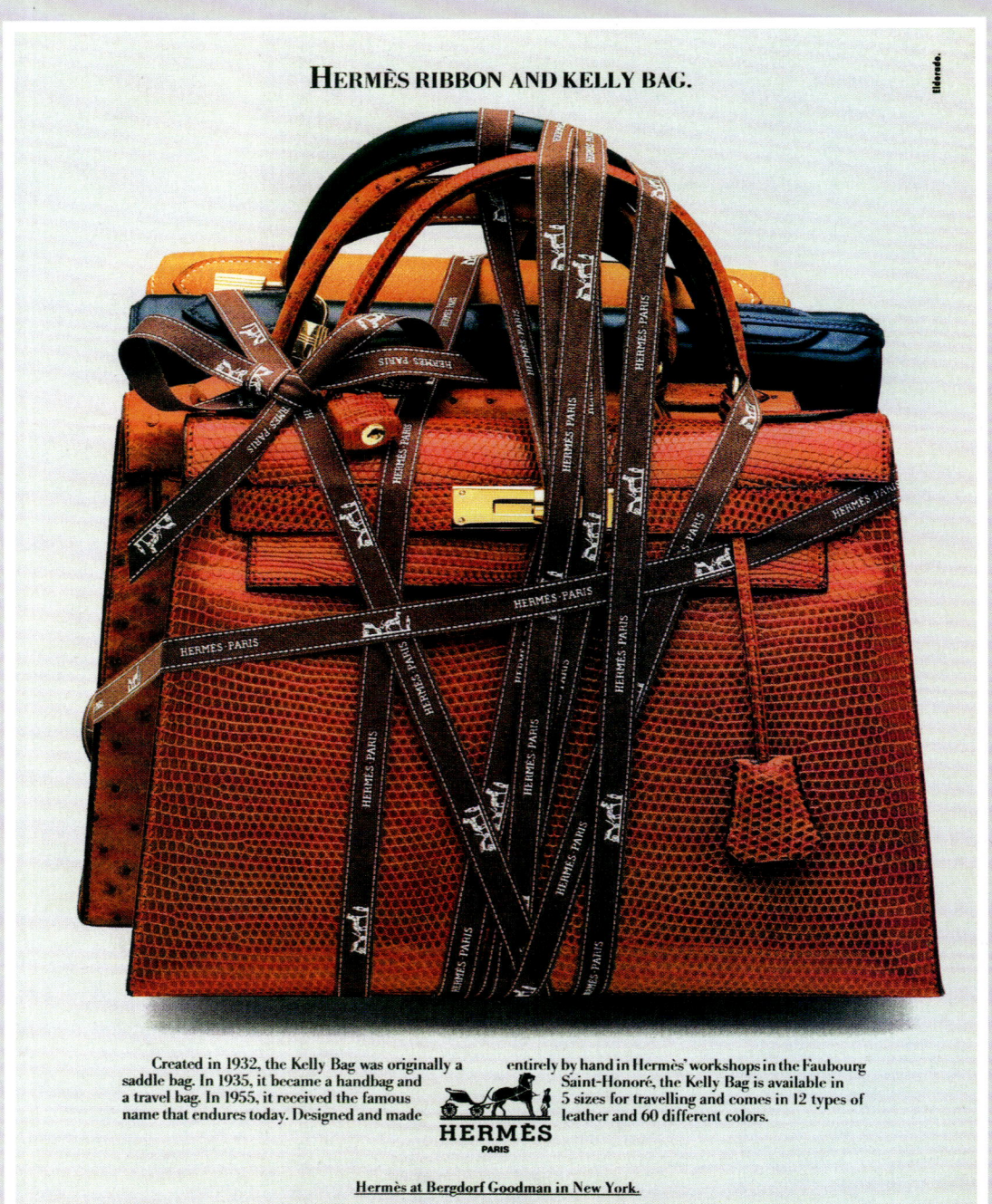

Advert for the iconic *Kelly* which presents the origins of the bag. *American fashion magazine*, c.1983.

A NECESSARY AND PERSONAL ACCESSORY

· · · · · · · · · · · · · · · ·

Venturing into the wide world of Hermès bags requires, as always, making choices.
This chapter inevitably presents the most famous styles, but rounds them out with a few that are
interesting in terms of their story and design.

Bags have a rich and varied history in the women's fashion universe. From a simple container to a style statement, this accessory has been handed down to the present day through eras and cultures, and it has carved out a central niche in the definition of any look.

Bags contain us, a part of us. Whether they carry practical items or purely aesthetic objects, they all belong to the personal sphere. Inside, bags conceal something which is part of the life of a person, something which that person always wants to have with them but not necessarily share with others. Bags belong to the 'private' sphere, just as their contents are personal. This meaning is even clearer if we take our cue from Sigmund Freud. In *A General Introduction to Psychoanalysis*, he wrote that 'the female genital is symbolically represented by all those objects which share its peculiarity of enclosing a space capable of being filled by something.'[1] Bags fall squarely within that category.

While the bag symbolically may represent a female component, historically it has been used by both women and men. Actually, it was men who first needed a container to carry items, given that they travelled for trade, politics or even war, activities which they did out in the world while rich women needed them much less because they generally spent much of their lives within the walls of the home.

Often used to carry money, documents or papers, bags are assigned a lot of value. It's no accident that the famous saying 'your money or your life' seems to put the two on equal footing, even if only symbolically.

Socially speaking, bags convey status in a figurative sense, and bags are often mentioned in various expressions in which they stand in for or are associated with money: being a 'moneybags' means being wealthy, and 'bags of money' refers to large sums of it.

Undoubtedly, through the bag she carries, a woman conveys her style and position in society.

"L'Art indien des plaines"
silk twill scarf.
"Kelly" bag in matt
alligator skin.
Riding jacket and trou-
sers in deerskin leather.
Boots in box calf.
Hooded zipped cardigan
in "Calèche" dévoré
velvet. "Kelly" mini clutch
bag in matt alligator skin.

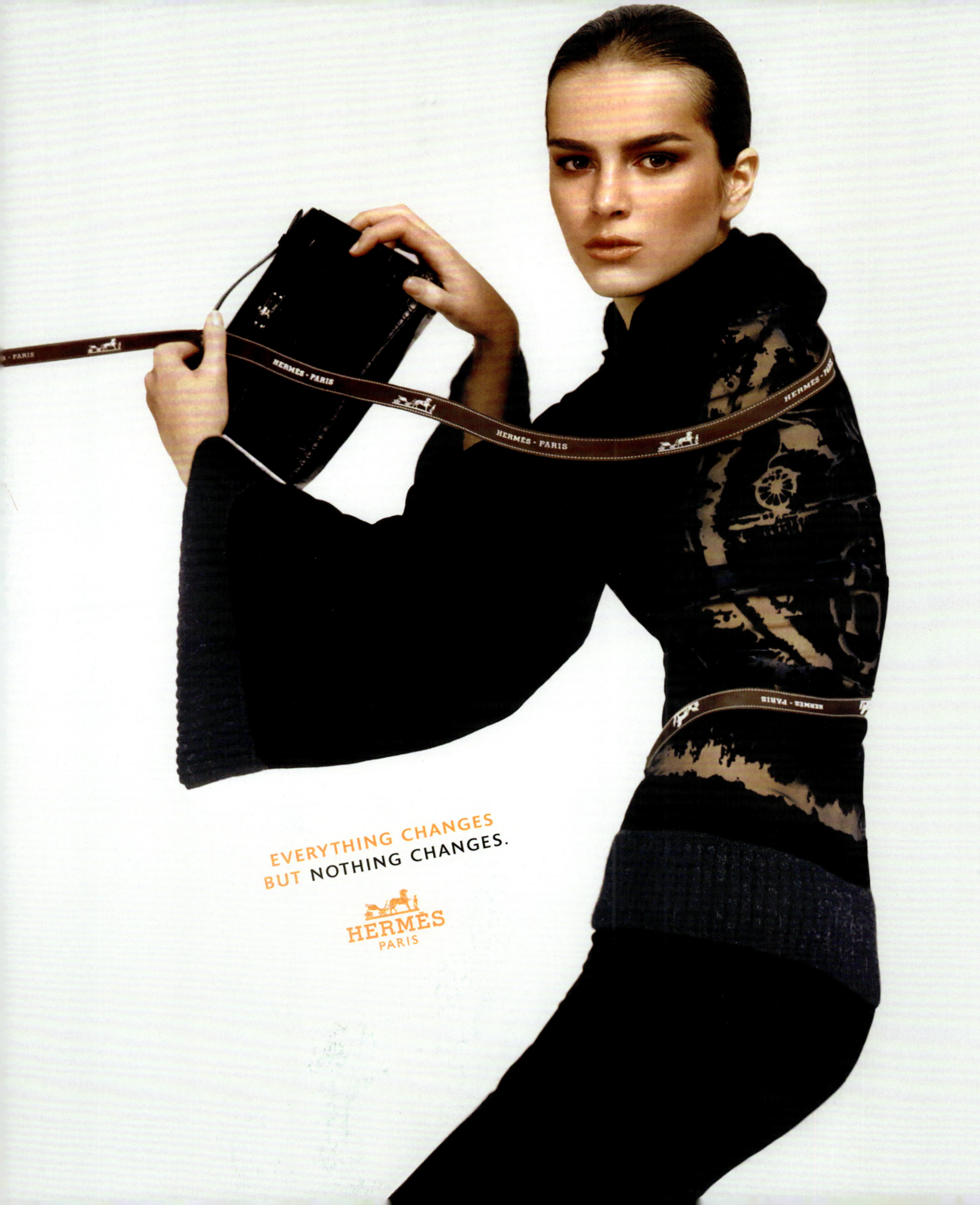

From a necessary object to a luxury item

Aside from symbolic considerations, which are also relevant, bags began to be part of women's wardrobes in the early 20th century, when women began to enjoy greater freedom. This was the moment when Hermès made a bet on the future of this accessory.

What sets great entrepreneurs apart is their ability to fully comprehend the time in which they are living and to interpret the needs of the society around them, often staying one step ahead and shaping desires through products defined by distinct aesthetics.

This was true of Émile-Maurice Hermès in the 1920s and 1930s, when he foresaw that bags would play a more important role in the lives of women than they ever had before.

Philippe Dumas, book author and illustrator, completed a sketchbook between the 1980s and the mid 1990s filled with drawings that portray items from the vast and highly prized private collection of his grandfather Émile-Maurice. A few pages are dedicated to small bags – or rather, to what were called the 'ancestors of women's bags of the future'.[2] Four historical bags are illustrated in the notebook, which is titled *La vie à l'aire libre* (*Life in the open air*), such as the *Sac à plombs* from the Louis XV era and the *Réticule fin XVIIIème*. The materials of each one (silk, fabric, metal and leather) are indicated, and they present an idea, a starting point for their creation. In the *La Route* sketchbook, we see a travel bag *en tapisserie* from the Romantic era, in addition to travel cases with all that's needed to set sumptuous tables, picnic baskets, and silverware containers.[3] In the *L'Exotisme* booklet, two entire pages portray a number of cross-body and travel bags, along with small and elegant pouches.[4]

Looking at these marvellous illustrations, we get a sense that the bag-object was part of the private cabinet of curiosities which the collector had created, and that these specimens from other eras were references for modern creations. The theme of travel, understood as exploration, discovery of the universe and freedom of movement, is central to the brand's philosophy. And through travel, whether by horse, carriage, sea, train or car, luxurious accessories were essential to making the experience enjoyable and gratifying.

Between the late 19th century and the early 20th century, travel bags for women were born, made from exquisite leathers and completed by multiple compartments. Their design was practical, designed for women who had begun to explore the world, bringing enormous suitcases with them. Hermès had introduced the *Haut à Courroies* in 1897, a bag designed to carry saddles and boots for horsemen, but which swiftly became a convenient bag for the transport of various objects. Suitcases, toiletry bags and shoe cases were part of the product range sold by the brand, a set of fine products destined for the lucky few who could afford to travel to new destinations.

However, a turning point occurred in the history of fashion, and consequently in the history of women's handbags, during the First World War. At that time, an entire generation of women was transformed from 'angels at the hearth' into te-

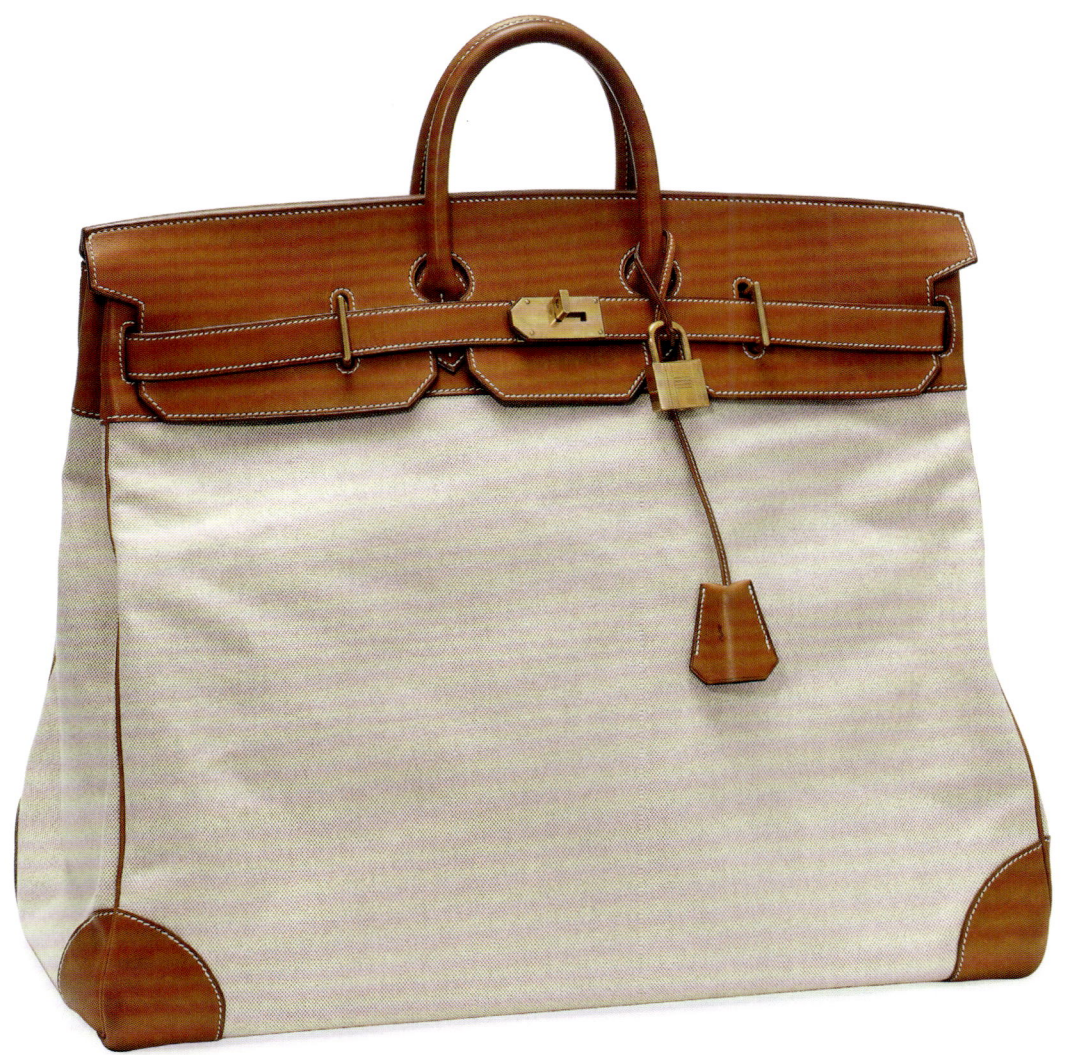

Haute a Courroies: a bag designed to carry boots and saddles, characterised by vertical and trapezoidal lines. Barenia natural leather and écru toile, 2003.

nacious workers, employed to save the economy of their home countries in industries which, up until then, were exclusively reserved for men. In the process, they gained awareness of what it was like to play an active role in society.[5]

In the 1920s, women gained greater independence and the freedom to move about. For the daytime, they chose small, envelope-style bags made of different materials (from antelope to snake or crocodile leather) with hardware in gold or silver, made to be worn with the new dresses that were both casual and short. They chose bags made in shiny fabrics with motifs in small diamonds or marcasite as their finery for afternoon visits, while for evening outings, they wore asymmetrical dresses with small *minaudières* made with metallic plaques or in precious metals decorated by ornamental motifs in precious or semi-precious stones or in lacquer. Some styles even had wrist loops.

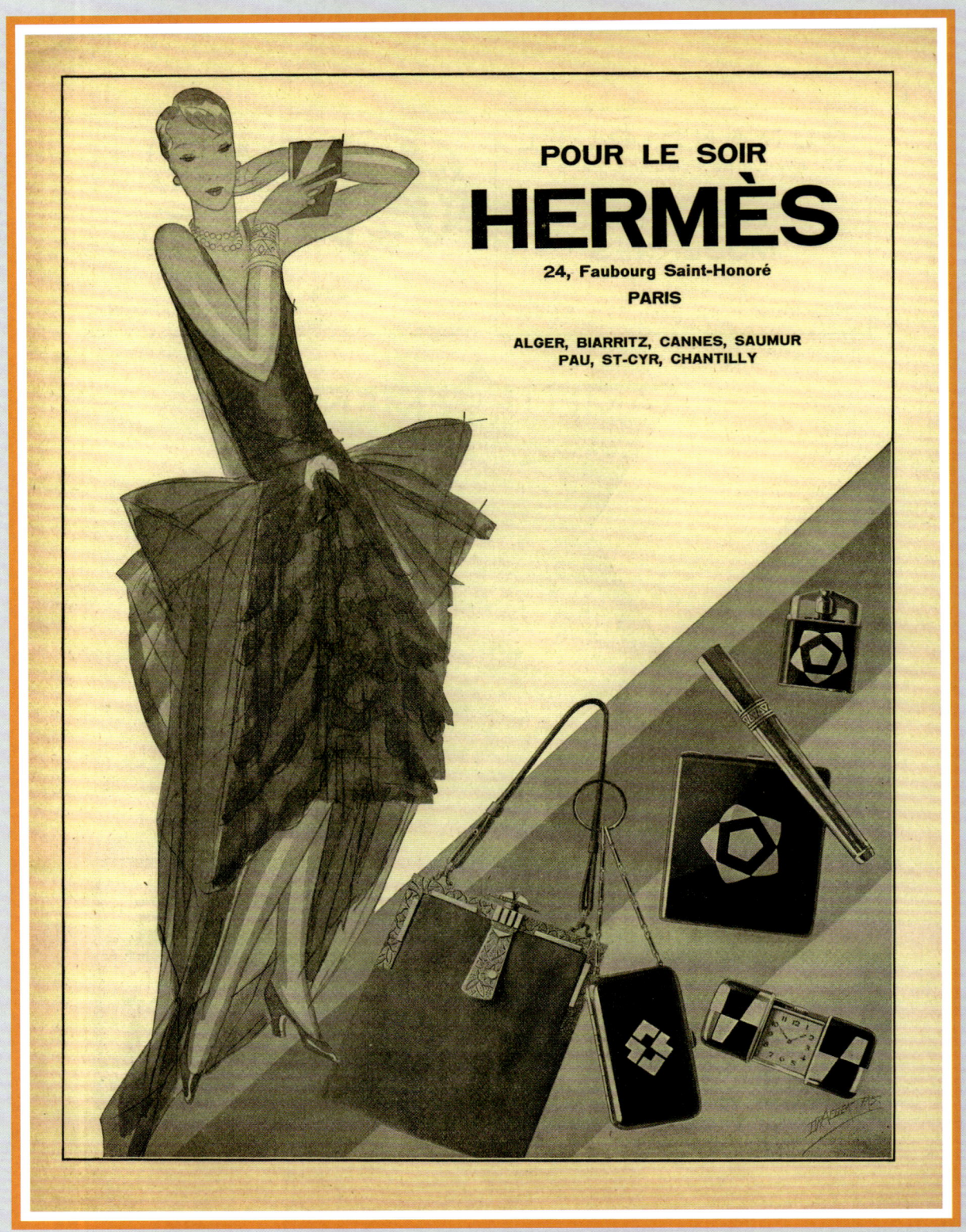

Hermès advert from 1929 showing different styles of small bags decorated with the geometric forms for which Art Deco is known.

However, the Hermès woman remained a traveller who needed elegant, large and capacious containers. Conceived of as a travel bag and destined for use by men and women, the *Bolide* created in 1923 was the first bag in the world to have a zip fastener, which Hermès imported from the United States.[6] Its rounded shape was inspired by the aerodynamic curves of cars at the time, and it was perfectly designed to fit into the boot of such vehicles. Also made for travel, the *Sac de dames à courroies* created by Hermès in 1930 was an evolution of the structure of a briefcase.

In the 1930s, women's bags became more structured while maintaining their sophisticated details and fine materials. The daytime 'envelope' clutches carried by hand or under-arm were often rectangular or trapezoid in shape. They were usually medium in size, large enough to hold the objects indispensable to modern women, such as a wallet, lipstick and a compact mirror. Bovine leather became the material of choice for daytime bags, alongside lizard and crocodile, with details and clasps in fine metals. With materials that were

innovative at the time, such as galalith and Bakelite, bags with new or imaginative shapes were made. Evening bags, on the other hand, maintained a more glamorous character: often smaller in size, they were made of luxuriant materials such as velvet, silk, and satin, and decorated with crystals or golden embroidery. Popular styles included *minaudières*, which were small rigid boxes in precious metals encrusted with diamonds, and contained inner compartments for small make-up accessories.

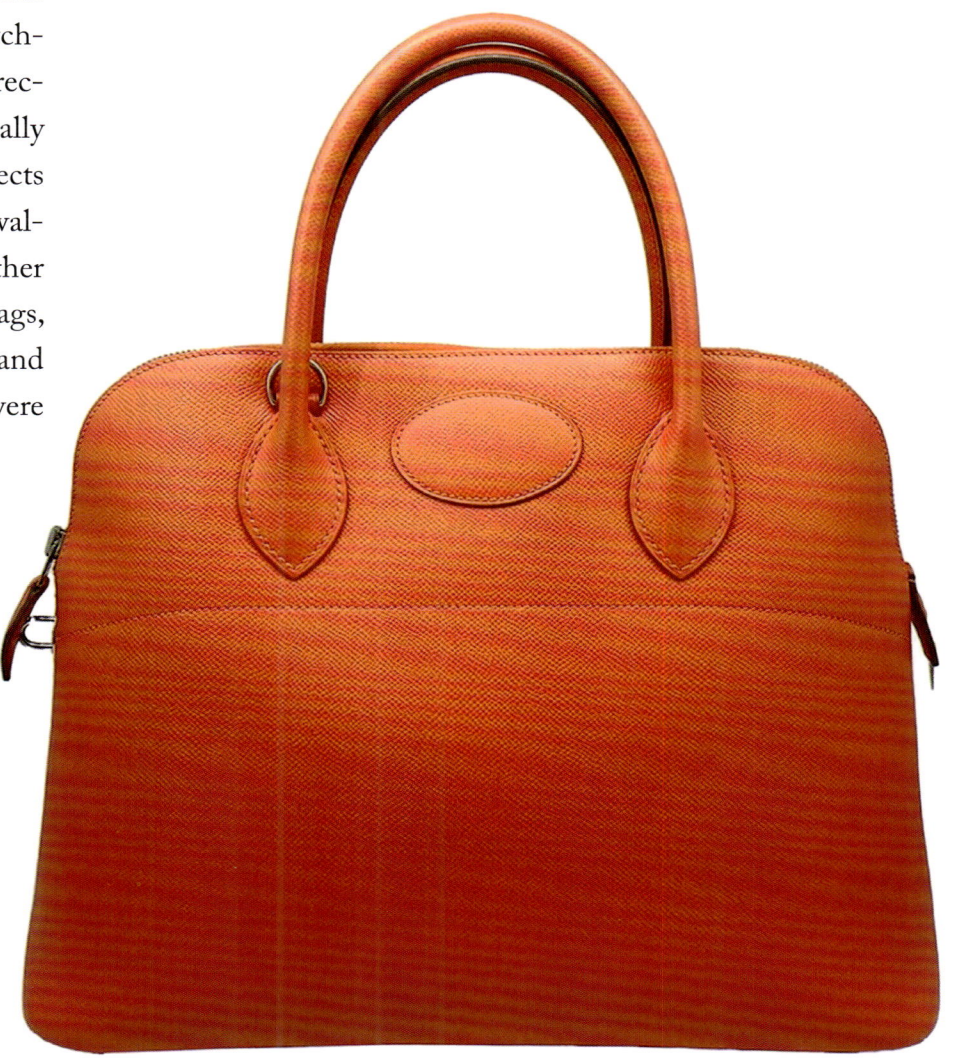

Still being made today, the *Bolide* bag was introduced in the 1920s. Practical and elegant, with rounded lines and plenty of room on the inside, it comes in different sizes and materials.

During the Second World War, scarce resources and the need for practicality deeply shaped fashion, accessories included. Bags became more robust and functional, medium or large in size, ideal for carrying personal items, documents and other items essential to women, who increasingly worked at jobs outside of the home. The materials used were often alternatives to leather, such as fabric, jute and canvas, while silhouettes were sober and without superfluous ornamentation, reflecting the austerity of the era. Nevertheless, bags were still elegant thanks to essential lines and meticulous details, such as topstitching and simple yet refined clasps. In the late 1940s, when the economy began to pick up again, bags began to regain a touch of glamour. Structured handbags were in vogue, often square and flat with short handles and metal clasps.

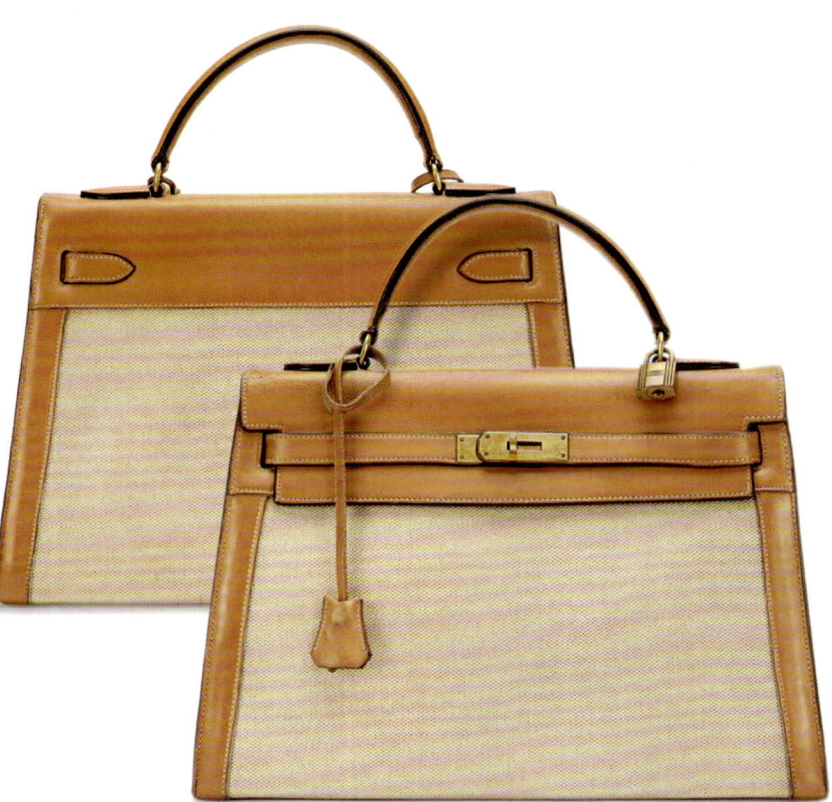

Evening clutches grew in popularity again too, enriched by details such as embroidery and beadwork.

Look at the extensive legacy of Hermès advertisements, and it's possible to see how the company created different styles in these decades, made for elite women who sought discreet elegance.

However, it wasn't until the 1950s that the brand created its own precise and impeccable identity in the bag industry, thanks to entrepreneurial intuition and a bit of lucky publicity: Grace Kelly was the unsuspecting subject of a photograph taken in 1956, in which she's holding a *Sac de dames à courroies* on one arm. That bag would later be renamed the *Kelly* in her honour.[7] In the 1950s, women's bags were refined, elegant accessories which characterised the era, symbols of renascent economic well-being and an ideal of feminine sophistication. For daytime, structured handbags prevailed: compact and geometric, often trapezoid or square, they had short handles and were designed to be carried on the arm or by hand. Fine materials such as calfskin, crocodile and lizard gave them a luxurious and impeccable finish. Small and discreet clutches were quite popular as accessories for the formal evenings, balls and cocktail hours which enlivened social life.

....

This page – A vintage *Kelly Sellier 32* in *Gold* Courchevel leather with gold hardware. The *Kelly Sellier* features topstitching and a rigid border, 1959.

Opposite page – Actress Grace Kelly at the Orly airport on 3 May 1955. She's wearing a Chanel skirt suit and is carrying the Hermès bag which hadn't yet been named after her.

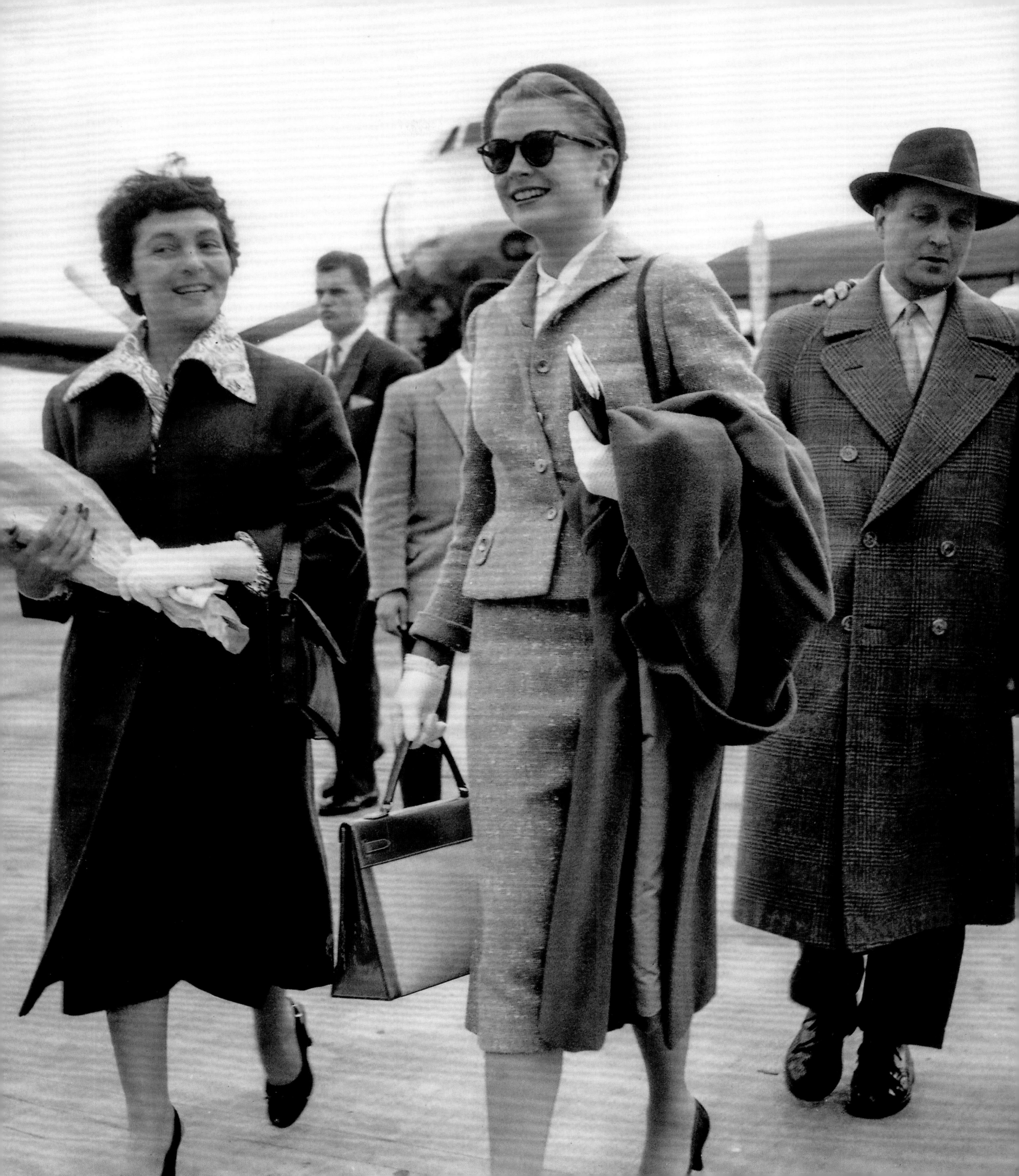

A classic with classic style

Distinguished by its essential aesthetic, the *Kelly* bag has become an Hermès icon.

Reflective of the style of the era in which it was made, the *Kelly* is structured, trapezoid in silhouette, and has just one handle which can be used to carry it by hand or on the arm. To close the top, a flap is overlapped by two buckle straps which are bound by a *touret* clasp and a padlock.

The seams are the classic saddle stitch, a double-needle stitch that requires know-how to create and which ensures the maximum durability of the structure.

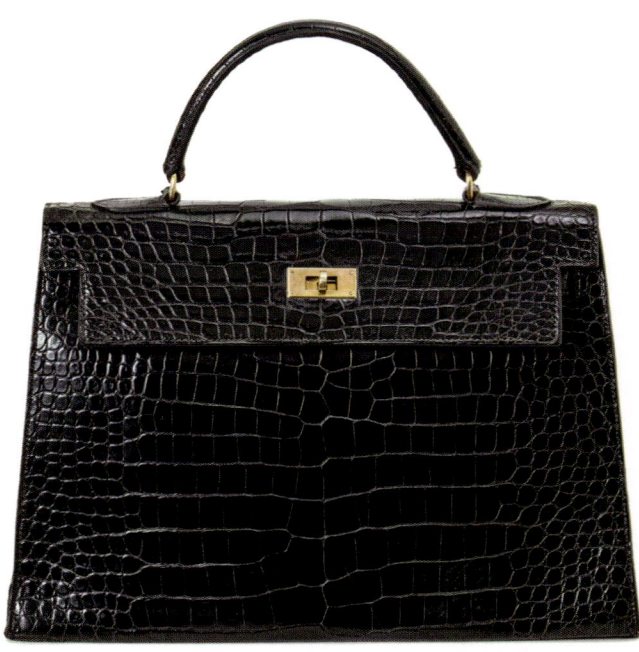

Kelly 32 in crocodile with golden hardware, Hermès. France, 1940s. The *Kelly* is a masterpiece of craftsmanship: every hand-made piece requires over 25 hours of work to complete.

Each bag is made by hand by an expert artisan who marks each part of the product with an identifying number, so that it is always possible to trace it to its creator. Every *Kelly* bag takes anywhere from 18 to 25 work hours to make. Among the many versions, the two main ones are the *Sellier* (with rigid, structured edges) and the *Retourne* (softer and rounder).[8] *Sellier* means 'saddler' in French. The name is a tribute to the origin of Hermès as the leading saddler and harness maker of French nobility. The *Kelly Sellier* is defined by topstitching (a technique in which the seams remain visible, on the outside, for decorative and functional purposes) and crisp, rigid edges. This gives them a more structured silhouette. The seams on the *Kelly Retourne*, on the other hand, are internal and covered by piping along the outer edges, offering a softer shape and thus a more casual look.

It comes in sizes which range from 40 cm to mini versions, and in different materials. Hermès offers it in different types of leather: Epsom, Togo, Clémence, Box, Swift, crocodile, ostrich and lizard. The brand constantly introduces new interpretations of this bag with versions in innovative materials and a vast range of colours.

However, the *Kelly* is one of the hardest bags to purchase. To get one, it's often necessary to be an Hermès client for a long time. Wait times depend on availability, and can range from months to years. For this reason, some vintage and rare versions are sold at auction for astronomical sums, exceeding their original price tags.

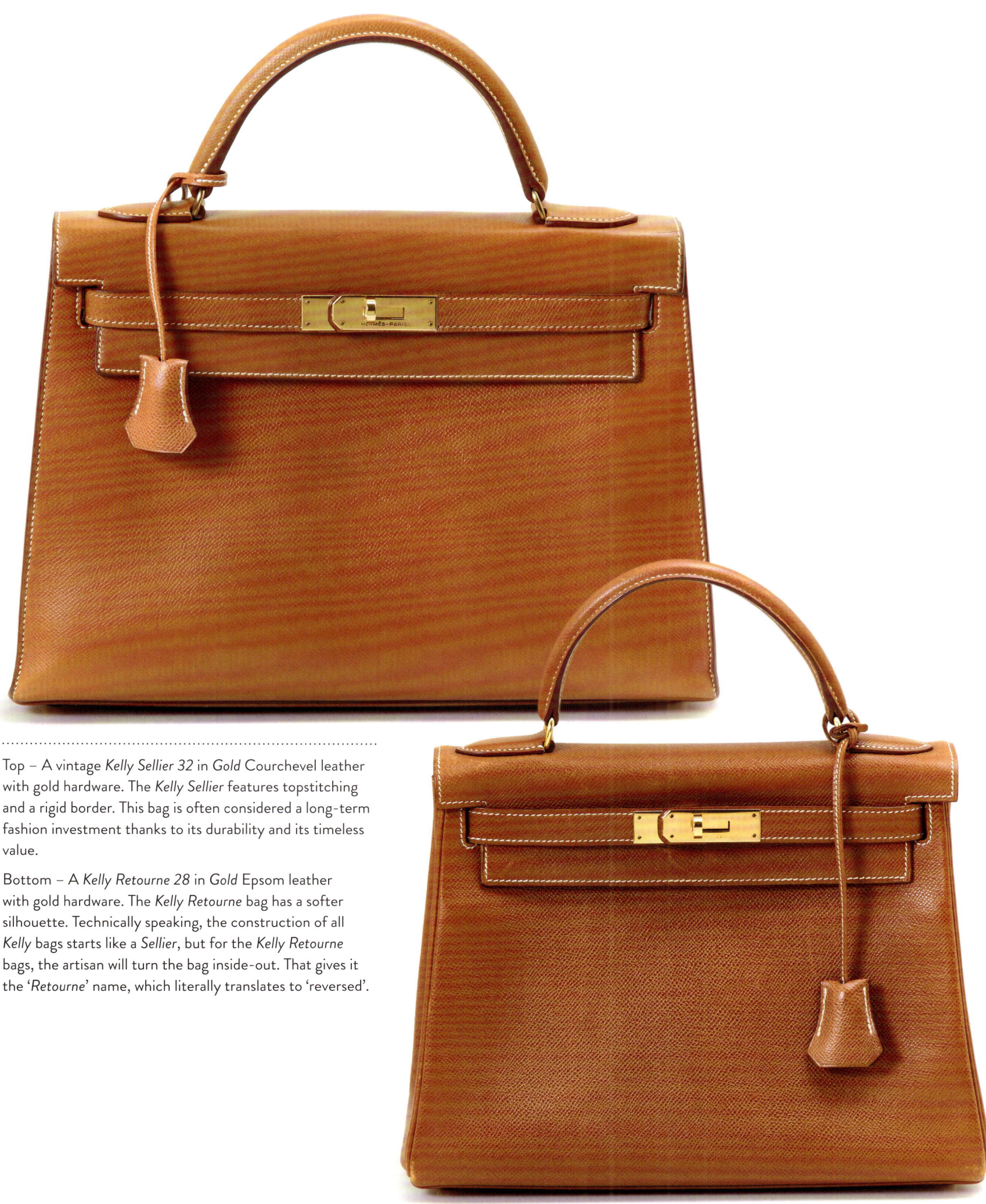

Top – A vintage *Kelly Sellier 32* in *Gold* Courchevel leather with gold hardware. The *Kelly Sellier* features topstitching and a rigid border. This bag is often considered a long-term fashion investment thanks to its durability and its timeless value.

Bottom – A *Kelly Retourne 28* in *Gold* Epsom leather with gold hardware. The *Kelly Retourne* bag has a softer silhouette. Technically speaking, the construction of all *Kelly* bags starts like a *Sellier*, but for the *Kelly Retourne* bags, the artisan will turn the bag inside-out. That gives it the '*Retourne*' name, which literally translates to 'reversed'.

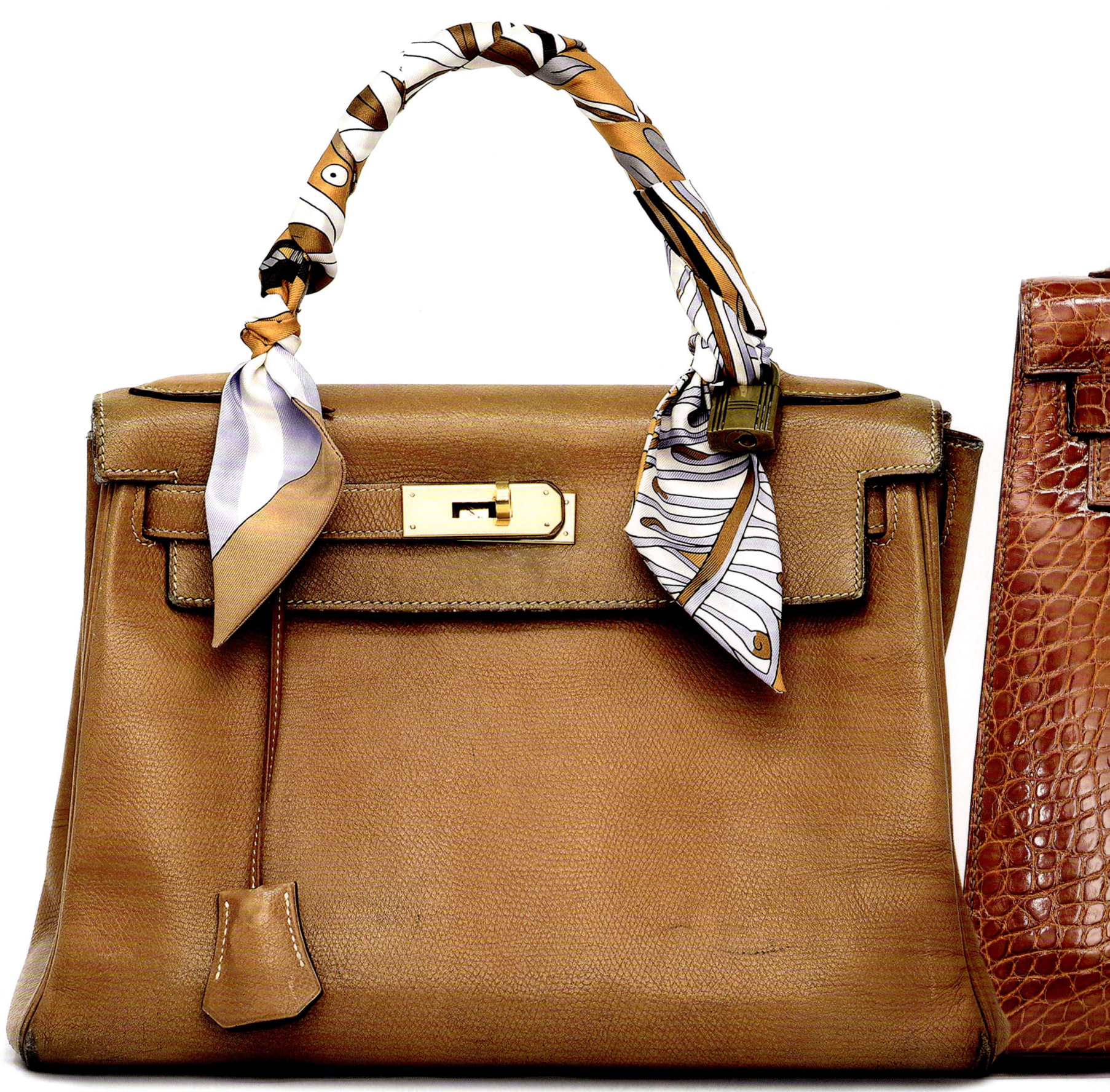

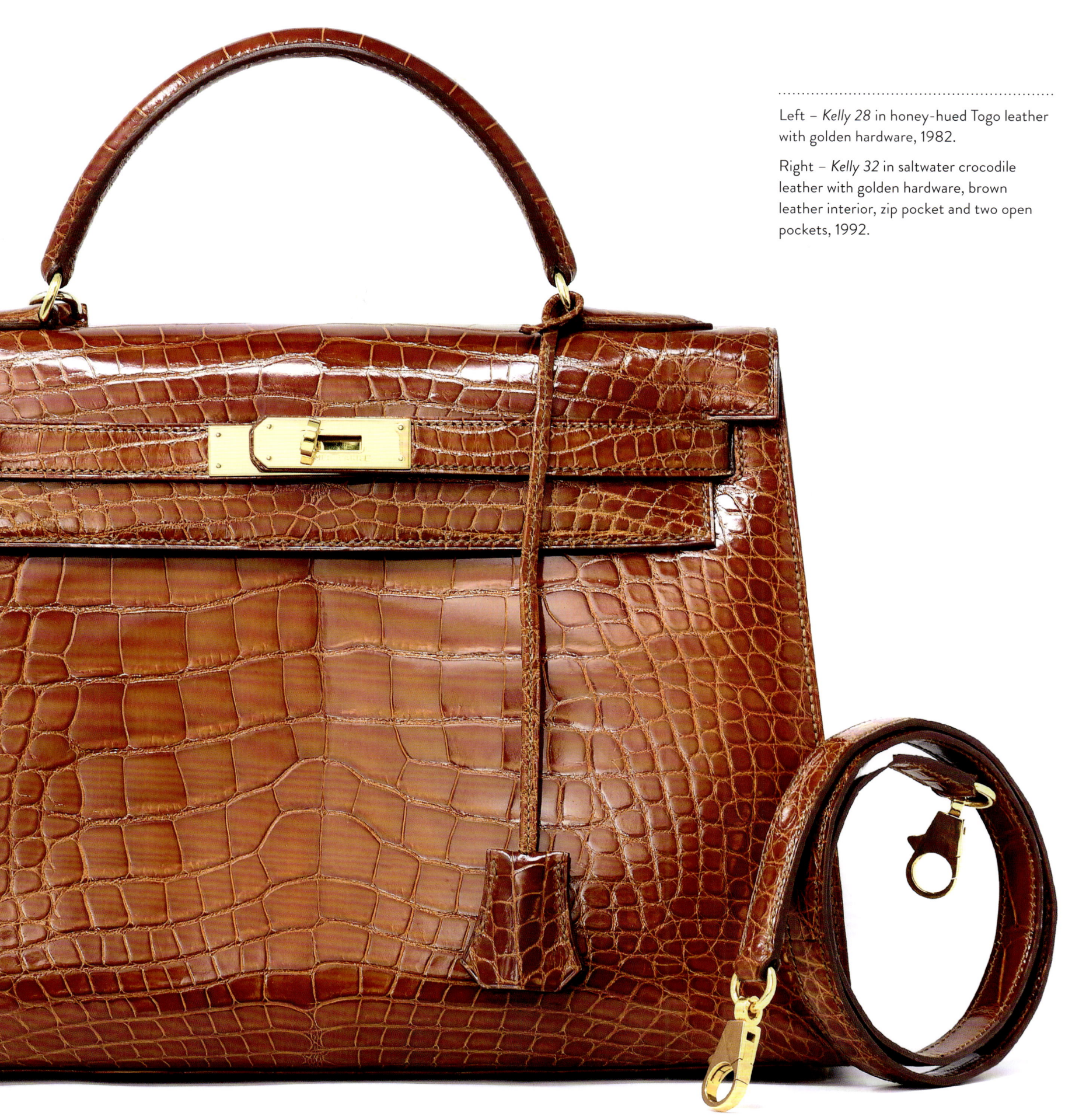

Left – *Kelly 28* in honey-hued Togo leather with golden hardware, 1982.

Right – *Kelly 32* in saltwater crocodile leather with golden hardware, brown leather interior, zip pocket and two open pockets, 1992.

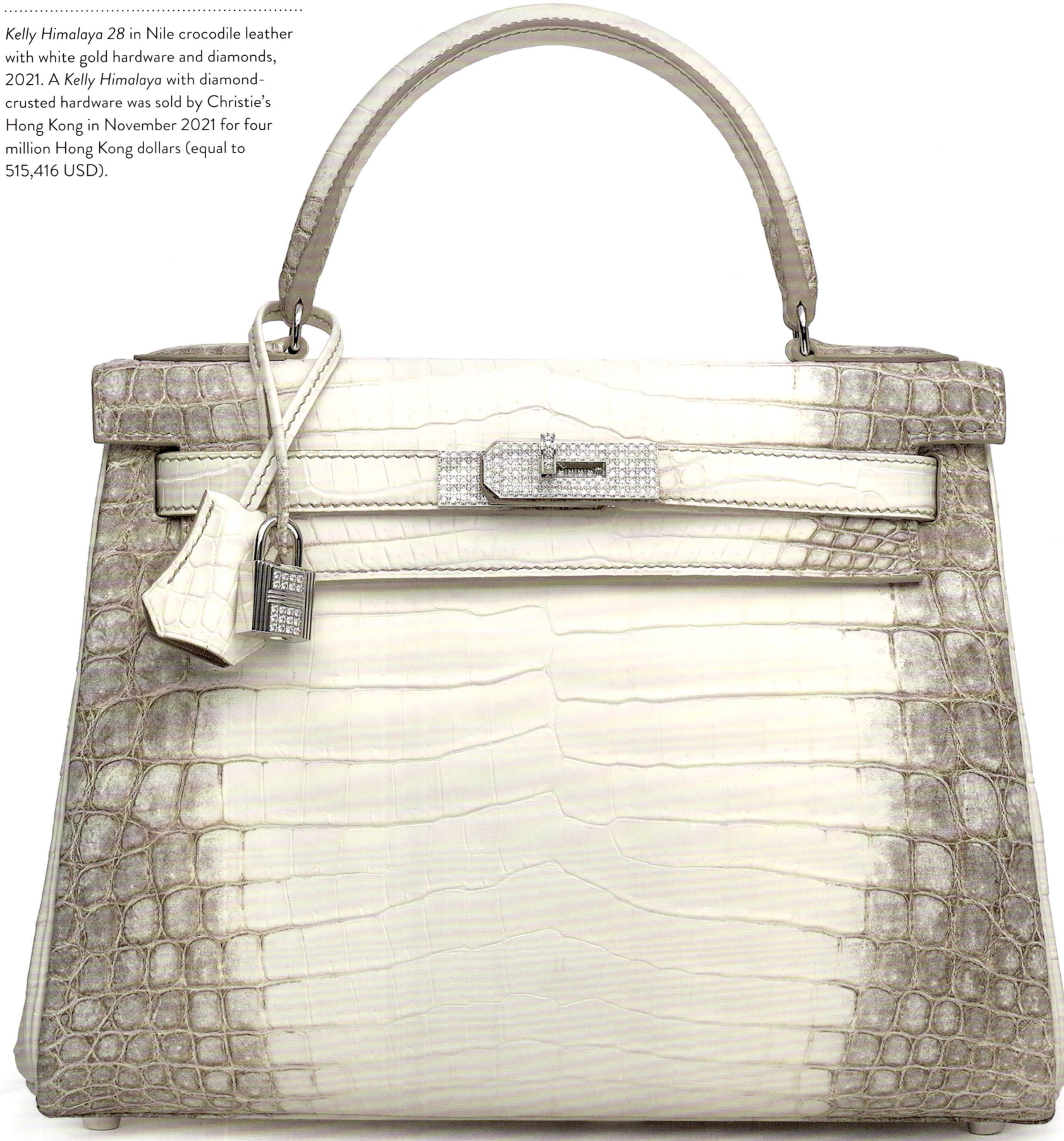

Kelly Himalaya 28 in Nile crocodile leather with white gold hardware and diamonds, 2021. A *Kelly Himalaya* with diamond-crusted hardware was sold by Christie's Hong Kong in November 2021 for four million Hong Kong dollars (equal to 515,416 USD).

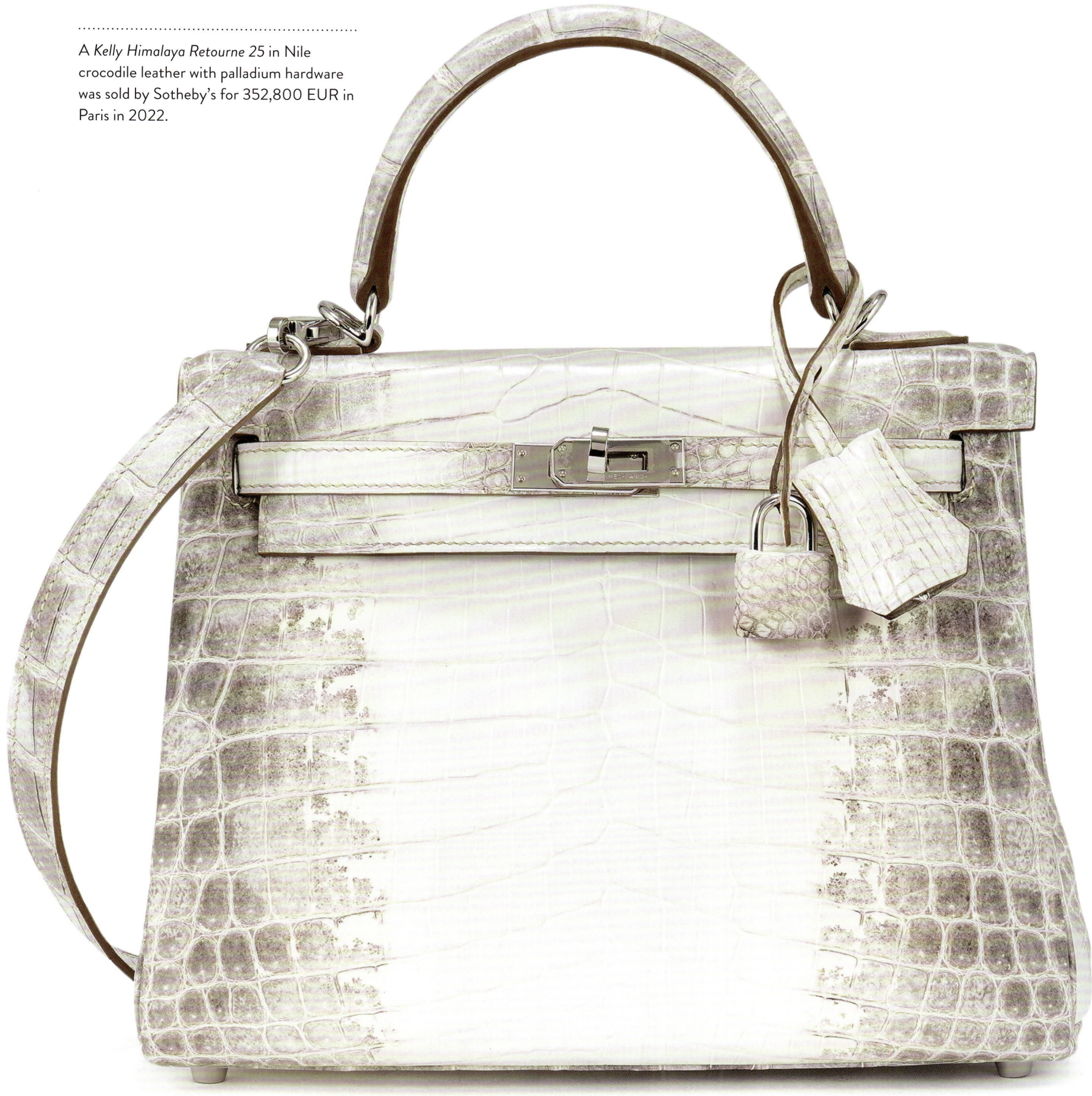

A *Kelly Himalaya Retourne 25* in Nile crocodile leather with palladium hardware was sold by Sotheby's for 352,800 EUR in Paris in 2022.

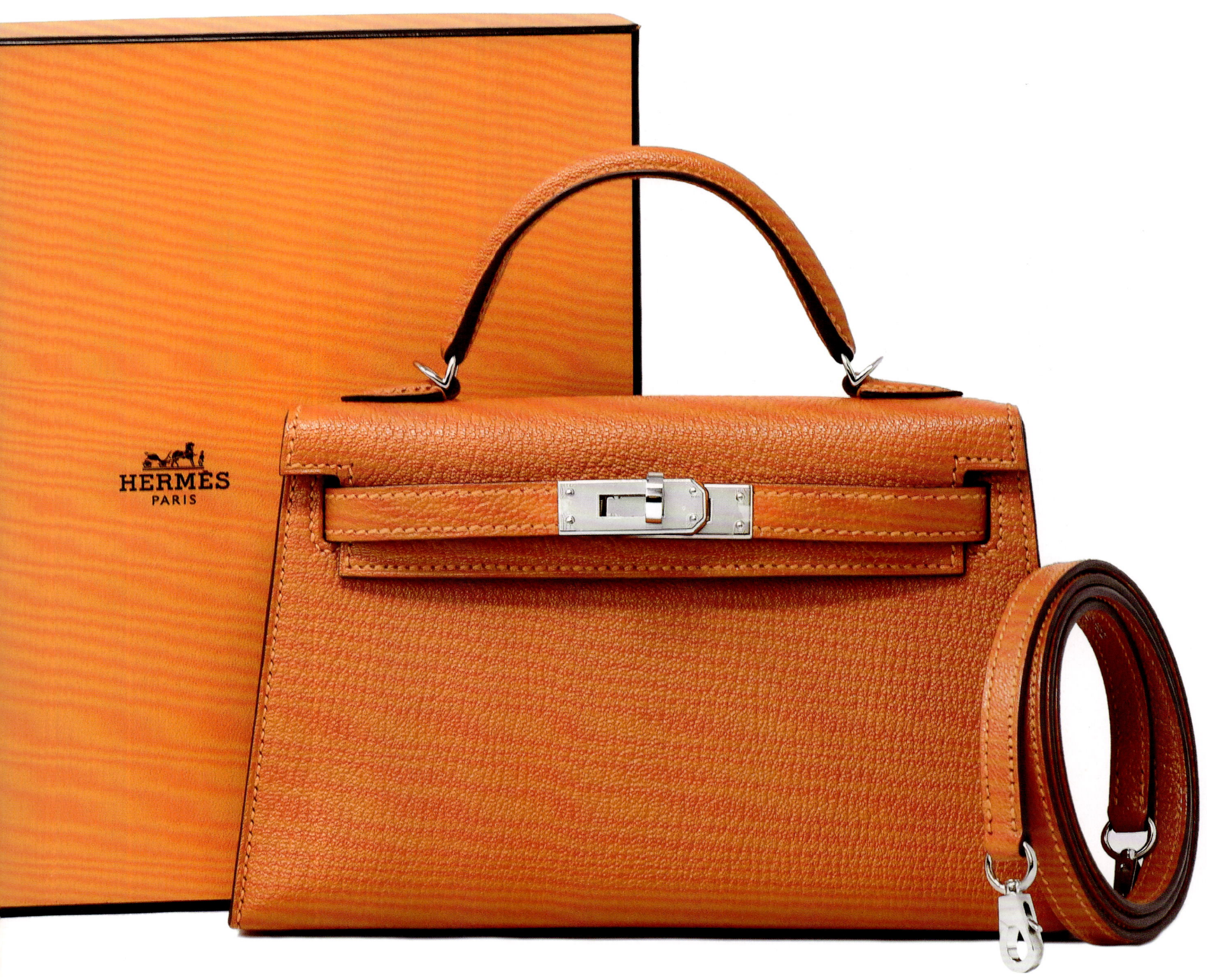

Hermès *Mini Kelly Verso* double 20, outer colour *Feu*, interior *Rose Eglantine*, with palladium hardware, 2019. The *Kelly Mini II*, an ultra-compact version of the *Kelly*, was a success among collectors and fashion lovers.

Opposite, top – *Mini Kelly Pochette 22* in Swift leather in *Blue France* with golden hardware, 2016. The *Kelly Clutch* by Hermès is a compact and refined version of the famous *Kelly* bag. It has the same elegant and distinct silhouette as the *Kelly*, but in a much smaller size.

Opposite, bottom – *Mini Kelly Pochette 22* in Epsom leather in *Rouge Casaque* with palladium hardware, 2016. The *Kelly Pochette* has a lock and clasp closure like the original *Kelly*, but it has a short top handle.

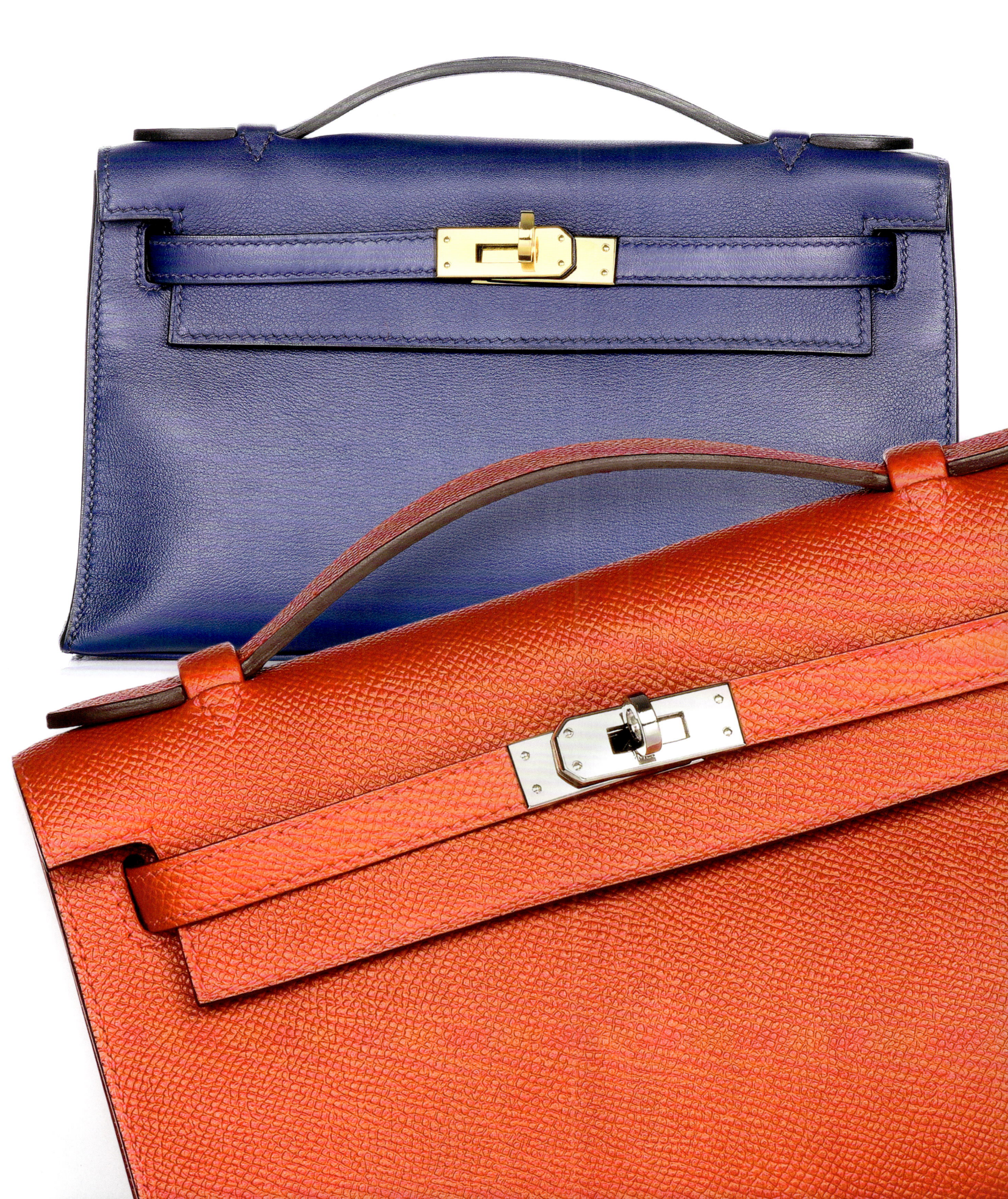

The H era

In the 1960s, bag styles (and thus their design) changed radically, to stay in line with the experimental zeitgeist. Fashion became bolder and more modern, embracing new shapes, materials and colours. Cross-body bags became very popular, suitable to the dynamic lifestyles of younger generations. Practicality was essential, and bags were upgraded with functional elements, such as multiple compartments and zip closures. This was the backdrop to the creation of the *Constance*, designed in 1967 by Catherine Chaillet and destined to become a classic Hermès style, characterised by its unmistakable H-shaped clasp. At the time, Chaillet was pregnant and she later decided to name the bag after her daughter, Constance.

Still being made today, it comes in different sizes, materials and colours. It's more than an accessory: it's also a coveted object for fashion connoisseurs and collectors. One version of this famous bag is the *1-24*, named after its 24-cm width. This measurement makes it slightly larger than other versions of the *Constance*, and it's perfect for those who need a slightly roomier bag, without sacrificing elegance and portability. The *Constance III Mini Bag* starts from the third generation of the Constance (hence the 'III'). It has a width of 18 cm while keeping the same classic silhouette with slightly rounded corners and a semi-rigid structure. The metal 'H' clasp remains the focal point of the bag – its distinct, recognisable touch.

Another quintessential style from the 1960s

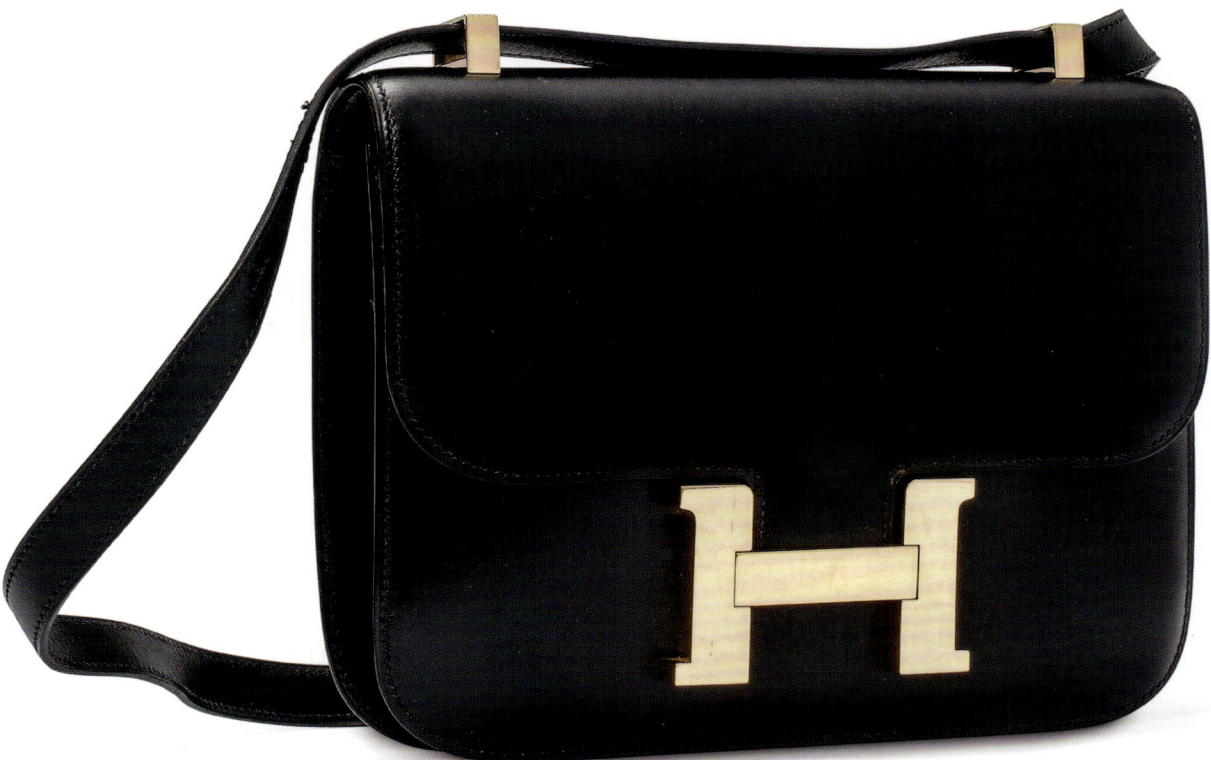

An Hermès classic, the *Constance* was born in the 1960s. Its structural and compact form, with an adjustable cross-body strap, makes it perfect for everyday use or more formal occasions.

is the *Boutonnière*, which gets its name from its menswear detailing. The word *Boutonnière* in French refers to the flowers or other decorative elements which men often wear in the button-hole of a jacket on formal occasions.

The casual *Garden Party* style, in leather and fabric or entirely in leather, was launched in 1964 and is still being produced in different sizes.

The *Drag* bag, introduced in 1965, is character-ised by its slightly trapezoid shape, which gives it an elegant silhouette. It is enriched by a dou-ble clasp, its defining characteristic. Initially de-signed to be a travel bag and introduced in this same decade, the *Plume* was inspired by a travel cutlery case from the 1920s. It is still in produc-tion. Its rectangular shape and slightly rounded corners give it a sense of simple sophistication. It's an accessory designed with enough room to hold the essentials, meticulously organised so as to ensure maximum practicality.

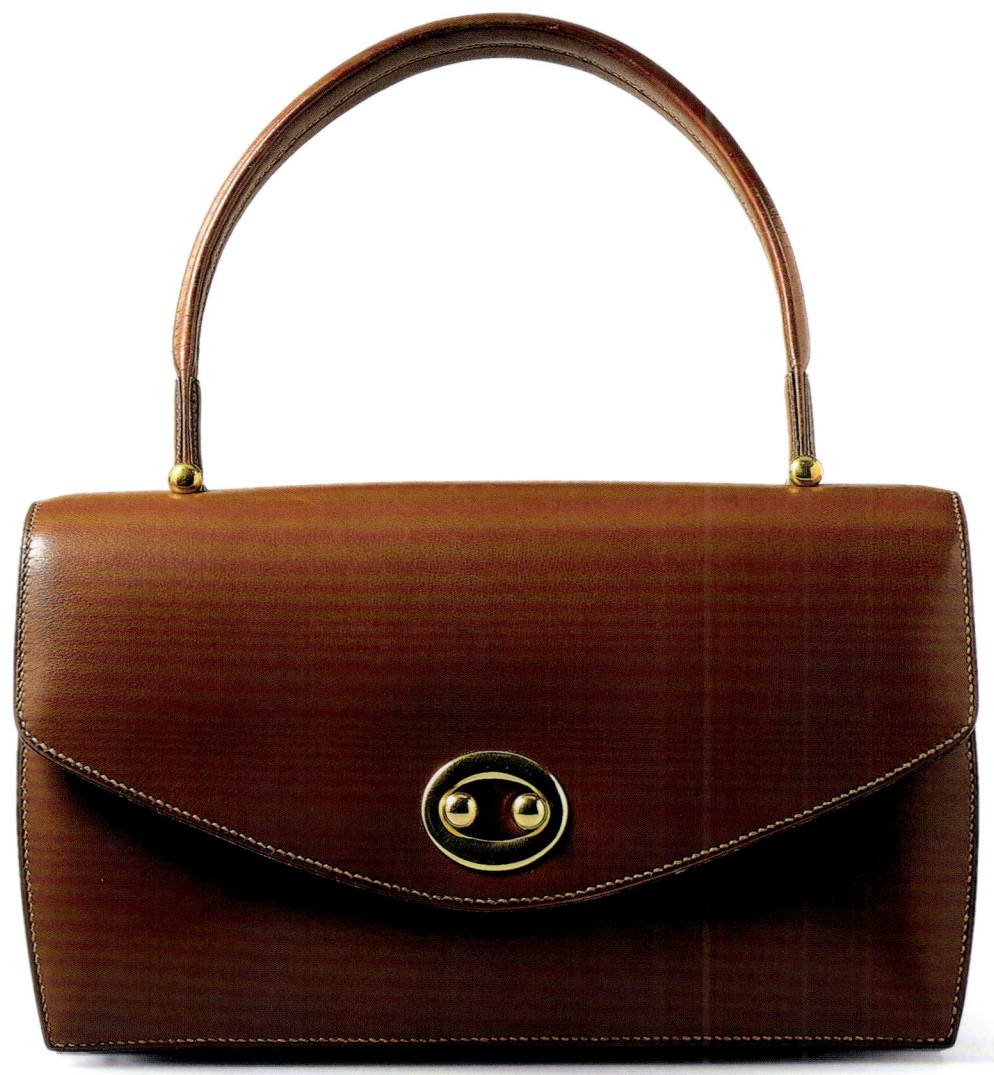

In the 1960s, the *Boutonnière* bag was produced in a limited quantity, making it an object of desire for collectors.

Garden Party 36 in Negonda canvas with *Pourpre Rose* Taurillon Clemence leather details and palladium hardware, lined in fabric and leather, 2018. This shopping bag with clean lines belongs to the more informal line by the fashion house.

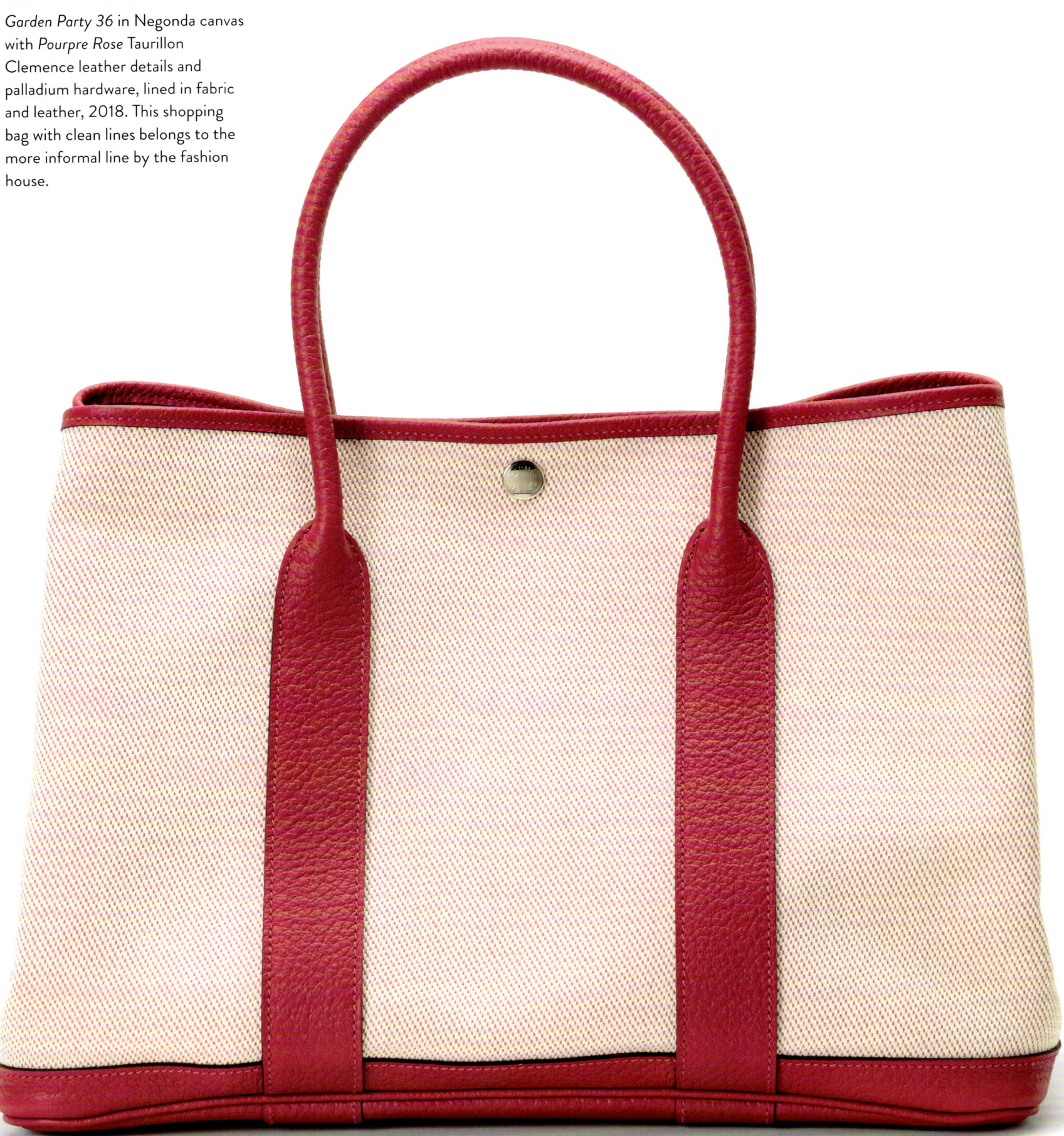

Plume in matt black saltwater crocodile leather, 2018. As lightweight as its name suggests, this bag is the ideal accessory for everyday use while remaining refined. It comes in different colours and sizes, and easily adapts to multiple needs and occasions.

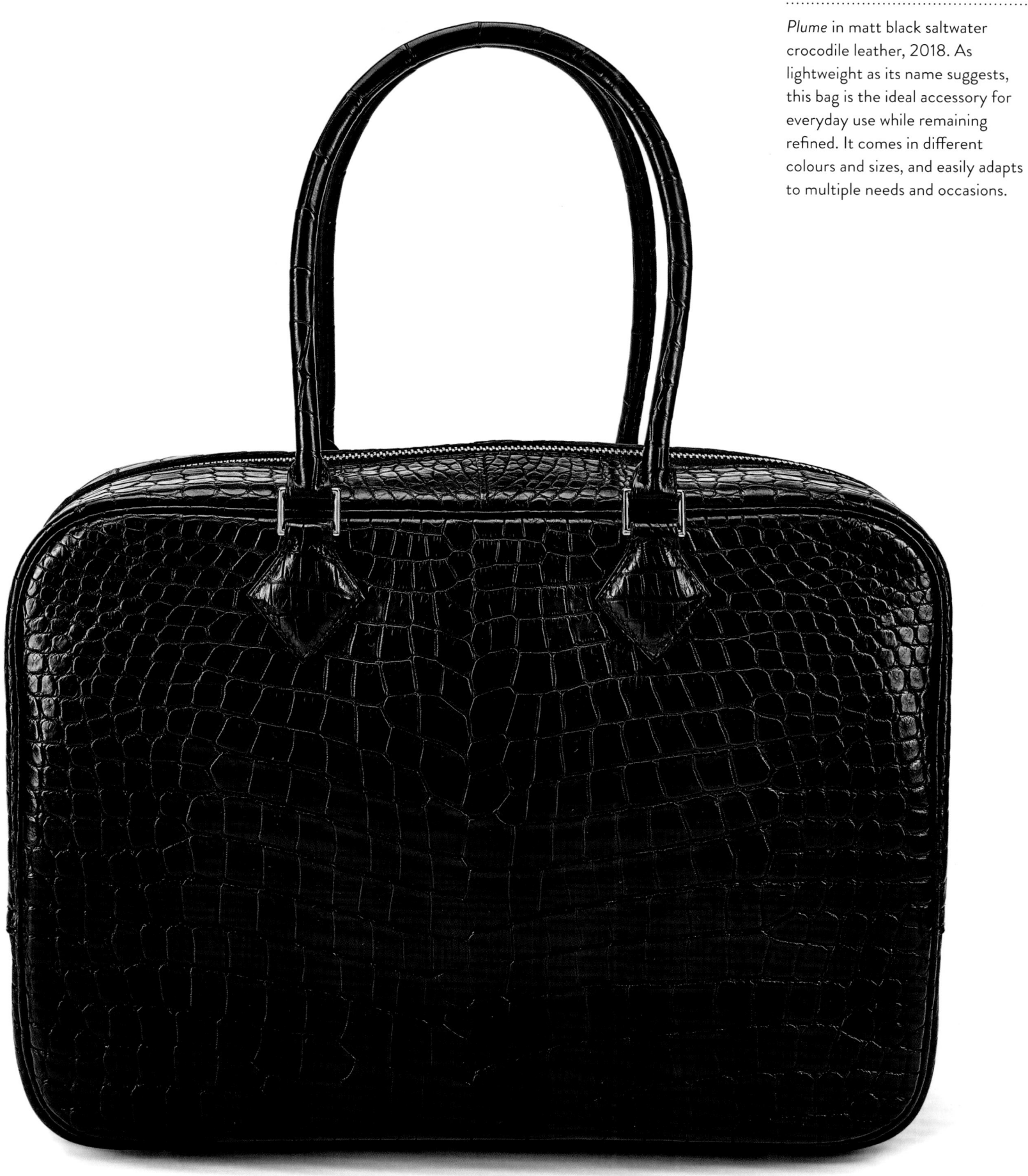

Casual styles

Hermès bags from the 1970s have a softer shape than those from the 1950s and 1960s. Hobo, bucket and cross-body styles were particularly popular, adored for their practicality and references to a dynamic and casual lifestyle. Bags adapted to the needs of a generation which prioritised practicality without sacrificing aesthetic taste.

During this decade, other styles were created which have shaped the history of Hermès, becoming classics. The *Jige* clutch (introduced in 1975) is one such example. It was created by Jean Guerrand, son-in-law of Émile Hermès, and gets its name from his initials: 'J.G.' Characterised by a flap closure with a stylised H, it's designed to be carried by hand. Made in different types of fine leather and in different sizes, the *Jige* is one of many examples of impeccable Hermès craftsmanship.

Another style which has stood the test of time

This page – *Jige* clutches in different colours. Introduced in 1975, this bag is now a classic.

Opposite page – *Évelyne* in dark brown with palladium hardware, an adjustable canvas shoulder strap, a strap closure in leather and snap fasteners. On the inside: brown suede lining and a bellows pocket in brown leather. This bag was designed to carry equestrian gear, but today it is reimagined as an object which blends function and style.

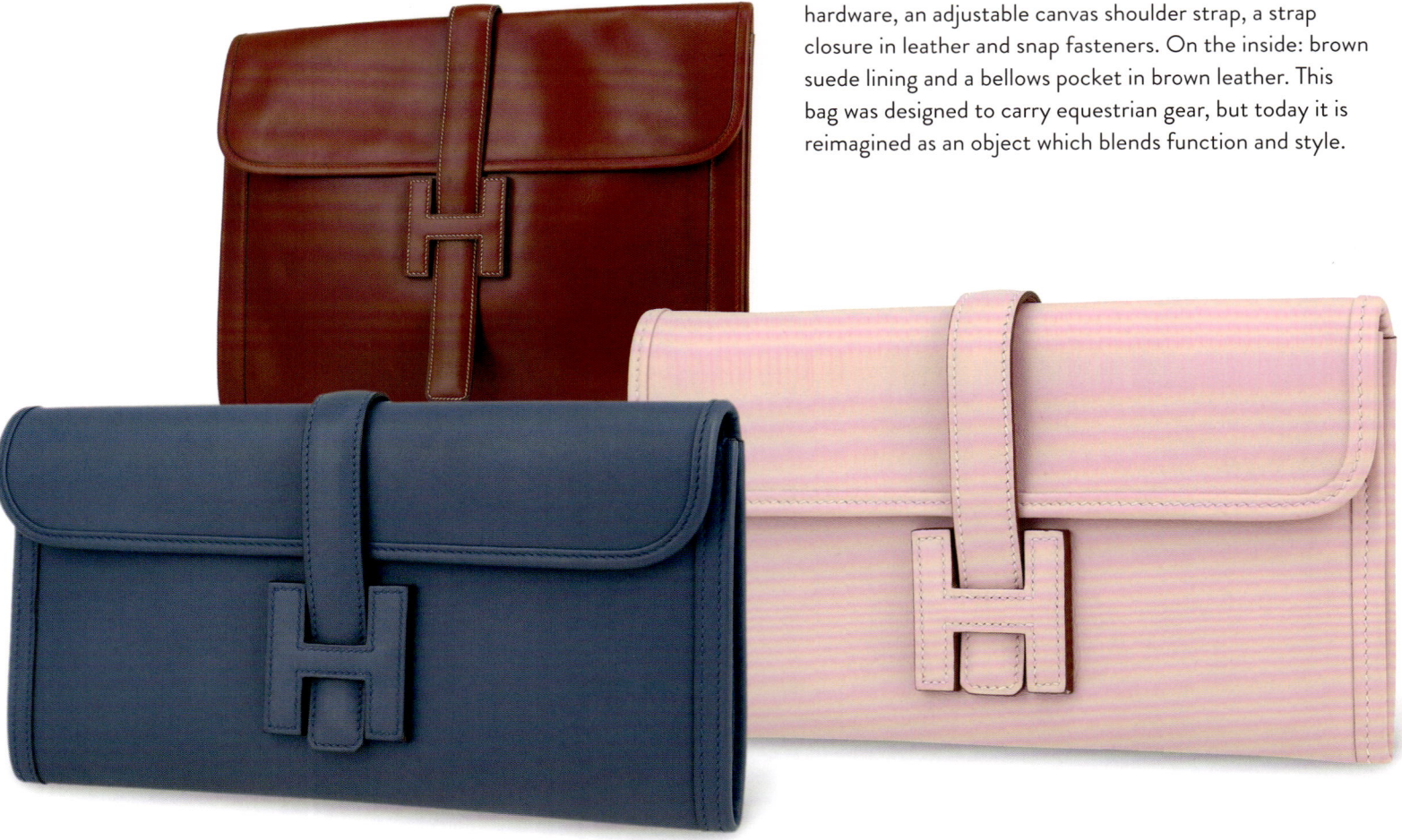

is the *Évelyne*. Designed in 1978 and dedicated to Évelyne Bertrand, the former head of the equitation department of Hermès, it was initially made to carry horse grooming equipment, with an openwork H designed to help the items inside dry quicker. While the first version of the *Évelyne* didn't have any outer pockets, those that followed certainly did.

The elements which have been carried over from Hermès' equestrian heritage to this sporty bag are the shoulder-strap/belt and the shape, which echoes the oval outline of a horseshoe.

In 2016, the *Évelyne* was made in a *Sellier* version with an embossed 'H diamant' emblem and polished raw-cut edges. It now also comes in PM and TPM versions.[9]

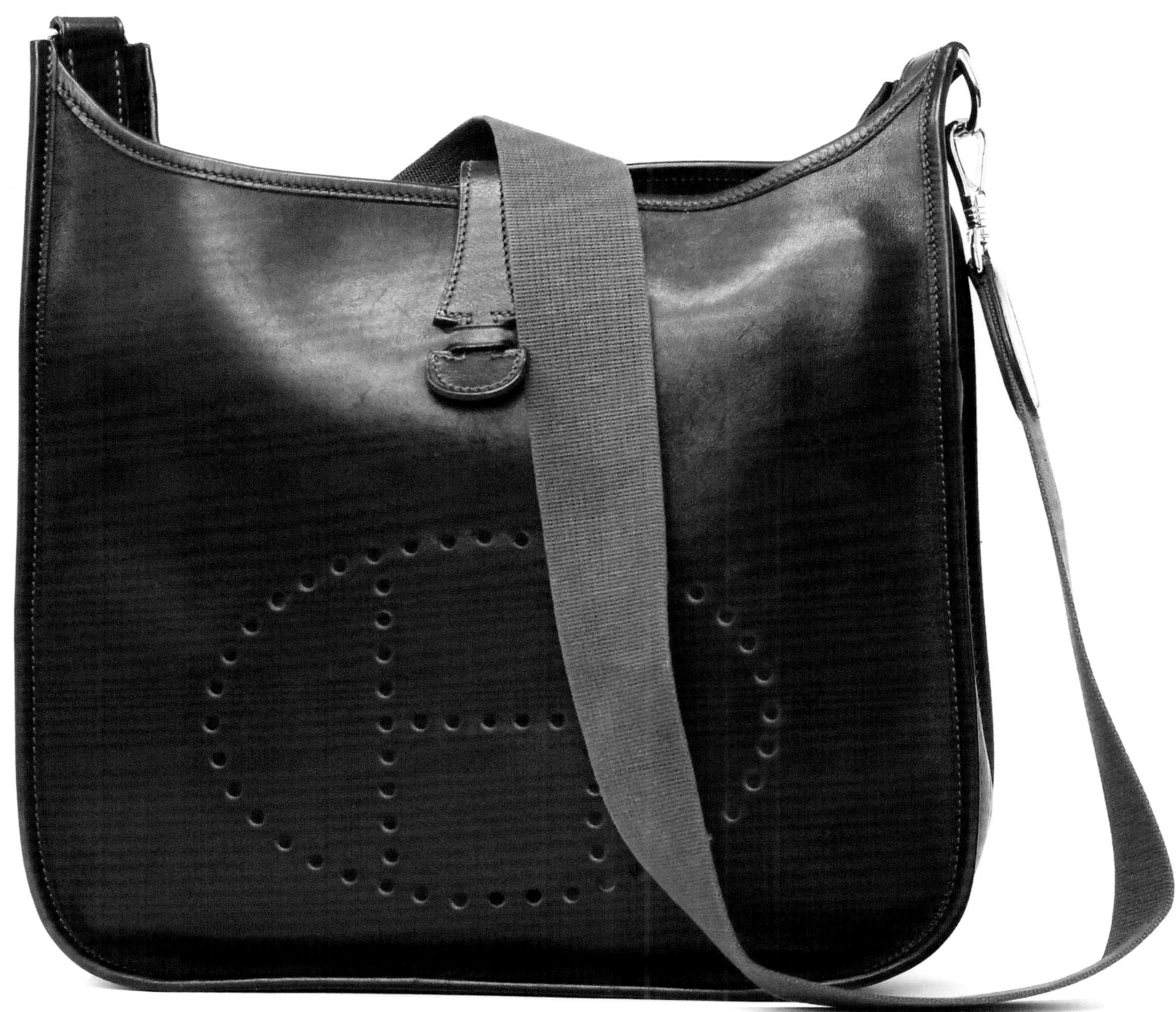

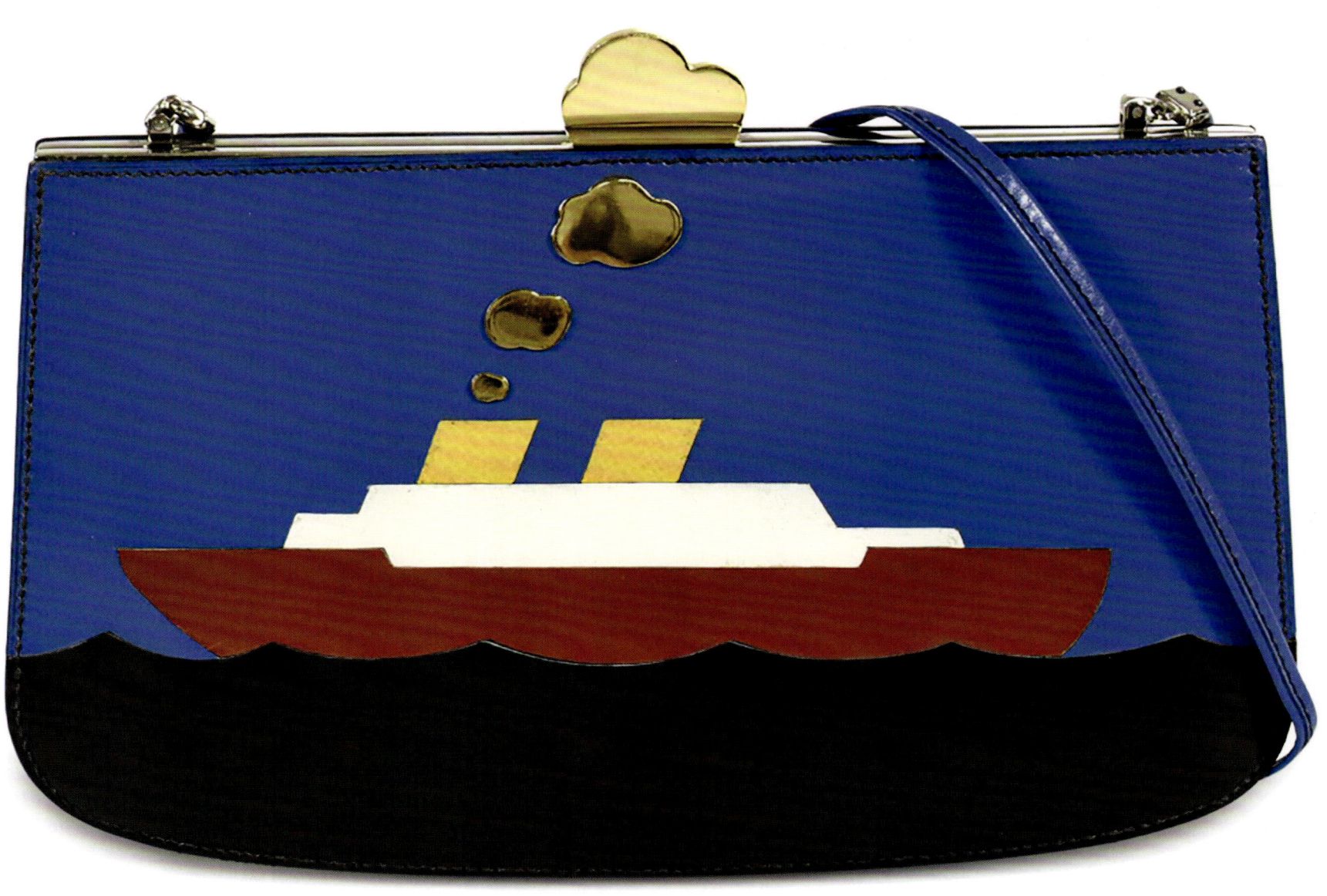

This page – *Sac à Malice* bag in *Blu Royale* leather with details in other hues. Playful and ironic, these bags were introduced in the 1980s.

Opposite page – *Sac à Malice* bag in lizard and Monsieur calf leather with palladium hardware, 2020. The bag depicts a multicolour rocket ship as it heads to a red planet which cleverly conceals a clasp.

Elegance and whimsy

The day bags from the 1980s were often large and structured, designed to be not just practical accessories, but also statement pieces. The most quintessential bag from this period is the tote: large and capacious, it was ideal for career women who needed an elegant yet functional accessory to carry files, papers, make-up and personal items. Shoulder and cross-body bags, with robust shoulder straps that were often adjustable, were a popular choice, especially for informal occasions. Bag design often focused on geometric shapes, while fine materials added a touch of luxury.

Structured clutches, used for glamorous evenings or elite events, became a must-have. Crafted in metal and glossy leather with jewel details, they were often worn with shimmering looks, in line with the exuberant style of the decade.

The *Sac à Malice* introduced by Hermès in the 1980s conveyed a playful, whimsical spirit. Its classic shape echoes that of the evening bags from the 1920s, inspired by the avant-garde art movements of the era. But what made these bags special was the decoration on the front panel, a three-dimensional element which changed depending on the style.

These decorations often depicted fun scenes or symbolic motifs, such as a bouquet of flowers, a shining sun or a playful ode to the animal kingdom, making each bag unique. The name, *Sac à malice*, means 'bag of tricks' in French, a perfect summary of the essence of this bag. On the inside, the bag is spacious and well organised, designed to easily hold essential items. Despite its rather eccentric design, it's an extremely functional bag which demonstrates that art and practicality can harmoniously coexist.

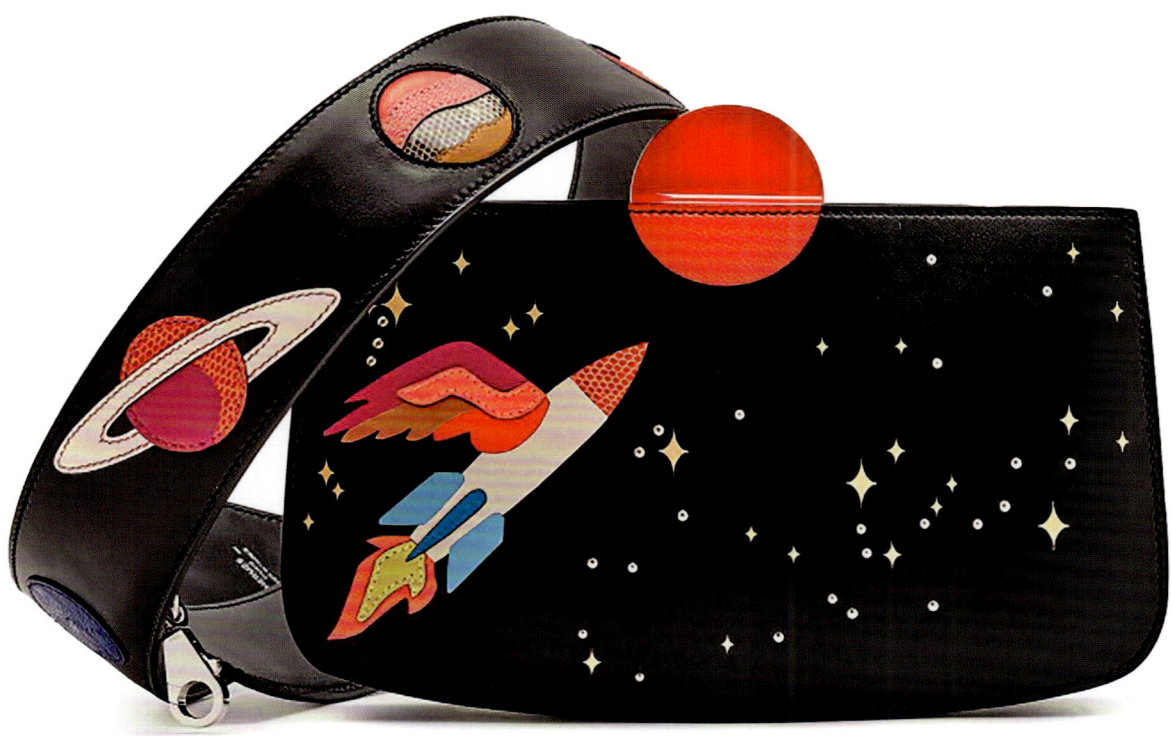

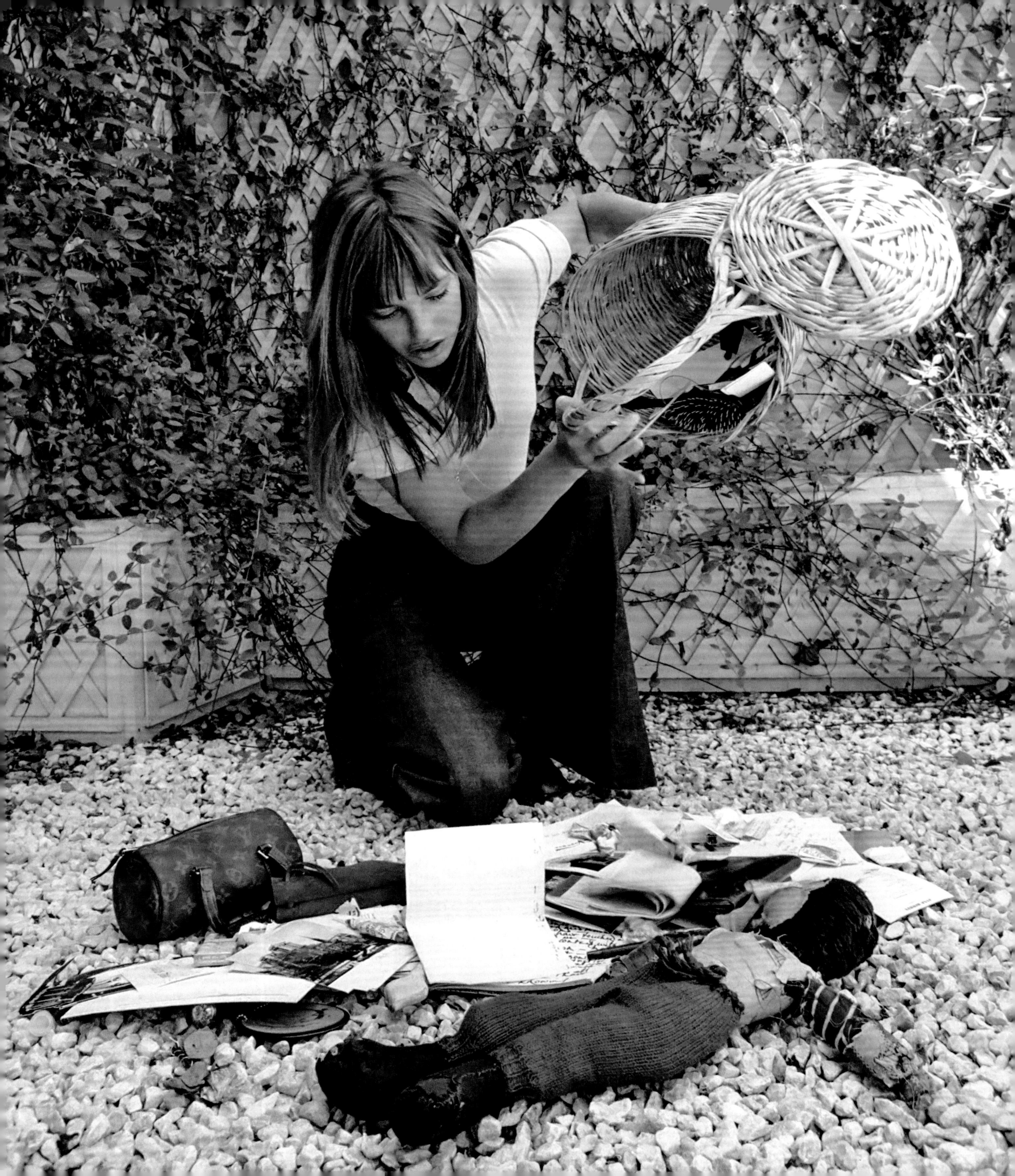

The Timeless Birkin

First sold in 1984, the *Birkin* was the result of a chance meeting between the British-French actress and singer Jane Birkin and Jean-Louis Dumas, who was then the Creative Director of Hermès, while on a Paris–London flight. The artist complained she was unable to find a practical and roomy yet also elegant bag, so Dumas designed one for her, with a supple and spacious rectangular body, burnished flap and *sellier* stitching.

The classic elements of a *Birkin* are: two handles, a top flap with cut-outs, two buckle straps, a *touret* clasp, a lock and four feet on the base to ensure stability.

Each bag requires approximately 25 hours of work to create, and all *Birkin* bags are made exclusively by the hands of highly trained artisans. One craftsman is responsible for the entire process from start to finish, and each one identifies their work with a unique ID made up of numbers, letters and symbols. To produce the *Birkin*, Hermes uses a rare type of leather with unique properties: *Vache Naturelle*, either smooth or *grainé*, which has an exceptionally clear finish that takes on a beautiful patina over time.

It has been produced in many different versions, in addition to the *Sellier*, which is characterised by topstitching on the outer edges for a more rigid and defined structure, and the *Retourne*, with seams concealed on the inside for a softer, more casual look. The *Birkin* bag now comes in four sizes, with widths of 25 cm, 30 cm, 35 cm and 40 cm. To be used as a travel bag, there's a 50 cm format also.

The *Birkin* is famous for its rarity: the waiting lists are long, and purchases are reserved for the lucky few. Its value grows over time, transforming it into an investment piece.

Opposite page – British-French singer and actress Jane Birkin often used wicker baskets as large bags before Hermès made her namesake bag.

This page – *Birkin* bag in brown leather with golden hardware, 2004.

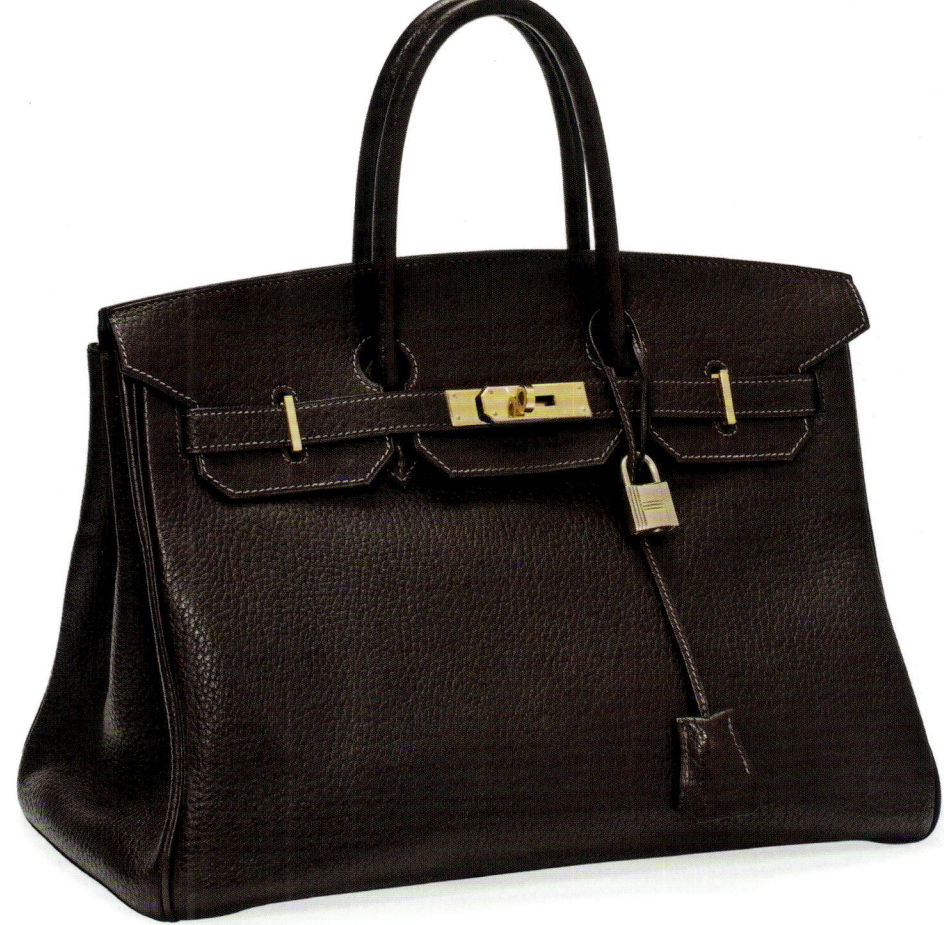

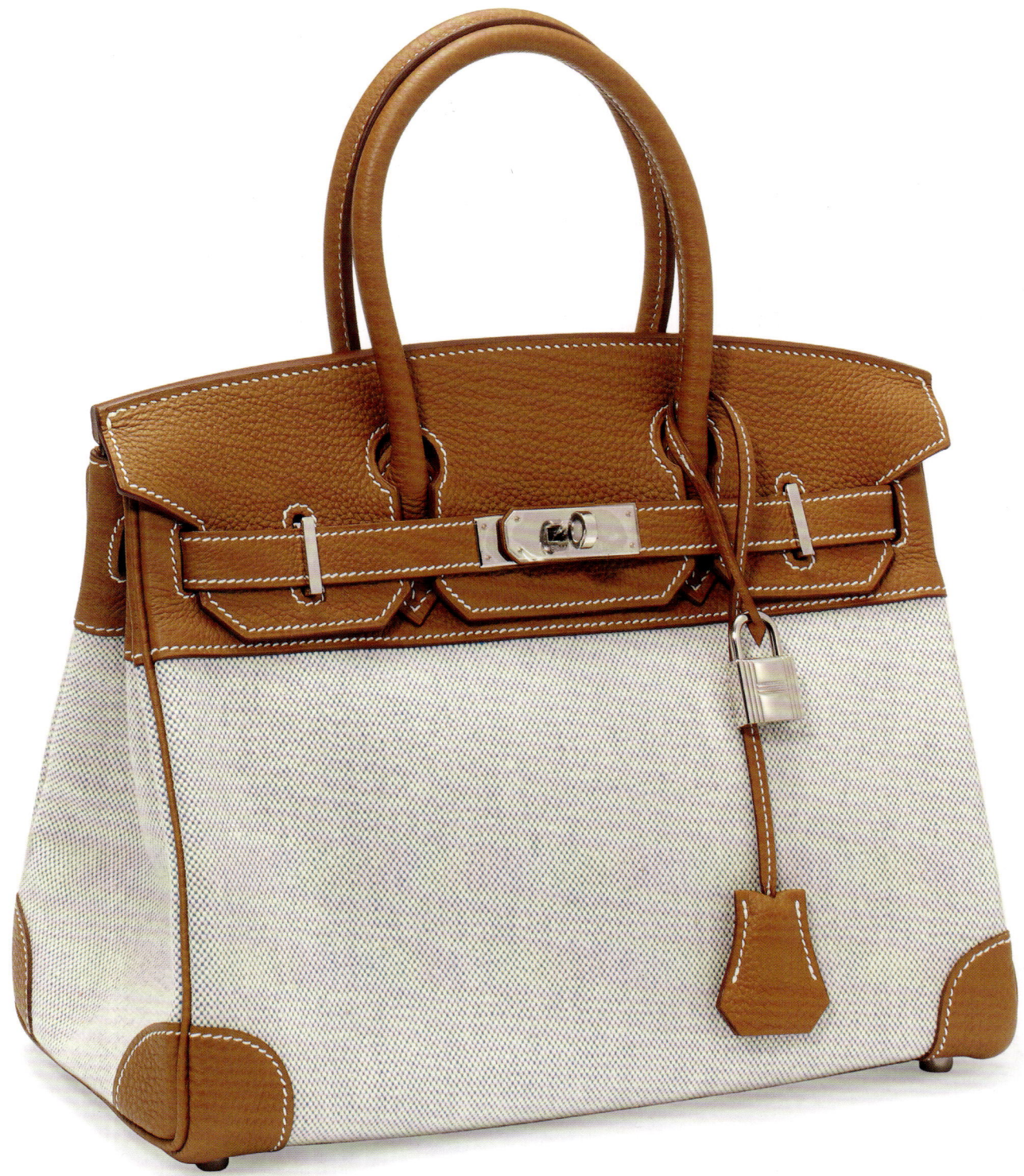

This page – *Birkin* bag in H canvas, golden Barenia leather and palladium, 2009.

Opposite – 'It starts with a dream' advert for the *Birkin* bag, 2019.

Following pages – The famous *Birkin* bag by Hermès has a belted strap and metal lock with a set of keys.

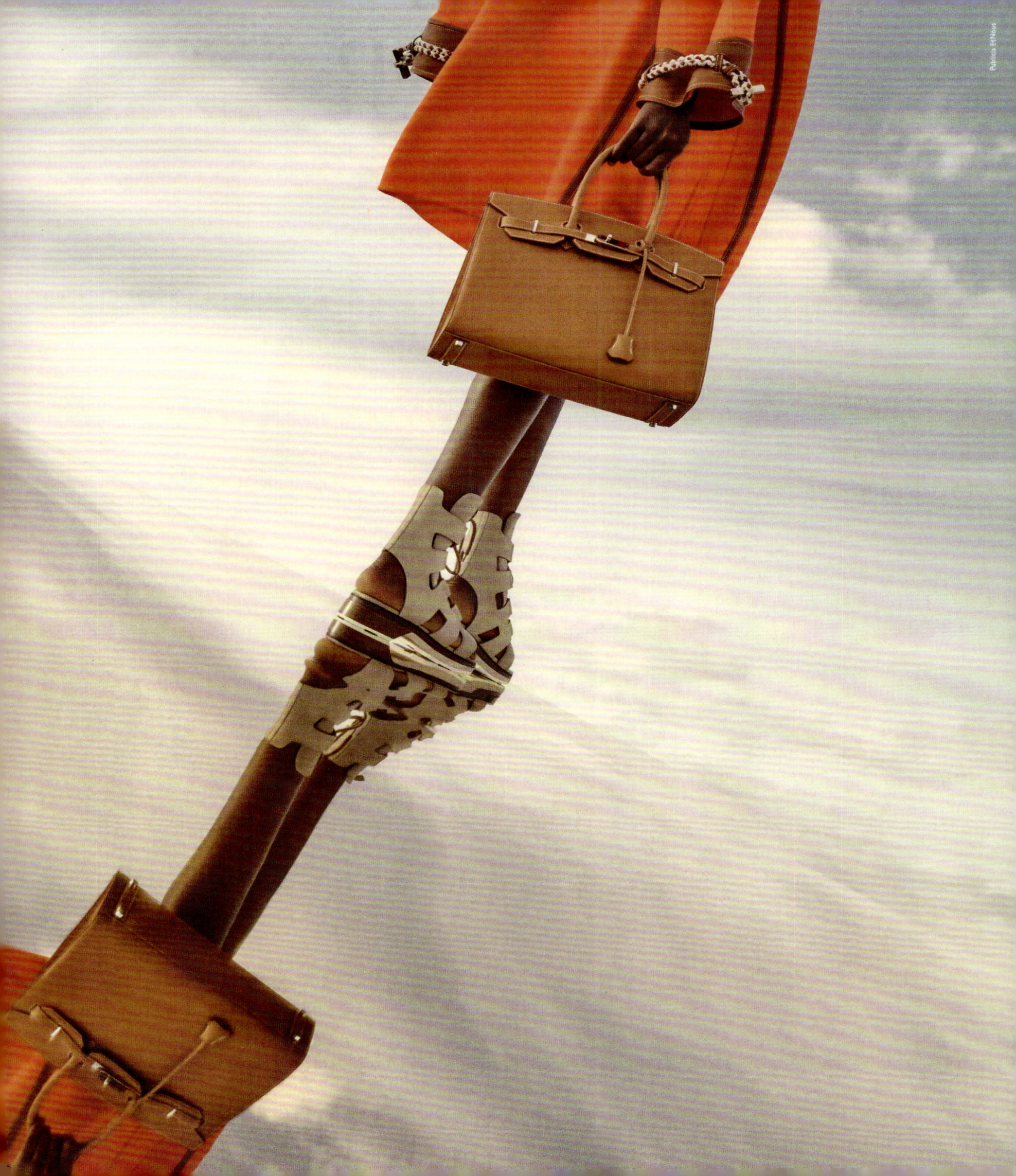

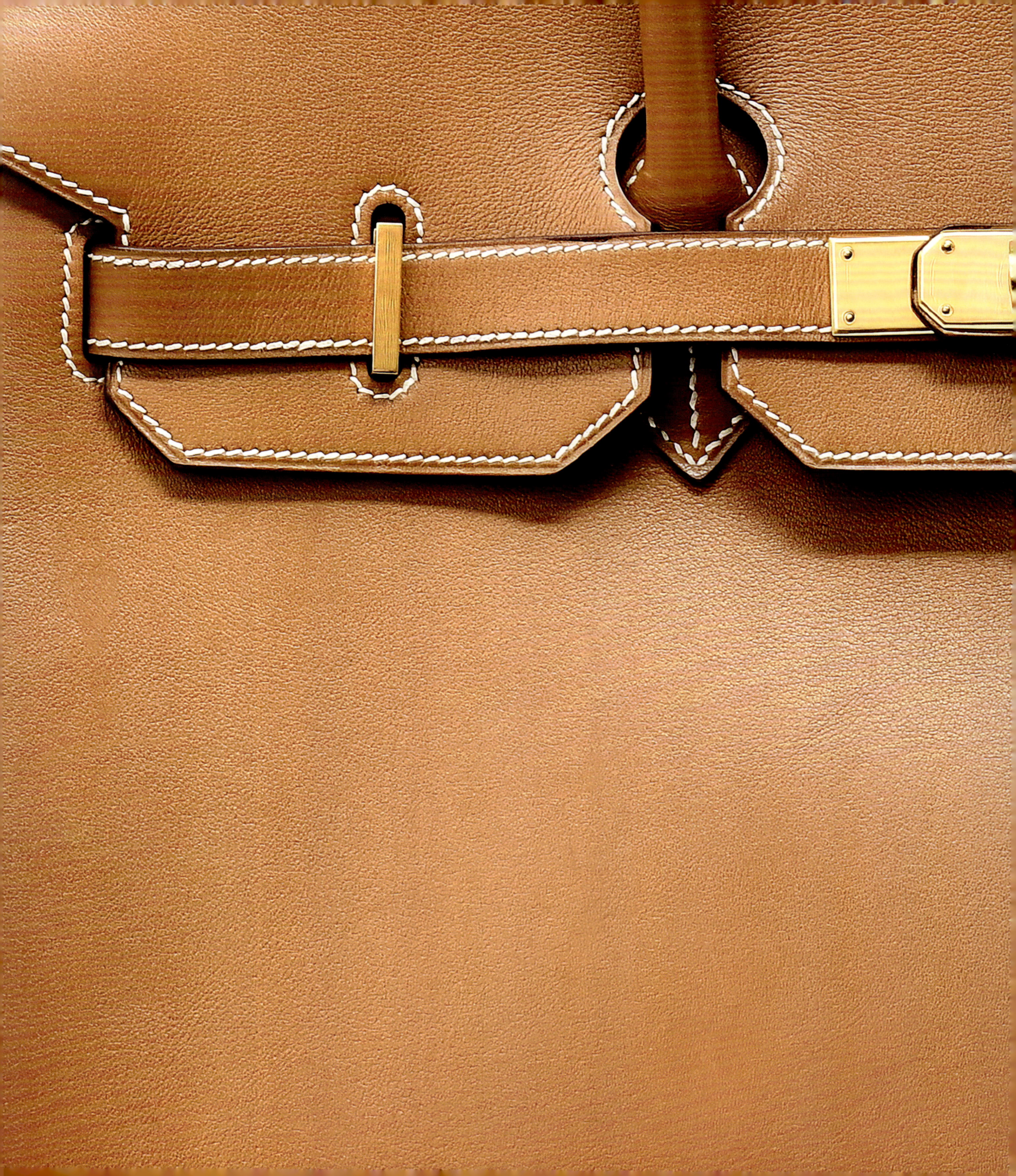

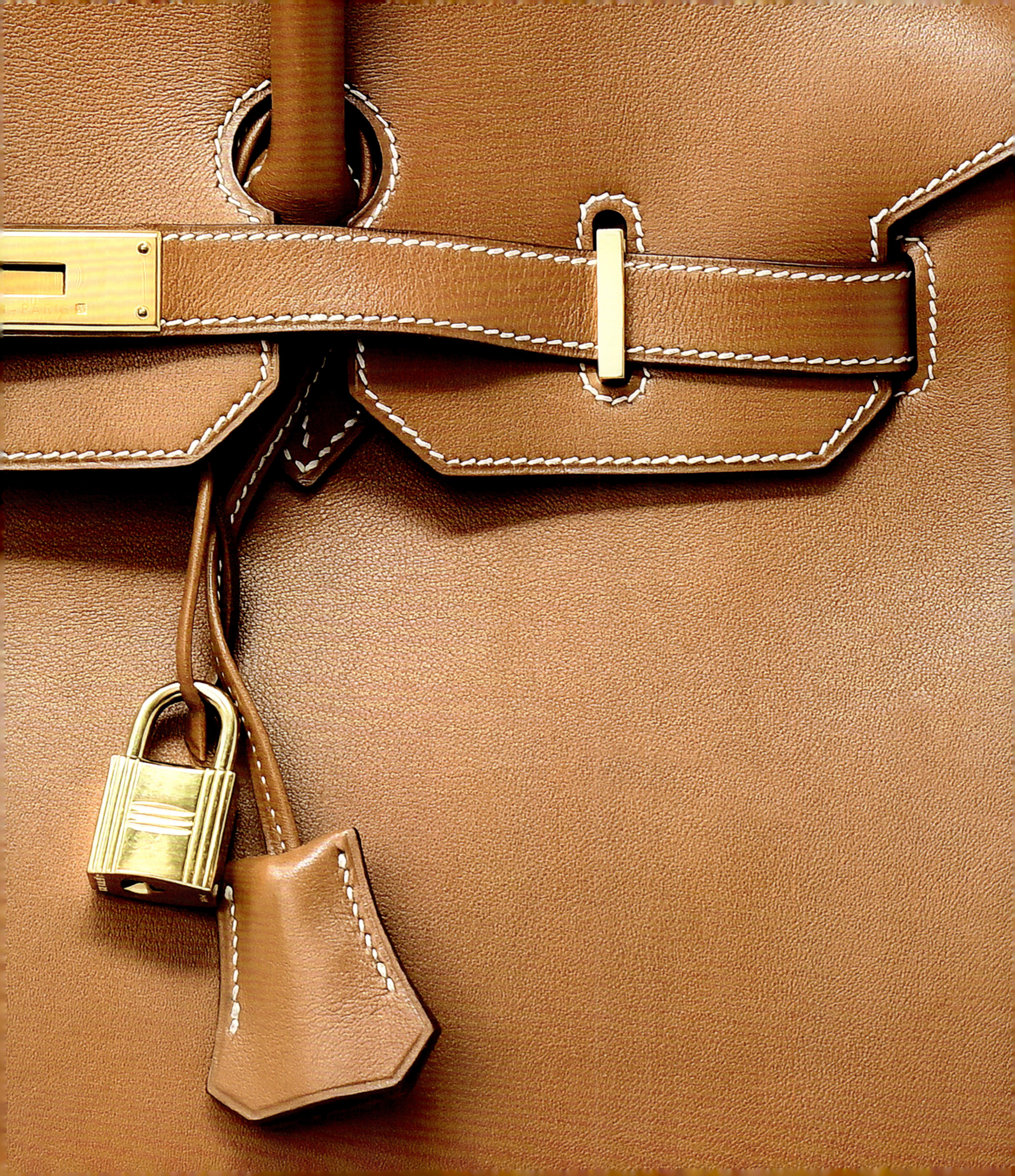

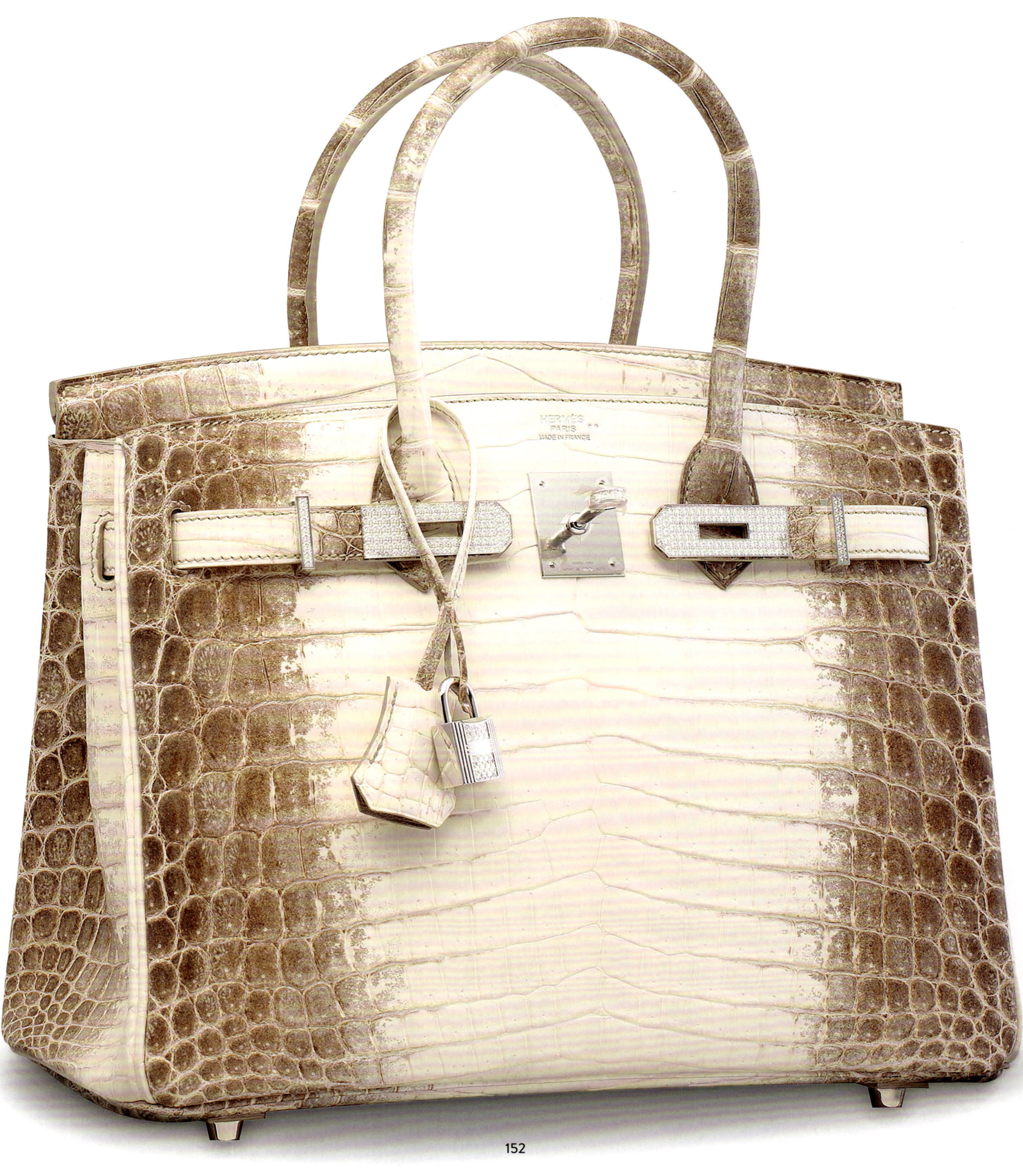

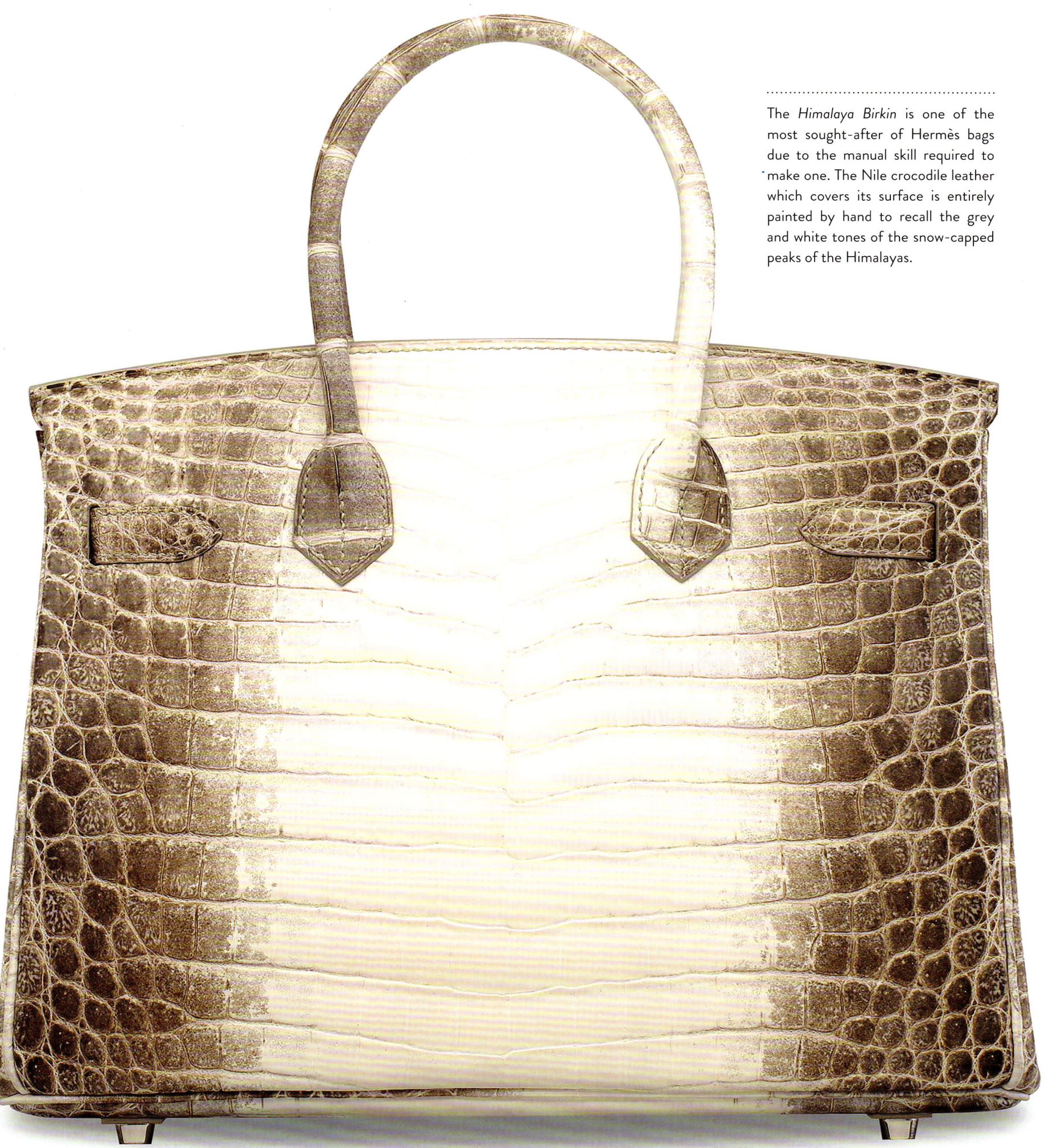

The *Himalaya Birkin* is one of the most sought-after of Hermès bags due to the manual skill required to make one. The Nile crocodile leather which covers its surface is entirely painted by hand to recall the grey and white tones of the snow-capped peaks of the Himalayas.

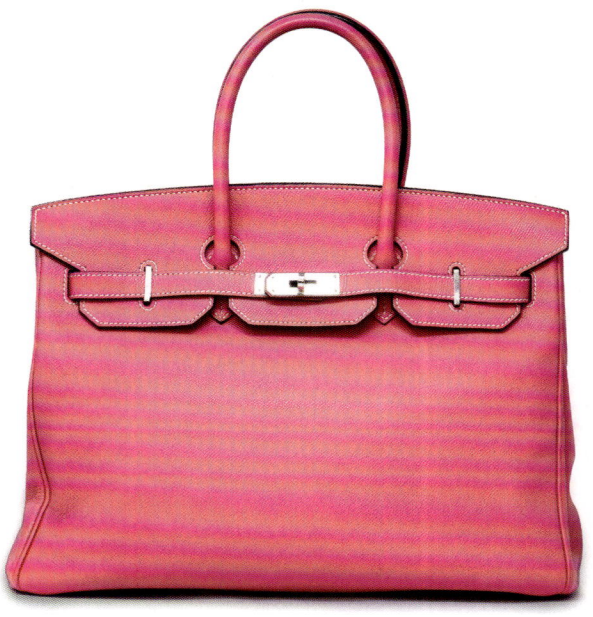

Birkin 35 in *Rose Tyrien* Epsom leather with palladium hardware.

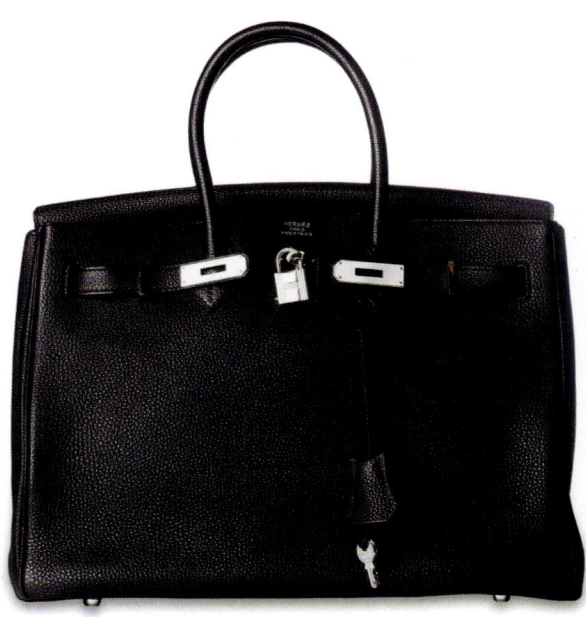

Birkin 35 in black leather.

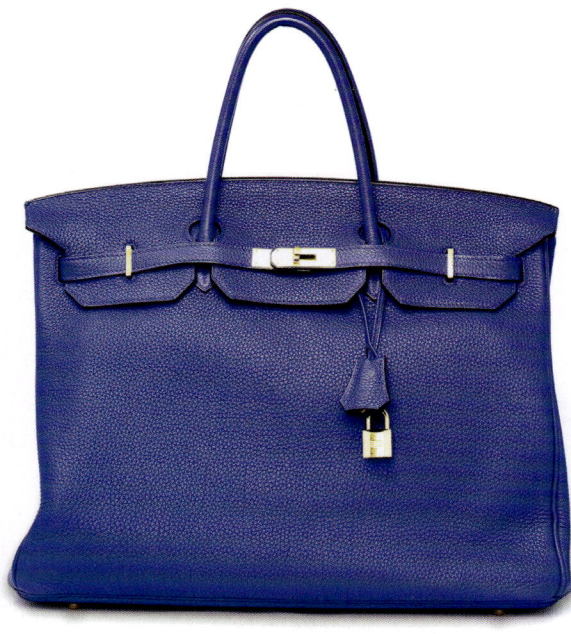

Birkin 40, in *Bleu Électrique* Togo leather with golden hardware.

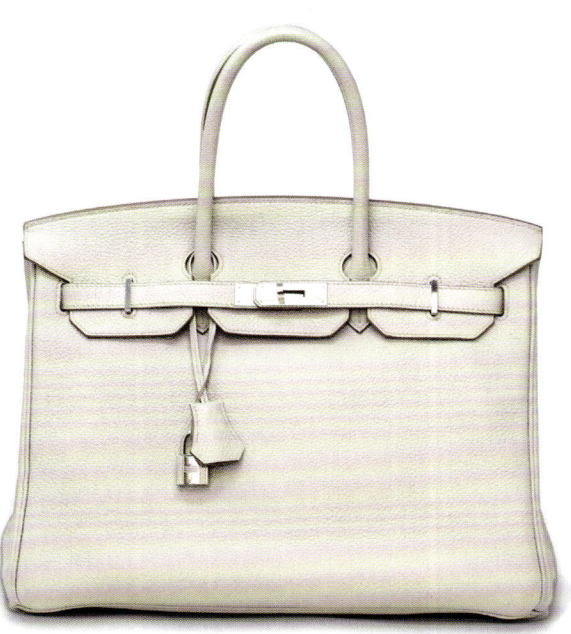

Birkin 35 in *Gris Perle* Togo leather and palladium details.

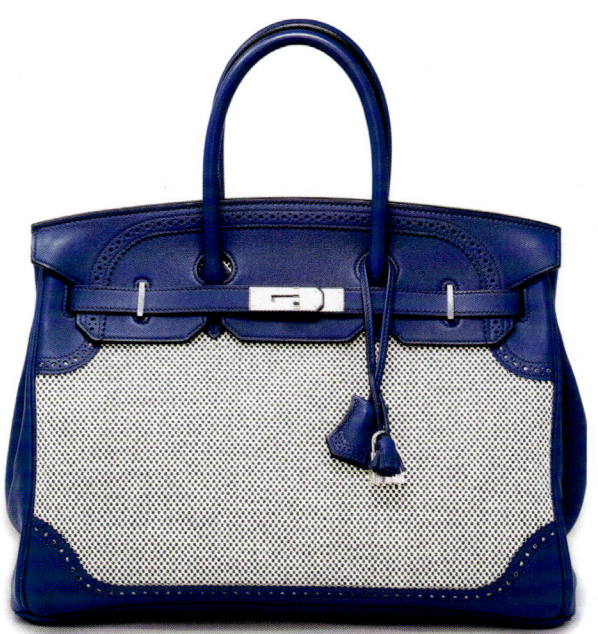

Birkin Phillies 35, Limited Edition, *Bleu Saphir* Swift leather and natural canvas with palladium hardware.

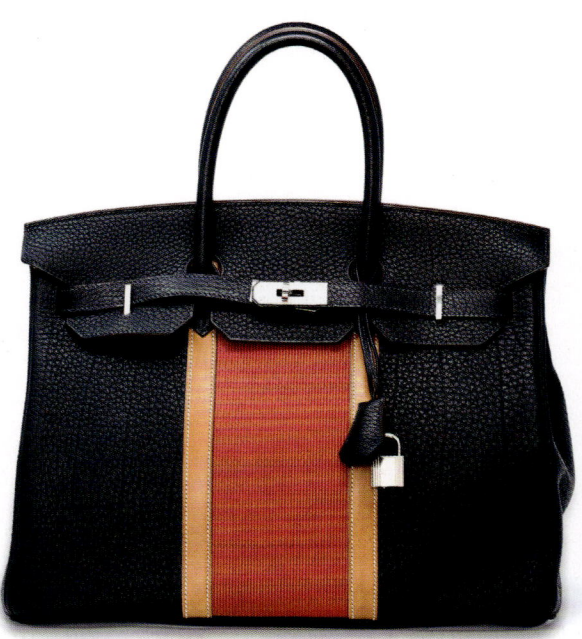

Birkin 35, Limited Edition, in indigo Ford leather with a strip in natural Barenia leather and *Rouge Casaque* Ottoman de Cren, with palladium details.

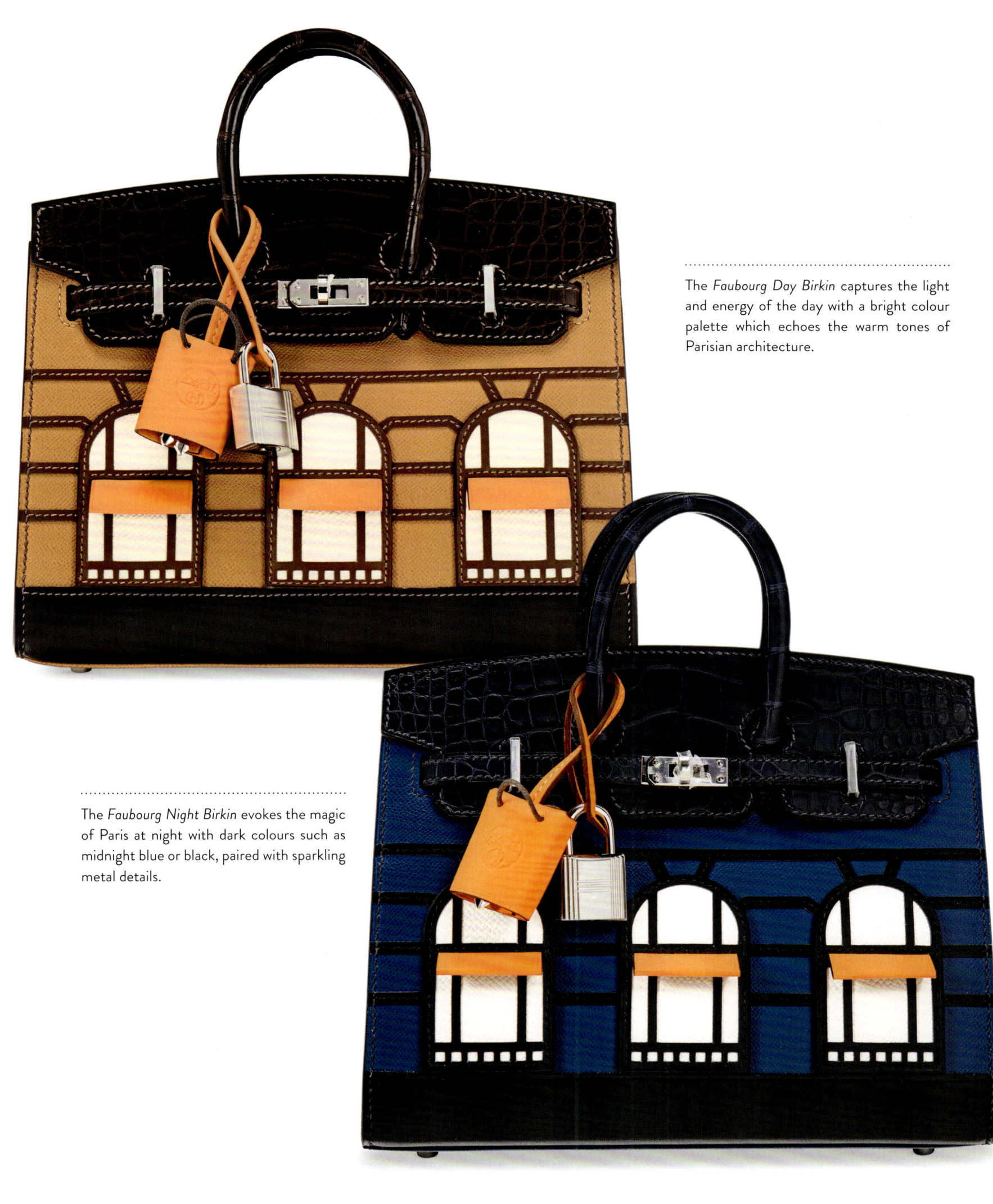

The *Faubourg Day Birkin* captures the light and energy of the day with a bright colour palette which echoes the warm tones of Parisian architecture.

The *Faubourg Night Birkin* evokes the magic of Paris at night with dark colours such as midnight blue or black, paired with sparkling metal details.

Hermès *Christine Envelope* in hammered leather, closed with a triangular flap and an Hermès saddle nail head in palladium, lined in leather with a bellows pouch and a hidden compartment. The bag is large enough to hold all everyday essentials, while remaining elegant and relatively compact.

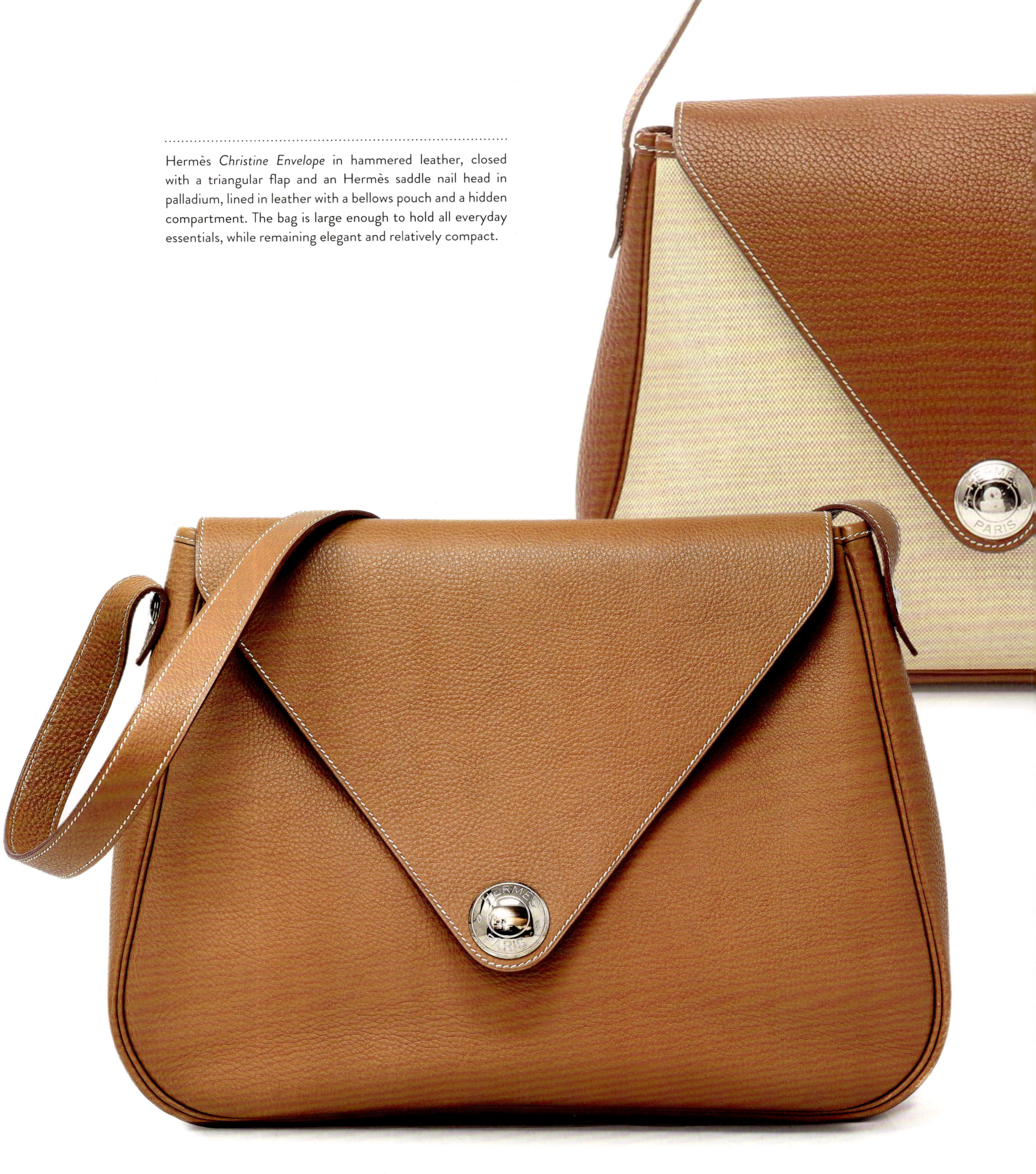

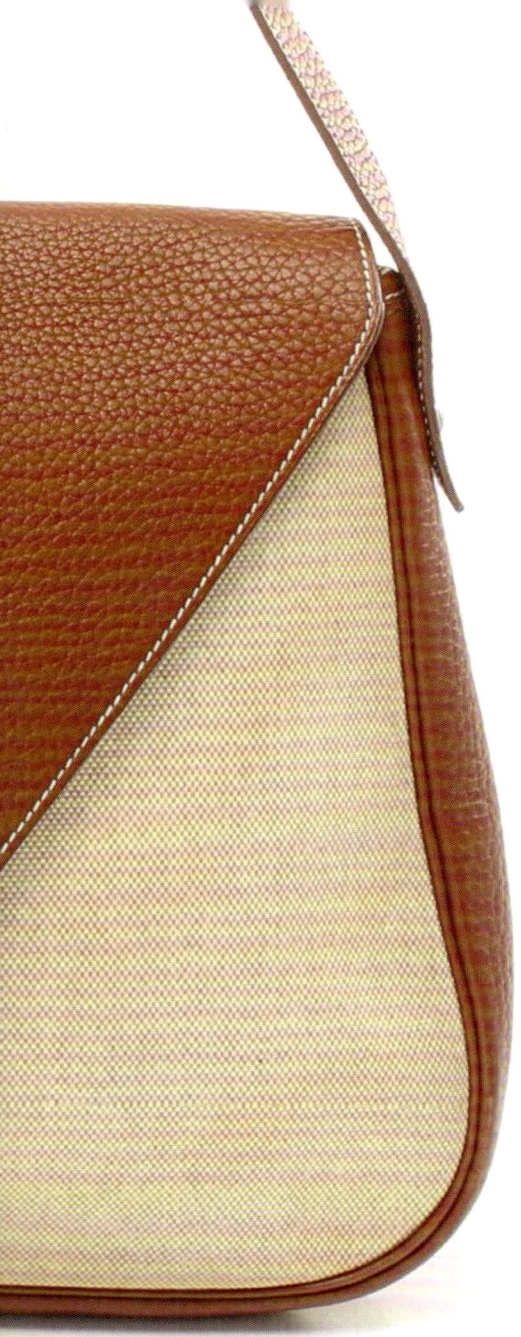

Minimalist luxury

In the 1990s, women's bags underwent a style revolution, reflecting the social and cultural changes of the era. This decade saw a mix of minimalism, experimentation and a return to luxury, which influenced the collections of the world's leading brands.

The emergence of pop culture and stars from TV programmes such as *Sex and the City* have influenced bag design. A bag was no longer just an accessory; it became a symbol of identity and aspiration. *'It's not a bag. It's a Birkin,'* a shop assistant once pretentiously said to Samantha Jones in an episode of *SATC*, almost suggesting that this bag is an object in a class of its own, something to be desired and worth waiting a long time to obtain.

During this era, Hermès explored more casual and practical designs, introducing the pared-back look of the *Christine*: its silhouette echoes that of an envelope, with an inverted triangle flap which firmly closes the main compartment. Its adjustable strap allows it to be worn on one shoulder or crossbody, making it an accessory which can adapt to different contexts.

Another bag from the 1990s, the *Herbag*, echoed some of the aesthetic elements of the *Kelly*, such as the trapezoid shape and the strap closure. However, the *Herbag* stands out for its more casual and versatile structure, crafted in a combination of canvas and leather for lightness and practicality.

The *Vespa* is another bag which was created in the mid 1990s. It stands out for its essential and practical design, conceived of as a sophisticated and versatile accessory for everyday use. Constructed in high-quality leather, it has a supple handle yet is resistant to wear, to ensure durability over time. Its clean lines are enriched by essential yet sophisticated details, such as the *chaîne d'ancre* closure.

The *Victoria* bag from 1997 combined functionality and an elegant design. Rectangular in shape, it conveys a sense of order and practicality while being very spacious. The double handles in leather offer hand or arm portability.

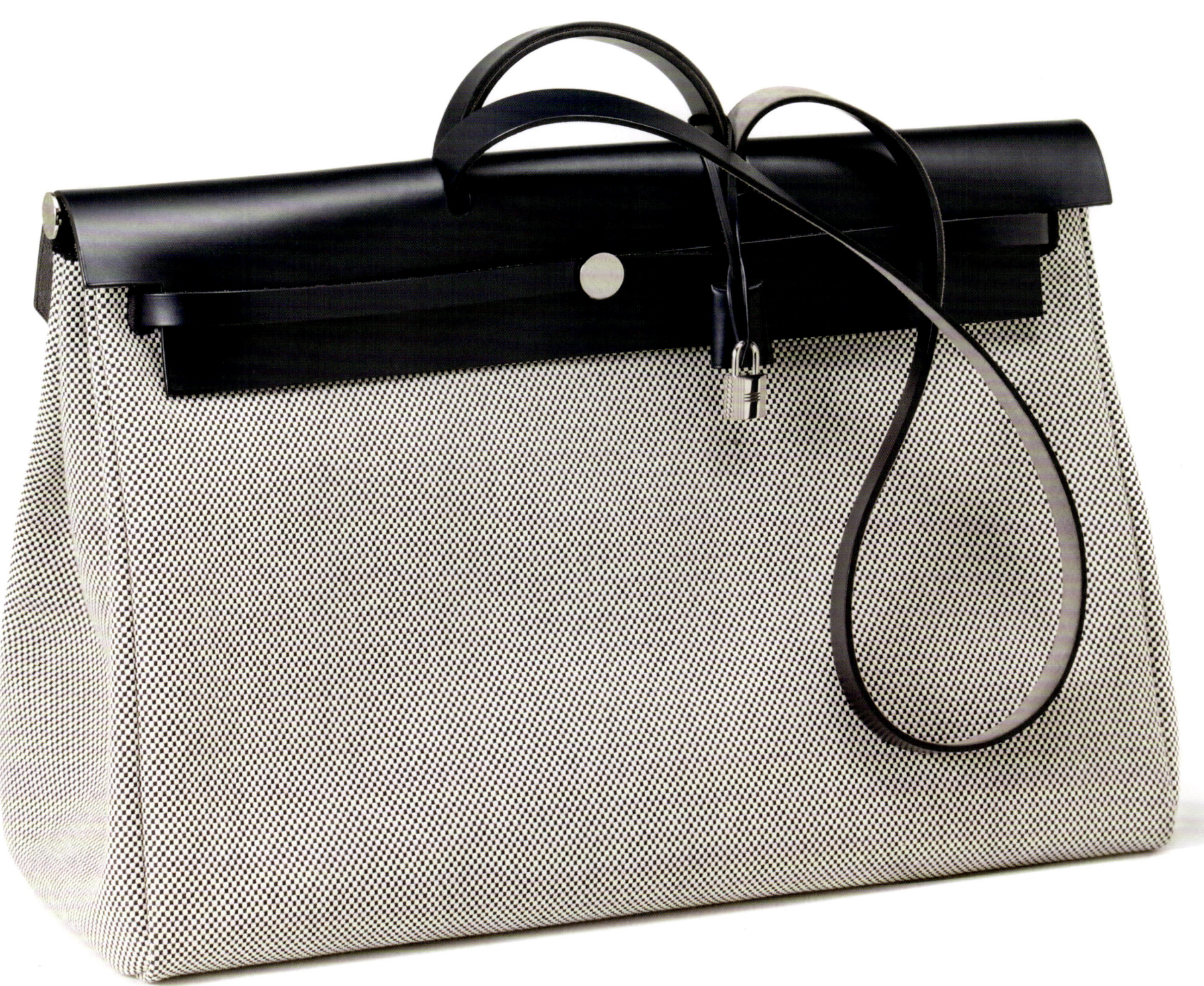

This page – *Hermès Herbag 52 Vache Hunter* in blue/ecru toile, Vache blue leather and checked toile with a large outer zip pocket on the back, fixed shoulder strap in matching leather, and palladium hardware. Loved for its casual-chic style and functionality, the *Herbag* is an elegant yet slightly sporty accessory.

Opposite page – *Hermès Vespa* bag in *Rouge Clemence* leather, 2000. Canvas shoulder strap, T-bar closure and golden hardware. Red suede lining and an internal pocket with a beige canvas flap.

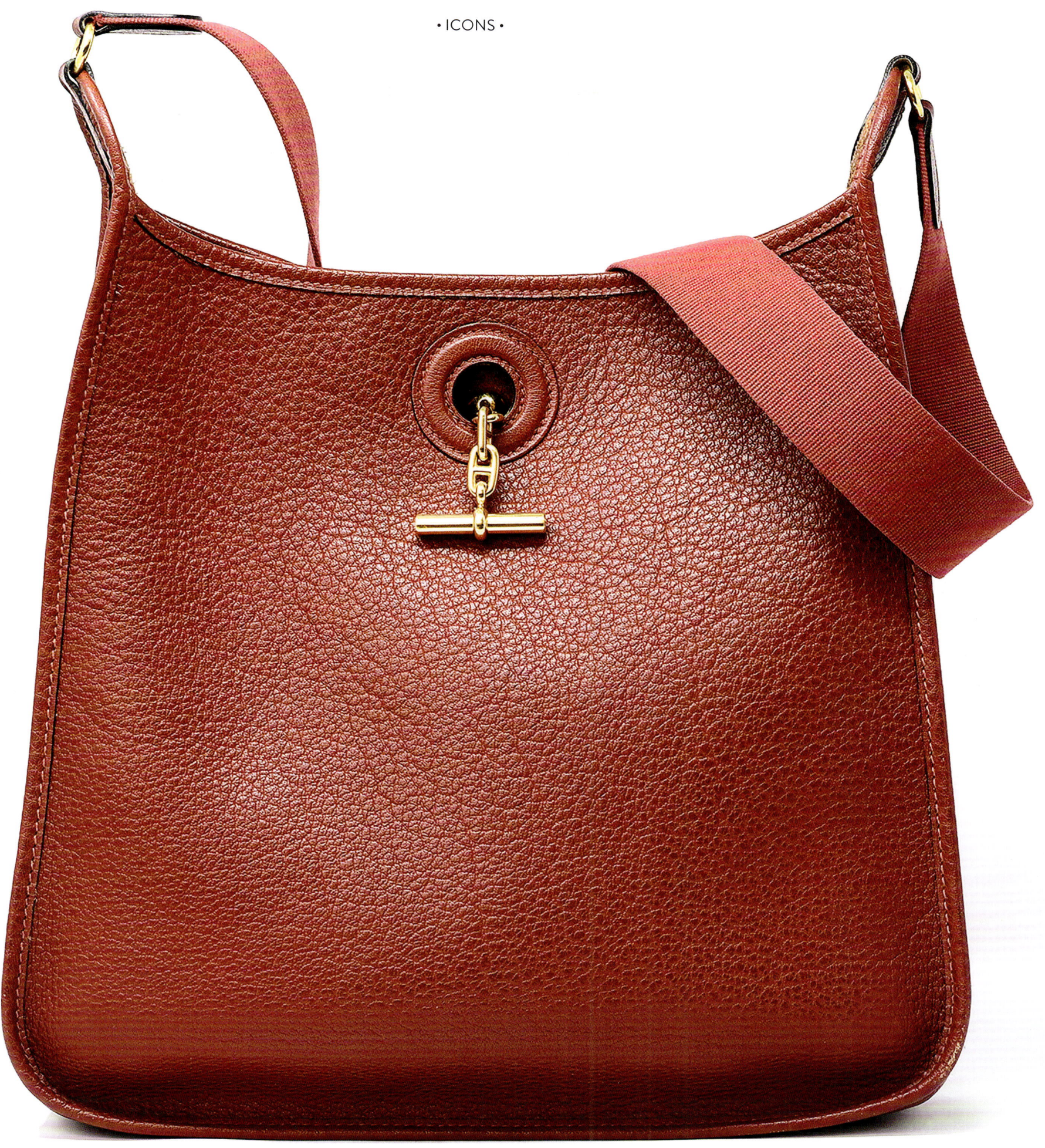

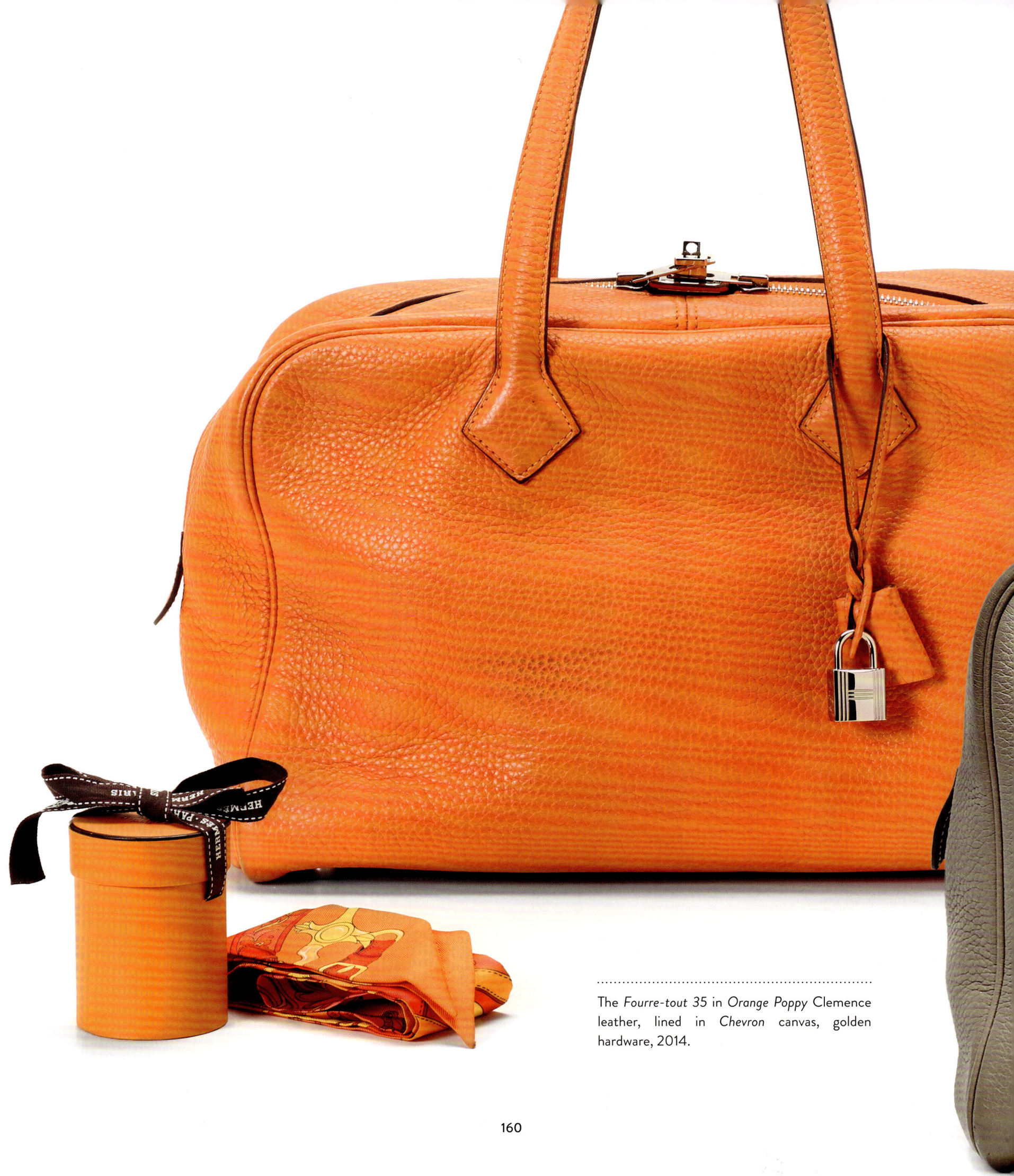

The *Fourre-tout 35* in *Orange Poppy* Clemence leather, lined in *Chevron* canvas, golden hardware, 2014.

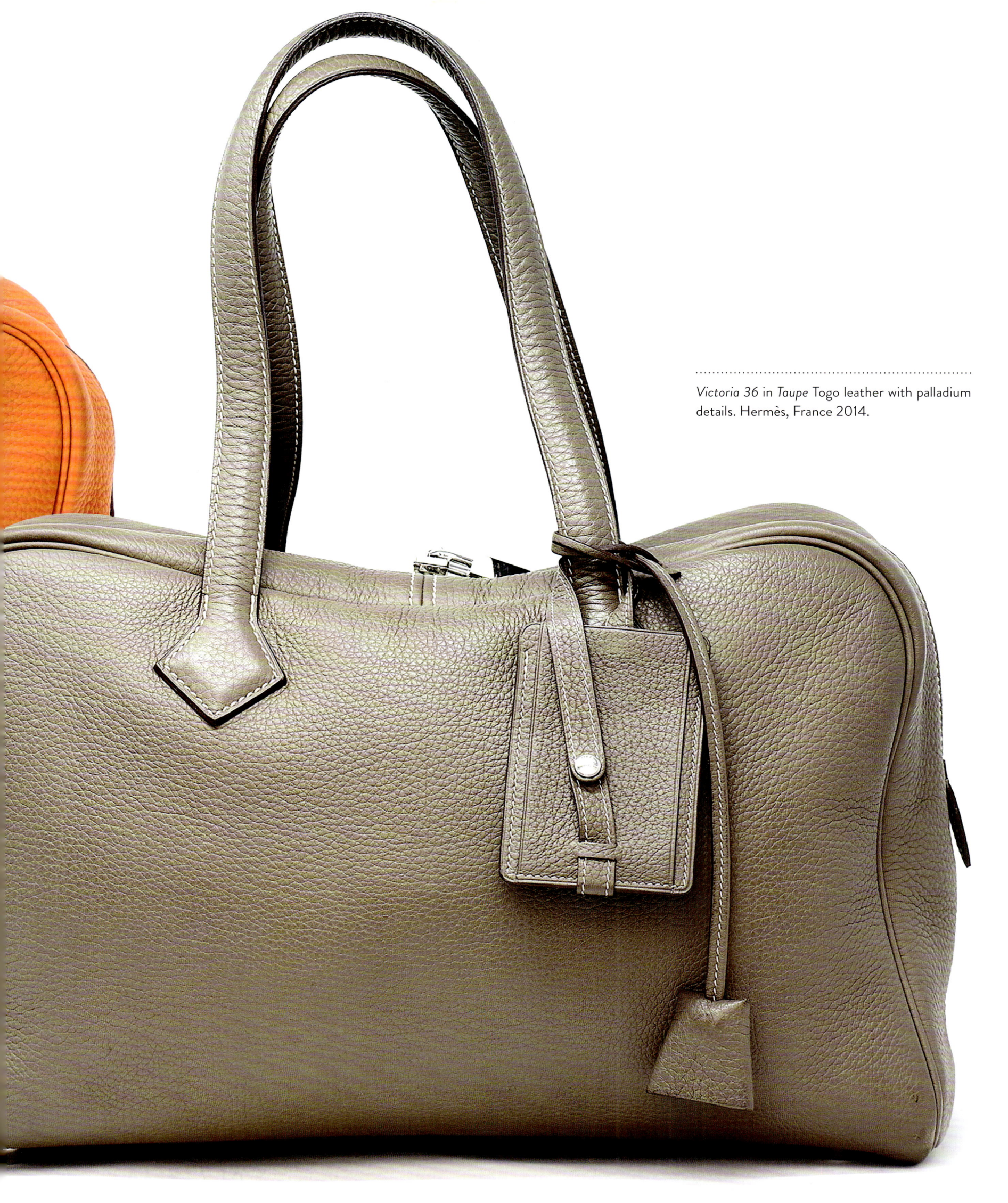

Victoria 36 in *Taupe* Togo leather with palladium details. Hermès, France 2014.

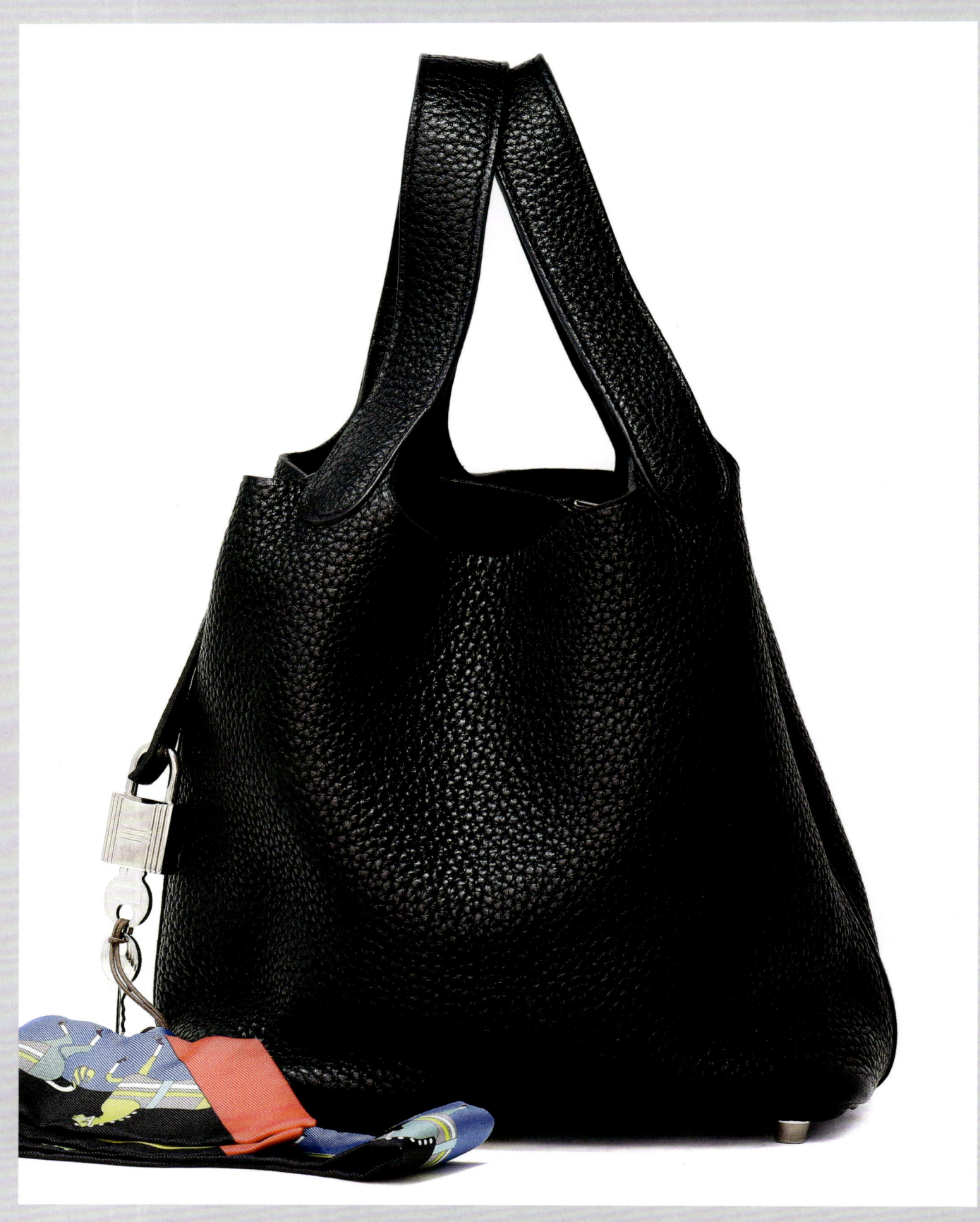

The 2000s

The phenomenon of the It bag dominated the 2000s. Thanks to the combination of long-standing tabloids and the nascent internet, celebrities and the first influencers had unprecedented impact on the style of bags, which, in many cases, bore a logo as the central element of their design, often reinterpreted in a creative way, or through bold colours. Hermès chose the latter form of expression and introduced versions of its historical bags in very bright hues.

In the early noughts, the maison introduced various new bags, such as the *Picotin* (2002), whose shape refers to the feed bags which contained oats for horses. Rounded, simple and minimalist, it has a strap along the top which makes it possible to adjust the width, and it comes in three sizes: 18, 22 and 26 cm.

In 2007, the *Lindy* was introduced, named after the famous Lindy Hop dance which was all the rage in the 1920s, underscoring its dynamic style. Its innovative design includes two handles placed on the very ends of the bag, which make it possible to fold it slightly when it's lifted.

The Lindy could be carried by hand or over the shoulder thanks to a detachable strap, and it had a twist lock and lateral zip pockets. It came in different sizes, including 26, 30, 34 and 45 cm. In 2019, a mini version measuring 20 cm was introduced.

From 2010 to today, women's bags by Hermès have evolved constantly, going through phases of reinterpretation of tradition and innovation inspired by sustainability. This period also saw the rise of new trends, transforming bags into cultural symbols and fine design objects which women love to collect.

The *Cabag* introduced in 2010 recalls the word *cabane* ('hut' in French), evoking an image of simplicity and versatility. The design of the *Cabag* is distinguished by its soft, roomy structure in cotton or linen canvas, embellished by calfskin details – quintessential materials which represent Hermès craftsmanship and heritage.

That same year, the *Jypsière* was born, which the fashion house describes as the 'union of a hunting bag and the iconic *Birkin*'. It's one of the creations by Jean Paul Gaultier, who at the time was the Creative Director of Womenswear at Hermès.

....

Hermès Picotin Lock 18 in Clemence Noir Taurillon leather, palladium hardware, 2013. The *Picotin Lock 18* is the smallest bag in the series, perfect as a refined evening clutch or for those who prefer a compact yet chic accessory. The short handle and the bucket design with a padlock closure give it a distinct elegance.

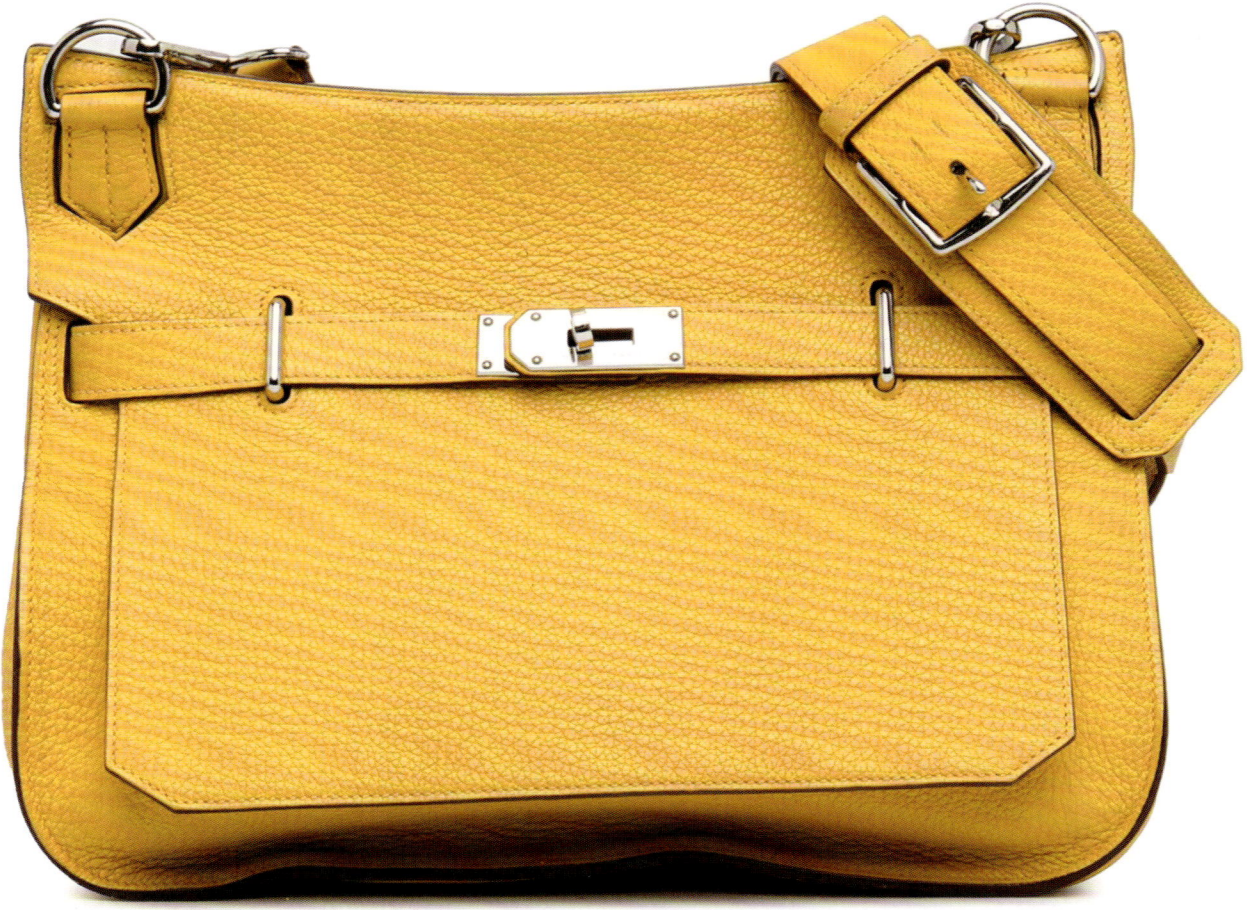

The *Jypsière* was inspired by details from saddle bags and travel bags, but with an elegant and modern design. Its rectangular silhouette and well-defined structure come in many versions and sizes, including a mini option. Demand for this style is high, especially when issued in limited editions or exclusive colours.

The *Médor* also appeared in 2010. Its bold design incorporates square studs and a closure inspired by dog collars, recurring elements of Hermès heritage. The use of studs from collars had been in the fashion house's inventory since 1927, eventually becoming a distinguishing feature of the brand. The *Médor* also came in a clutch version.

The *Toolbox* bag from 2012 was inspired by just that – toolboxes. It is distinguished by its structured square shape and the bellows opening, which makes it easy to access the items held inside, is entirely functional, and accentuates the

originality of its design. It can be carried by hand via the short top handles, but it also includes a detachable strap for shoulder or cross-body portability.

The *Roulis*, introduced in 2011, is a minimalist yet well-balanced bag characterised by the distinctive *chaîne d'ancre* closure, a signature detail which honours Hermès' sailing heritage and which takes on a more elongated shape here.

First produced in 2014, the *Convoyeur* bag stands out for its compact design and structured rectangular silhouette with a spring-loaded clasp. Originally designed for a practical purpose (the transportation of riding boots and tack), it underwent a transformation to become a sophisticated fashion accessory. The mini *Convoyeur* is characterised by a compact silhouette with a leather flap that's folded over and closed with a metal detail.

The *Oxer* Bag was also created in 2014. It was inspired by the equestrian world, a theme dear to the fashion house. In particular, the name 'Oxer' refers to a sort of jump often seen in horseback riding competitions.

Presented in 2017, the *Cinhetic* bag resembles a pretty make-up box via its square shape, plus a curved handle and a chain which can be used for cross-body or shoulder carry. But what makes the *Cinhetic* special is the asymmetrical H clasp that echoes the movement and energy of the dynamic and lively lines which give the bag its name. It's a perfect example of Hermès' modern approach to design, in which bold geometric lines are combined with refined details and hand crafts-manship.

The *Della Cavalleria* bag, introduced in 2021, takes its name from a treatise on horsemanship. It was inspired by the brand's equestrian heritage and its origins in saddlery. This bag borrows elements of the utilitarian bags used by horseback riders, such as the curved shape, the flap and the Verdun half-bit with rounded corners.

Also from 2021, the *In the Loop* bag is charac-terised by soft lines and a rounded structure, while the handles were inspired by *chaîne d'ancre* links, which also form the base of the bag. Even the closure of the bag takes the shape of the famous chain link.

Named after traditional Japanese sandals which feature a raised wooden base and a minimalist de-sign, the *Geta* bag was introduced in 2022. This inspiration can be seen in its geometric shape and the H-shaped clasp which is mirrored on two sides of the bag. The click on closing the bag is meant to mimic the click of the wooden sandals.

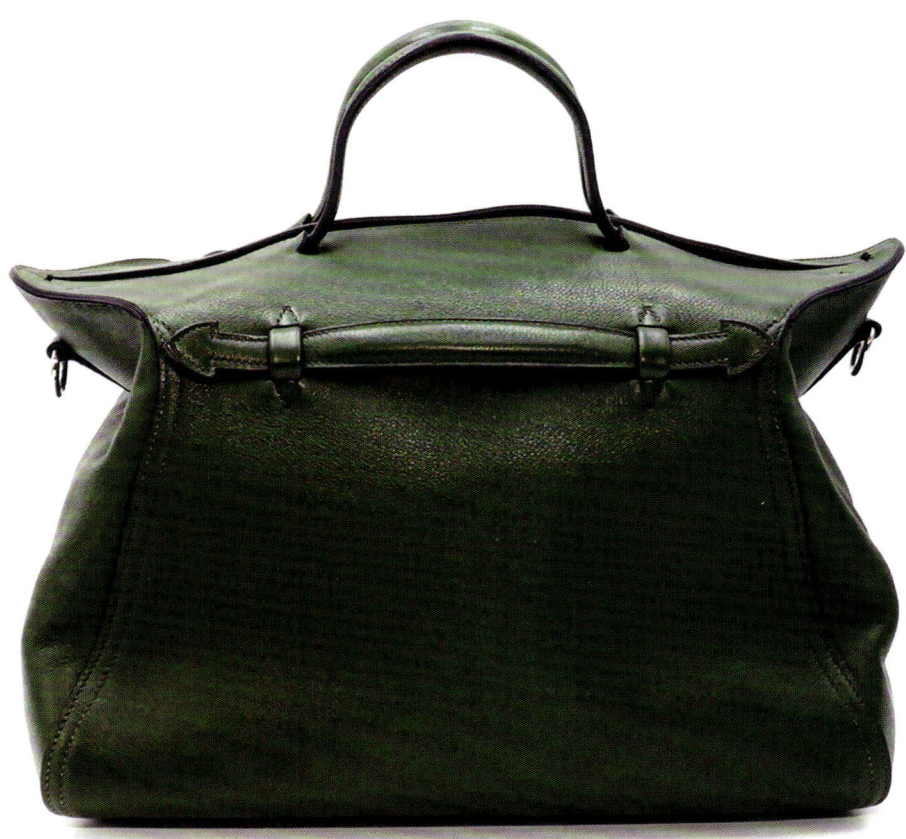

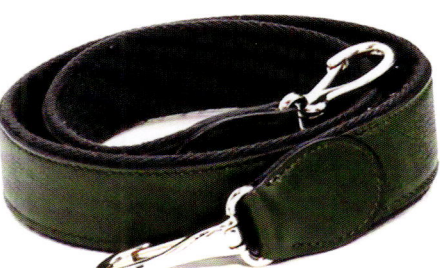

Opposite page – *Jypsière* bag in *Jaune de Naples* leather and shiny metal hardware. This creation by Jean Paul Gaultier is a true icon.

This page – The *Oxer* bag from 2014 comes with four handles and a cross-body strap.

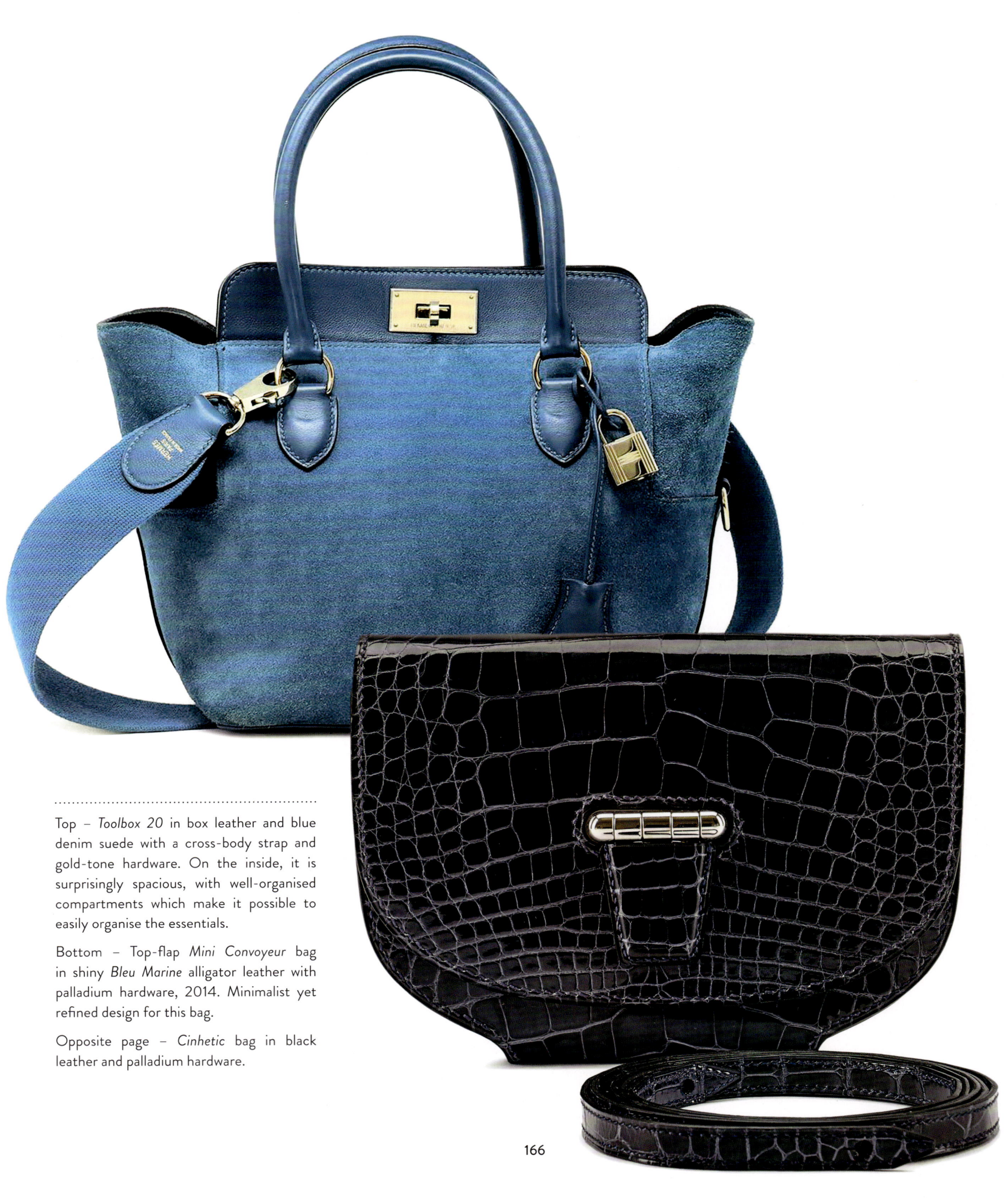

Top – *Toolbox 20* in box leather and blue denim suede with a cross-body strap and gold-tone hardware. On the inside, it is surprisingly spacious, with well-organised compartments which make it possible to easily organise the essentials.

Bottom – Top-flap *Mini Convoyeur* bag in shiny *Bleu Marine* alligator leather with palladium hardware, 2014. Minimalist yet refined design for this bag.

Opposite page – *Cinhetic* bag in black leather and palladium hardware.

166

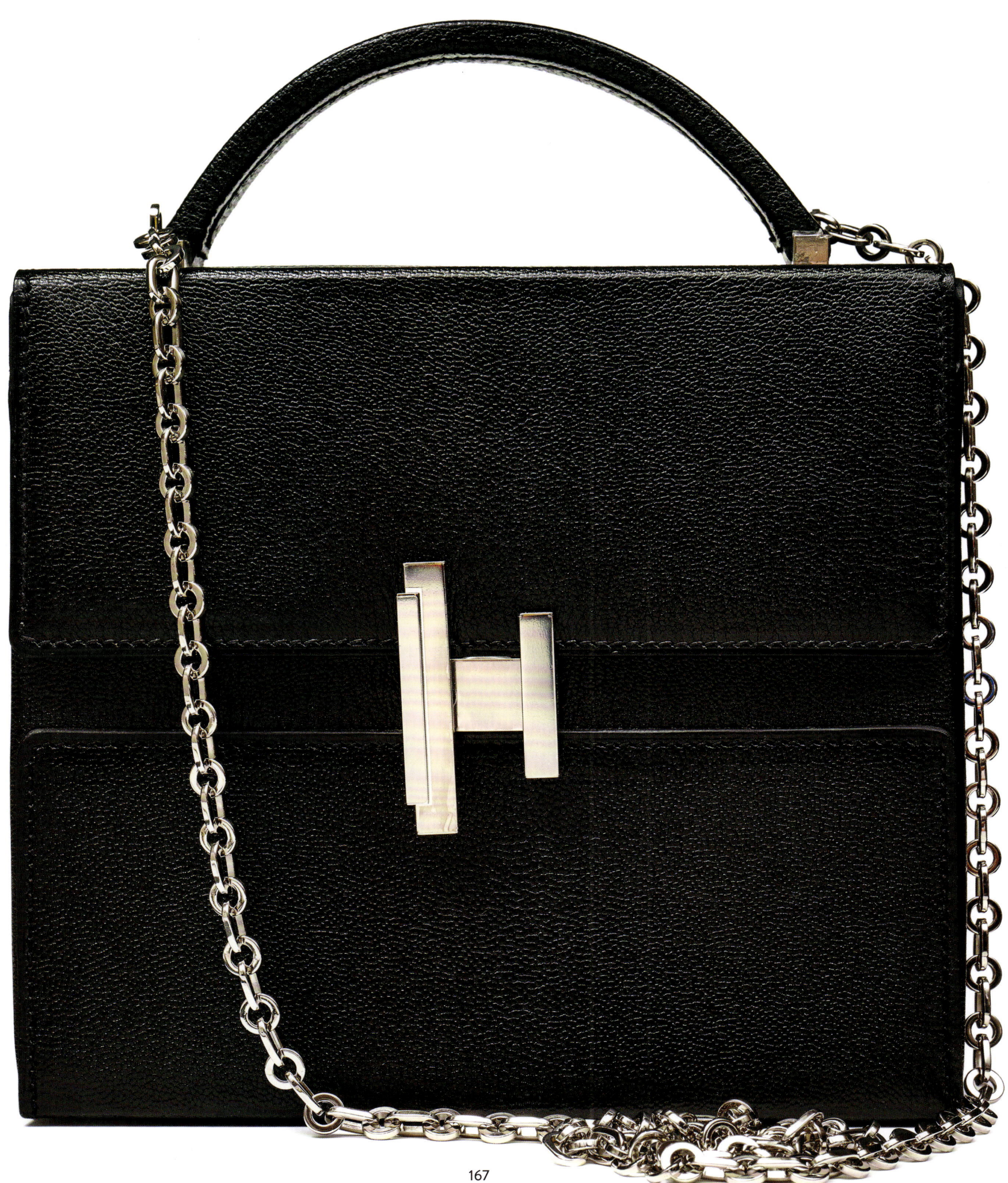

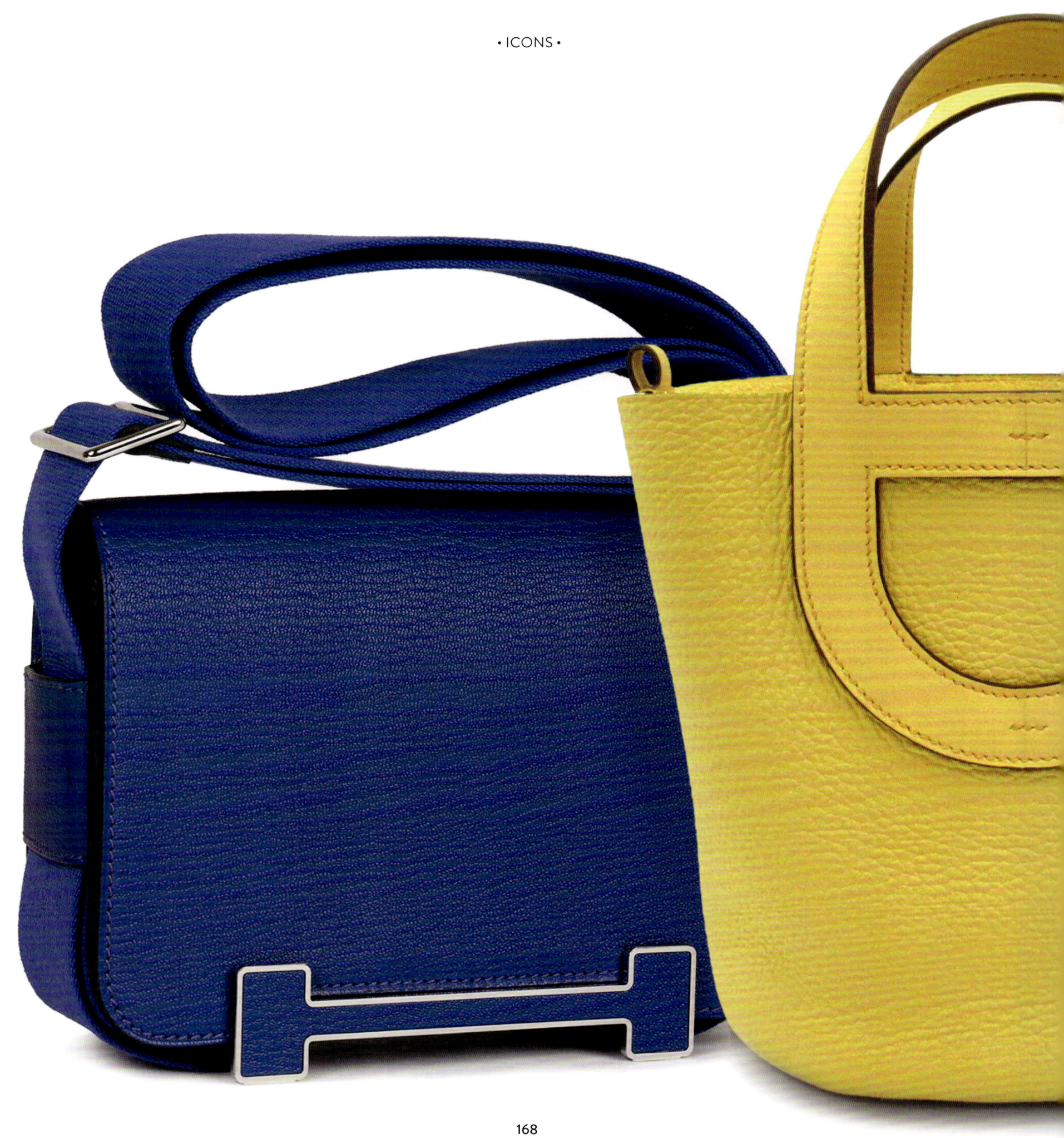

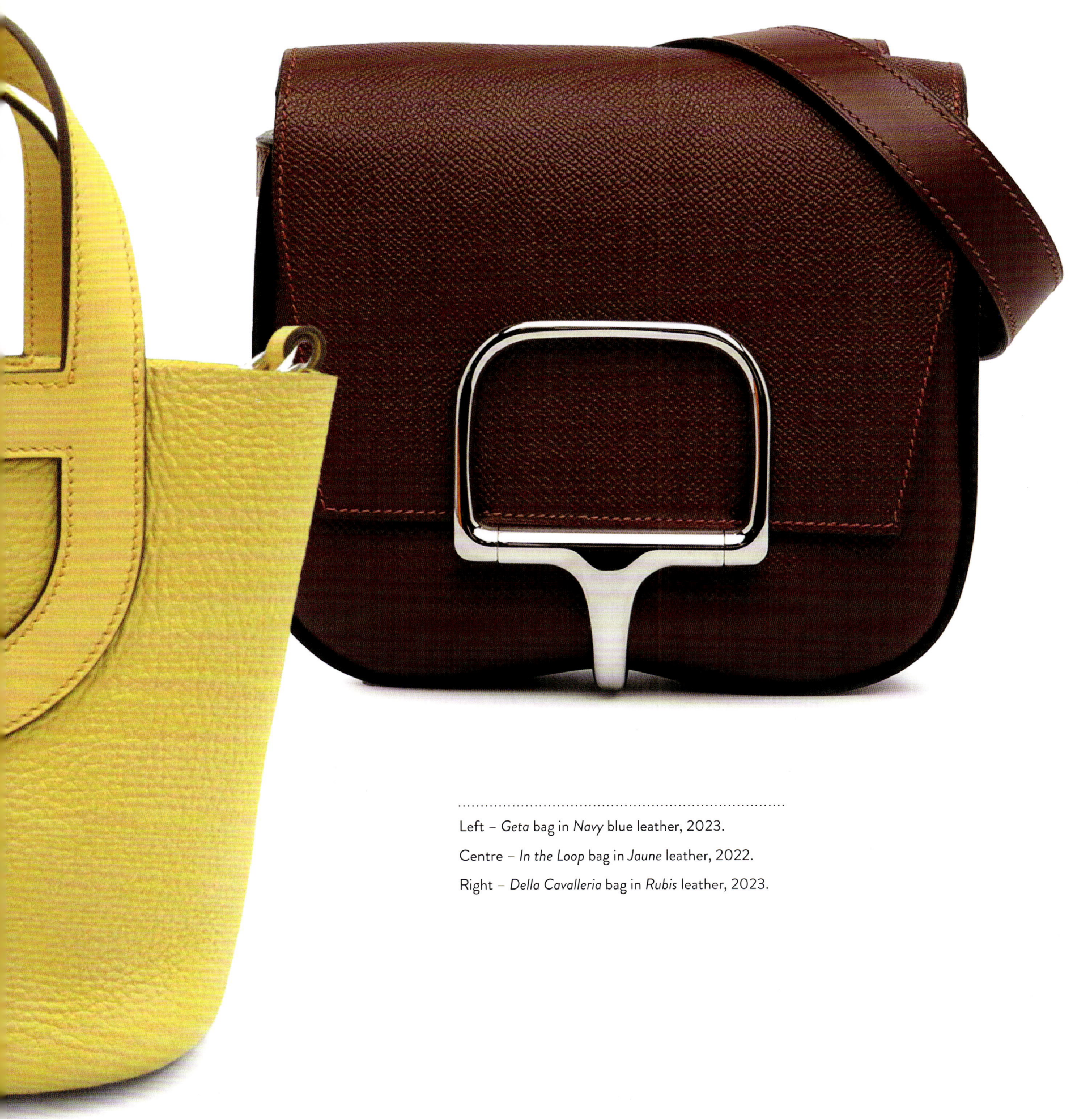

Left – *Geta* bag in *Navy* blue leather, 2023.

Centre – *In the Loop* bag in *Jaune* leather, 2022.

Right – *Della Cavalleria* bag in *Rubis* leather, 2023.

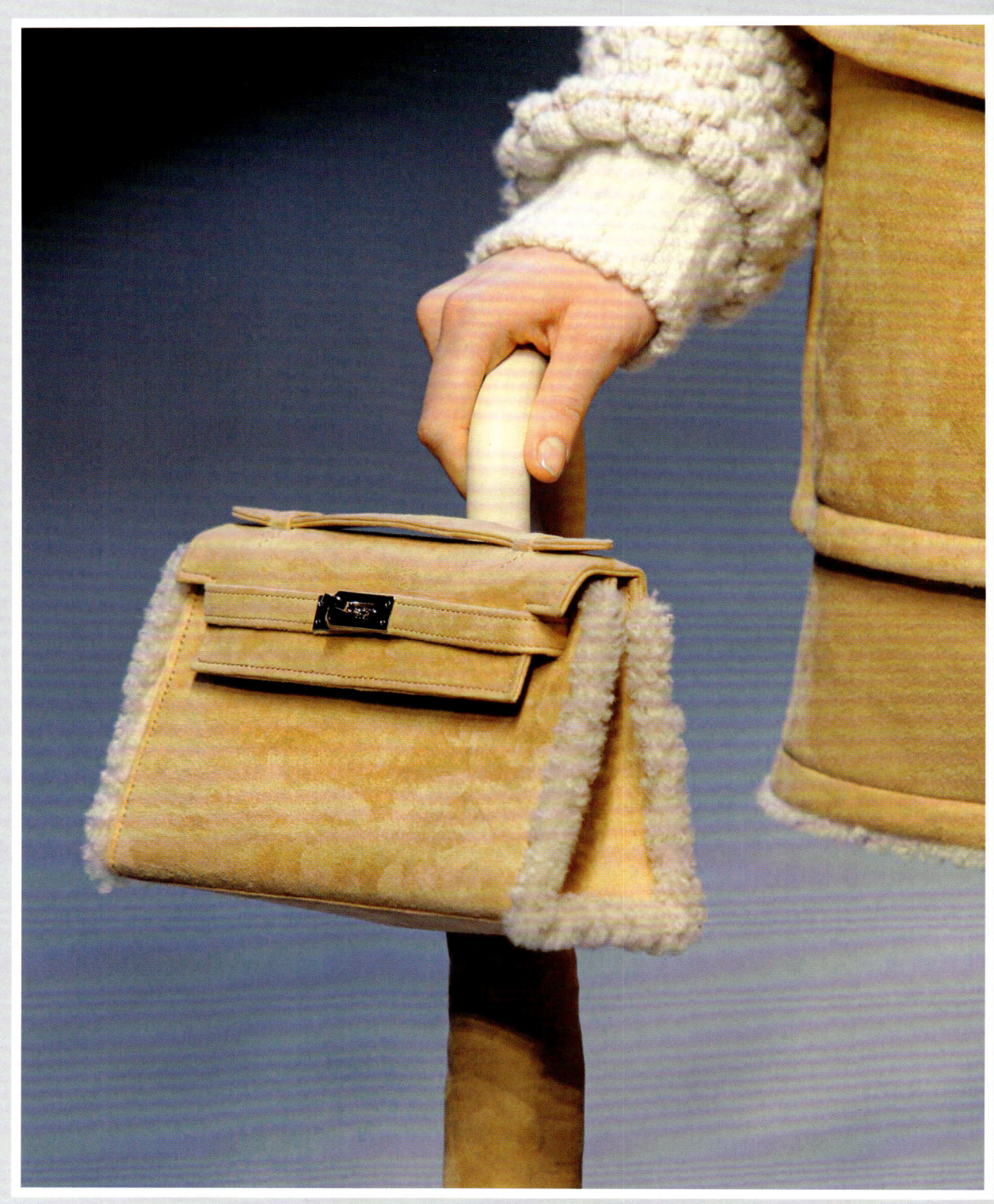

The *Teddy Kelly* on a runway. The *Teddy Kelly* was dreamt up by Jean Paul Gaultier, and in 2005 he made the design in a small, limited collection in shearling with kidskin details. The *Teddy Kelly* is an ode to the know-how of Hermès and the ability to reinvent its classics.

Beyond fashion and time

Hermès bags are known not just for their quality, but also for their value as an investment. Unlike many luxury goods, these objects tend to increase in value over time. In recent years, the vintage luxury bag market has seen significant growth, and a new trend has emerged: that of buying bags as an investment. Today, some Hermès products are considered safe places to park a sum of money, on par with real estate, fine art and watches. The *Kelly* and the *Birkin* are among them. One of the factors which feed into the legendary nature of Hermès bags is their inaccessibility. Despite their elevated costs, these bags are almost impossible to buy. To get a *Birkin* or a *Kelly* and a few other iconic styles, especially in limited editions, special materials or in-demand colours, customers often have to join a waiting list or be a regular Hermès customer. This policy reinforces their status as symbols of the elite.

Moreover, their scant availability has ensured that an ever-growing number of people are turning to auction houses to buy them, especially when it comes to limited editions, famous vintage styles, or bags in particularly exclusive materials.

In terms of auction purchases, some analysts also underscore the 'thrill of the chase', which stimulates the buyer. Hunting down a rare vintage piece or a special style can itself turn into a satisfying quest, offering as much satisfaction as at the moment of purchase.

The *Birkin Himalaya* and the *Kelly Himalaya* have become cult items for collectors.

Both of these bags are made of hand-dyed Nile crocodile leather. The name isn't linked to the place of origin of the materials, but rather to the white and grey shading of the crocodile leather, which echoes the snow-capped Tibetan mountains.

The *Birkin Diamond* is a version of the *Birkin* which combines classic design and the opulence of diamonds. This exclusive style is made from different types of fine leather, such as Niloticus (Nile) or Porosus (saltwater) crocodile leather, and it's embellished by sparkling elements: the twist clasp and the hooks of the straps are studded in white diamonds, often set in white or yellow gold.

Today, collectors know the evolution of the fashion house and its bags, collections and designers quite well, and they know why a certain object is important historically and in terms of fashion design. Some of the most sought-out vintage styles are the *JPG Shoulder Birkin* or the *Teddy Kelly*, both designed by Jean Paul Gaultier. Gaultier also created other styles which are highly sought out at auction, such as the *Birkin Shadow*. First introduced in 2009, this style stands out for its innovative design, which plays with three dimensionality and optical illusions. The most iconic characteristic of the *Birkin Shadow* is the 'bas relief' representation of its functional elements, such as the handles and the straps, which seem to emerge from the surface of the bag but which are actually embossed directly in the leather. The famous designer is also to be credited with the *Kelly 35 Osier Picnic* introduced to the market in 2011, made of leather and wicker.

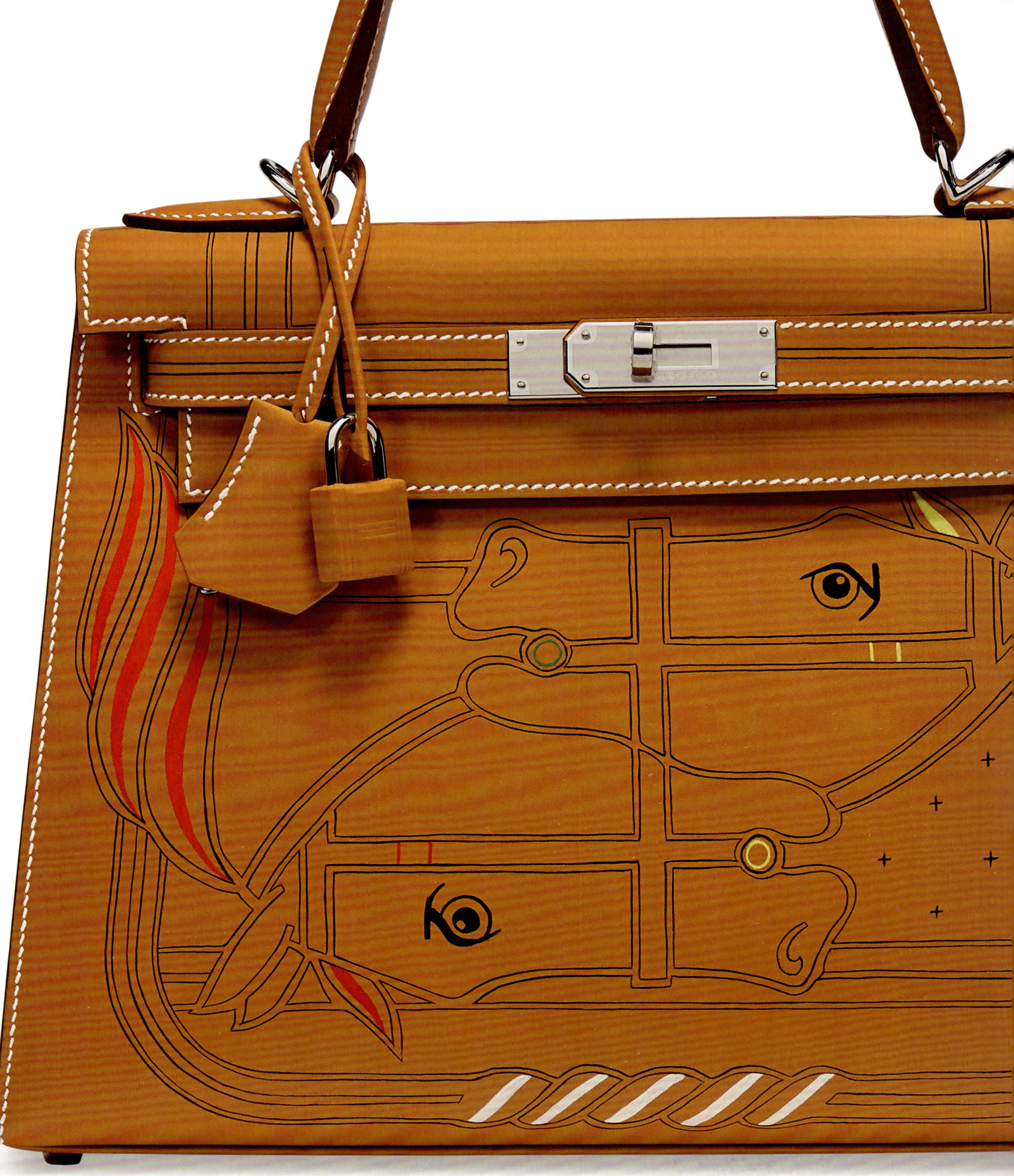

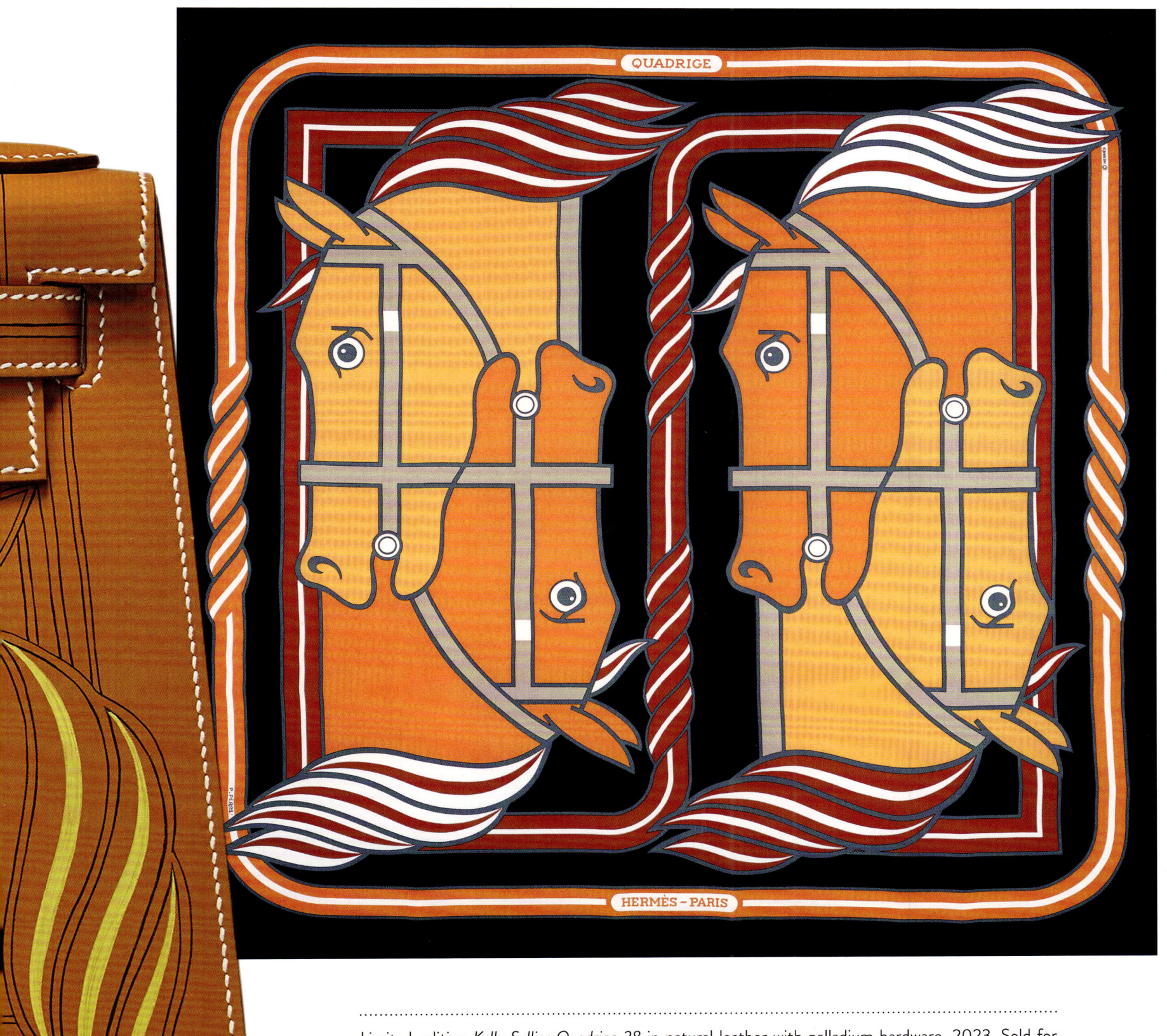

Limited-edition *Kelly Sellier Quadrige 28* in natural leather with palladium hardware, 2023. Sold for 37,800 USD in September 2024. The *Kelly Quadrige* takes up the motif of the *Quadrige* silk scarf which was first introduced in the 1970s. This design stands out for its iconic style: two horse heads intertwined by tack, arranged in a way that creates the look of a puzzle. The motif was inspired by the equestrian traditions that form one of the pillars of the Hermès brand. The design was later reissued many times, strengthening its position as one of the most popular motifs by Hermès.

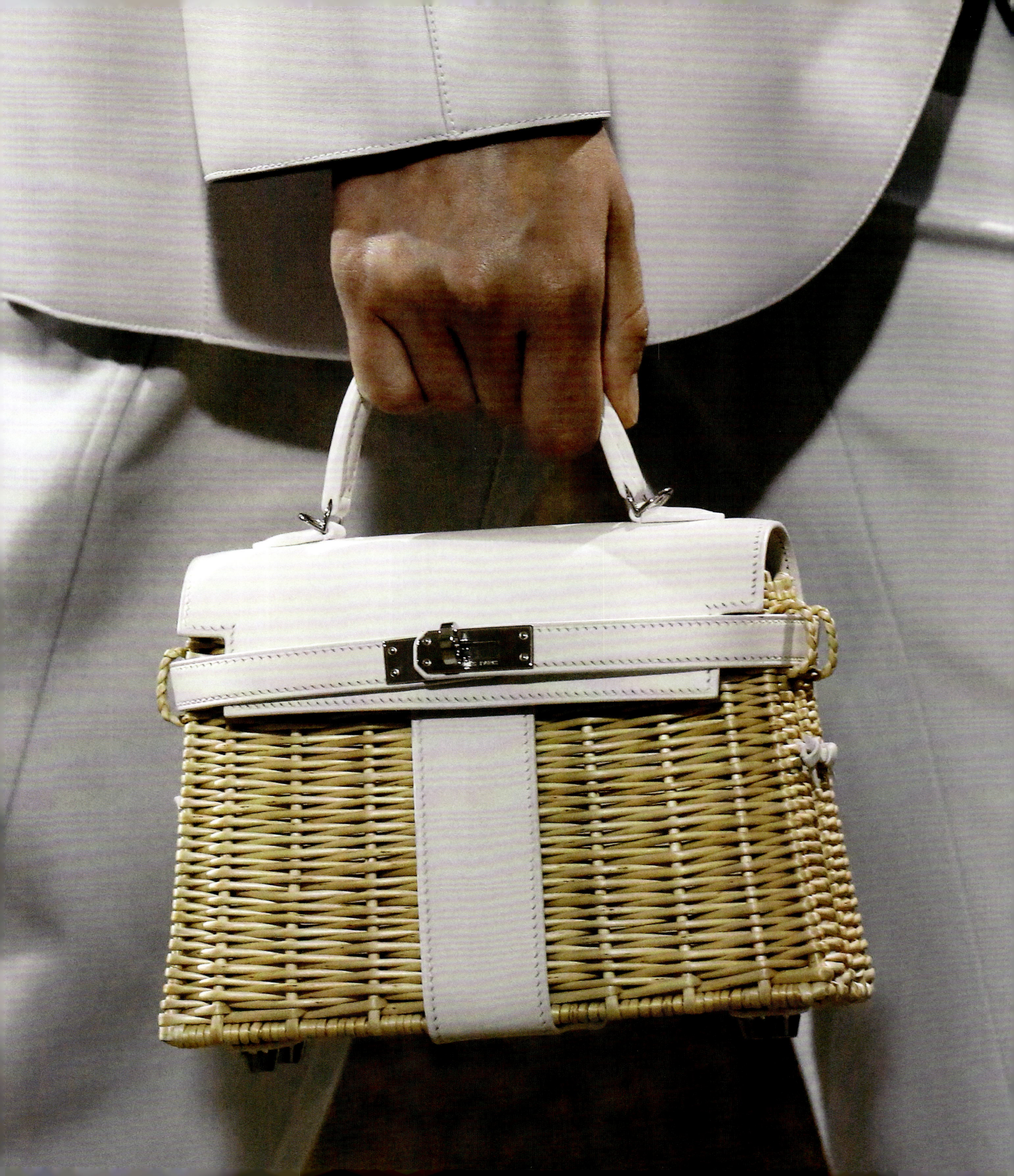

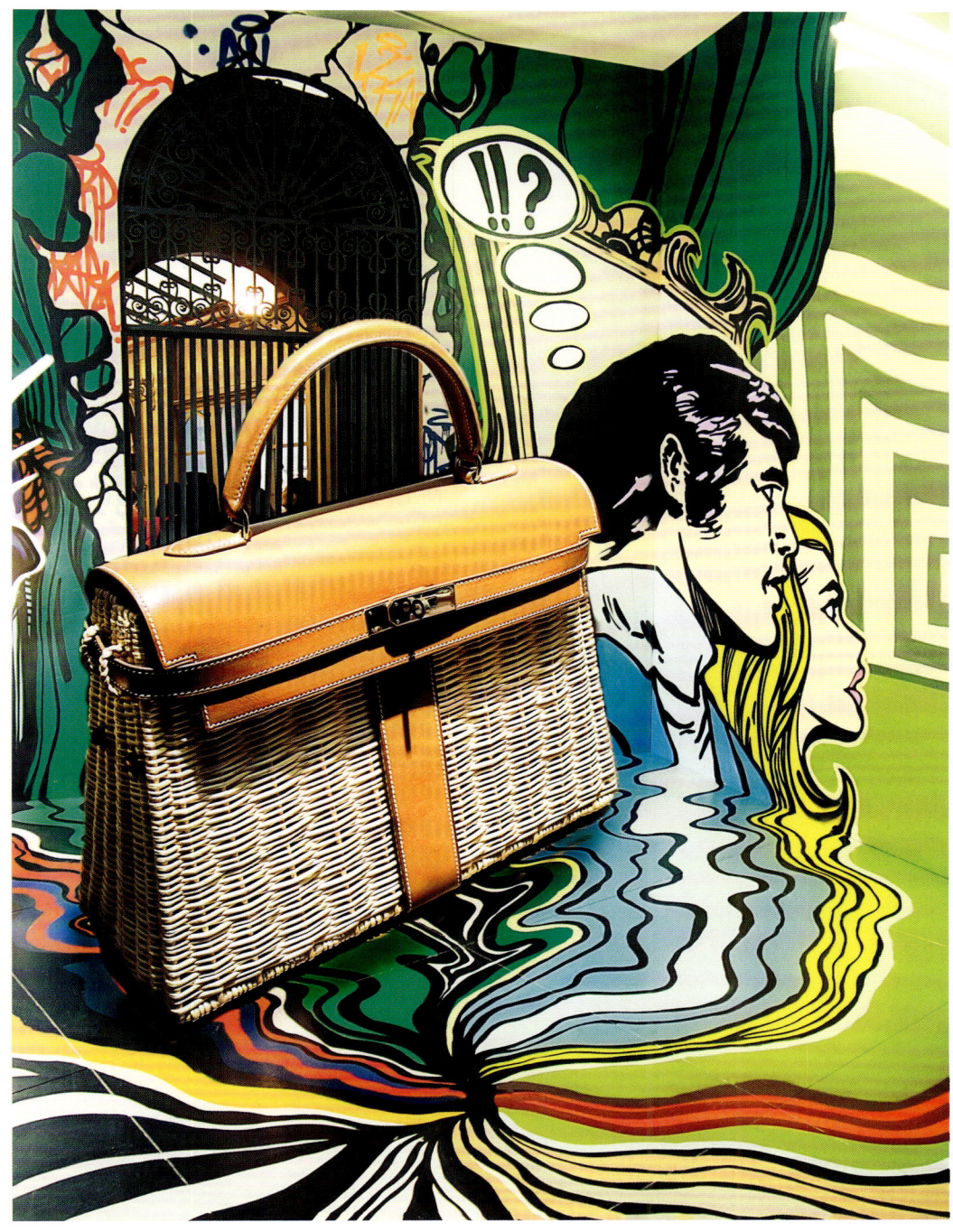

Opposite page – The *Kelly Picnic* bag is characterised by its Osier wicker structured trimmed by Swift leather. It has a flat top handle in leather, a flat detachable cross-body strap in leather, a leather flap closure and an inner envelope flap.

This page –The *Kelly Picnic* bag, designed by Jean Paul Gaultier in 2011.

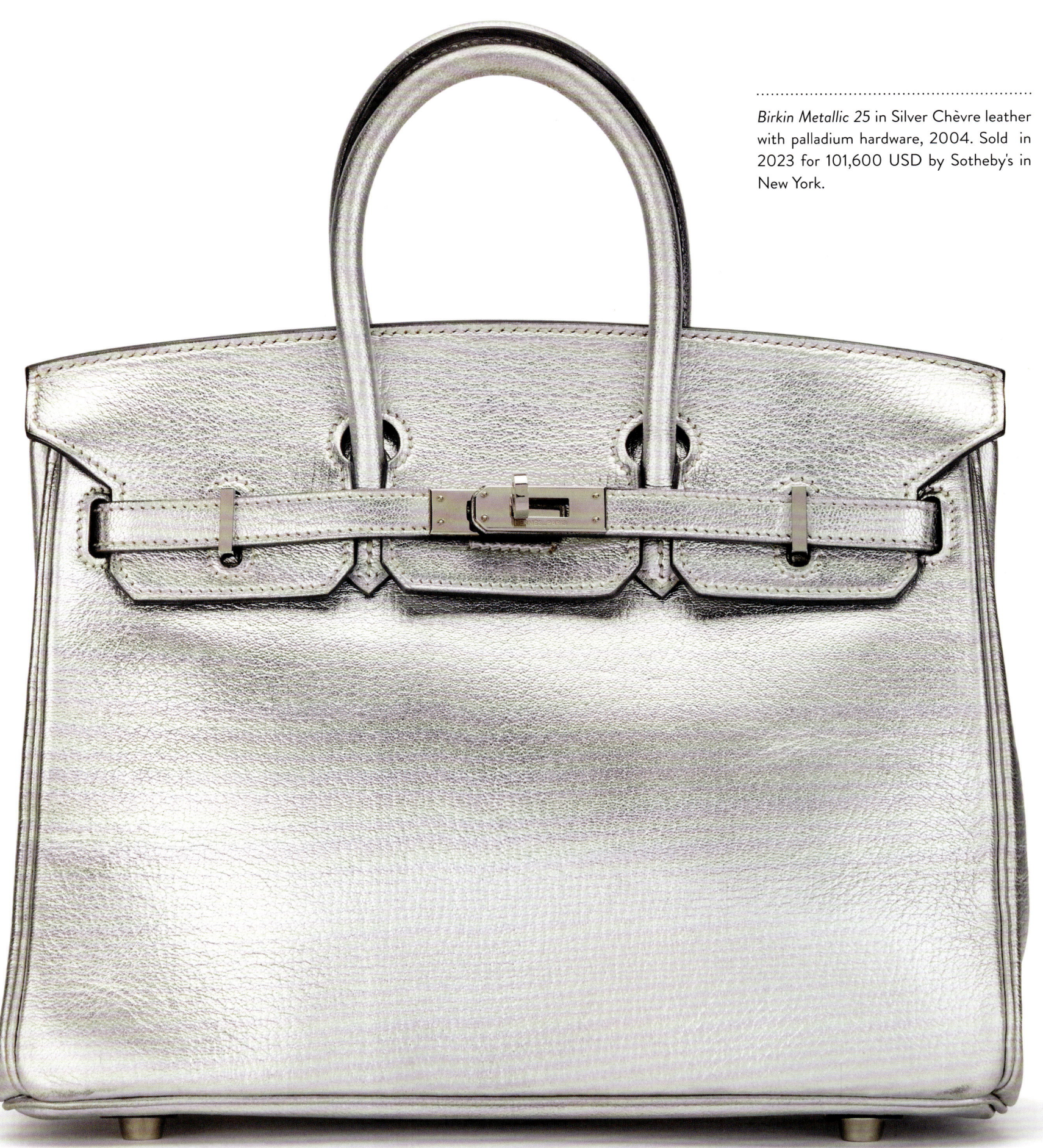

Birkin Metallic 25 in Silver Chèvre leather with palladium hardware, 2004. Sold in 2023 for 101,600 USD by Sotheby's in New York.

The *Quelle Idole bag*, also known as the *Kelly Doll*, is another one of the rare pieces which fetches high prices at auction. It was introduced in 2000 and designed by Jean-Louis Dumas, Creative Director and Chairman of Hermès from 1978 to 2006.

The *Birkin Metallic*, made only in 2004, is another popular milestone in the brand's history.

Among the limited editions, the *Birkin HAC (Haute à Courroies)* should be mentioned. Taller and narrower than the original *Birkin*, it was initially designed to carry saddles. Then there's the *So-Black Birkin* in black leather with black metal hardware. Another limited edition, the *Cargo Birkin* is the most functional version of this iconic bag, crafted in lightweight canvas with five sporty outer pockets.

Particularly coveted is the *Birkin Faubourg* introduced in 2019 as a limited edition inspired by the famous Hermès flagship shop at 24 Faubourg Saint-Honoré, Paris. The base of the bag represents Parisian pavements, while the top recalls the structure of the building, complete with windows and awnings. The *Night* and *Day* versions of the *Birkin Faubourg* are two extraordinary interpretations of the same theme, expressed via different day and night atmospheres with varied colour palettes which emphasise architectural details through tones of grey, orange and midnight blue.

In 2021, the *Sous la Neige* and *Faubourg Midnuit* versions of the *Faubourg* were introduced. The first recreates the building under a mantle of snow, with refined, one-of-a-kind details such as snowy roofs and lights in windows. The later celebrates the charm of the night-time through an intense colour palette, dominated by tones such as black, midnight blue and silvery accents. The

Birkin Faubourg Disco, on the other hand, was created in 2024. It unites the iconic design of the *Birkin* with the sparkling energy of the lights of a nightclub, crafted in black leather which sees the shapes of the famous façade on its surface, in the form of white graffiti.

Interest in these bags is constant over time and so important that the fashion house, looking at its precious heritage, creates quite popular new editions.

Experts at auction houses also point to other styles in limited editions or unique colours, such as the *Constance*, the *Roulis*, the *Picotin*, the *Herbag*, the *Convoyeur* and the classic *Vespa*, as being some of the most sought-after.

They are joined by *HSS* (*Horseshoe Stamp Special*) versions.[10] These unique pieces are customised as requested by clients, including colours and special details. Every season, a predetermined selection of Hermès bags can be customised, using a set of materials and colours. After having decided on the customised combinations, the final project is sent for approval before production begins.

Special orders are often created in the most popular colours of a given season, and they often feature contrast hues on the inside, or, in a few cases, surprising two- or three-tone colourways.

Another type of customisation may include the addition of contrast stitching or custom hardware, such as brushed gold, brushed palladium or rose gold plating. Details such as the position of the pocket, the length of the buckle straps and the addition of initials are additional customisable options offered to the lucky few.

For many collectors, the value of a luxury bag lies in owning a piece of fashion history, rather than in the bag's practical use.

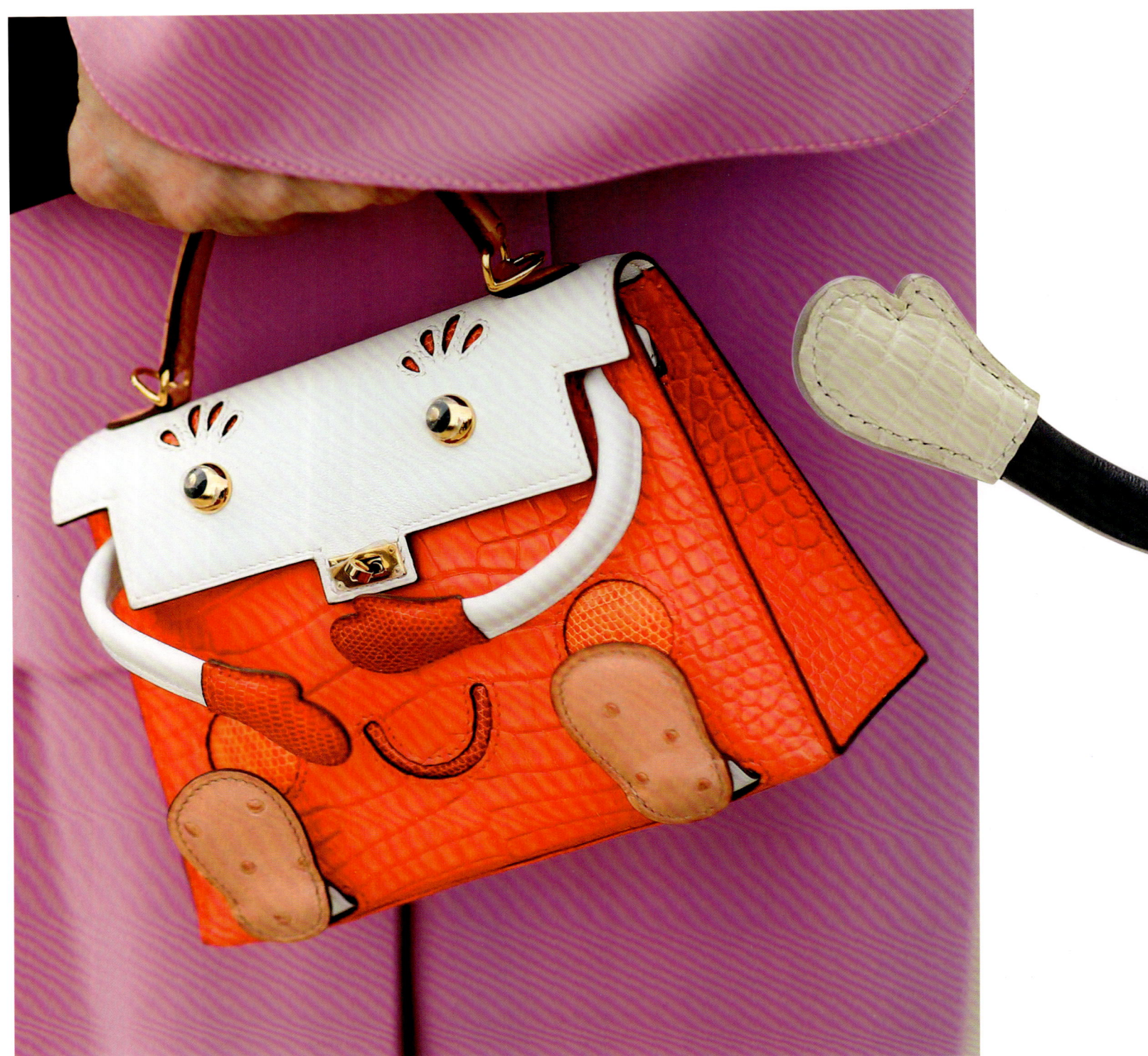

This page – In 2015, Hermès presented a set of five *Quelle Idole* bags at the *Leather Forever* exhibition in Singapore. These *Kelly Dolls* bags, embellished by embroidery, beads, exotic leather and other unique elements, went viral among Hermès collectors. They were subsequently auctioned off for charity. This is an example of these exclusive bags.

Opposite page – Custom Edition *Quelle Idole* bag by Matte Béton in crocodile and black Swift leather with palladium hardware, 2019. Sold for 2,205,000 HKD in 2024. Made available for custom orders, this style is very exclusive.

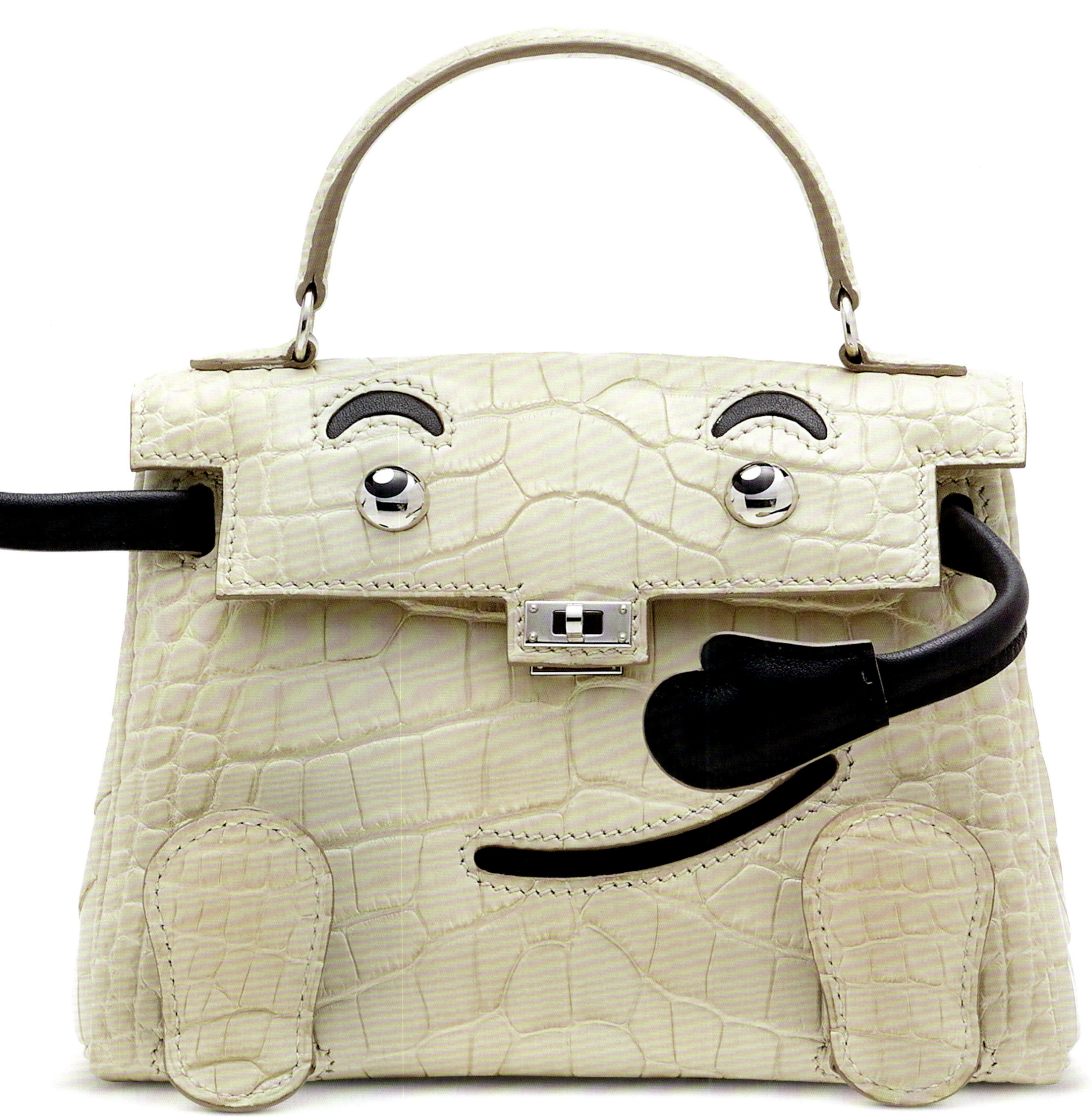

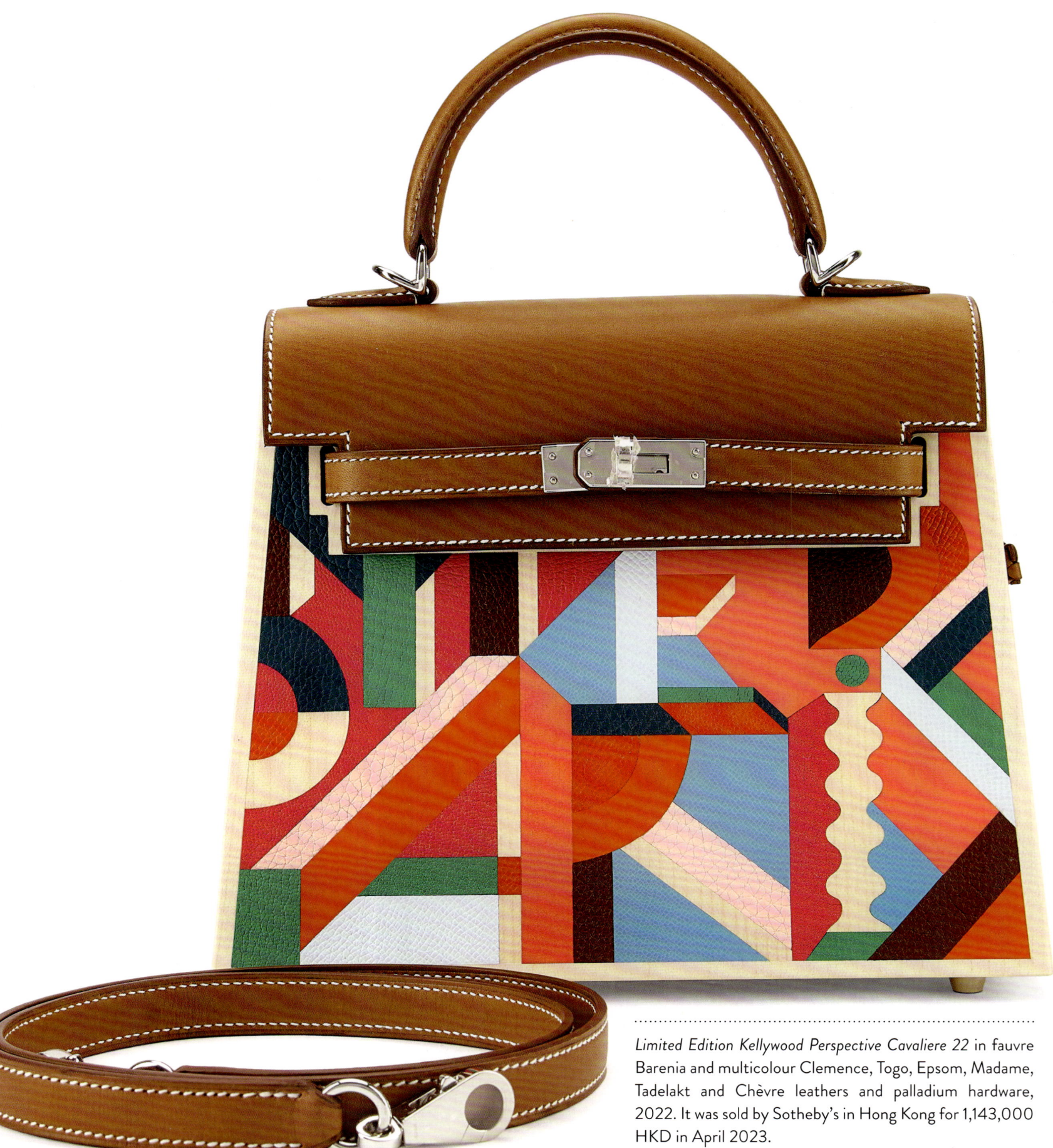

Limited Edition Kellywood Perspective Cavaliere 22 in fauvre Barenia and multicolour Clemence, Togo, Epsom, Madame, Tadelakt and Chèvre leathers and palladium hardware, 2022. It was sold by Sotheby's in Hong Kong for 1,143,000 HKD in April 2023.

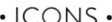

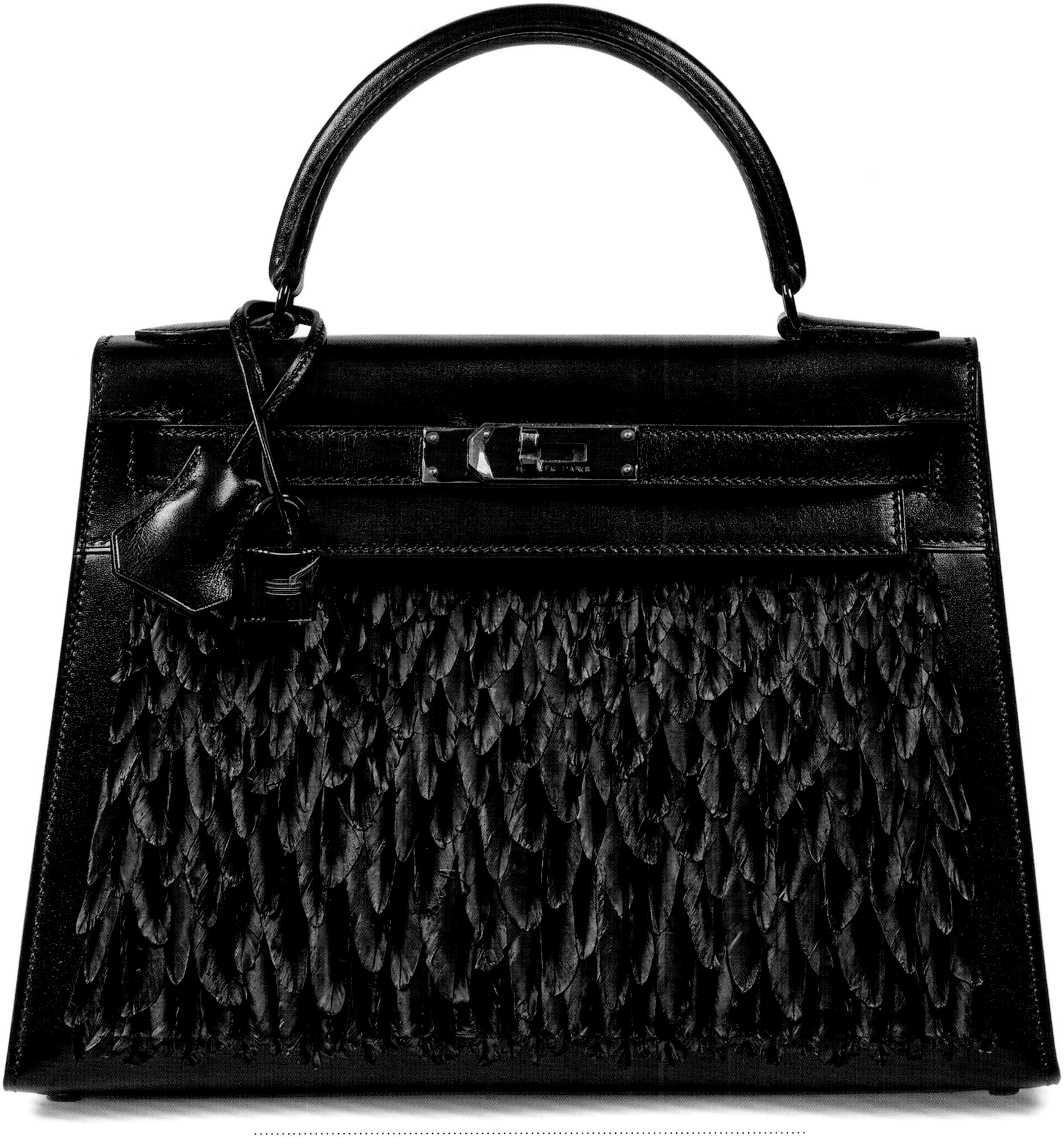

Limited Edition *Kelly Sellier 28* in black calfskin and feathers with black PVD hardware, 2010. Sold for 277,200 EUR in 2022 in Paris.

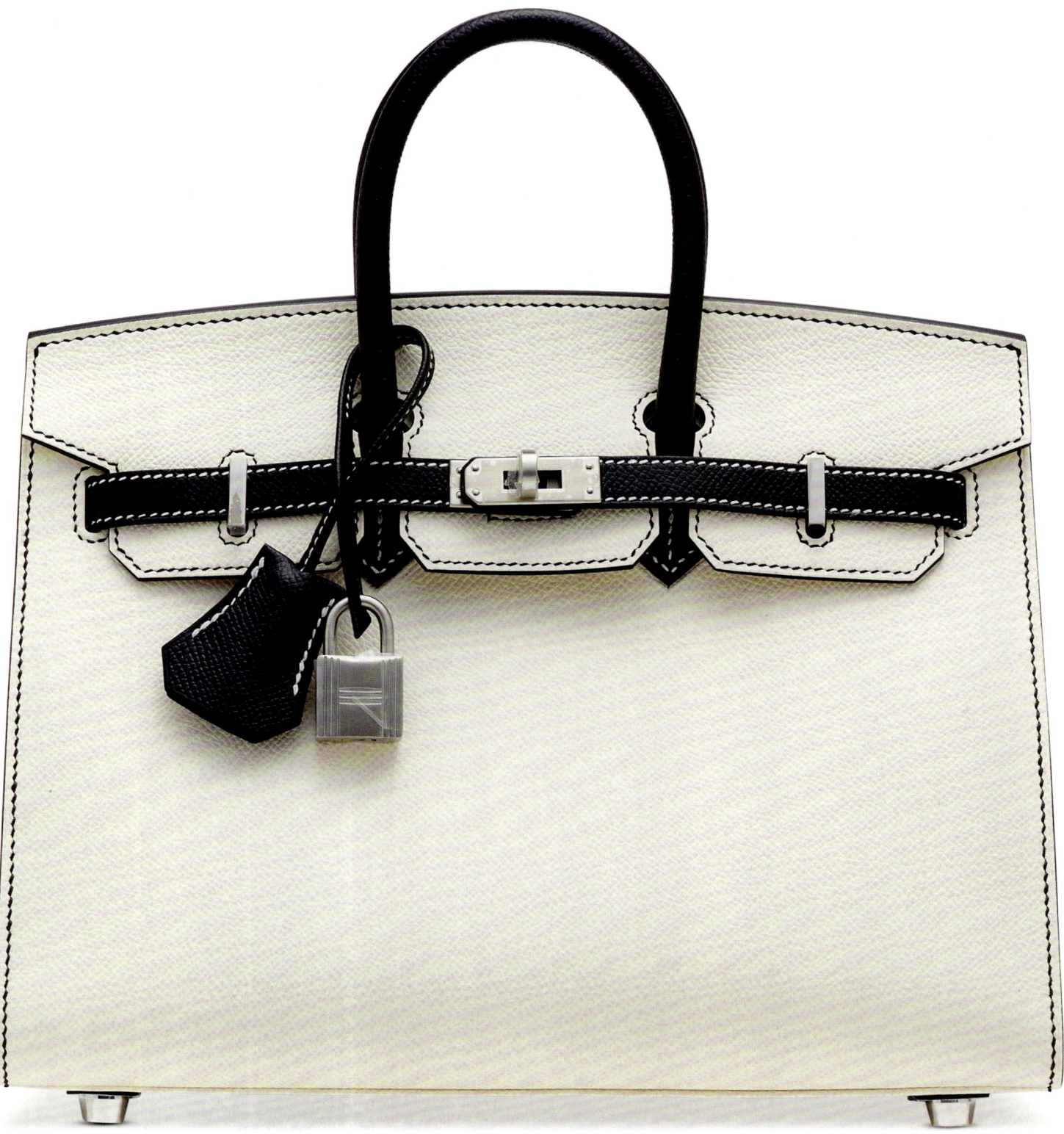

This page – Custom Edition *Birkin 25* in natural and black leather with brushed palladium hardware, 2021. Sold in Hong Kong for 239,400 HKD in May 2024.

Opposite page – Limited Edition *Touch Birkin 25* in matt black crocodile and Togo leather with gold hardware, 2018. Sold in Hong Kong for 302,400 HKD in May 2024. The *Touch* versions of the *Birkin* and *Kelly* bags have a main compartment in leather, combined with details such as straps in lizard, alligator or crocodile in the same colour.

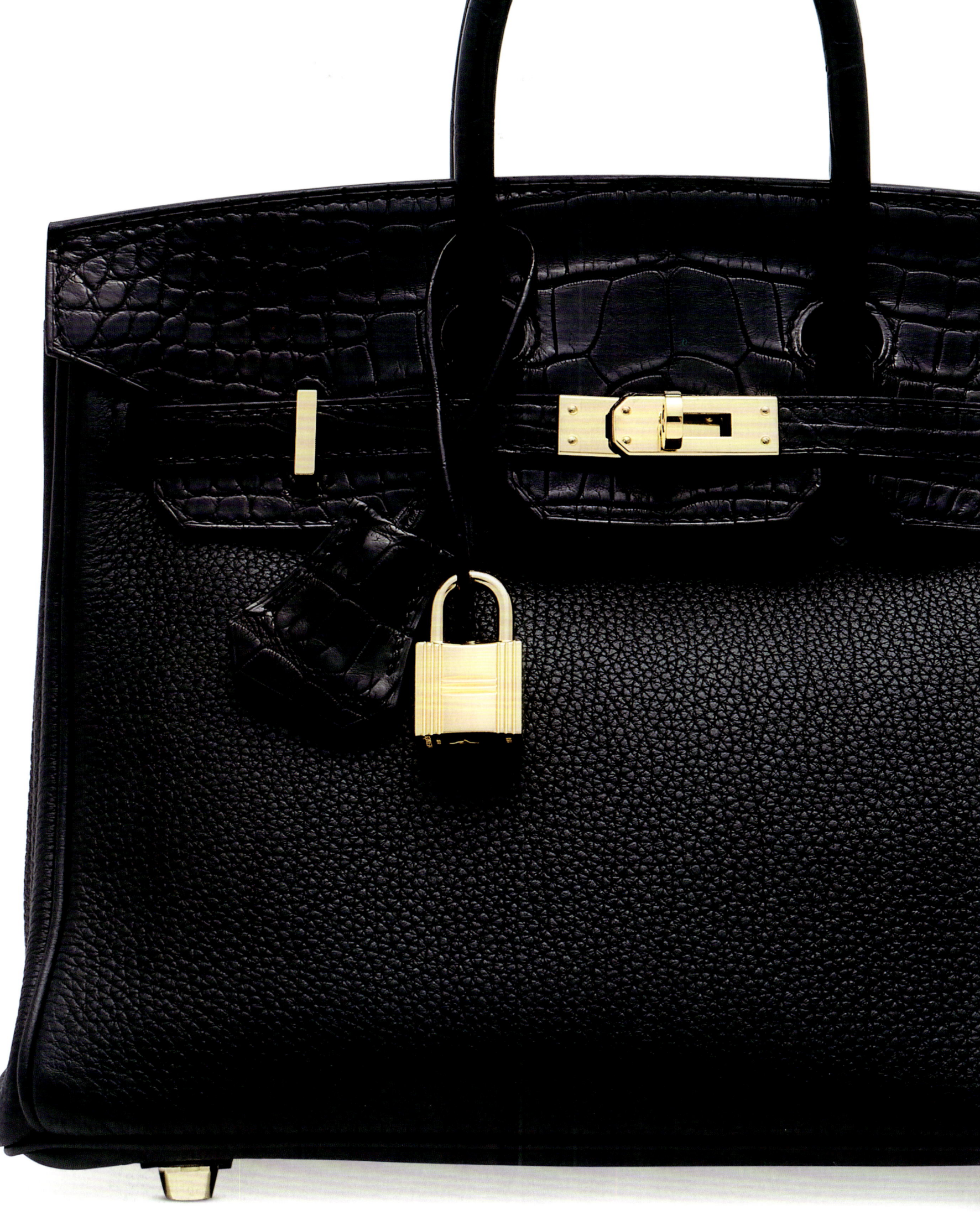

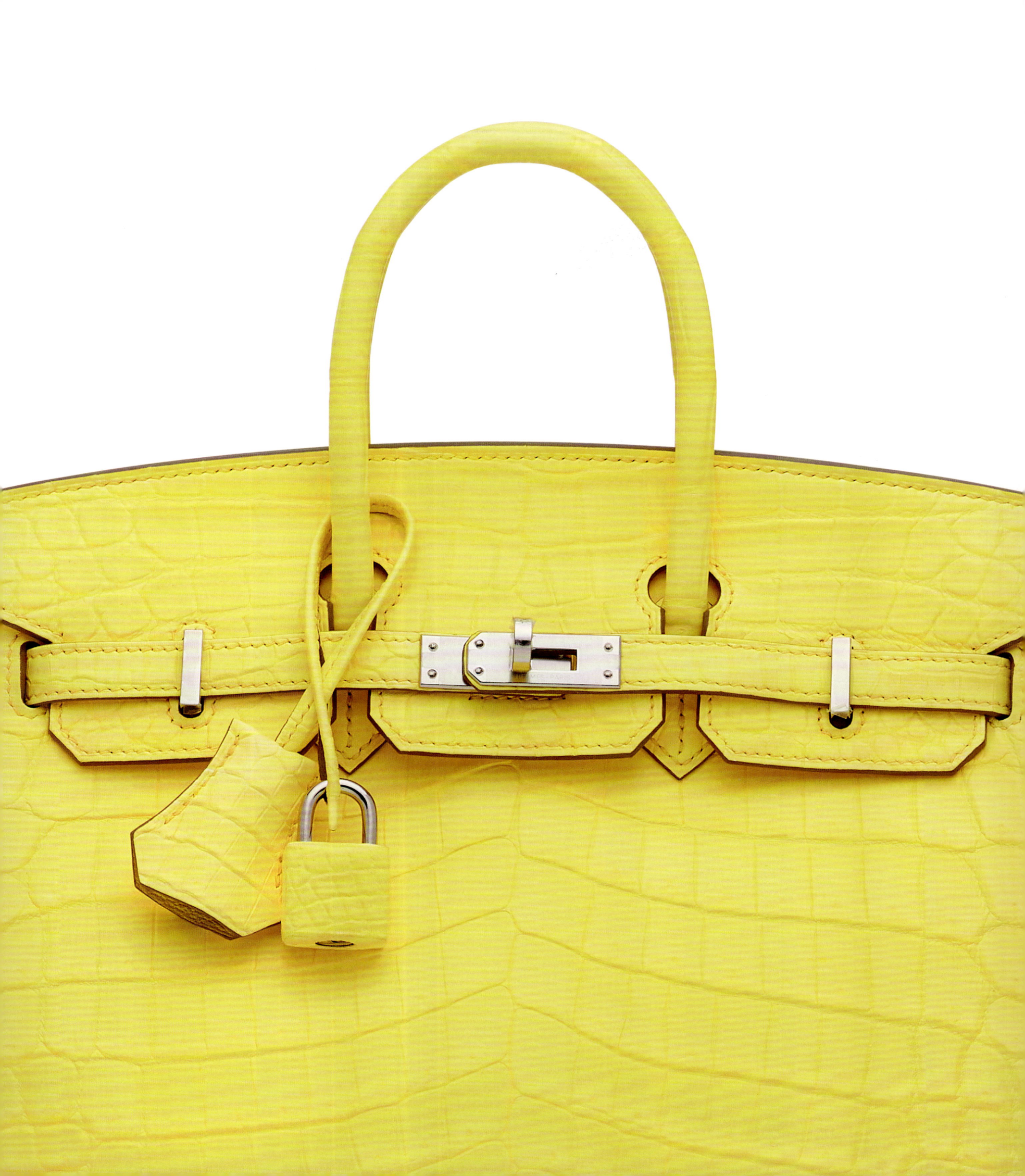

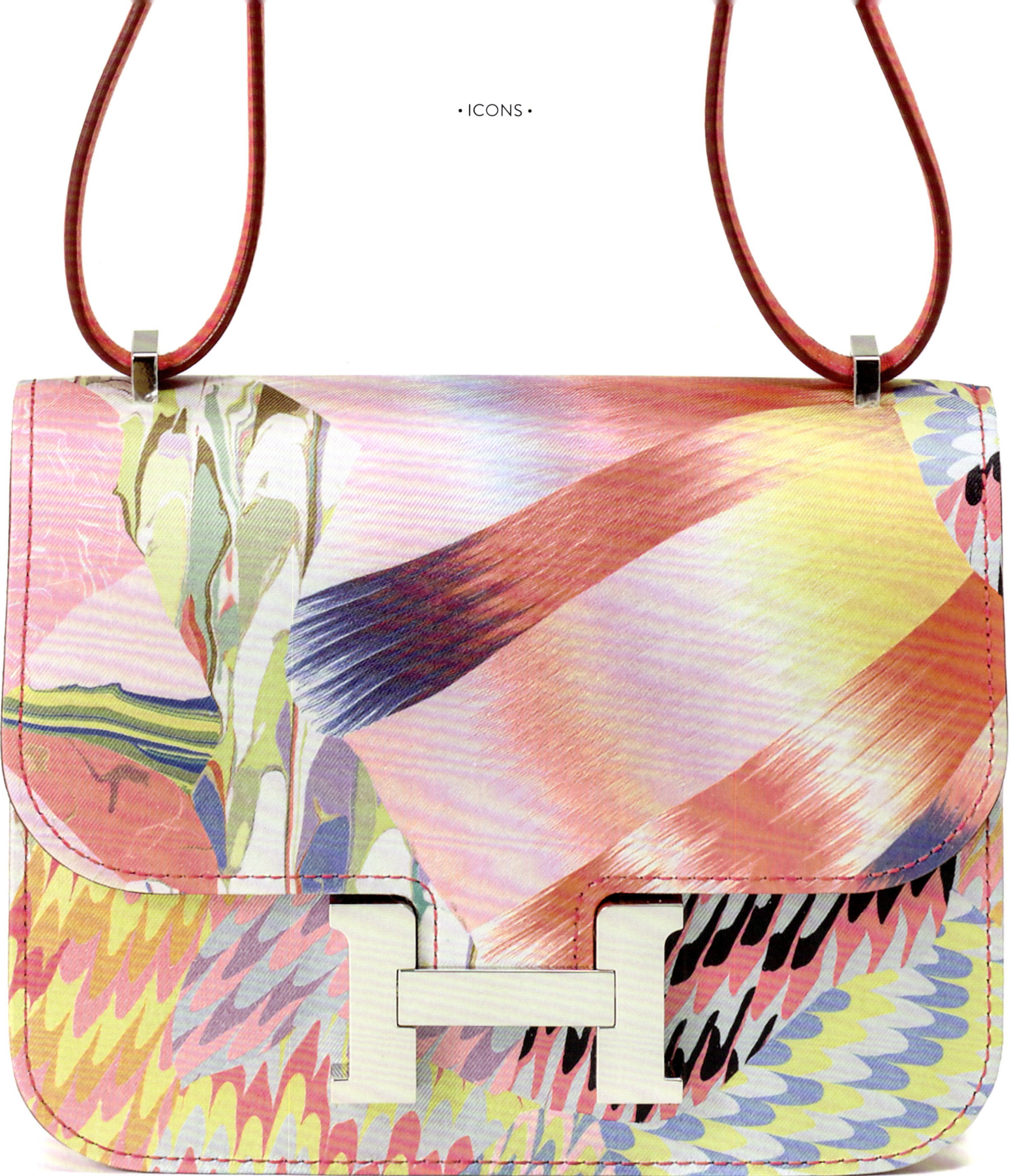

Opposite page – Unique Edition *Birkin 25* in matt satin-finish boreal *Jaune Citron* Nile crocodile leather with palladium hardware, 2022. Sold for 655,200 HKD in May 2024.

This page – Limited Edition *Constance 18* in Marble Silk and Rose Swift leather. Carré silk on the outside and fuchsia Swift leather on the inside, palladium hardware, 2022. Marbled silk arises from a Japanese technique which requires incredible skill to give rise to a flowing, sparkling, colourful pattern. Made in an extremely limited number, this rare bag reflects the constant dedication of Hermès to innovation, based on traditional techniques.

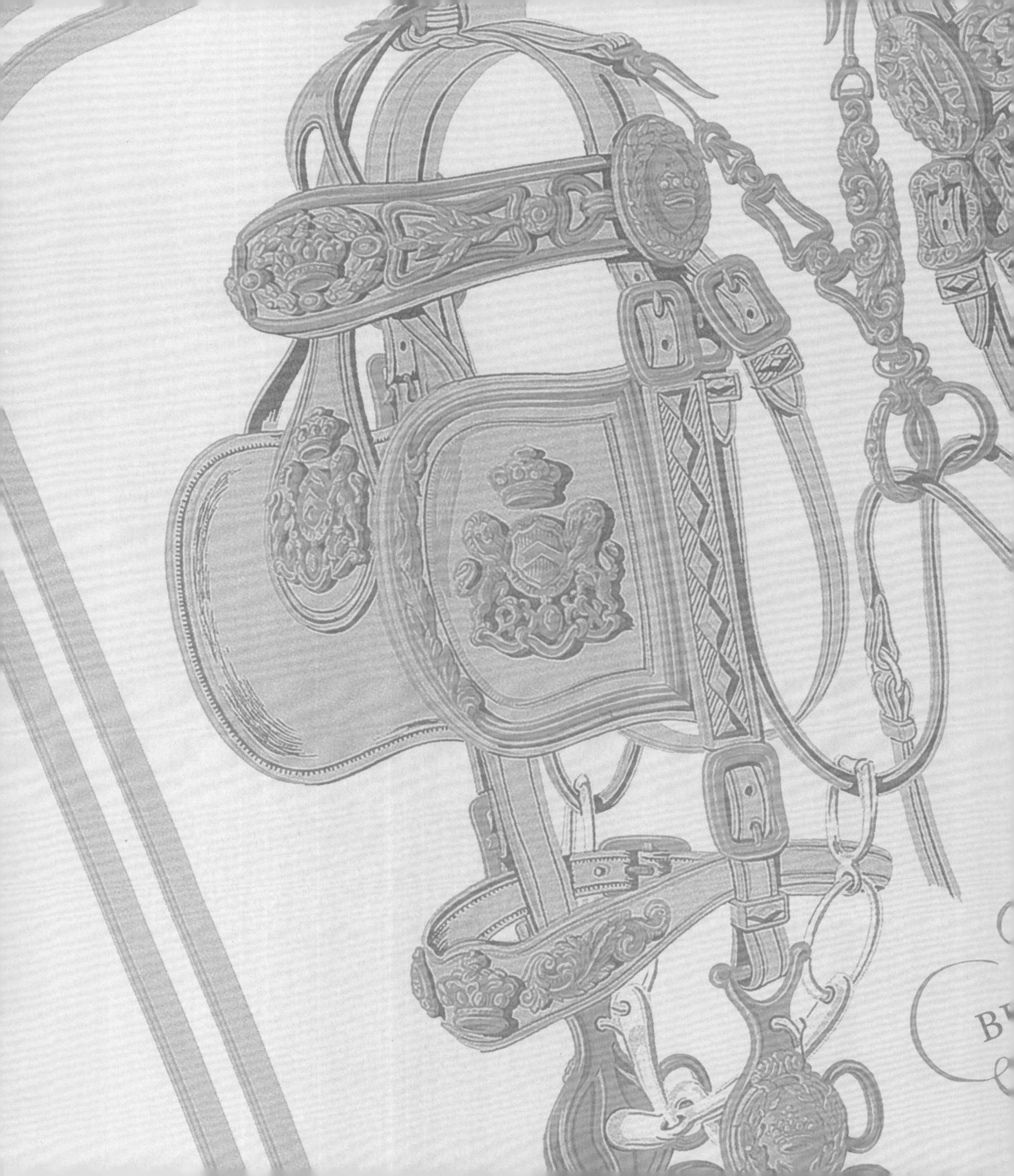

Jewellery

·················

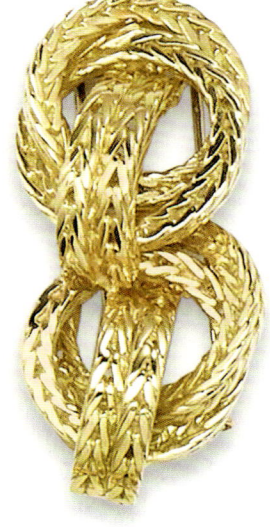

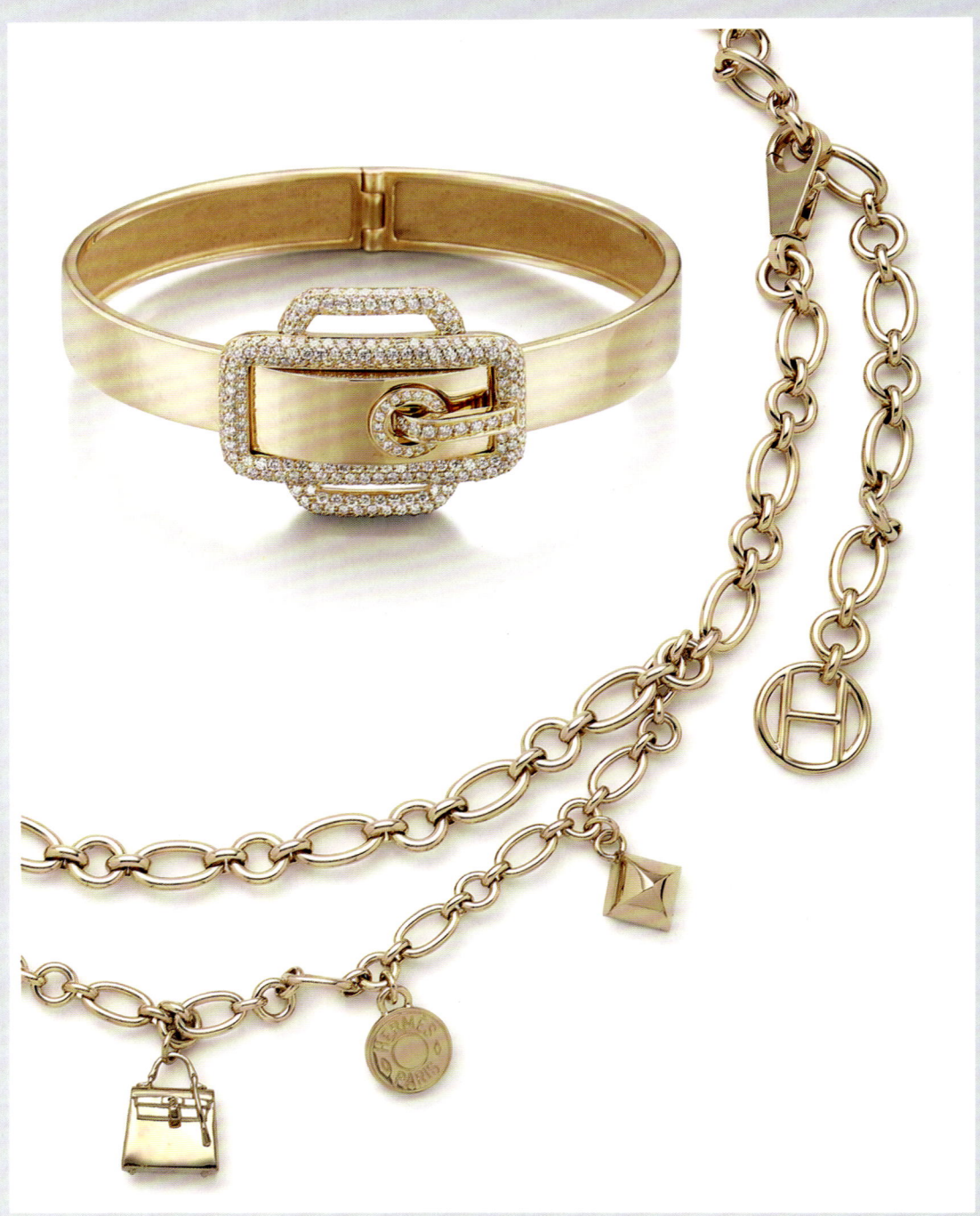

Top – *Attelage D'Or* bracelet in gold with diamonds. The shape of this bracelet is inspired by the rings on a harness found on the attachments for multiple horses. This piece has 270 set diamonds for a total of 1.59 carats.

Bottom – *Olga* belt in metal with five charms which are shaped after a few of the brand's iconic elements, including a padlock, a *Kelly* bag, a *Médor*, and anchor chain and a *Clou de Selle*. Silver and palladium. It can also be worn as a necklace.

PRECIOUS
AND CREATIVE

....

'At Hermès, the goal has never been to make the "object of the moment", the kind of thing you see everywhere and which then disappears after a few months, and that's equally true for bags and shoes as it is for necklaces and bracelets.'

Pierre Hardy, Creative Director of Hermès jewellery

Famous for its luxury products and impeccable craftsmanship, the French fashion house in Rue du Faubourg Saint-Honoré has expanded its range of products over the years and begun to sell jewellery with the same dedication to quality and fine design as its other creations.

Hermès began to explore the world of jewellery, or rather of fine bijoux, in the 1920s, with the first *Filet de Selle* bracelet in silver and leather. It was presented in 1927[1] and was overtly inspired by the equestrian world, which has been the universe of reference for Hermès since it was founded in 1837.

Almost one decade later, Robert Dumas (the son-in-law of Émile-Maurice Hermès, and the man who would eventually become the brand's Creative Director), introduced another important reference for the brand: the nautical world. History has it that Dumas, a sailing enthusiast, was looking at the anchor chains which kept boats docked along the coast of Normandy when he was inspired to design the outlines of the *Chaîne d'Ancre* bracelet, introduced in 1938. Crafted in silver, it would become one of the French brand's most symbolic accessories.

In so doing, the company made its début with fashion jewellery before introducing fine jewellery.

Between the First and Second World Wars, the haute bijouterie industry was quickly developing due to restrictions on the use and circulation of precious materials arising from the economic downturn and the political situation. The first non-precious fashion jewellery was created by Paul Poiret. In the 1910s, he had introduced pieces which didn't necessarily take the shape of true jewels; instead, they were conceived of as complements to dresses. They referred to the style, colour and type of fabric, which is why they were updated with every season and every collection.

The example set by Poiret was soon followed by Madeleine Vionnet. *Bijoux de couture* came into its own in the 1930s thanks to personalities such as Coco Chanel and Elsa Schiaparelli, who both managed to be successful while exploring entirely different creative paths.

On the other hand, given the economic situation, the number of people shopping at jewellers had dropped notably and imitation jewellery began to fall out of fashion in favour of more creative options. This meant that, in order to be successful, prodcuts had to continually be updated, interpreting and influencing public taste. In this context, the culture of the time made space for *bijoux* as fashion items, pieces in which style surpassed their intrinsic value.

Hermès stands alone in that, positioning itself in the luxury and refined accessory sector, it introduced silver jewellery but didn't follow the rhythms of fashion and continuous changes in style. Instead, it integrated these new products within its world of reference, which didn't change with the frequency of *couturiers*.

The birth of precious jewellery

In the early 1940s, due to the war, the production of jewellery practically came to a standstill, at least in Europe. Only after the war would jewellery make a comeback.

In those years, Hermès proposed lines of precious jewellery made in gold and gemstones, to the point that they appeared in advertisements of the time along with famous jewellers, such as Cartier, Van Cleef and Boucheron.

The 1950s began with a boom, the economic kind: people were hungry to rebuild and to be creative in different ways, from literature to architecture and design. Paris once again was the capital of luxury. Post-war, fashion dictated that women wear very feminine garments which accentuated their figure. In 1947, Dior introduced the New Look: it was defined by rounded shoulders, a cinched waist, and calf-length skirts. This style soon spread around the globe. Shoes, bags, scarves and jewels had to be perfectly harmonious with clothing, and fashion dictated rather discreet and small accessories. In the 1950s, however, there were very precise codes in terms of garments. In the morning, people wore shirt-dresses in soft fabric, held in place by small belts, or outfits composed of pencil skirts and cropped open jackets; there were dresses with short yet ample skirts for the afternoon, elegant dresses for the early evening, and dresses with deep necklines or a corset-like torso for special occasions.

In this sumptuous, opulent decade, gold jewellery was very popular, but with special textures and plaits; the smooth surfaces and shiny finishes of the 1940s were replaced by soft, sinuous shapes. Gold was twisted like thread, woven like rope or cut into small even pieces, each one placed at intervals with small coloured stone or diamond inserts.

The array of subjects in this new decorative style of daytime jewellery was inspired by nature. Flowers and animals appeared often, especially in brooches and clips, though there was no shortage of bows, lace edging, knots, draping, curls and so on. The most frequent bracelet styles in the 1950s were cuffs, with buckle motifs and large links, often with *charms*. Short chokers to fill in deep necklines were semi-rigid and had delicately finished surfaces. The items made by Hermès can be traced back to this style, in line with the items made by the big names in jewellery. Elegant chains in gold and silver were embellished with charms that echoed the iconic motifs of Hermès, such as stirrups, bridles and bits. These details weren't just decorative; instead, they were symbols of the brand's heritage. Some objects included enamelled elements, a technique which began to be widespread in Hermès jewellery. The *Collier de Chien* line, introduced in 1949, reimagined the belt made in 1927 and celebrated its sculptural, modern volumes.

In this decade, the division between jewellery to wear in the day and jewellery to flaunt at night and on special occasions was greater than ever. The former was mainly yellow gold ornamentation; while worldly occasions such as cocktail parties and benefit galas required platinum and diamonds. Yet it doesn't seem that Hermès presented necklaces with the qualities of *haute joaillerie* (high jewellery) at that time. Indeed, *haute joaillerie* was an area in which creations were rather stagnant, to the degree that, in the following decade, they tended to adhere to a tried-and-true formal repertoire. In the 1960s, the jewellery market became increasingly segmented. Alongside large jewellery brands, other trends arose, with a wide variety of characteristics, purposes and styles. These would soon become the stars of the jewellery market alongside more traditional items.

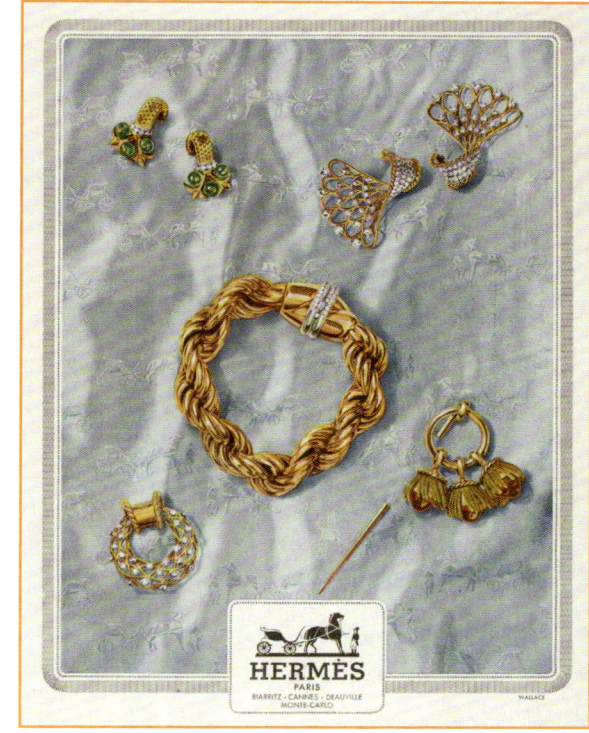

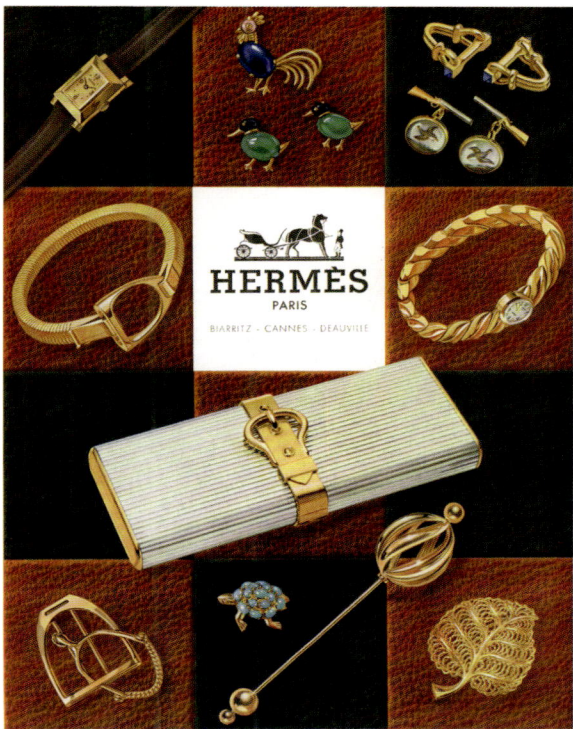

Hermès jewellery adverts from 1948 (top) and from 1950 (bottom).

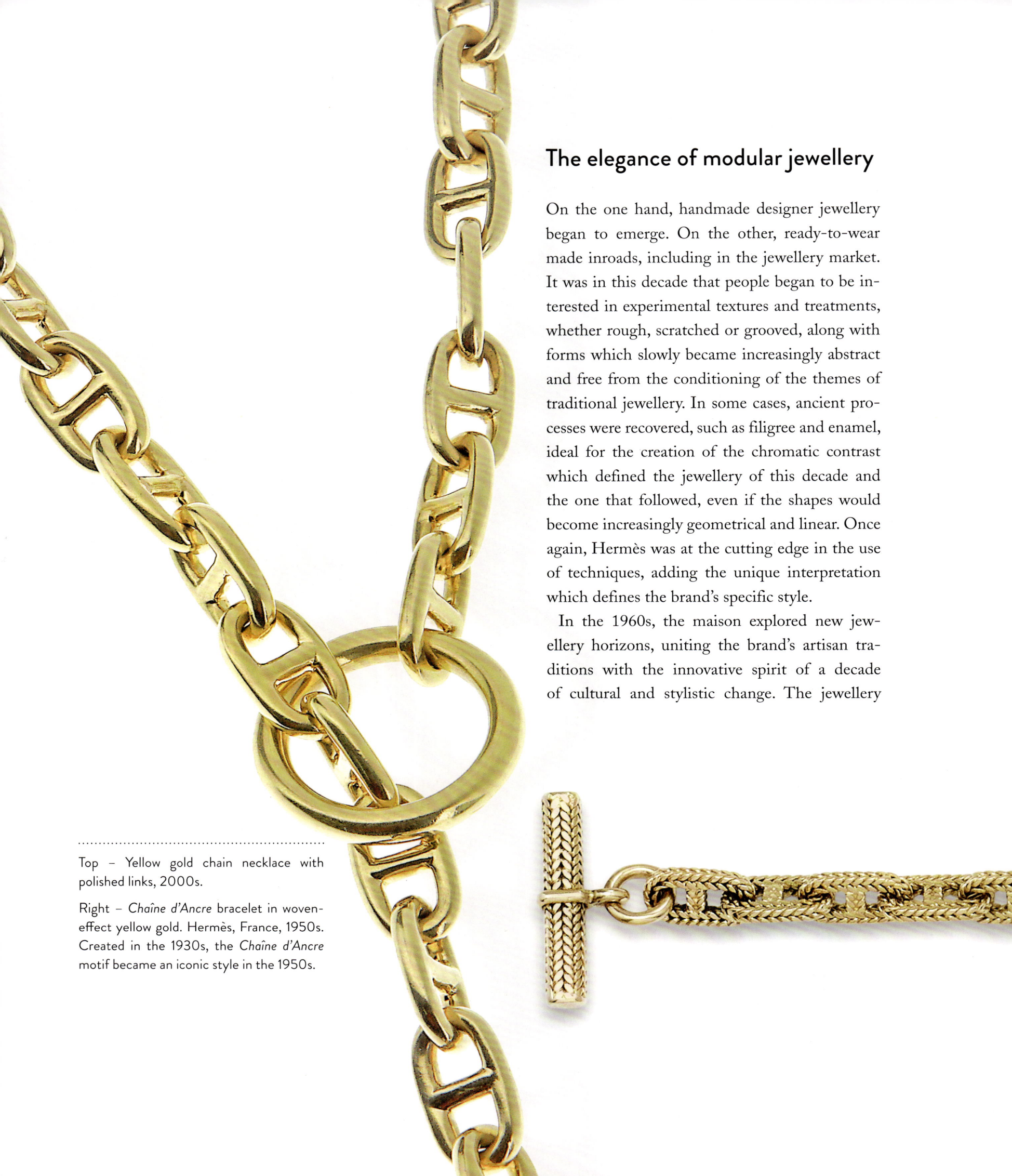

The elegance of modular jewellery

On the one hand, handmade designer jewellery began to emerge. On the other, ready-to-wear made inroads, including in the jewellery market. It was in this decade that people began to be interested in experimental textures and treatments, whether rough, scratched or grooved, along with forms which slowly became increasingly abstract and free from the conditioning of the themes of traditional jewellery. In some cases, ancient processes were recovered, such as filigree and enamel, ideal for the creation of the chromatic contrast which defined the jewellery of this decade and the one that followed, even if the shapes would become increasingly geometrical and linear. Once again, Hermès was at the cutting edge in the use of techniques, adding the unique interpretation which defines the brand's specific style.

In the 1960s, the maison explored new jewellery horizons, uniting the brand's artisan traditions with the innovative spirit of a decade of cultural and stylistic change. The jewellery

Top – Yellow gold chain necklace with polished links, 2000s.

Right – *Chaîne d'Ancre* bracelet in woven-effect yellow gold. Hermès, France, 1950s. Created in the 1930s, the *Chaîne d'Ancre* motif became an iconic style in the 1950s.

from this period reflected sober yet bold elegance, characteristic of the understated luxury that has always been a hallmark of Hermès. Its necklaces in the 1960s were defined by versatile designs which often took on the shape of a precious buckle, or they were designed into softly geometric lines.

Bracelets were among the starring pieces of Hermès jewellery in the 1960s. The *Chaîne d'Ancre* motif, which was introduced in the 1930s and reinterpreted with variations in the following decades, remained one of the brand's iconic pieces thanks to its balance of simplicity and sophistication. In this decade, Hermès began to reimagine its historic aesthetic, starting to use three-dimensional and sculptural forms. This includes the *Tête de Cheval* bracelet (1966), offered in gold and silver. The rings from the 1960s expressed refined elegance, with motifs which echoed the equine world or abstract patterns. The use of semi-precious stones, such as agate and onyx, gave jewels modern allure, while gold and silver dominated as the main materials.

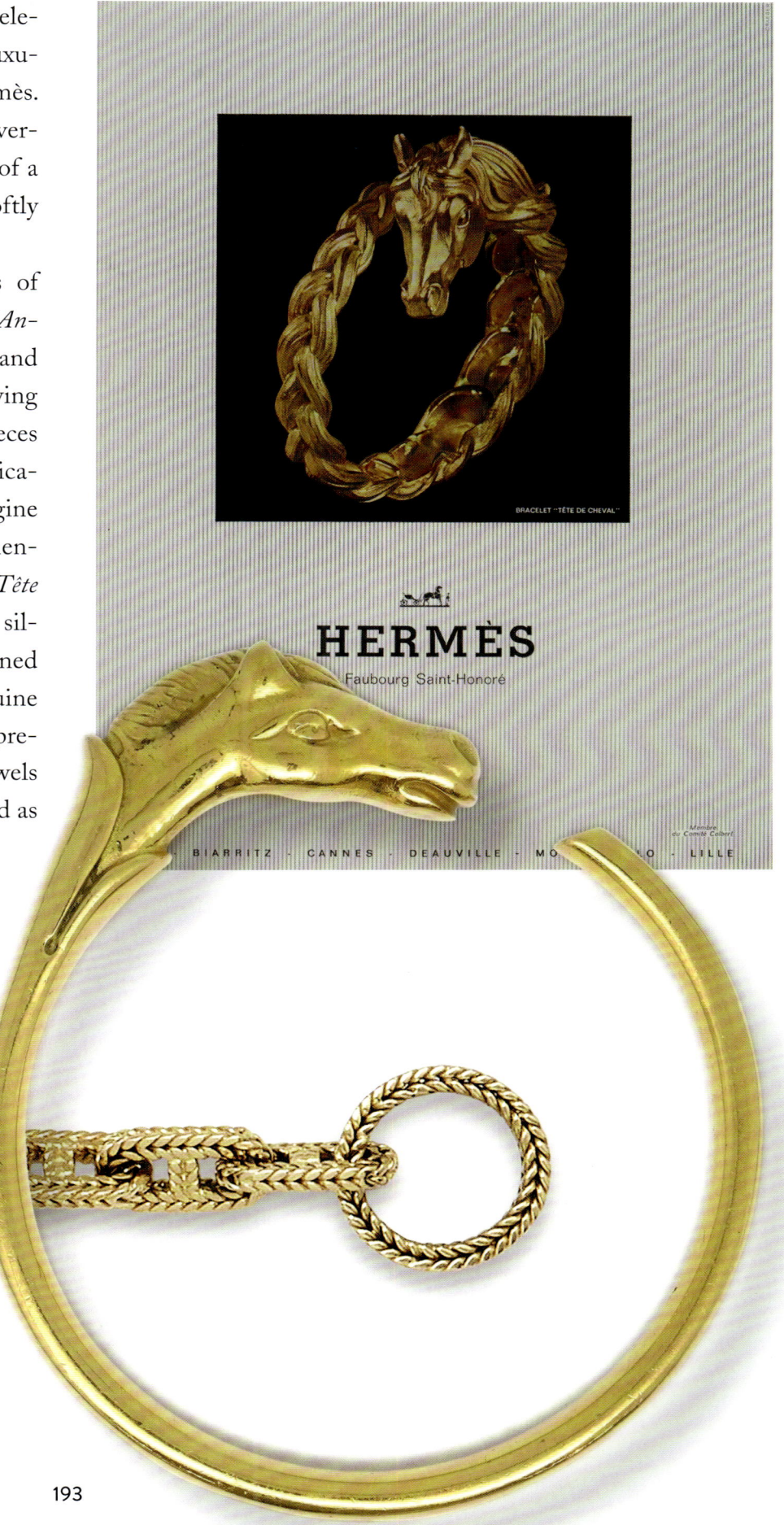

Top – Full-page advert for the *Tête de Cheval* bracelet, 1966.

Bottom – *Tête de Cheval* bangle in gold-plated metal, 1970s to '80s.

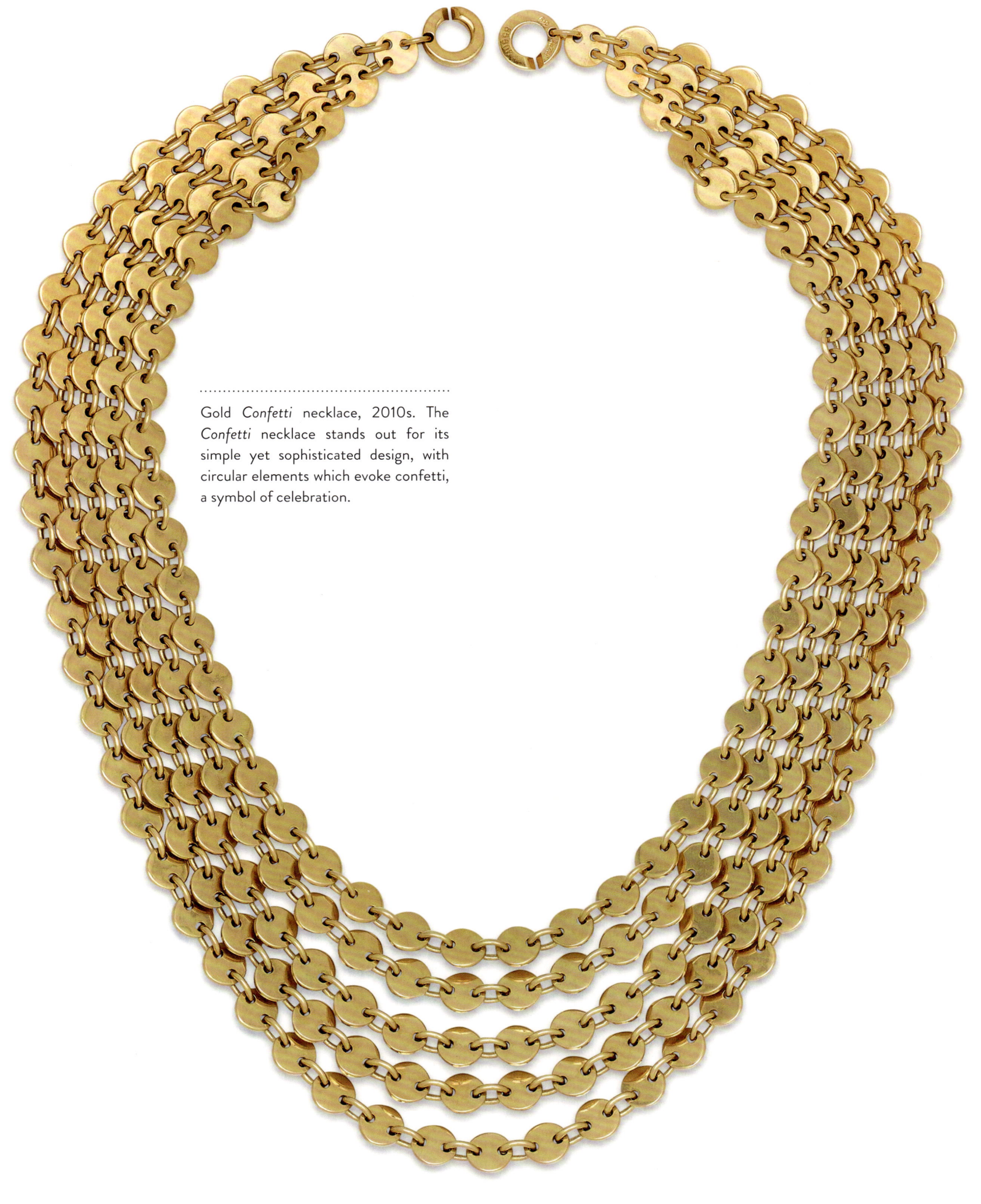

Gold *Confetti* necklace, 2010s. The *Confetti* necklace stands out for its simple yet sophisticated design, with circular elements which evoke confetti, a symbol of celebration.

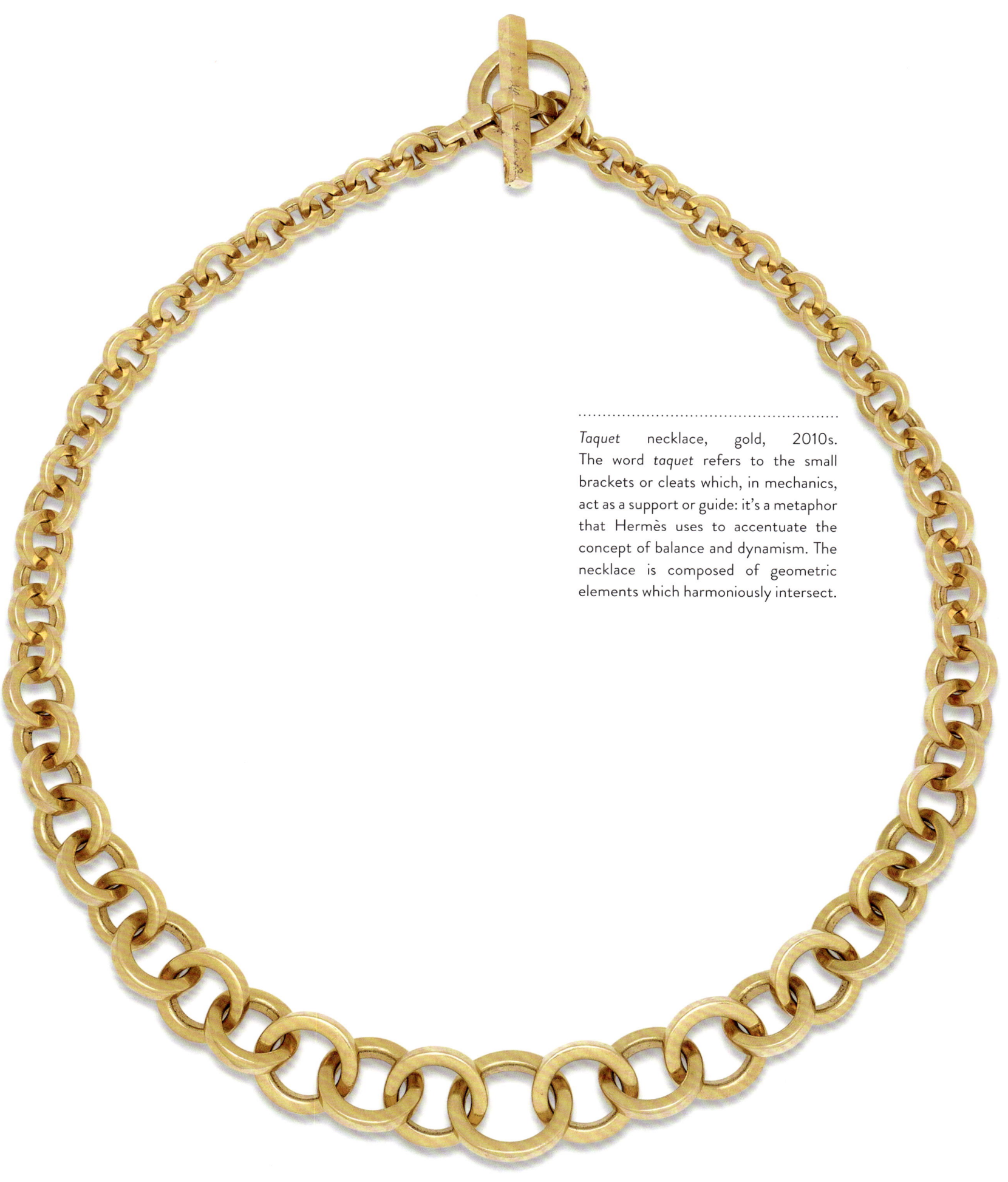

Taquet necklace, gold, 2010s. The word *taquet* refers to the small brackets or cleats which, in mechanics, act as a support or guide: it's a metaphor that Hermès uses to accentuate the concept of balance and dynamism. The necklace is composed of geometric elements which harmoniously intersect.

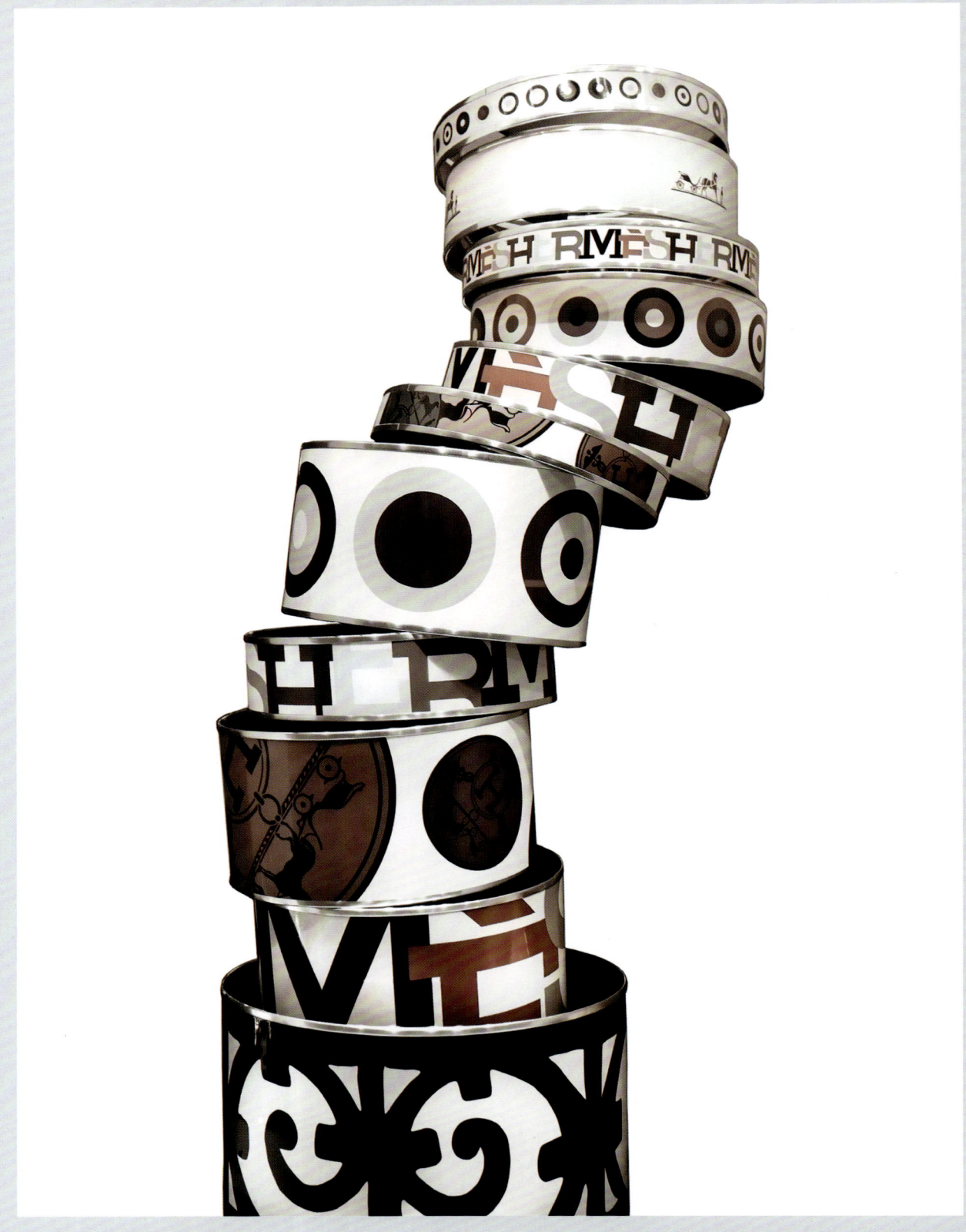

Hermès poster with a stack of enamelled bracelets.

Modern collections

Controversial, challenging, cut through with social tension and also ideologies and a new bodily and spiritual freedom, the 1970s were years with a dual spirit, in fashion as in many other areas of life. One was more nonconformist, the other more elegant, which emerged mainly at the end of the decade. As such, in parallel with fashion which expressed political ideals and corresponded to the feminist decision to wear garments that wouldn't draw attention to the body, a look emerged that stood alongside hippy style but which was still chic.

Jewels transformed to adapt to the new needs of liberated women. Jewellers chose modern, linear designs for their creations, elevating them through exquisite and interesting finishes and processes. Jewellery came in yellow gold for both day and evening, with a market which was oriented around goldsmithing to the detriment of traditional jewellery – understood as unique pieces with highly valuable stones. The surface of the gold was often embellished with incisions or brushed, and often included semi-precious stone inserts such as lapis lazuli, jade, tiger's eye and coral.

To meet the demand for colour, Hermès introduced its first enamelled bracelets.[2] With a metal base (generally gold-plated brass), they were hand decorated with traditional fired enamel methods, giving each piece a unique, long-lasting finish. Many of the motifs of Hermès' enamelled bracelets were inspired by its famous silk scarves, with equestrian, floral or abstract themes evoking the luxury and refinement for which the brand is known. The colours used were intense and often contrasting, giving the necklaces a vibrant and modern look while still maintaining ties to traditional craftsmanship. These bracelets were designed to be worn alone or in combination, so as to create personalised bold looks which were in line with the style of this freedom-loving era.

Reflecting the times – i.e. elegant but simple in its lines – the *Nausicaa* bracelet was born in 1971. Its name evokes the sea, but with a design inspired by equitation. Originally created by Jean-Louis Dumas, it is still being made and sold today.

The jewellery of the 1980s was characterised by imposing shapes and bold aesthetics. Large-link chains, colourful stones and majestic compositions were in vogue again. In this multifaceted context, there was an interest in reinterpreting elements that came from the past with pieces which were inspired by 1940s styles, reworked with large proportions: jewellery took on three-dimensionality, becoming sculptural and voluminous.

In this decade, Hermès stood out in the world of jewellery with creations that echoed the spirit of the times. The famous bracelets in enamel, decorated with geometric, floral and equestrian motifs, continued to be in demand, even if they were marked by intense hues and imposing dimensions. *Gourmette* chains were the stars of bracelets and chokers once again. Jewellery became larger with smooth and rounded surfaces in metal, continuing to embody the defined and immediately recognisable design which served as the foundations of the brand's style.

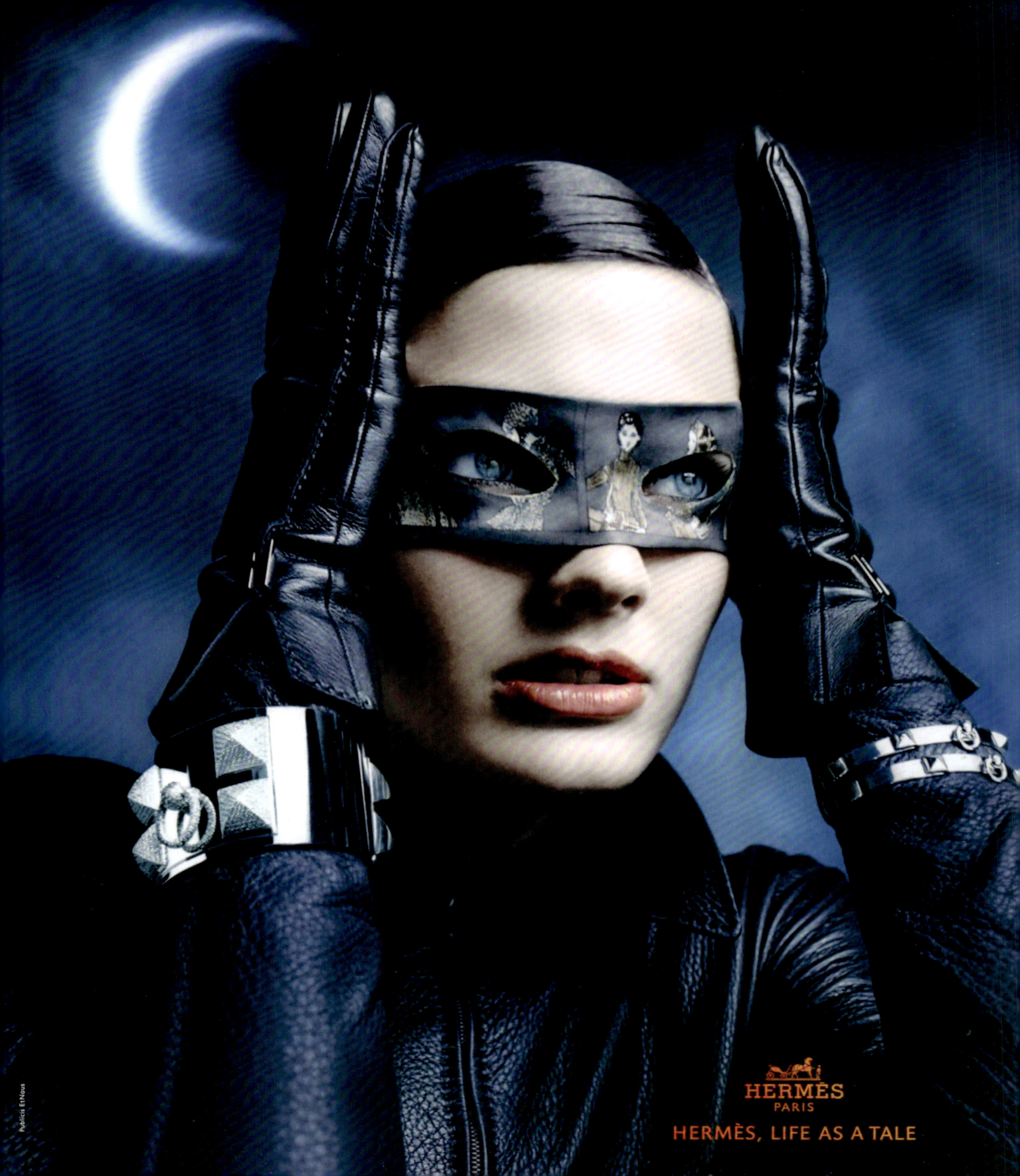

HERMÈS
PARIS

HERMÈS, LIFE AS A TALE

Renewal goals

Jewellery in the 1990s was composed of simple shapes, elementary geometries and modular structures. It was distinguished from styles of the 1980s by softer, less structured thematic combinations and motifs. Many different types of gold were used in different hues: from yellow to red, white to rose. And different materials were combined and juxtaposed, such as gold with leather and gold with steel, or even gold with horn. In parallel to material experimentation, formal research corresponded to a conceptual aesthetic which united different inputs coming from design, graphics and even art and fashion. Jewellery was produced which interpreted volumes, sizes and materials with a narrative scope, like veritable applied arts.

To further expand its reach in the jewellery market, Hermès purchased the historical silversmith Puiforcat in 1993.[3] The 1990s saw Hermès bolster its position as a luxury jewellery leader thanks to distinct creations which combined precious materials and innovative designs, within the framework of its traditions.

The necklaces from the 1990s are distinguished by simple yet elegant designs with details which evoke the equestrian world and Hermès traditions. They include many versions in links in white or rose gold to create bracelets or long necklaces which can be worn in different ways and which easily adapt to casual and formal looks. In the 1990s, the *Médor* bracelet, inspired by the famous *Collier de Chien*, was introduced. The aesthetic of this accessory is characterised by square studs which decorate the leather band, making it iconic and easy to recognise.

Enamelled bracelets continued to play a starring role in the jewellery line-up, with decorations inspired by the motifs seen on the brand's silk scarves, including geometric, floral and abstract patterns. These accessories came in different widths, from slender to more robust, ideal for more subtle looks and for bolder *statements*. The strength of Hermès jewellery in this decade was its ability to combine tradition and modernity. Its pieces evoked the long history of the brand, but they adapted perfectly to the contemporary spirit of the 1990s thanks to clean lines and innovative materials.

Advert for the *Médor* leather and metal bracelet from the 'Life as a tale' campaign, 2010–2011.

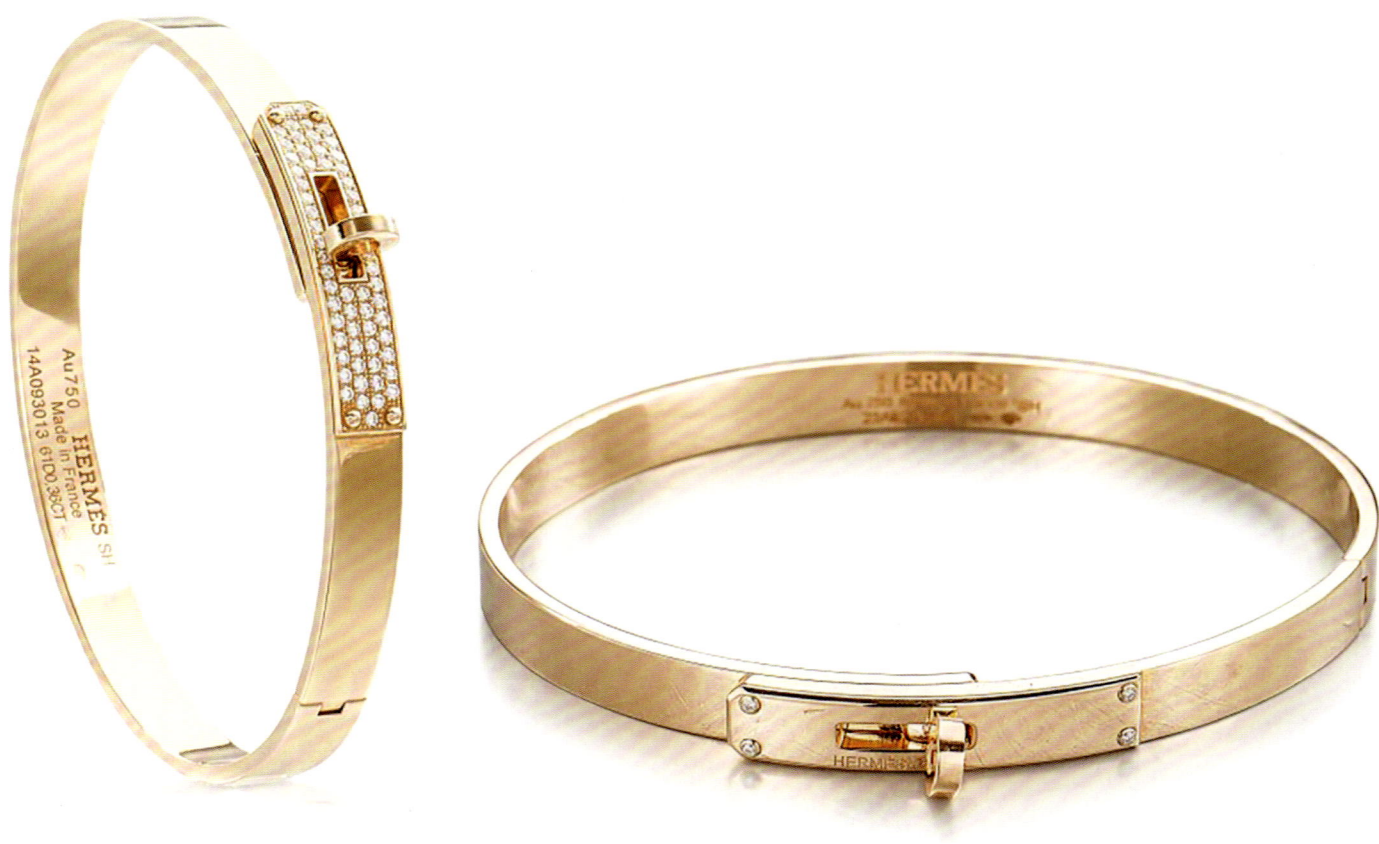

The *Hermès Clic H* bracelet was presented in 2000 as part of the brand's enamelled jewellery collection. It was an evolution of the first enamelled bracelets inspired by the company's vintage silk scarves, launched in the 1970s. Its design, characterised by the famous H-shaped clasp, has made it one of the brand's most recognisable pieces.

Since the 2000s, moreover, Hermès has been inspired by its lines and iconic elements to create its jewellery. The *touret* clasp, the straps and the *clochette* of the *Kelly* were thus reinterpreted in silver and gold. Through its collections, the history of the bag is reinvented and enriched, remaining in constant evolution.

....

This page – Two *Kelly* bracelets: rose gold and diamonds (left), rose gold with four diamonds (right), 2020.

Opposite – Advert for the gold *Médor* bracelet from the 'Dance with the orange ribbon' campaign, 2007.

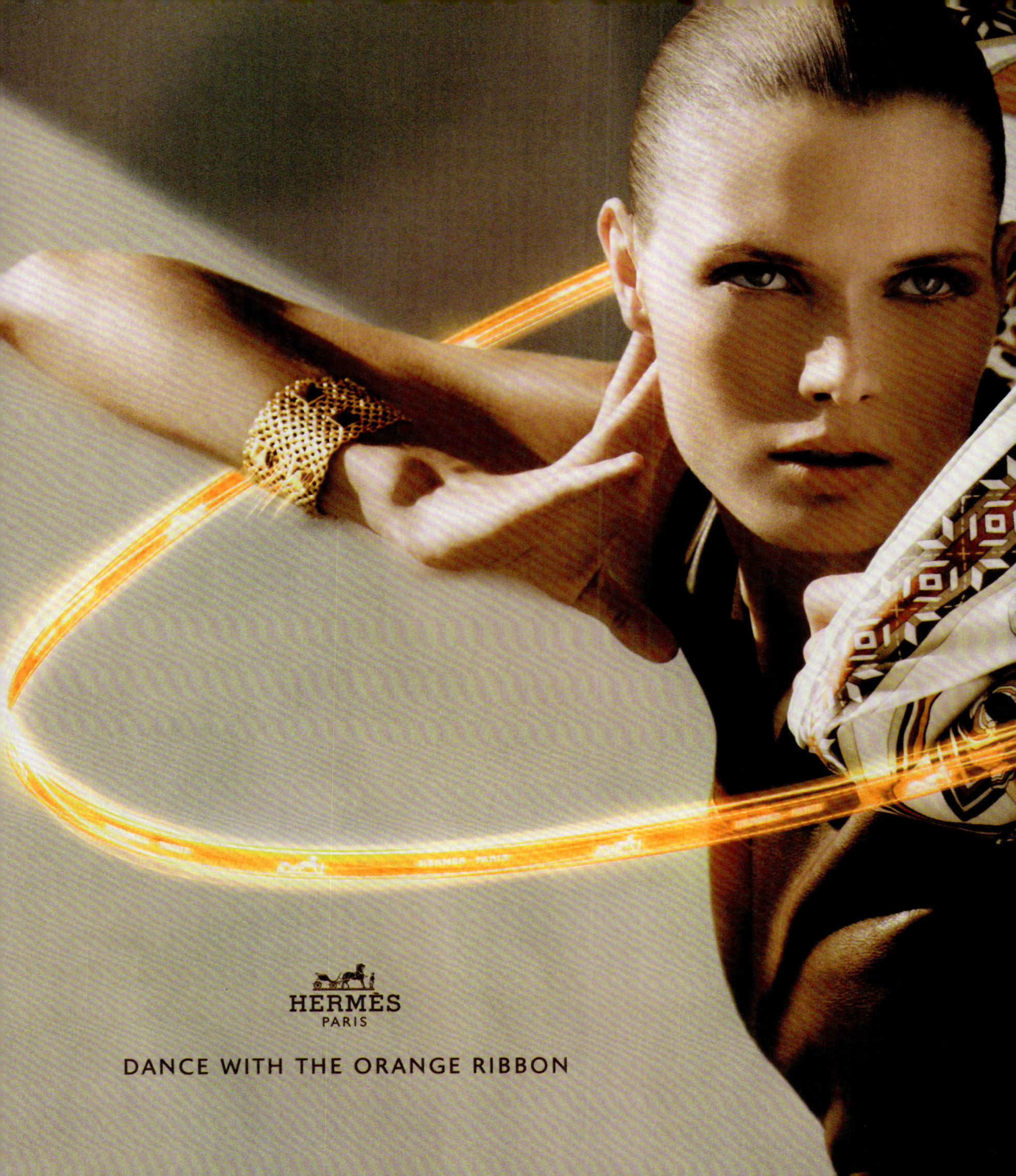

Iconic Design

Hermès jewellery is known for its impeccable quality and distinct design. Each piece is the result of an attentive selection of materials and meticulous handcrafted workmanship. In terms of design, Hermès is inspired by its equestrian *heritage*, reinterpreting the shapes of stirrups and bits, alongside 'nautical' motifs such as knots and those linked to sport, movement, and life spent outdoors. In general, the fashion house is inspired by the beauty of nature and everything which helped create a refined image.

Today, Hermès jewellery includes the fashion jewellery collection, which is part of the women's clothing line and is made up of high-quality items in materials such as wood, leather, metal, silk and enamel. The high jewellery collection, on the other hand, is sub-divided into silver, gold and haute bijouterie.

One line is dedicated to silver jewellery which takes shape in four different themes: *Chaîne d'Ancre, Kelly, The Equestrian, The Wonders.* The *Chaîne d'Ancre* motif is reimagined in infinite versions and sizes, becoming modern in a punk interpretation; while the *Kelly* collection is an ode to the famous bag: short and long necklaces in contemporary, sculptural proportions, earrings, rings and pendants explore its details. The equestrian realm embraces the *Collier de Chien* motif introduced initially as decoration in 1949 and now an Hermès jewellery icon, along with the *Ex-Libris* which Émile-Maurice Hermès had drawn in 1923 and which became one of the most famous silk scarf designs. The items in the *Wonders* collection, on the other hand, depart from classic leather goods, such as the *Birkin*, the *Kelly* and the *Constance*, transforming them into precious pieces.

In addition to the four themes (*Chaîne d'Ancre, Kelly, The Equestrian* and *The Wonders*), the gold jewellery line explores the same reference shapes with smooth, soft surfaces or encrusts them with shimmering diamonds. It also includes the *Precious Moments* collection, which mainly features rings with colourful stones and diamonds, wedding bands and pieces which evoke affectionate bonds.

The most recent arrival to the scene is the *Haute Bijouterie* line, introduced in 2010. It includes the most precious pieces made in the brand's ateliers, as imagined by French designer Pierre Hardy.[4]

Kelly Chaîne Choker in rose gold and diamonds, 2020s. The *Kelly Chaîne Choker* was inspired by the famous Kelly bag, a symbol of elegance and craftsmanship for the French brand.

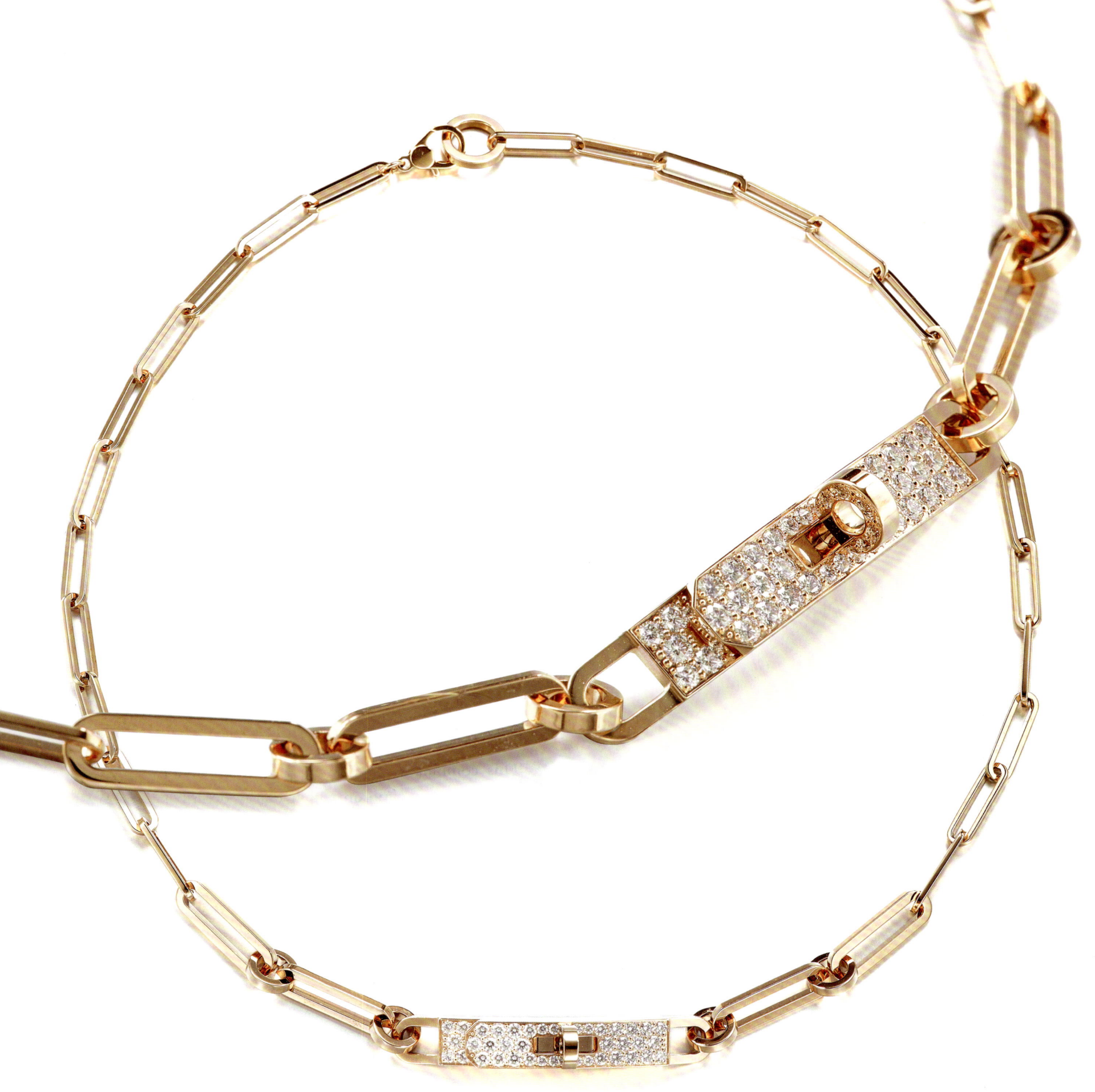

In the world of gems

In 2001, Hardy was named Creative Director of Jewellery. He had joined the fashion house in 1990 as the Creative Director of Footwear, but early on in the new millennium, the then Chairman Jean-Louis Dumas asked him to start designing jewellery too.

Hardy's aesthetics are distinguished by precise geometric shapes, chromatic contrast and a balance of modernity and craftsmanship.[5]

The designer began his path in this *métier* by working with fine silver jewellery. Having worked for Hermès for a few years, he had the time to get to know the brand's relevant universe. For his first collection, he went to the root of the shapes which had formed the aesthetics of the maison. For his first silver collection, he worked on the brand's historical motifs, such as the *Chaîne d'Ancre*, the *Clou d'H*, the *Kelly* bag, the padlock and the *Collier de Chien*, before eventually approaching the world of high jewellery. For his silver jewellery collection, Hardy created the *Galop bracelet* (an ode to Hermès' first industry), which takes the shape of a sculptural horse head.

Hardy's first high jewellery collection for Hermès on the other hand, came out in 2010. This *Haute Bijouterie* line included the *Fouet* (whip) necklace, with its sinuous, tactile shape, covered in diamonds, braided like a rope and in the shape of a whip, and the *Centaure* ring, a graphic interpretation of a horse hoof. Both are references to the equestrian heritage of Hermès.

From then on, however, through increasingly complex concepts and sophisticated techniques, Hardy continued to construct a completely new visual style for Hermès jewellery, finding diverse and relevant creative expressions. To Hardy, 'a piece of jewellery contains the idea of shining a light on a specific part of the body: a wrist, a joint, a collarbone. The jeweller's craft is to capture this light and reflect it.'[6] Over time, Hardy began to experiment with more radical ideas to imagine an entirely new way to interpret the style and history of Hermès. 'Everyone has an image of the typical Hermès vocabulary. I wanted to bring it to life, perhaps invent new words, new shapes, a new way of integrating the Hermès universe.'[7]

The *Black to Light* fine jewellery collection, presented in 2019, represents a stylistic turning point for Hermès. It explores the contrast between the darkness of black gems and the luminosity of rose gold.

There are more than 20 pieces, from necklaces to bracelets and rings, which juxtapose rough black jade and black spinels with the elegance of rose-coloured metal. This combination creates an effect of 'radiant darkness', an oxymoron which Hardy describes as encapsulating the modern essence of the collection.

Among the most distinct pieces, the *Niloticus Lumière* bracelet and necklace in rose gold, black jade and diamonds evokes the elegance of Nile crocodiles.

The collection reinterprets four emblematic shapes from the Hermès repertoire: *Chaîne d'Ancre*, the *Kelly* motif inspired by the famous bag, *Galop*, which takes the shape of a horse's head, and *Collier de Chien*.

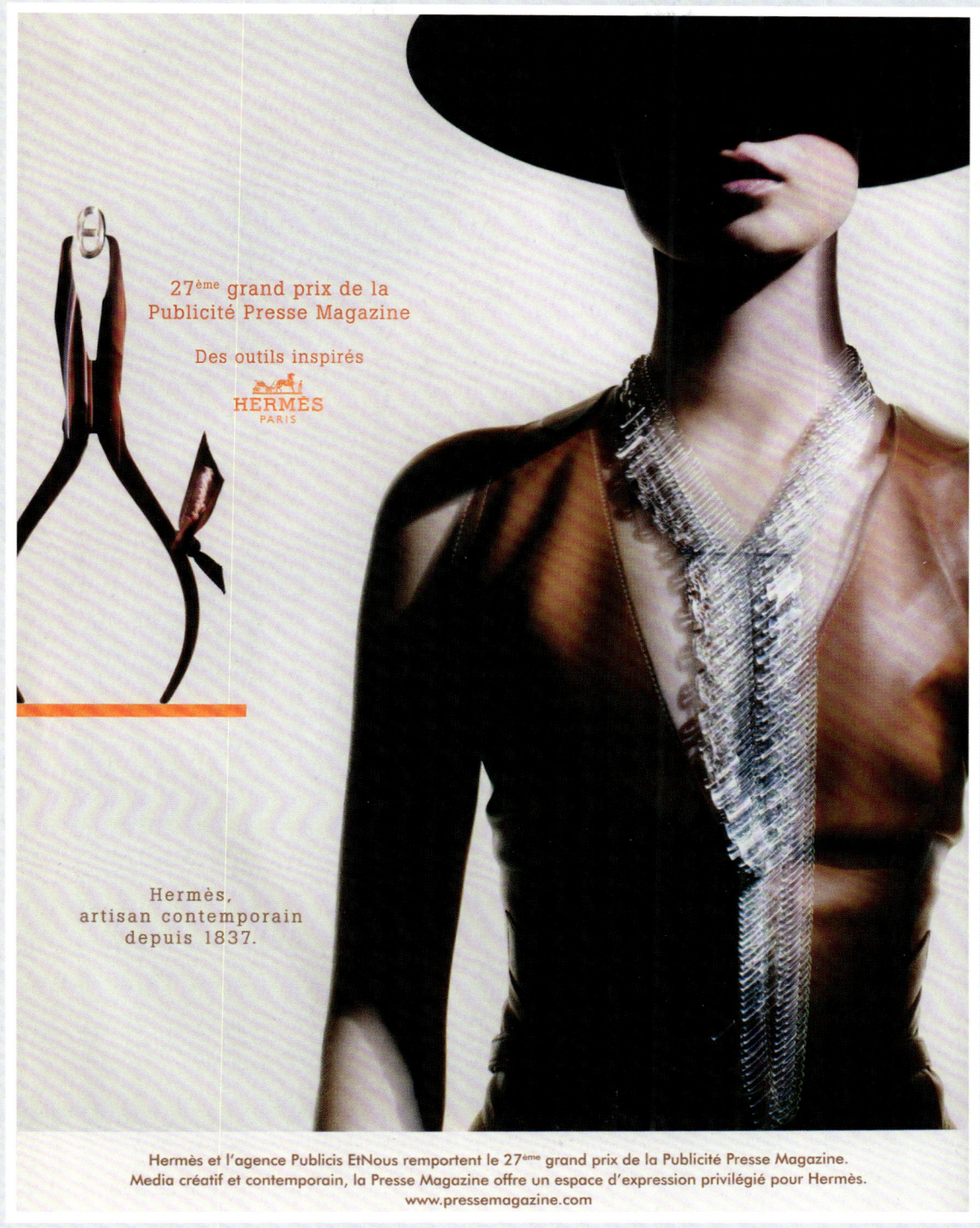

With its Inspired Tools campaign on the subject of craftsmanship, created with the Publicis EtNous agency, Hermès won the 27th Grand Prix de la Publicité Presse Magazine in 2012.

The innovative use of black gemstones, which require notable skill to be cut and polished, gives the jewellery a sophisticated contemporary aesthetic, demonstrating Hermès' ability to fuse tradition and modernity in timeless creations.

The *Lignes Sensibles* collection marked Hardy's desire to explore the emotional and physical connection between jewellery and the body. Composed of 45 pieces which are divided into five lines (*À l'écoute, Ondes miroirs, Hermès Réseau lumière, Contre la peau* and *Filière sensuelle*), it features necklaces, bracelets, rings and earrings which follow the natural curves of the body, emphasising the symbiosis between ornament and skin. The creations use rose gold and stones in delicate hues, such as green prehnite, tourmaline and diamonds, echoing the shades of the flesh and eyes.

Sensuality, a playful spirit, light and lightness are the hallmarks of the *Kellymorphose* collection, which has become a travelling exhibition sent to the most prestigious Hermès locations. For this project, Hardy analysed the distinctive elements of the *Kelly* bag: its trapezoid shape, its closure, the straps, the key and the key-carrying *clochette*, to give shape to the jewels. One of the most emblematic pieces is the *Kelly Gavroche* necklace, which takes the shape of one of the bag's straps, knotted to the side like a scarf and completely encrusted in diamonds in different cuts.

The *Les Jeux de l'Ombre* collection (2022) was inspired by the interplay of light and shadow, making the intangible, tangible. Composed of 53 pieces, it uses precious materials such as rose gold, diamonds, sapphires and black spinels to create jewels which seem to project shadows on the body of the wearer.

This combination of light and dark adds depth and dimension to the creations. Among the most symbolic pieces, the *Fouet Ombré* necklace in rose gold embellished by brown diamonds and midnight blue sapphires stands out for its reinterpretation of the motif of a horse whip, an iconic Hermès element.

The *Les Formes de la Couleur* collection (2024) is centred around the exploration of colour and the relationship between colour and shapes. Hardy has returned to his artistic training, referencing colour theory and using colourful gems to create powerful and sensual compositions. Made up of 22 pieces, the collection is divided into distinct chapters, each one with a unique aesthetic. The *Portraits de la Couleur* chapter offers rings with surprising combinations of geometric shapes and colours, such as square rubies, triangular beryls and circular sapphires. *Fresh Paint* features jewellery that imitates the look of painted stones, with meticulous craftsmanship which creates arabesques and shaded textures. *Arc en Couleurs* offers pieces in undulating, soft forms which adapt to the curves of the body. It is made with a gradient of almost 1,400 stones in soft colours. The *Hermès Diaprés* chapter includes rings, bracelets and necklaces composed of emerald-cut diamonds or sapphires, accentuated by mother-of-pearl and baguette-cut stones. *Supracolor* presents architectural pieces which demonstrate the dispersion of light waves, such as a unique necklace with rutilated quartz and a triangle-cut diamond.

Thanks to his creative vision and respect for artisan traditions, Hardy continues to influence the world of fashion with iconic creations which unite functionality and pure aesthetics, applying the maison's philosophy to his creations: invisible luxury.

'My rule is to design jewellery which always reflects the Hermès mantra: being as discreet as possible and leaving maximum freedom of movement to the wearer. It's a philosophy which I truly understood when I saw how the horseback riding saddles are created: everything is designed to leave the horse free to move. The concept is the same. Even if, in theory, jewellery is worn to get noticed.'[8]

This page – Cuffs in rose gold and black baguette-cut spinel (left) and in white gold with baguette-cut diamonds (right). Both from the *Kellymorphose* collection, 2022.

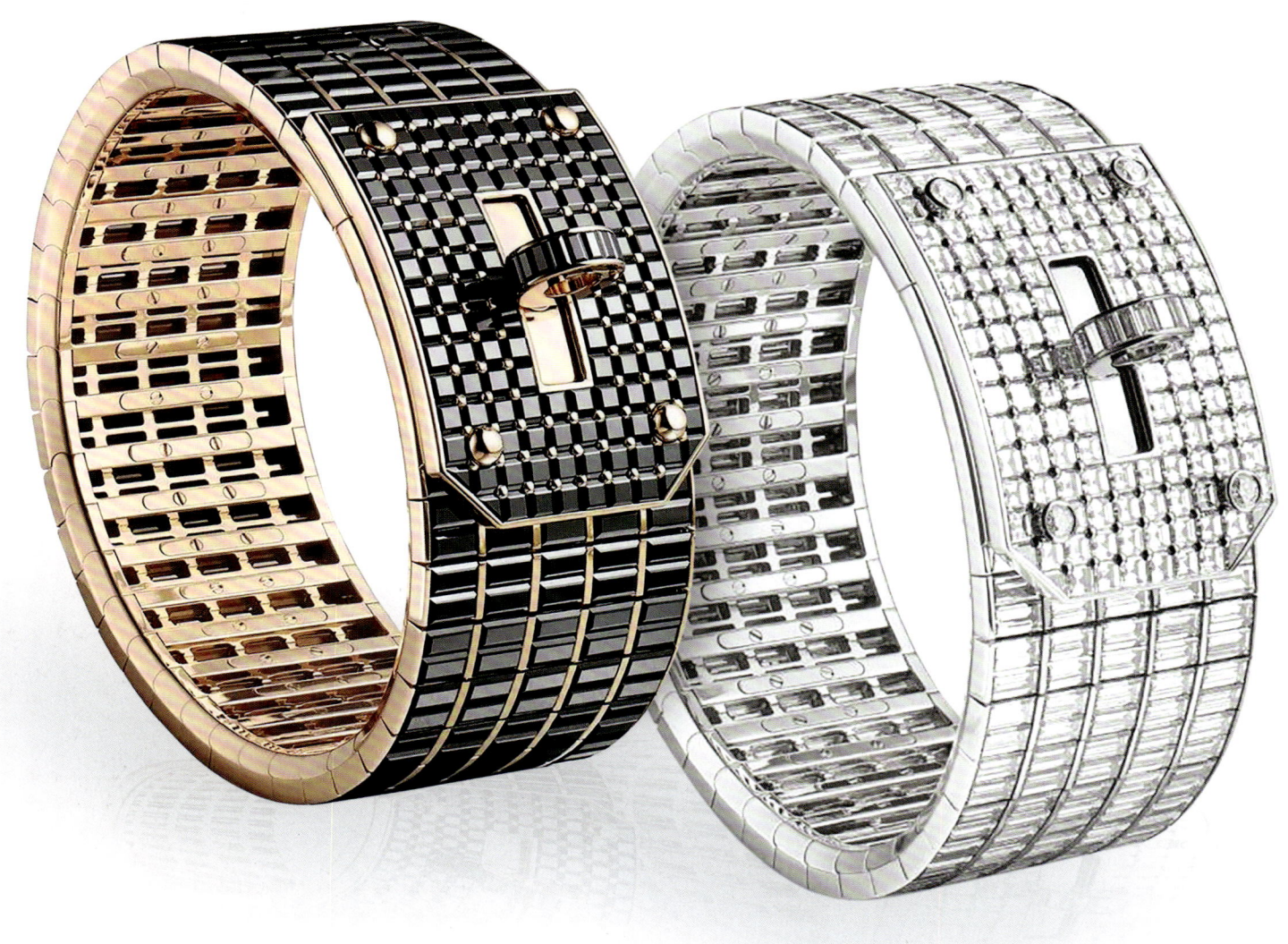

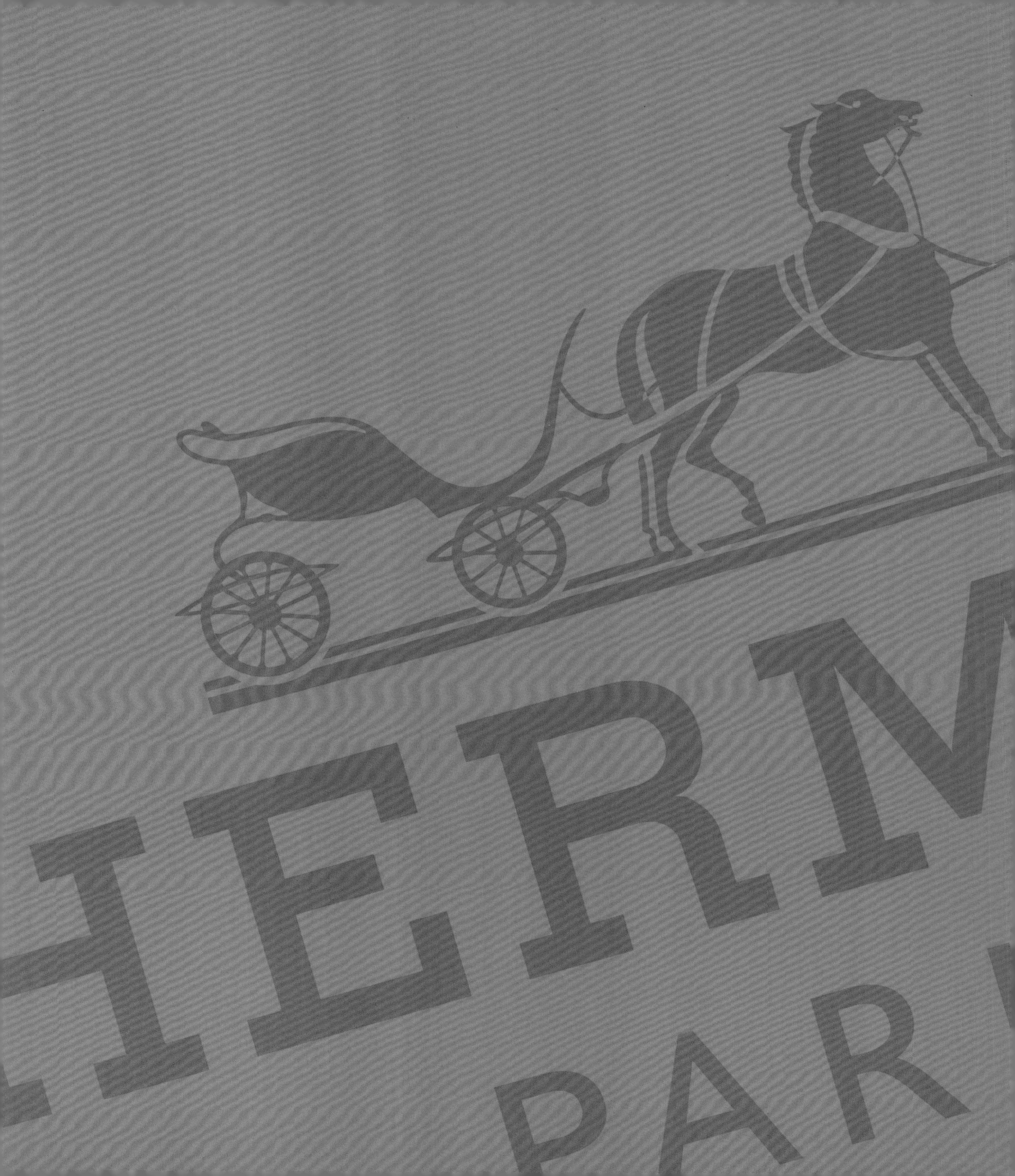

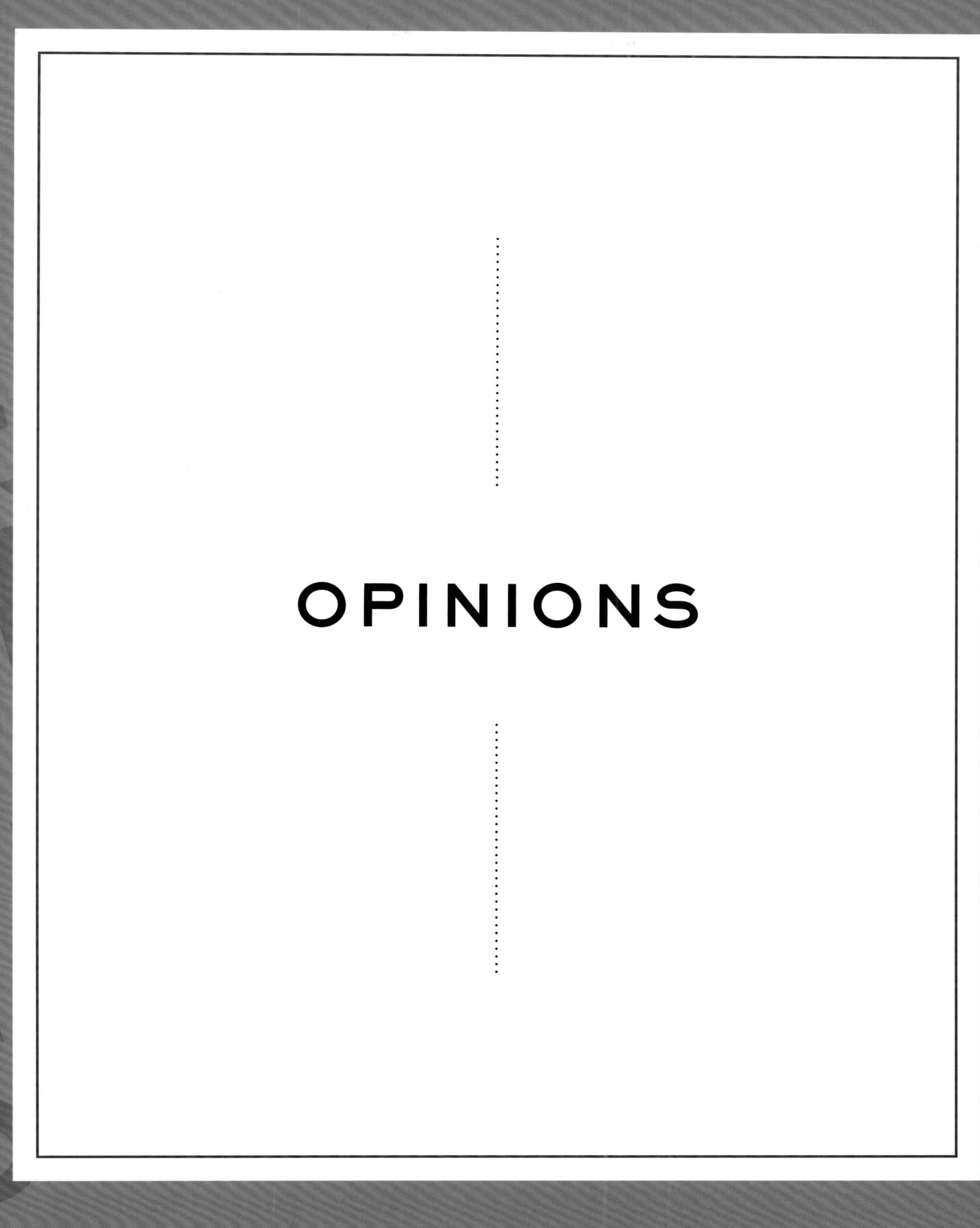

OPINIONS

Rachel Koffsky

—

ACCESSORIES AS WORKS OF ART

Appointed Senior Vice President and International Head of Handbags & Accessories at Christie's in 2022, Rachel Koffsky began her career at the auction house in 2014 as a Bags and Accessories specialist. She will help us understand the values which Hermès bags and jewellery have come to represent.

Since the mid 2000s, the second-hand luxury bag market has grown significantly, transforming into an economically important industry. Different factors have driven this phenomenon, including greater environmental awareness, the seeking out of economic value and the increasingly widespread cultural acceptance of second-hand items.

According to a Future Market Insights (FMI) report published in 2023, the global second-hand bag market is worth about 6.3 billion USD and is expected to reach 11.4 billion USD by 2033, with a compound annual growth rate (CAGR) of 6.10% in the projected period. It's easy to imagine that Hermès will play a key role in all of this.

'The secondary market is the most dynamic segment of the fashion and accessories industry. Such impressive growth is tied to a radical change which has taken place in relation to items bought second hand. If "vintage" was once seen as less desirable than "new", today this category, which has a "second life", connotes exclusivity, rareness and uniqueness', remarks Koffsky.

The idea of buying second-hand items is widely accepted in society today. Celebrities and influencers often promote the purchase of vintage or second-hand products, thereby helping to promote this practice, even making it glamorous.

One of the factors which has contributed to the growth of the second-hand luxury bag market is increased sensitivity to environmentally sustainable habits.

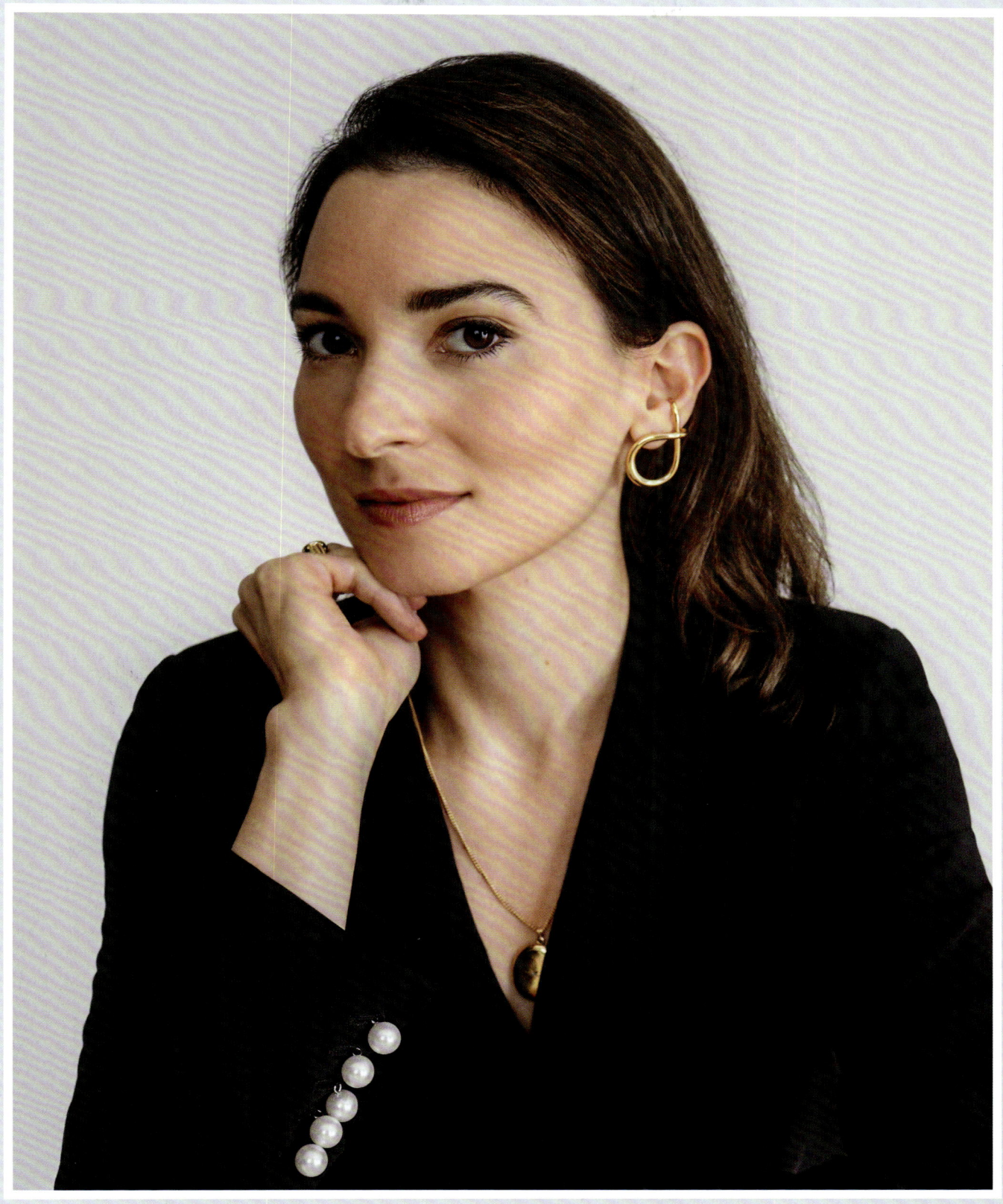

Rachel Koffsky, Senior Vice President and International Head of Department, Handbags & Accessories, Christie's.

Consumers are ever more aware of the environmental impact of the production and consumption of luxury items. Purchasing second-hand bags is seen as a way to promote sustainability through re-use, contributing to economic circularity and easing the pressure which the production of new goods places on the environment.

Another aspect to consider in any analysis of the vintage market is that luxury accessories can be a significant investment. The purchase of second-hand goods makes it possible for consumers to obtain high-quality products at lower prices. Moreover, some luxury items which were produced in limited editions, or those which were customised or discontinued, can increase in value over time.

'The draw of Hermès bags is their rarity, their quality materials and the value of the brand. For example, a limited-edition or customised Birkin, made with exotic leather and embellished with precious metals or stones, can reach a price at auction which well exceeds its original value. Often available only to select clients and with waiting lists which last for years, the exclusivity of these bags helps them become objects of desire and increases their market value,' Koffsky confirms.

The value of consistency

These elements alone, however, aren't enough to explain the passion of collectors and their behaviour. A brand can be described as the sum of intangible product attributes: its name, packaging, price point, heritage, reputation and advertisements. Hermès is unique in its reputation for quality, style, exclusivity and imagination.

'The story of the fashion house began in 1837 when Thierry Hermès founded an atelier specialising in the production of harnesses, bridles and reins; from that moment up to today, led by the six generations after him, the brand has excelled in craftsmanship,' recounts Koffsky. 'The saddles they make today are done in such a way that they're almost indistinguishable from those made in the late 19th century. Double-needle point *sellier* stitching, invented in the Hermès workshop in the early 1800s, is still used for Birkin bags and all others crafted by hand in the atelier in Pantin. This process, which creates a singular, durable, precise stitch, cannot be executed on a sewing machine. Moreover, it's an element which embodies the value and recognisability of the fashion house.

'To create the unique identity of the brand and define it over time, the iconic orange boxes certainly have done their part (they were a product of necessity, caused by the lack of paper in other hues during the war). Today, they are as famous and recognisable as the blue boxes of Tiffany. To understand the power of the brand, all

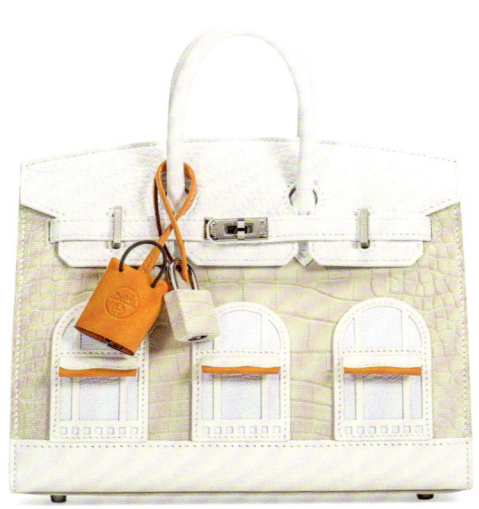

Launched in 2019 as a very limited edition, the *Faubourg Birkin* is characterised by its unmistakable design: an ode to the façade of the flagship Hermès boutique in Paris, at 24 Rue du Faubourg Saint-Honoré, completed by the famous lock and keys and protected by a leather Hermès dust bag in the brand's signature orange. Trimmed by sellier topstitching, the *Faubourg Birkin* is the first *Birkin* to be made in the 20 cm size.

we need to do is consider the "pilgrimages" which Hermès fans take to reach the headquarters at 24 Rue du Faubourg Saint-Honoré to admire the sumptuous window displays, the incredible mosaic flooring and the wide selection of items inside, which over the years has expanded to include various product categories, all of them luxury accessories. Hermès is loved by collectors, who are attentive to and passionate about their scarf, jewellery, porcelain and, most importantly, bag collections.'

Customer trust and loyalty are integral to the history of the brand, motivated and explained by the consistent values which the brand continues to embody. Founded as a saddler, the brand has evolved over the decades, expanding its range of products to include clothing, accessories, perfume, watches, jewellery and leather goods. Despite its diversification, Hermès has remained extraordinarily consistent over the years, and has built its reputation upon products which are not only luxurious, but which also last over time, offering tangible and durable value to customers.

'This is particularly true for the bags, which are much more than practical containers: they become works of art you can wear. The 1950s Kelly bags and those made today are extremely similar in their style, design and manufacture. At auction, Birkin and Kelly bags from the 2020s are found next to similar items from the 1970s, 1980s and 1990s. Few other fashion houses can boast such consistency. While many brands go through peaks and valleys in terms of success and popularity, Hermès has always had a high level of consensus.'

Created for the opening of the Hermès Store on Madison Avenue in 2022, the *Bolide on Wheels* embodies the most whimsical side of Hermès creativity. Some limited-edition versions have fetched over 20,000 USD at Christie's New York.

Wearable works of art

As Koffsky sees it, Hermès accessories challenge the idea that fashion isn't art. Historically speaking, the prevailing opinion was that art is the result of individual creation, the fruit of higher spiritual inspiration and thus in a class above commerce. Fashion, on the other hand, was considered an industry whose main mission was to meet the needs of everyday life and the market. As explained in detail at the beginning of this book, sociologists and philosophers such as Georg Simmel, Roland Barthes, Thorstein Veblen and Jean Baudrillard debated the value of fashion in society and its relationship with art, with different visions over the centuries.

In the 1980s, critics such as Michael Boodro and Rémy G. Saissel posited that art is in a category above the money and trade of the market; it exists for its own sake. It isn't created for function: instead, it has the sole scope of being contemplated, standing the test of time and lasting forever. Fashion is therefore the exact opposite because it is created to fulfil a function and because it is, by nature, constantly changing.

But more recent thought includes the idea that fashion and art, at least initially, share a similar genesis which can be traced back to the creative act. Only later on do they head down different paths. And of course, we mustn't forget that even fine art is subject to market logics.

The 'eternal' nature of Hermès accessories makes it possible to see them as elements in which two different worlds intertwine, their lines blurring. Fashion, like any other artistic activity, therefore asserts itself as a component worthy of the aesthetic domain, whose codes fully belong among those of contemporary expression, with accessories such as bags and jewellery poised as a decisive component in the social construction of the self. Hermès is often seen as eternally immune to trends. *Kelly* and *Birkin* bags are essential and iconic pieces which never go out of fashion.

Exceptional results

According to Koffsky, the *Birkin* and the *Kelly* are seen as some of the most coveted bags in the world, with custom and limited editions among the most sought-after, like the Himalaya versions, considered the 'Holy Grails'. In November 2021, a *Himalaya Birkin* with diamond-encrusted hardware fetched four million HKD (515,416 USD) at Christie's Hong Kong.

'The *Himalaya* is a collector favourite,' explains Koffsky. 'The sale took place at a time when the market was particularly lively, because after the pandemic many new collectors began looking to the world of auctions. Once reserved to an elite inner circle, this industry is seeing real growth, attracting an ever-greater public thanks to digitalization. Recently, the *Kelly Clutch* joined the list of most-coveted, as did the *Faubourg Birkin* and the *Bolide on Wheels*.'

Created in 2019 for VIP customers and produced in a limited edition of 50, the *Faubourg Birkin* was inspired by the Hermès boutique in Paris. A white *Faubourg Birkin* was sold for 189,000 USD at Christie's New York in May 2024, while the sea blue and the brown, gold and orange versions claimed 163,800 USD and 151,200 USD at the same auction.

The *Kelly Clutch* designed by Jean Paul Gaultier in 2004 is at the top of its category: one of them was sold by Christie's New York for 52,000 USD in May 2024.

Jewellery and Silk Scarves

In addition to bags, Christie's has recorded important sales for Hermès jewellery and its famous silk scarves. Hermès jewellery has timeless allure, characterised by minimalist yet sophisticated designs which excite fashion collectors and enthusiasts. Pieces such as the iconic *Collier de Chien* bracelet or the *Chaîne d'Ancre* necklace have been sold for record prices, reflecting the growing recognition of Hermès jewellery. The fashion house's silk scarves are famous for their intricate and artistic designs, which often tell a story through detailed and symbolic imagery.

Such record-setting sales at Christie's highlight a broader trend in the luxury market, one in which items that combine the brand's signature details, craftsmanship and exclusivity are increasingly seen as valuable investments.

In conclusion, the long-lasting appeal of the brand and its position as a luxury market status symbol have carried it over into a world which is closer to that of fine art than fashion. This trend is evidenced by the sales of Hermès bags, jewellery and silk scarves at Christie's, sales which reflect the growing trend to see high-range fashion and accessories as an investment opportunity, thanks to their rarity, craftsmanship and historical significance.

Morgane Halimi

—

A BRAND THAT HAS STOOD THE TEST OF TIME

The insight of Morgane Halimi, Global Head of Handbags and Fashion at Sotheby's, is particularly relevant to understanding the market of second-hand luxury bags and accessories and the central role which Hermès plays within it.

The rapidly growing secondary luxury bag market is an increasingly important part of the global luxury industry. Driven by factors such as sustainability, financial value and changes in consumer habits, this once-niche market segment is quickly proving to be an essential component of the global luxury industry. With increasing demand and new opportunities, it's destined to remain a key focus of high-end brands and investors for years to come.

Such is the view shared by Morgane Halimi, who joined the Sotheby's team in 2021 with the goal of creating the Handbags and Fashion Department. She says that the second-hand bag market is the one showing the most interesting growth, confirming that the Hermès brand is able to maintain its primacy even as sales begin to increase.

'Between 2022 and 2023, we doubled our turnover linked to vintage handbags. The percent linked to Hermès bags, however, has remained unchanged: 90% of vintage bags sold at Sotheby's are Hermès.'

That trend is seen across all channels, from traditional in-person auctions to online sales and even the bricks-and-mortar points of sale which Sotheby's has opened in different cities, including Zurich and London. They are joined by the Sotheby's Maison which recently opened in Hong Kong, where the Sotheby's Salon concept store takes up the entire first floor. In it, the retail experience has been carefully designed to present multiple objects from different categories within the same space: rare books, African art, natural history objects, pottery, bags and so much more.

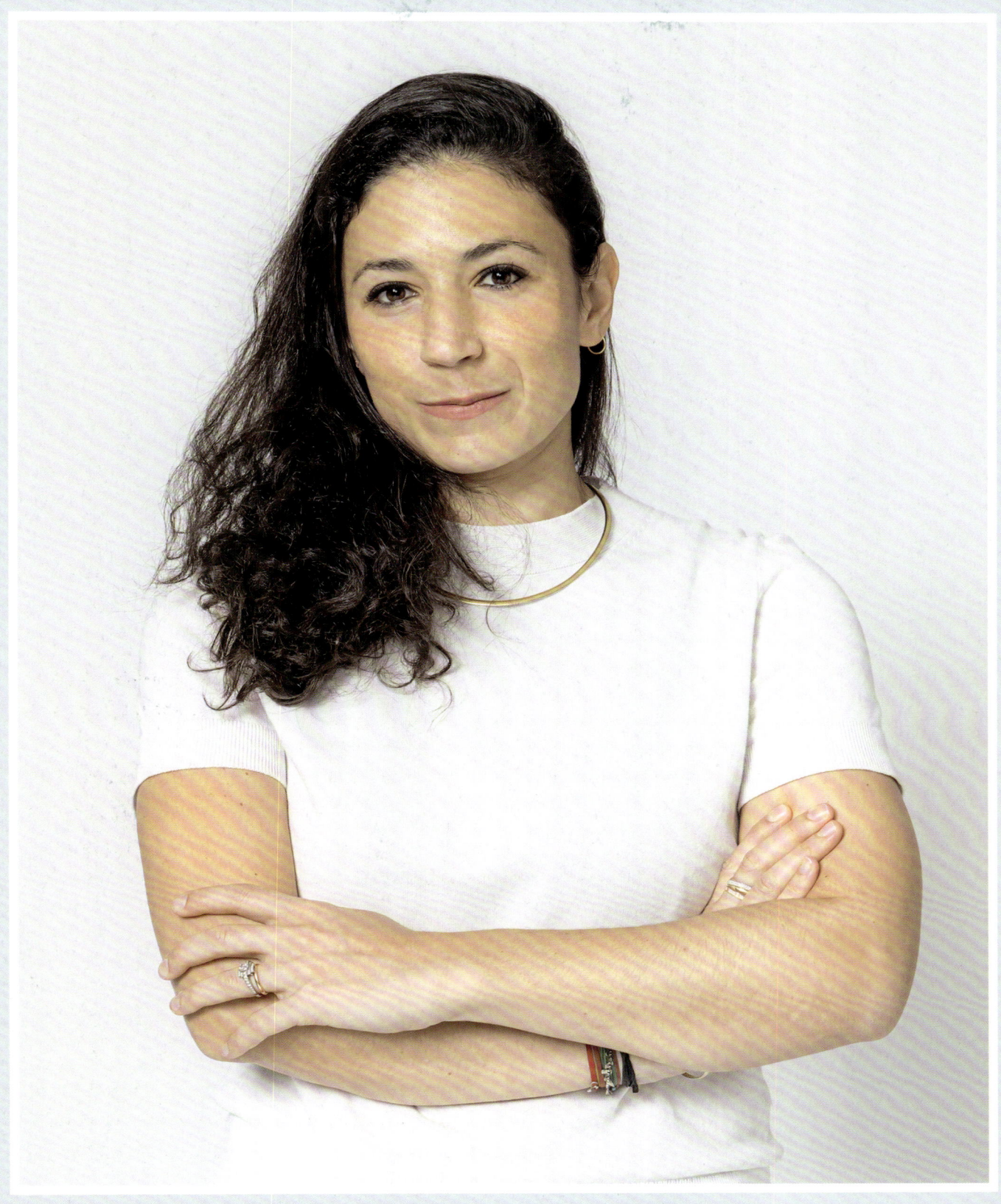

Morgane Halimi, Global Head of Handbags and Fashion, Sotheby's.

Secondary market luxury bag auctions represent a very appealing market segment for collectors, investors and fashion enthusiasts. This industry, once reserved for a close inner circle of elites, is growing considerably, attracting an ever-expanding consumer base thanks to digitisation and the growing cultural acceptance of second-hand items. Digital technology is also bringing massive change to the auction industry. Online platforms and mobile apps have made it easier than ever for participants to watch auctions and bid in real time from anywhere in the world.

Moreover, as Halimi confirms: 'many people seem to appreciate and even have fun with the "game" of auctions.'

Pre-owned luxury bag auctions offer numerous unique advantages compared to traditional sales channels, including the opportunity to purchase rare or discontinued pieces which are no longer available in official boutiques or authorised shops. For many collectors, the value of a luxury bag is more than its practical use: it's a question of owning a piece of fashion history. For some clients, on the other hand, it's a matter of accelerating the path to obtaining the item desired, whether that's an exclusive piece or a classic *Birkin*. The fixed-price sales which take place through the Buy Now online platform help clients who want to purchase a luxury object without the pressure and uncertainty of bidding. The same logic is applied to purchases at Sotheby's bricks-and-mortar sales points, which include galleries, showrooms and exhibition spaces. They offer clients the chance to see and interact, physically and in person, with the luxury items being sold – an experience that can't entirely be replicated online. The chance to see a work of art, a piece of jewellery or a fine design product up close makes it possible to appreciate its details and the quality of its craftsmanship, crucial aspects for informed purchasing decisions. In addition, the staff members at physical sales points act as consultants for customers. Sotheby's offers personalised services, including advice on purchases, sales and collecting, benefiting from the experience of its specialists in various fields.

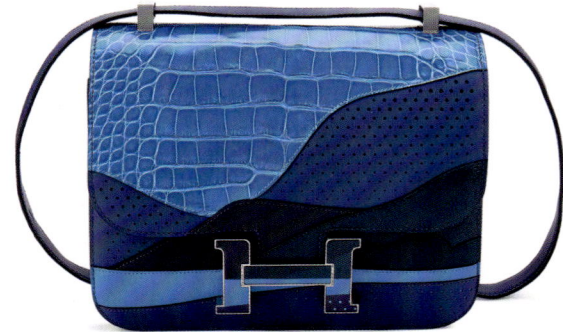

Limited Edition *Constance 24 Au Bout du Monde* in Swift, Box, alligator, lizard, Sombrero and Chèvre leathers, in a combination of *Bleu Encre*, *Bleu Zellige*, *Bleu de Malte*, *Bleu Nuit*, *Vert Cypres* and Black, with enamelled metal hardware. Hermès, France, 2020. This bag was sold by Sotheby's in Hong Kong for 30,240 EUR in April 2024. The *Constance Au Bout du Monde* version was inspired by the design of the silk scarf of the same name, created by Antoine Carbonne in 2016. It mimics its blue and green colourway.

Size and colour: global preferences

Across international markets, there is a clear preference for smaller bags. As a result, Hermès has made most of its iconic models in miniature versions, from the *Bolide* to the *Lindy* – and, at the top of this trend, of course, the sought-after *Mini Kelly II*, released in 2016. Preferences for Hermès bag colours and sizes widely vary from one country to the next, influenced by the local culture, climate and socio-economic factors.

Halimi notes that body shape and size are particularly relevant when it comes to choosing such a personal object. In the United States, the physical structure of women is generally, heftier and, as a consequence, despite the interest in mini bags, women prefer much larger silhouettes. Moreover, many Americans prefer capacious bags that can hold everything they need for a day out and about, due to a lifestyle which often revolves around the use of a car, a reality that explains why the *Birkin 35* or the *Kelly 32* are among the most popular.

In terms of colours, Hermès bags are preferred in a broader range of hues in the United States, as customers are more open to bright tones. Red, orange and green are commonly chosen, reflecting a cultural trend towards personal expression and a taste for the unique. This bolder approach to fashion is boosted by cultural diversity and the ample spectrum of lifestyles seen across the country.

In Europe and Asia, women tend to be smaller and, as a consequence, they tend to opt for more contained bags. In Europe, mid-size bags are particularly common, such as the *Birkin 30* or the *Kelly 28*. They're practical for everyday use and spacious enough to hold essential items, without being too bulky. The importance of functionality and a preference for classic elegance guide the choices made by European consumers.

On the Old Continent, the bestselling colours are classic, sober hues such as gold, black, beige, grey and dark blue. These colours are loved for their versatility, as they can be easily paired with a wide range of clothes and styles. Europe has a long tradition of discreet and refined elegance, and these neutral tones reflect a cultural preference for minimalism and understatement.

'Bags in classic colours which recall earth tones, different shades of cream, black, and golden hues in standard sizes are appreciated in Europe and around the globe in general, making them the most sought-after and sold. The second-hand market is particularly important because it includes pieces which are hard to find in boutiques,' explains Halimi.

In Asia, Hermès bag preferences are influenced by different factors, including climate, culture and the sizes of people's homes. In many Asian cities, where space is limited and people often use public transportation, small and compact bags like the *Kelly 25* or the *Mini Kelly* are very popular. These small sizes are considered elegant and practical, easily adapting to urban lifestyles. In most countries in the Far East, Hermès bags are very popular among men, especially the *Birkin 40* and the *HAC* styles.

In terms of colours, there's a marked preference for light, delicate tones such as white, light beige, pink and light blue. These colours are seen as symbols of purity

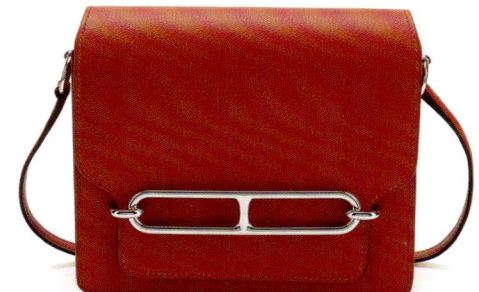

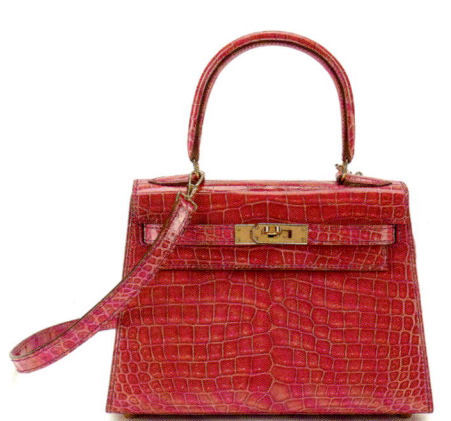

Top – Limited Edition *Mini Roulis 18* bag in ruby red and violet pink leather, palladium hardware. Hermès, France, 2022. A limited edition *Roulis Mini* bag was sold by Sotheby's in Hong Kong for 60,960 HKD in October 2023.

Bottom – *Mini Kelly 20* in bonbon pink saltwater crocodile leather with gold hardware. Hermès, France, 1997. This bag was sold by Sotheby's in Hong Kong for 1,206,500 HKD in February 2023.

and refinement, values which are greatly appreciated in many Far Eastern cultures. Moreover, lighter hues are preferred in warm and humid climates, as they reflect the light of the sun and help create a cool, fresh feel.

Halimi explains: 'In the Orient, pink and green are beloved colours. For this reason, Hermès creates bags in these tones each year. Shades such as Sakura Pink, which recalls the colour of cherry blossoms in full bloom, and Bubblegum Pink are favourites in the Far East. Different shades of red, on the other hand, are popular in the Middle East.'

In the Middle East, Hermès bags are often chosen as a status symbol. Rich and vibrant colours such as burgundy, royal blue and emerald green are bestsellers, reflecting a taste for opulence and exuberance. These tones are often associated with royalty and prestige, values which are in line with the local culture. Smaller models are preferred like everywhere else in the world, though there is also interest in larger sizes, such as the *Birkin 35*.

Three record-breaking categories

In terms of value, there are three categories which fetch the highest prices.

Of course, there are bags that have become the Holy Grail, such as the diamond hardware versions of the *Kelly* and the *Birkin*, or the *Himalayan* collections. The *Himalaya Kelly* is particularly prized for its crocodile leather, which is dyed to obtain a colour gradient which goes from white to grey, evoking the Himalayas. The complexity and the time required to produce such a bag increase its value, making it a true masterpiece of craftsmanship.

One notable example is the *White Matte Niloticus Crocodile Himalayan Kelly 25 Retourné Palladium Hardware*, which sold for €352,800 in Paris in 2022. Its price tag can be attributed to the rarity of the bag, the complexity of its production and the prestige associated with the Hermès name.

The second category is that of 'vintage masterpieces', which includes the most coveted styles from the past, usually no longer in production but in perfect condition. This category includes a few iconic styles from the Jean Paul Gaultier era, such as the 2005 *Teddy* collection. One notable example is the *Matt Alligator So Black Birkin 35* from 2011, which sold in June 2024 in New York for 132,000 USD.

The third highest-selling category at auction is that of limited editions. They usually include bags which embody the creativity of Hermès and the brand's ability to reinvent the classics. At the top of this category is the *Faubourg Birkin 20*, which exists in five colours, and the *Kellywood*, in wood as the name suggests. These limited editions also exist for other styles, such as the *Constance*.

Different variables influence the final prices of Hermès bags auctioned by Sotheby's. Rarity is decisive: limited editions or bags made with exotic or hard-to-find materials, such as crocodile, ostrich or lizard leather, tend to fetch higher price tags. The condition of the bag is crucial: those in excellent condition, preferably with original packaging and accessories, are particularly sought-after.

In addition to an object's tangible qualities, the history and provenance of the bag can impact its value too. Bags which were owned by celebrities or presented at important cultural events can fetch record prices. The story behind each bag can add intangible yet substantial value which goes beyond the physical object.

'It's so difficult to buy a Hermès bag that, when a customer gets one, they feel like they've become part of an exclusive group of people who share the same values: discreet, sustainable luxury which leads them to select an object which is recognisable for its design, though not too flashy in the display of the logo.

'Moreover, the brand stays true to its promise: *A Hermès bag is forever*. Using it properly, it can always be repaired, making it new again. It's a meticulously crafted item which can be compared to a work of art. The fact that Hermès constantly renews all its collection is another asset for its customers.'

Accessories and the value of design

At Sotheby's, silk scarves by Hugo Grygkar, Dimitri Rybaltchenko and the Comme des Garçons limited editions have fetched record prices. Even Hermès jewellery is now also seen as collection-worthy.

Hermès jewellery sales follow the same dynamics as bags, explains Halimi, as they are classic, timeless items. Whether in gold or silver, the fine design of these vintage collections makes them very popular.

Jan Schoormans
& Peter van der Bel

—

THE PERSONALITY PROFILE OF HERMÈS

The Big Five personality theory classifies Hermès as a luxury brand which embodies creativity, precision, empathy and stability, with a propensity for quiet elegance over blatant showiness.

The OCEAN model (also known as the five-factor model of personality or simply 'Big Five') is a psychology-based theory according to which five main traits are used to define the fundamental personality of an individual. Those traits are: *openness, conscientiousness, extroversion, agreeableness* and *neuroticism*. This model is widely used in psychology to understand human behaviour, personal relationships and individual differences.

Openness reflects a person's intellectual curiosity, imagination and openness to experience. People with a high score in this area tend to be creative, inquisitive and willing to explore new ideas. Those with low openness scores are often more traditional and less inclined to change.

The *conscientiousness* category measures the tendency to be organised, disciplined and goal-oriented. Conscientious people are reliable, meticulous and self-disciplined. Those who have a low conscientiousness score, on the other hand, might be seen as impulsive, disorganised or prone to procrastination.

Extroversion refers to a person's degree of sociability, energy and seeking out of social stimuli. Extroverted people love to spend time with others; they're enthusiastic and assertive. Introverts, on the other hand, prefer calm settings and they tend to be more reserved and reflective.

Agreeableness measures a person's ability to be empathetic, cooperative and kind to others. Those with a high score in this area are generally altruistic, trusting and

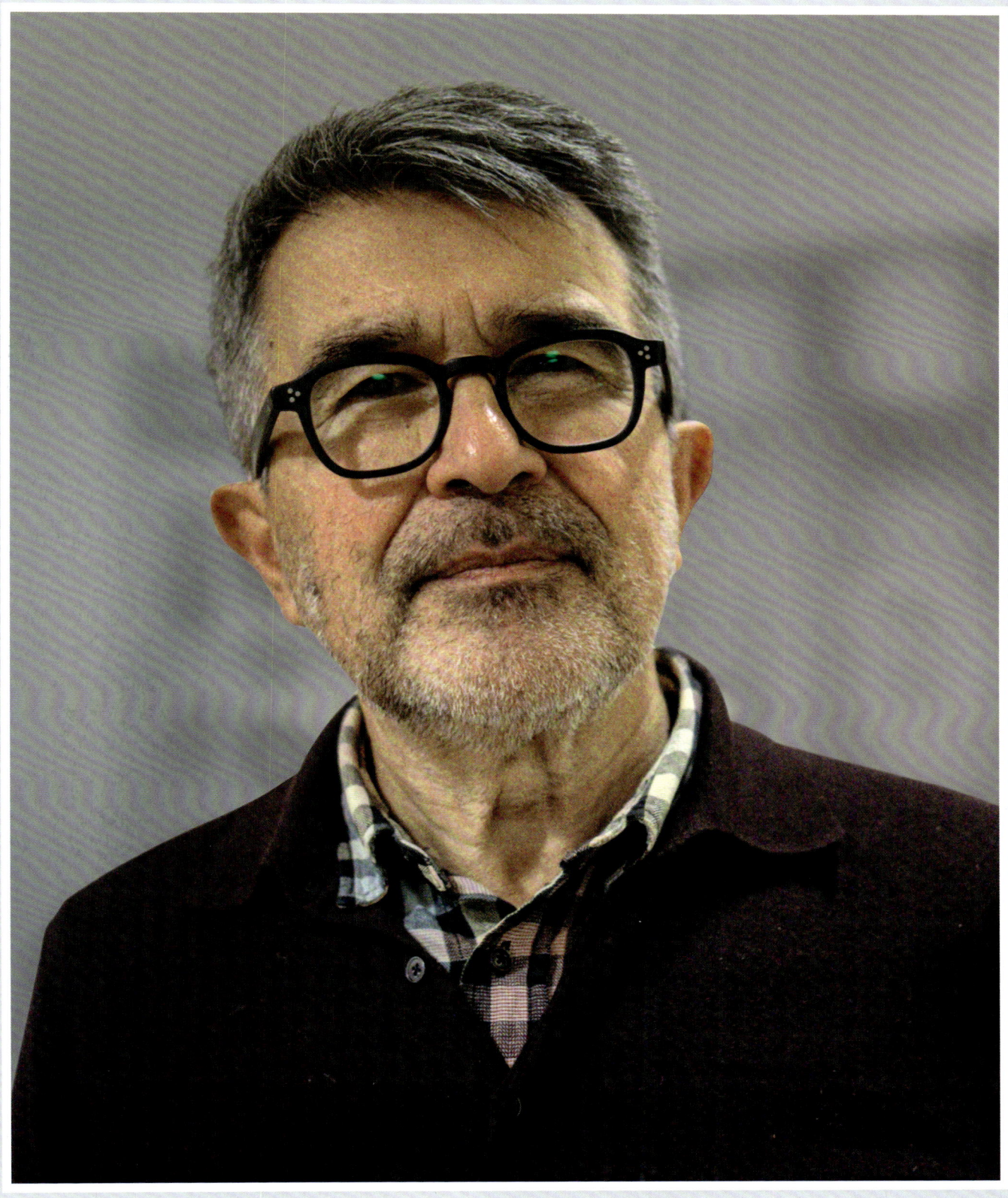

Peter van der Bel, a specialist in the application of language to behavioural science, is co-founder of the Centre for Applied Product Personality Research, headquartered in Amsterdam.

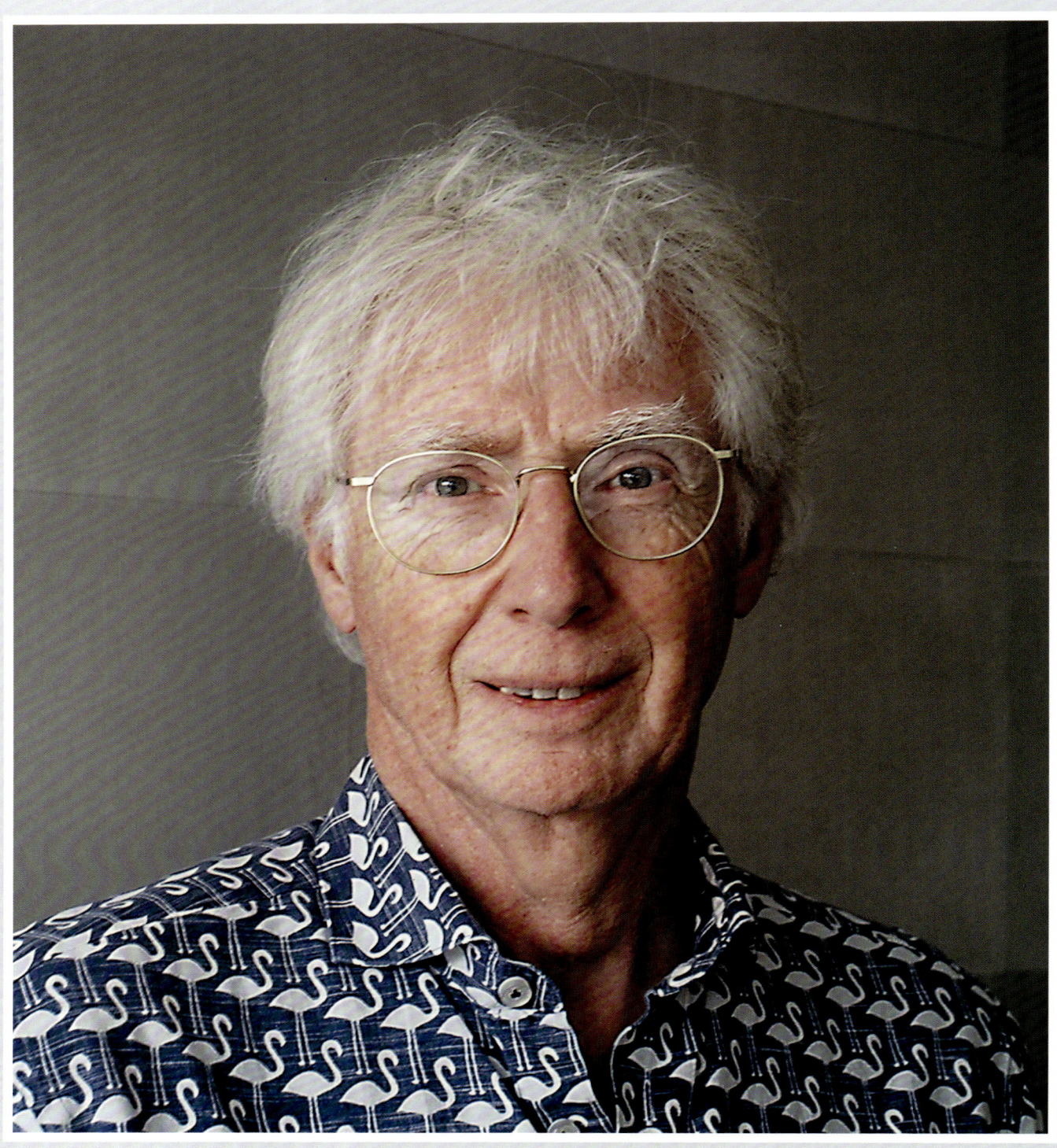

Jan Schoormans is a professor of consumer research and behaviour at Delft University of Technology in the Netherlands. Over the years, his research has focused on the development of the concept and the visual assessment of product personality. His research has demonstrated that there is a correlation between the personality of individuals and the products they choose. In 2011 he founded, with Peter van der Bel, The Centre for Applied Product Personality Research (CAPPR). The centre develops and uses evaluation methods to classify the personalities of people, products and services.

collaborative. People with low scores, on the other hand, may be seen as critical, competitive and less inclined to compromise.

Neuroticism refers to low emotional stability and the tendency to feel negative emotions. Individuals with high levels of neuroticism are more vulnerable to stress, while those with low scores tend to be calmer and more emotionally resistant.

The OCEAN model is used in various fields, from staff recruitment to psychological counselling and academic research. Its strength lies in its ability to offer a clear and scientifically validated overview of individual differences, allowing for a deeper understanding of human behaviour and social dynamics.

Jan Schoormans, who is a professor of consumer behaviour at Delft University of Technology in the Netherlands, and linguistics expert Peter van der Bel have applied the model to the world's leading fashion and luxury brands, thereby assigning them a personality profile.

According to these two experts, product and brand personalities can be described by using terms similar to those used for human personality traits. That makes it possible to identify specific products, compare them with others, and identify potential correlations. The personality of a brand is meaningful because it reflects the user's preferences.

According to van der Bel and Schoormans, 'this idea is based on the concept of "similarities attract".[1] A large number of psychological studies have indeed demonstrated that the affinity between the personalities of two individuals notably increases their interest in getting to know each other and starting a relationship. Research indicates that the same phenomenon is found with regards to the personality of a person and that of a product. That means that, in general, consumers tend to prefer products with a personality similar to theirs. This is also true for Hermès.'

These experts have created a Big Five personality for the luxury brand Hermès, explaining the associated values for each trait.

Openness is high for the French brand. Craftsmanship and creativity characterise the work of Hermès, which is famous for its dedication to workmanship and innovation, through which it produces timeless pieces with a creative character that unites tradition and innovation. Another sign of the maison's propensity for experimentation is its enthusiasm for artistic collaboration, through which it explores new horizons. A third aspect that confirms its high degree of openness is its decision to promote innovation through tradition: despite being deeply linked to its history, Hermès adapts to contemporary tastes through fresh interpretations of classic styles, demonstrating a high level of mental openness.

For this luxury brand, van der Bel and Schoormans have calculated a very high conscientiousness score. *Conscientiousness* is found in each and every product made by the brand. In terms of workmanship, Hermès is known for its precision, attention to detail, and the scrupulous and knowing use of the finest materials. Indeed, the fashion house consistently embodies the values of reliability and responsibility towards its customers. Likewise, over time Hermès has upheld a profound commitment to quality: the brand's strict quality controls and designs which outlive trends are the result of careful planning. They are also proof of a long-term vision. The brand's dedication to sustainability further reinforces the concept of conscientiousness, having opted for sustainable practices, guaranteeing that its products are not just luxurious but also made in an ethical and responsible way.

The brand's *extroversion*, on the other hand, is moderate and it could not be otherwise considering how important the aura of exclusivity is for the company. Hermès' communication style is selective: the brand uses discreet but effective marketing campaigns focused on storytelling and exclusivity instead of relying on aggressive advertisements. The Hermès communication style is characterised by understatement and elegance, and by messaging which exalts the history and heritage of the brand. This results in a consistent, well-defined media presence which reinforces the image of the brand as a symbol of refined luxury. Likewise, the shopping experience in Hermès boutiques is meticulously curated. These intimate and welcoming settings reflect the elegance and the heritage of the maison, and the entire experience is designed to create meaningful interaction with clients instead of just closing sales. The coherence and consistency of the brand is also reinforced by its distribution strategy. In spite of its global reach, Hermès has always been selective in its distribution, limiting the availability of its products and rigorously controlling its sales channels. This choice not only upholds the exclusivity of the brand; it also guarantees that every sales point reflects the quality standards imposed by the group's parent company and identity.

The brand's *agreeableness* is high thanks to a philosophy which puts the client first. Hermès prioritises highest-level service which is focused on building long-term relationships with its clients. The maison has developed an easy-to-recognise aesthetic characterised by elegant design and clean lines, thereby satisfying a wide range of people while maintaining its identity. This consistency has made it possible to construct empathetic communication between the brand and its customers over time. Agreeableness is reinforced by the behaviour of the brand, which projects the values of a 'family': it sources its materials responsibly and adheres to equal work practices. These choices reflect the image of a highly ethical entity.

The luxury brand's *neuroticism* score, on the other hand, is low, as its identity is quite stable. Visual identity is maintained in a consistent manner across all its products and communication tools. This in turn creates deep aesthetic consistency, but also conveys a sense of calm and security. Thanks to meticulous quality standards, the brand keeps product defects to a bare minimum, which gives rise to a sense of reliability and trust among customers. Hermès is also known for the tactful and professional management of challenges, thereby avoiding scandals and an unstable image.

In conclusion, van der Bel and Schoormans highlight how the continuity and coherence of Hermès as a brand is the result of the harmonious integration of tradition, quality craftsmanship, aesthetics and innovation. Through unwavering attention to detail, an exclusive distribution strategy and refined communication, Hermès has managed to keep its identity intact, despite the expansion and changes in the global market. This consistency has not only helped build a strong reputation, but has also allowed Hermès to stand the test of time: it continues to be a symbol of luxury and quality, even today.

....

Scan the QR code to take a quick test to see how your personality aligns with that of Hermès.

Beppe Vicenti

—

CONSISTENCY AND AUTHENTICITY IN THE HERMÈS PHILOSOPHY

Authentic brands stand out in a crowded market by presenting their values and by putting a unique and defined identity on display.

Creating a brand identity that reflects the founding values of the brand means building a solid bridge between what the company wants to convey and the way it's perceived by its audience. Once well defined, this identity not only increases brand recognition and consistency, it also facilitates communications which directly reach those who share the same values and principles.

Identifying the fundamental values of a brand's identity is a crucial first step in the construction of an authentic corporate identity. In addition to defining the essence of the brand, these values guide many decisions, from marketing strategies to graphic design, which help create the brand's image (in the broadest sense of the word): how people know and recognise it.

According to Beppe Vicenti, an expert in the semantic processes which enliven the universe of brands and advertising, the Hermès philosophy can be summarised in a single quotation from the former CEO, Jean-Louis Dumas: 'We don't have a policy of image, we have a policy of product.'

The brand's identity is deeply rooted in luxury and exclusivity and, using these principles as a foundation, Hermès has always avoided mass production. According to Hermès, every single product released under its name must reflect the complex and meticulous work carried out by its artisans.

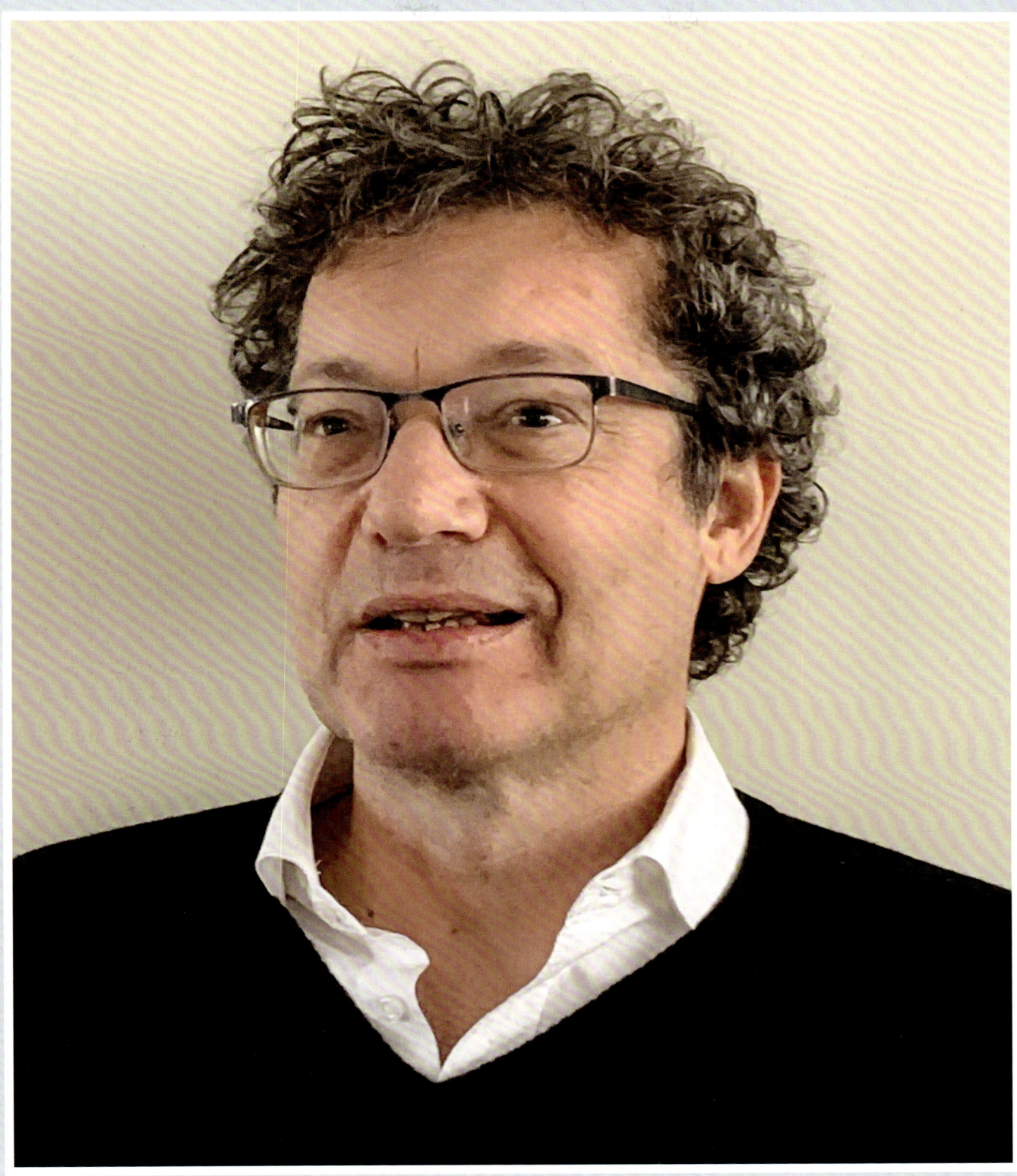

For over 30 years, he has studied the evolution of markets and other complex exchange systems, with a special focus on how the processes of meaning and communication change from within. Constantly focused on the profound dynamics which determine purchasing and consumption behaviours, Vicenti now helps companies to develop innovative marketing strategies. Among the many educational activities he carries out at universities and specialised schools, he has been a guest lecturer at the Jewellery History workshop at the University of Milan. He also worked with White Star on the publication of *Rolex Philosophy*.

Craftsmanship and exclusivity

One of the key values of Hermès is craftsmanship, a factor which holds highest ranking in the sense that it determines the final quality of each object.

Every Hermès product is made with painstaking care by highly skilled artisans, many of whom were trained within the company itself. The professionalism of all its *métiers* is considered a carefully guarded company asset. This level of quality and craftsmanship is not only a sign of excellence; it's also a key element in terms of brand uniformity. Hermès has built its reputation upon products which are not only luxurious, but which also last over time, offering tangible and durable value to customers.

Attention to detail is manifested in every seam, in perfect details and in harmonious proportions. Unlike brands that focus on flashy logos, Hermès chooses understatement, where luxury is expressed through materials, clean lines and intrinsic quality. Such timeless style has allowed Hermès accessories to stay relevant for decades.

The fashion house's products are known for their elegant simplicity. This simplicity is the result of careful design that places practicality of use and ergonomics at the centre, without ever neglecting well-defined harmony. This design philosophy, which unites form and function across all Hèrmes product categories, gives the brand distinct character.

Handcrafted processes and absolute quality take time, and Hermès has added 'patience' as one of the pillars of its strategy. Customers can't expect to walk into a boutique and leave with a *Birkin* or a *Kelly*. They must instead place an order and wait a few months for it to be made.

'Some economists see this strategy as a way to boost the sales of "consolation" products, such as wallets, belts and other accessories,' explains Vicenti.

Quality and singularity are values coherent with the company's positioning in the exclusive luxury world, reinforced by its distribution strategy. Hermès has always been selective in its distribution, limiting the availability of its products and rigorously controlling its sales channels. This choice not only upholds the exclusivity of the brand; it also guarantees that every sales point reflects its quality standards and identity. The customer experience in a Hermès boutique is curated in exacting detail to offer shoppers a place that reflects the brand's elegance and traditions.

Moreover, Hermès often introduces limited editions, which help generate interest among its enthusiasts and fans.

Even its financial strategy bolsters brand coherence. Hermès has always asserted its independence in its shareholding structure and family ownership. As such, it can maintain control of all its activities and implement its long-term vision.

Symbols and storytelling

Hermès is also known for its iconography and for its symbolic decorative motifs, which are often inspired by the world of horses, fine art and nature. They're used in a consistent manner on an entire range of products, from silk scarves to details on bags which often have easily identified references. Founded in 1837 as a saddlery, the fashion house got its start producing harnesses for horses and saddles and other tack for horseback riding. This initial connection with the equestrian world has become a recurrent and distinctive theme for Hermès. Elements such as bridles, stirrups, buckles, saddles and even feed bags or sacks to carry boots have been turned into symbols which echo the origins of the brand and which, still today, characterise many of its products.

The buckles decorating many Hermès bags, such as the *Kelly* or the *Birkin*, are based on the shapes of horse harnesses. These metal details are more than a stylistic element: they evoke a sense of robustness and the functionality that characterises equestrian accessories. Stirrups become decorative elements in bags such as the *Steeple*, where its curved shape echoes the tack used by horsemen; the *Picotin*, inspired by feed bags; or the *Évelyne*, which echoes the structure of grooming bags. The *touret* clasp, seen on iconic bags like the *Birkin*, evokes the mechanisms used for straps on saddles. This element is functional but also a symbol of security and durability. Hermès uses heraldic motifs linked to its logo and its history, integrating them into fabrics and details on bags. The themes which reference the world of sailing are also pertinent. Inspired by a ship's anchor, the *Chaîne d'Ancre* motif was introduced in the 1930s and has been reimagined on many bags over the decades. These themes are more than just decorative: they also reflect the historical and cultural depth of the brand, creating a unique visual identity.

The inclusion of historical symbols in the design of its products is one of the fundamental elements which distinguish the brand in the global luxury landscape. It goes beyond decoration, embracing narration. Every detail tells a story: a past of craftsmanship, a present of luxury and a future of innovation.

Aesthetic uniformity

Hermès has developed an easy-to-recognise aesthetic, characterised by elegant design, clean lines and the use of orange, which has become emblematic. This visual identity is seen in the brand's packaging and product displays also. 'Just think of the logo and how it could seem obsolete in other contexts,' Vicenti notes. 'Instead, it encapsulates all the messages of the brand.'

The Hermès logo, known as *Le Duc Attelé*, which depicts a horse-drawn carriage with a nobleman next to it, is an iconic symbol that reflects the historical roots of the company and its patrimony of fine craftsmanship. It isn't a mere homage to the equestrian origins of the brand; it also evokes the idea of a refined and aristocratic world in which luxury was associated with life on horseback and travel via horse-drawn carriage. The man standing next to the horse recalls a coachman, underscoring the concept of service and attention to detail which has always distinguished the brand.

Le Duc Attelé has become a global emblem of prestige. More than a distinct trademark, it's a symbol of an era and traditions which live on in Hermès, uniting past and present in the name of craftsmanship and luxury.

The tone of voice chosen for communications must be consistent with the values and personality of the company. Cohesion between the tone of voice and identity is essential to the creation of authentic and credible communications.

'Hermès' communications are characterised by understated elegance, and by storytelling which exalts the history and heritage of the brand. Hermès creates advertising campaigns which are based on evocative storytelling, often on themes which are in line with its history. *Flâneur Forever, Leather Forever, J'aime mon Carré* and *Seek the Orange* are just a few examples. This results in a consistent, distinct media presence which reinforces the image of the brand as a symbol of refined luxury.

'Just think of the legendary shop windows, which hold displays that look like three-dimensional paintings, the kind to stop and admire, the kind which tell a story co-starring the product. This visual platform is very robust in terms of demonstrating the exquisite style and artisan patrimony of the brand,' Vicenti continues.

Heritage and innovation

Hermès regularly goes back to its roots when it needs inspiration for the creation and launch of new products, as if the past were an expansive, inexhaustible container of creativity. *Heritage* is one of the elements which most distinguishes the identity of Hermès.

'Every fashion brand has a wealth of heritage in its past, which takes on value internally, as it is testimony of the company history, and externally, as fashion has the ability to tell the story of society through the historical evolution of style. The *heritage* of a fashion brand includes not only the garments created, but everything which over time has been produced around the brand's image. It is thus a rich gathering of audiovisual materials, texts and even creative processes, studies which have led to the creation of collections and their promotion and distribution. Every creative director, in their work, must consider this past, with the knowledge that what they produce will also become part of it,' Vicenti confirms.

While the heritage of a brand can be seen as a present process which negotiates, builds and rebuilds identity, social and cultural values and the meaning assigned to them, it is also true that this process must look to the future and lay its foundations precisely upon connecting the past and present in an engaging way.

Another crucial aspect of Hermès consistency is its ability to innovate without betraying its roots. Hermès has managed to uphold the balance between respect for tradition and openness to innovation. This is clear in creative collaborations and new products launched by the brand, which introduce modern elements without abandoning the fundamental values of quality and craftsmanship. One example of this synergy is the Hermès watch collection, which unites traditional elegance with cutting-edge technology while staying true to the distinct style of the brand.

The uniformity of Hermès as a brand is the result of the harmonious integration of tradition, quality craftsmanship, aesthetics and innovation.

Authenticity means telling consumers a story that reflects the brand's values – being true to oneself and expressing transparency. The brand's authenticity arises from creating trust, connecting on a deeper level with consumers and promoting meaningful relationships.

Hermès has proven quite successful in this regard.

NOTES

Hermès. Never trendy, always in fashion

[1] *Giacomo Leopardi (1798–1837) 'Dialogo della Moda e della Morte' in* Operette Morali, *Mondadori, Milan 2017. Leopardi imagines a conversation between two allegorical figures: Fashion and Death. Fashion, personified as a light-hearted and frivolous character, symbolises the human tendency to embrace the transitory and the superficial. Death, on the other hand, introduces a profound critique of fashion and its capacity to distract man's attention from life's existential questions.*

[2] *Roland Barthes,* Il Sistema della moda *in* Il senso della moda, *Einaudi, Turin, 2006.*

[3] *Federico Rocca,* Hermès – L'avventura del lusso, *Lindau, Turin, 2011.*

[4] *Georg Simmel,* Sulla psicologia dell'ornamento, *in* Sull'Intimità, *Armando Editore, Rome, 2004, p. 108 [1ˢᵗ ed. 1908].*

[5] *Leibenstein, H. Bandwagon,* Snob, and Veblen Effects in the Theory of Consumers' Demand. The Quarterly Journal of Economics, *Vol. 64, No. 2, 1950.*

[6] *Suleman Anaya,* The Humanity of Hermès. *https://www.businessoffashion.com/articles/news-analysis/humanity-hermes/, 2014.*

History

[1] *In early 2024, Hermès' net profit was 2.4 billion EUR, demonstrating significant growth over the same period the year before. This substantial increase in net profit underscores the brand's strength and success in the luxury market. (Source: Hermes Finance).*

[2] *The 16 Hermès crafts – known as* métiers *– are: leather goods and saddlery, women's silk, men's silk, women's ready-to-wear, men's ready-to-wear, shoes, belts, hats, gloves, jewellery, watches, perfumes, beauty products, furnishings and arte di vivere, tablewear and Petit h.*

[3] *Pierre Sommet,* Sur les traces de Thierry Hermès: Une histoire franco-allemande par excellence, *Editions Complicités, Paris, 2023, p.4.*

[4 and 5] *Pierre Sommet,* Sur les traces de Thierry Hermès: Une histoire franco-allemande par excellence, *Editions Complicités, Paris, 2023.*

[6] *During the Second Empire (1852–1870), the emperor and his wife Eugénie revived the splendour of Versailles and reinforced public support for his rule through numerous celebrations. Parisian life revolved around the large balls held by the court, entertainment for the upper middle class, and the many performances put on by the city's theatres.*

[7] *Charles-Émile had retired in the late 1800s, and his sons Adolphe and Émile-Maurice had renamed the company Hermès Frerès in 1902. Adolphe, despite being the majority stakeholder, would sell his shares to his brother just a few years later. He died in 1933.*

[8] *An advertisement from 1929 shows the Bradka case, a product designed to carry the shoes of sophisticated women. It could be hung on the wall of the bedroom or in the closet so that the right shoes were always to hand with each outfit change.*

[9] *During the war, Hermès even kept its workers on its payroll.*

[10] *The Hermès magazine appeared for the first time in 1973. Created in Germany under the name* Die Welt von Hermès, Le Monde d'Hermès *appeared in France two years later. Currently translated into 10 languages,* Le Monde d'Hermès *is distributed around the world.*

[11] *Bergère worked for Hermès from 1977 to 1980.*

[12] *Among them, the* Pippa *foldable armchair in wood and leather would become internationally renowned, even added to the collections of museums.*

[13] *Rena Dumas (1937–2009) was a French-American architect and interior designer, known for her eclectic and innovative style. Born in France, she founded the famous Rena Dumas Architecture Intérieure design studio in Paris. She was the wife of Jean-Louis Dumas.*

[14] *Martin Margiela, founder of Maison Martin Margiela, embodied an avant-garde vision: deconstruction, reinterpretation of aesthetic canons, and the use of unusual materials were his stylistic hallmarks.*

[15] *Yet, despite their apparent simplicity, each collection revealed subtle complexity: the cuts were designed to adapt perfectly to the body, the fabric used was the finest available, and every seam was an expression of artisan attention to detail. Margiela managed to express luxury which was almost 'spiritual', far from ostentation and close to the idea of a 'dress as a second skin', where every piece was meant to be experienced rather than simply worn.*

[16] *Gaultier's style codes were corsets, ethnic prints, sexy sailors and collaborations with culturally relevant artists from the international pop scene.*

[17] *While he was at Hermès, Gaultier created collections which have remained imprinted on the fashion house's history, reinventing classic garments such as the trench coat and the suit. The most emblematic pieces from this era were the deconstructed trench coat updated in leather, which combined French elegance and a bolder, more dynamic attitude. Gaultier also introduced the use of bondage elements in a subtle way, playing with buckles, belts and laces, adding an unexpected seductive touch to womenswear by Hermès.*

[18] *In addition to the* Birkin 25, *some of the pieces which became iconic and sought-out by collectors are the* JPG Shoulder Birkin, *the* Kelly Pochette, *the* Médor *clutch and the* Lindy, *and even the* Kelly Cut, Danse *or* Picnic. *No matter the style, he managed to interpret luxury with carefree whimsy.*

[19] *'Each one of my projects begins with research about the country, the city and the street where the building will be, to conclude with a true journey within it, without ever neglecting a fundamental element: the light,' explained Rena Dumas regarding the way she approached her work. After her death in 2009, other important architects collaborated with Hermès.*

[20] *For Puech and the other Hermès scions, the goal was clear: Arnault was poised to conquer. After all, his aggressive acquisitions of historical brands earned him the nickname of the 'wolf in cashmere'. For the fifth- and sixth-generation owners of Hermès, ceding their empire to a competitor would have been serious enough on its own. And losing it to what they considered to be an excessively flashy group with a business merely based on marketing was a 'revolting' option, as Thomas said at the time, while he was CEO of Hermès (Fashion Network, 12 December 2023).*

[21] *Hermès 'plays in a league of its own', Citigroup Inc. analyst Thomas Chauvet once said, after its rapid third-quarter growth, even in China. Attention to craftsmanship, a finely calibrated perception of exclusivity and the mastery of the scarcity – real or managed – of its products are all elements which flow into what has proven to be a winning strategy (Fashion Network, 12 December 2023).*

Silk scarves

[1] *Born in Germany in 1907, Grygkar was from a Czech family which moved to France in 1914. After having studied at the Académie des Beaux-Arts of Paris, he spent time at Residence La Ruche. In Passage Dantzig in the 15th arrondissement, it was the place where all the artists of the Montparnasse quarter met, lived and exhibited their work.*

[2] *Ledoux was born in Sheffield, England in 1903 to French parents. His family returned to France in 1915. His artistic talent was recognised and encouraged at a young age by his mother, Marie Villaret, who herself was an expert watercolourist and illustrator of children's books. Ledoux studied at the Académies de Peinture et de Dessin in Paris. In 1947, Dumas hired him to design for Hermès. Ledoux died in 1975 in a motorcycle accident. His last two silk scarves, La Marine (a Rames) and Les Trois Mousquetaires, were completed by his nephew, Vladimir Rybaltchenko. Numerous* carrés *designed by Ledoux were produced by Hermès after his death.*

[3] *Working with Hermès for 45 years, she first signed her work with a simple 'Caty', later changing to 'Latham'.*

[4] *After having worked as an independent designer, Pesce began collaborating with Hermès in 2005.*

[5] *Active since 1985, Ardmore is one of the most characteristic artist collectives in the vibrant African art scene.*

[6] *Josef Albers (1888–1976) was a famous painter, lithographer, colour theorist, writer, teacher and the artist with the longest appointment at the Bauhaus (1920–1933).*

[7] *In 2000, Buren had opened* La Verrière *in Bruxelles, a space dedicated to contemporary art. Six years later, the fashion house asked him to open a new space. So, for the Hermès atelier in Dosan Park, Seoul, he created the site-specific installation titled* Filtres Colorés.

[8] *To transfer the photographs to silk fabric, Hermès chose inkjet printing, a method which makes it possible to take advantage of an infinite number of colours, compared to traditional screenprinting, which does not allow for an unlimited number of colours.*

[9] *The first Hermès-Sugimoto collaboration took place in 2003, with the exhibition* L'histoire de l'histoire, *in the Forum space of the Hermès boutique in the Ginza district of Tokyo. Sugimoto's research is a continuous exploration of the resources of age-old know-how, intended to spark creative dialogue between history, a tradition, and tradition itself.*

[10] *Born in 1928 in Mendoza, Argentina, Le Parc lives and works in Cachan, France. A leading proponent of geometric and kinetic art in the 1960s, Le Parc was a founding member of GRAV (Groupe de Recherche d'Art Visuel, 1960–1968). His work explores movement, light, optics and even the relationships which are forged between the work of art and the observer.*

[11] *Lella Scalia, A beautiful square. Interview with Bali Barret,* Vogue Italy, *30 July 2020. https://www.vogue.it/moda/article/un-quadrato-di-bellezza-intervista-bali-barret-carre-hermes*

[12] *The classic silk scarf measures 90 × 90 cm; then there are those measuring 70 × 70 cm, the gavroche measuring 45 × 45 cm, the bandanna measuring 55 × 55 cm, and the large scarf of 140 × 140 cm. The strips of silk known as Twilly scarves measure 5 × 86 cm or 5 × 165 cm, and some come in at 7 × 89 cm (Hermès website, viewed November 2024).*

[13] *The Double Carré is printed on both sides, inspired by the lightweight, packable silk fabric maps used by parachutists in the Second World War.*

Bags

[1] *Sigmund Freud,* 'Symbolism in the Dream' *in* A General Introduction to Psychoanalysis, *Library of Alexandria, 1953.*

[2] *Philippe Dumas,* Musée Hermès – Carnet de Croquis de Pilippe Dumas illustrant le theme: La vie à l'air libre, *Actes Sud, Arles, 2014 [1ˢᵗ ed. 1990], pp.14-15. In this book of sketches on the theme of life outdoors, we see illustrations of carriages, bridles, saddles, boots, walking stick handles and bags.*

[3] *Philippe Dumas,* Musée Hermès – La route dans la collection H. par Philippe Dumas, *Actes Sud, Arles, 2014 [1ˢᵗ ed. 1995], pp.14-15.*

[4] *Philippe Dumas, Carnet de Voyage – Regard sur* L'Exotisme du Museé Hermès, *Actes Sud, Arles, 2014 [1ˢᵗ ed. 1988], pp.6-7.*

[5] *Elisabetta Chiodini,* 'Dettagli di Moda ossia "Nonnulla Eleganti"', *in* Dettagli di Moda – Gli anni Venti e Trenta nella Collezione Mangiameli, *Umberto Allemandi, Turin, 2010, p.21.*

[6] *This bag was originally called the* Bugatti *to celebrate the collaboration between the auto maker and the fashion house. Later on, it was renamed the* Bolide.

[7] *Hermès officially renamed the bag* Kelly *in the late 1970s.*

[8] *Vanessa Walt,* Your Guide to the Top 10 Hermès Bags, *Sotheby's website.*

[9] *'PM' and 'TPM' are acronyms used by Hermès to indicate the sizes of some of their bags and accessories. PM stands for* Petit Modèle *(small) and TPM stands for* Tres Petit Modèle *(extra small). Generally the smallest versions of a specific design, they're made for those who prefer lighter bags which are easier to carry, without sacrificing style and functionality.*

[10] *Customised pieces, known as* HSS *bags, feature a special horseshoe stamp to the left of the Hermès stamp within the bag. The emblem may be small, but it notably increases the bag's value. This made-to-measure option is offered exclusively to a select number of high-level collectors. These tailor-made pieces generally take six months to arrive, even if some collectors wait up to three years.*

Jewellery

[1] *In 1927, upon the request of the design house Callot Soeurs, Hermès created a belt inspired by its fine dog collars, to which leads were attached by dangling rings.*

[2] *The success of these enamelled bracelets laid the foundation for subsequent creations, such as the famous* Clic H, *introduced in 2000.*

[3] *Puiforcat was founded by Emile and Joseph-Marie Puiforcat in Paris in 1820 as a producer of fine silver jewellery. In the late 19ᵗʰ century, it won over the upper echelons of society, with European nobility and royal families among its customers, all thanks to Louis Victor Puiforcat. For its high-level clientele, the jeweller produced pieces in silver in the Louis XV and Regency styles.*
The international consecration of the brand, however, took place under the leadership of Jean Puiforcat, appointed master silversmith in 1920. Jean lived in an era with boundless sources of inspiration, both cultural and artistic: the influence of this context and his close friends, such as architects and designers René Herbst and Le Corbusier, led him to create a revolutionary formal style, a personal form of expression similar to Art Deco and characterised by pure and simple lines in addition to practicality.

[4] *Pierre Hardy is a French designer known for his innovative and bold take on the fashion world, especially in the creation of footwear and luxury accessories. Born in Paris in 1956, Hardy studied fine art, developing an eye for visual arts and architecture that would deeply influence his style. In the 1980s, Hardy entered the world of fashion as an illustrator for magazines, working subsequently for important fashion houses.*
He is currently the head of footwear and jewellery at Hermès.

[5] *In 1999, Hardy founded his namesake brand, launching footwear and accessory collections which reflect his love of contemporary art and experimentation.*

[6] *Pierre Hardy. https://www.hermes.com/us/en/content/187456-artisans-of-enlightenment/*

[7] *Vivienne Becker, Ten Meets Pierre Hardy, Hermes's Jewellery Extraordinaire. https://10magazine.com/ten-meets-pierre-hardy-hermess-jewellery-extraordinaire/*

[8] *Serena Tibaldi, Pierre Hardy: Designer del Lusso tra Arte e Astrazione. https://www.repubblica.it/moda-e-beauty/d/2023/09/19/news/pierre_hardy_designer_gioielli_hermes-413612525/*

Opinions

[1] *A natural law also exists, called the law of similitude and known as 'like is cured by like'.*

PHOTO CREDITS

BIBLIOGRAPHY

BOOKS

Robert Anderson, *Fifty Bags That Changed the World: Design Museum*, Conran Octopus, 2011

Marco Barel, *New Brand Fundamentals. How Great Companies Design and Develop Unique and Distinguished Identities*, GBR™, 2021

Roland Barthes, *The Fashion System*, University of California Press, 1990

David Bennett and Daniela Mascetti, *Understanding Jewellery*, Antique Collectors' Club Ltd, Woodbridge, Suffolk (UK), 1989

Romano Cappellari, *Marketing della moda e dei prodotti lifestyle*, Carrocci Editore, Rome, 2016

Mara Cappelletti, 'Un quadrilatero d'oro', in *Stile Milano*, exhibition catalogue, Nexo, Milan, 2020

Mara Cappelletti (ed.), *Gioielli di Gusto*, exhibition catalogue, Nexo, Milan, 2015

Elio Carmi, *Brand 111. Centoundici domande e risposte per sapere di più sulla brand e sul suo futuro*, Fausto Lupetti Editore, 2020

Luc Chabrin, *Hermès: Straight from the Horse's Mouth*, Abrams Books, NY, 2023

Elisabetta Chiodini, 'Dettagli di Moda ossia "Nonnulla Eleganti"' in *Dettagli di Moda – Gli anni Venti e Trenta nella collezione Mangiameli*, Umberto Allemandi, Turin, 2010

Caroline Cox, *Bags: An Illustrated History*, Aurum, 2007

Andrea Da Venezia, *Digital marketing del lusso. Comunicare e vendere il lusso attraverso il Web, le app e i social network*, Edizioni Lswr, Milan, 2016

Amy De la Haye, Tobin Shelley, *Chanel the couturière at work*, Victoria & Albert Museum Press, London, 1975

Carlo De Sio, *Come creare un Brand, oggi: Corso intuitivo di Brand management*, independently published, 2017

Philippe Dumas, *Carnet de Voyage – Regard sur L'Exotisme du Museé Hermès*, Actes Sud, Arles, 2014 [1ˢᵗ ed. 1988]

Philippe Dumas, *Musée Hermès – Carnet de Croquis de Pilippe Dumas illustrant le theme: La vie à l'air libre*, Actes Sud, Arles, 2014 [1ˢᵗ ed. 1990]

Philippe Dumas, *Musée Hermès – La route dans la collection H. par Philippe Dumas*, Actes Sud, Arles, 2014 [1ˢᵗ ed. 1995]

Deanna Farneti Cera, *I gioielli della fantasia. Ornamenti del XX secolo nell'arte, nel costume, nella moda*, Idea Books, Milan 1991

Laia Farran Graves, *Story of the Hermès Scarf*, Welbeck Publishing Group Ltd, London, 2023

Sigmund Freud, 'Symbolism in the Dream' in *A General Introduction to Psychoanalysis*, Library of Alexandria, 1953.

Sophie Gachet and Inès de La Fressange, *The Handbag Book: 400 Designer Bags That Changed Fashion*, Abrams, New York, 2024

Eugenio Gallavotti, *I racconti delle borse: Lessico illustrato dalla Birkin allo Zaino*, Franco Angeli Edizioni, 2023

Sofia Gnoli, *Moda: dalla nascita della haute couture ad oggi*, Carocci, Rome, 2012

Gaetano Grizzanti, *Brand identikit. Trasformare un marchio in una marca*, Fausto Lupetti Editore, 2020

Megan Hess, *The Bag*, Hardie Grant Books, Sydney, 2023

Karen Homer, *Little Book of Hermès: The Story of the Iconic Fashion House*, Welbeck Publishing Group Ltd, London, 2022

Paola Jacobbi, *Pazze per le borse! Perché alle donne non bastano le tasche*, Sperling & Kupfer, Milan, 2005

Alison James, *Hermès: The Fashion Icons*, Sona Books, Solihull (UK), 2024

Anna Johnson, *Handbags: 900 Bags to Die For*, Workman Pub Co, New York, 2002

Carl Gustav Jung, *The Archetypes and the Collective Unconscious*, translated by R.F.C. Hull, Princeton University Press, 2nd edition, 1981

Immanuel Kant, *Anthropology from a Pragmatic Point of View*, translated by Robert B. Louden, Cambridge University Press, 2006

Jean-Noël Kapferer, *Kapferer on luxury: how luxury brands can grow yet remain rare*, Kogan-Page, London, 2015

James Laver, *Costume and Fashion. A concise history*, Thames & Hudson, 5ᵗʰ edition, London, 2012

Harvey Leibenstein, 'Bandwagon, Snob, and Veblen Effects in the Theory of Consumers' Demand' in *The Quarterly Journal of Economics*, Vol. 64, No. 2, Oxford University Press, 1950

Giacomo Leopardi, 'Dialogo della Moda e della Morte' in *Operette Morali*, Mondadori, Milan, 2017

Suzanne Lussier, *Art Deco Fashion*, V&A Publications, London, 2003

Thierry Paquot, *Elogio del lusso. Ovvero l'utilità dell'inutile*, Alberto Castelvecchi Editore, Rome, 2007

Govers Pascalle and Jan PL Schoormans, 'Product personality and its influence on consumer preference' in *Journal of Consumer Marketing*, 2005

Govers Pascalle, Paul Hekkert and Jan PL Schoormans, 'Happy, cute and tough. Can designers create a product personality that consumers understand?' in *Design and Emotion*, 2003

Claire Phillips, *Jewellery From Antiquity to the Present*, Thames & Hudson Ltd, 2ⁿᵈ edition, London, 2004

Sylvie Raulet, *Art Deco Jewelry*, Rizzoli International Publications, Inc., New York, 1989

Arthur Rimbaud, *A Season in Hell*, Penguin Classics, New edition, 1995

Federico Rocca, *Hermès – L'avventura del lusso*, Lindau, Turin, 2011

Emanuela Scarpellini, *L'Italia dei consumi. Dalla Belle Époque al nuovo millennio*, Editori Laterza, Rome-Bari, 2008

Georg Simmel, *La moda*, Mimesi, Sesto San Giovanni, 2015

Georg Simmel, *On the psychology of fashion*, Divisare, 2017

Pierre Sommet, *Sur les traces de Thierry Hermès: Une histoire franco-allemande par excellence*, Editions Complicités, Paris, 2023

Lars Fr. H. Svendsen, *Fashion: A Philosophy*, translated by John Irons, Reaktion Books, 2006

Dana Thomas, *Deluxe. How luxury lost its luster*, Penguin Books, Reprint edition, 2008

Richard Thompson Ford, *Dress codes. How the Laws of Fashion Made History*, Simon & Schuster, 2022

Thorstein Veblen, *The Theory of the Leisure Class*, Oxford University Press, reissue edition, 2009

Julia Werner and Sandra Semburg, *For the Love of Bags*, Te Neues Pub Group, 2022

Klaus-Peter Wiedmann, Nadine Hennings, and Astrid Siebels, 'What is the value of luxury?' in *Psychology & Marketing*, 2012

Claire Wilcox and Sara Hodges, *Bags*, V&A Publications, London, 1999

Stefano Zecchi, *Il lusso. Eterno desiderio di voluttà e bellezza*, Mondadori, Milan, 2015

ARTICLES

Suleman Anaya, *The Humanity of Hermès*, https://www.businessoffashion.com/articles/news-analysis/humanity-hermes/

Vivienne Becker, *Ten Meets Pierre Hardy, Hermes's Jewellery Extraordinaire*, https://10magazine.com/ten-meets-pierre-hardy-hermess-jewellery-extraordinaire/

Christie's, *What every collector needs to know about Hermès handbags*, https://www.christies.com/en/stories/hermes-handbags-collecting-guide-e7f2b17272e144c98136ee3946005b8d

Pierre Hardy, https://www.hermes.com/us/en/content/187456-artisans-of-enlightenment/

Serena Tibaldi, *Pierre Hardy: Designer del Lusso tra Arte e Astrazione*, https://www.repubblica.it/moda-e-beauty/d/2023/09/19/news/pierre_hardy_designer_gioielli_hermes-413612525/

Vanessa Walt, *Your Guide to the Top 10 Hermès Bags*, https://www.sothebys.com/en/articles/your-guide-to-the-top-10-hermes-bags

Lindsey Weiss, *Top Five Most Popular Hermès Leather*, https://www.sothebys.com/en/articles/top-five-most-popular-hermes-leather

Lindsey Weiss, *The Many Shades of Hermès Pink*, https://www.sothebys.com/en/articles/the-many-shades-of-hermes-pink

MARA CAPPELLETTI

Mara Cappelletti hails from Milan. She holds a degree in Foreign Languages and Literature from Milan's IULM University and studied the history of jewellery and of Eastern art at Sotheby's Institute of Art in London.

Cappelletti is a freelance journalist and the author of several books on the history of jewellery, ethnic jewellery and watches from various publishers, including *24 Ore Cultura*, *Nexo*, *ACC Art Books* and *White Star*.

She designs and curates exhibitions on the themes of jewellery and fashion and also conducts research for catalogues. One of these was *Gioielli di Gusto e Stile Milano – Storie di eleganza (Jewellery of Milanese Taste and Style – Stories of Elegance)*, at Palazzo Morando – Milan's Museum of Costume, Fashion and Image.

Mara Cappelletti is President of the Associazione Culturale Stile e Storia (Cultural Association of Style and History), which focuses on research and the promotion of historical heritage, highlighting the relationship between art, fashion and jewellery as part of the customs of a given time period.

Since 2019, she has worked as an adjunct professor teaching the History of Jewellery at the University of Milan as part of its Master's programme in Publishing and Communication, Fashion Cultures. Since 2020, she has been collaborating with the Raffles Milano Fashion and Design Institute, teaching the history of jewellery. She also holds conferences and workshops at museums, cultural associations and art galleries.